WORKSHOP MANUAL

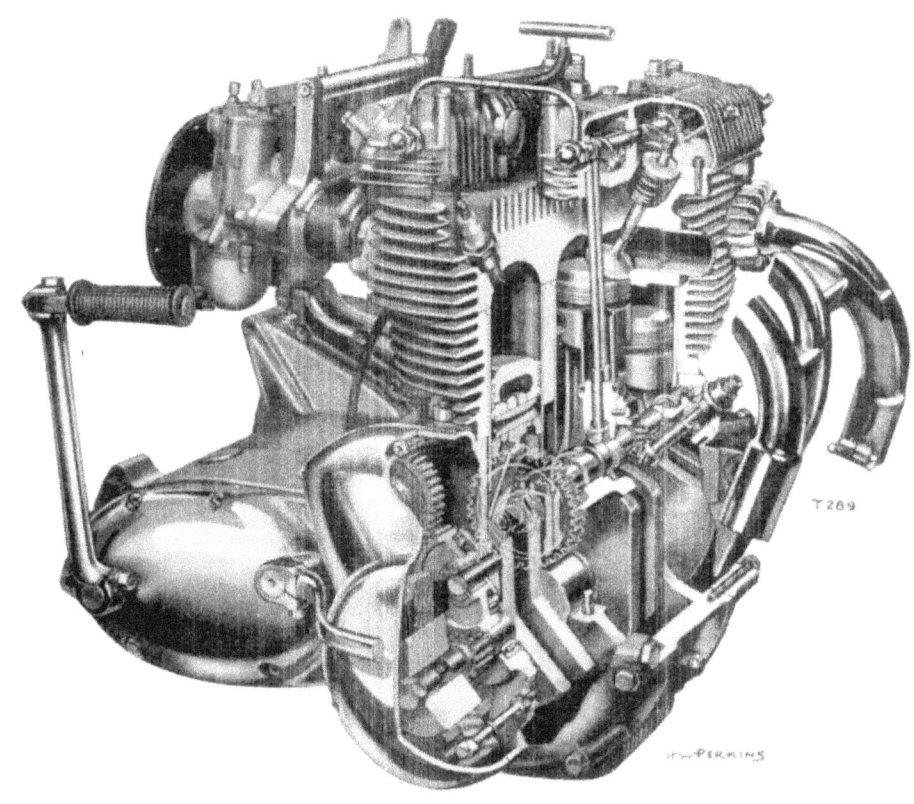

THREE CYLINDER MODEL T150
750 c.c. (45 cu. in.)

TRIDENT

FROM ENGINE NO. T150T101

TRIUMPH ENGINEERING CO LTD

MERIDEN WORKS · ALLESLEY · COVENTRY · ENGLAND

TELEPHONE MERIDEN 331
COVENTRY 20221

TELEGRAMS "TRUSTY" COVENTRY
TELEX "TRUSTY" 31305

Part No. 99-0963
(incorporating 99-0887
and Supplement 00-4223)

INCORPORATING

SUPPLEMENT

FOR

1973 MODELS.

750c.c. (45cu.in.)

THREE

CYLINDER

WITH
FIVE SPEED GEARBOX

IMPORTANT: The supplemental data and/or information may be merged into the appropriate section of this manual. If not, it will be appended to the end of the section and identified by the use of double alpha characters, for example 'AA' etc.

IMPORTANT

PRIOR TO UNDERTAKING ANY MAINTENANCE OR REPAIR TASKS THE READER IS INSTRUCTED TO REVIEW THE INFORMATION REGARDING ENGINE NUMBERS ON THE REAR COVER OF THIS MANUAL.

PUBLISHER'S INTRODUCTION

Welcome to the world of digital publishing ~ the book you now hold in your hand was printed using the latest state of the art digital technology. The advent of print-on-demand has forever changed the publishing process, never has information been so accessible and it is our hope that this book serves your informational needs for years to come. If this is your first exposure to digital publishing, we hope that you are pleased with the results. Many more titles of interest to the classic automobile and motorcycle enthusiast, collector and restorer are available via our website at www.VelocePress.com. We hope that you find this title as interesting as we do.

NOTE FROM THE PUBLISHER

The information presented is true and complete to the best of our knowledge. All recommendations are made without any guarantees on the part of the author or the publisher, who also disclaim all liability incurred with the use of this information.

TRADEMARKS

We recognize that some words, model names and designations, for example, mentioned herein are the property of the trademark holder. We use them for identification purposes only. This is not an official publication.

INFORMATION ON THE USE OF THIS PUBLICATION

This manual is an invaluable resource for those interested in performing their own maintenance. However, in today's information age we are constantly subject to changes in common practice, new technology, availability of improved materials and increased awareness of chemical toxicity. As such, it is advised that the user consult with an experienced professional prior to undertaking any procedure described herein. While every care has been taken to ensure correctness of information, it is obviously not possible to guarantee complete freedom from errors or omissions or to accept liability arising from such errors or omissions. Therefore, any individual that uses the information contained within, or elects to perform or participate in do-it-yourself repairs or modifications acknowledges that there is a risk factor involved and that the publisher or its associates cannot be held responsible for personal injury or property damage resulting from the use of the information or the outcome of such procedures.

WARNING!

One final word of advice, this publication is intended to be used as a reference guide, and when in doubt the reader should consult with a qualified technician.

INTRODUCTION

THIS manual has been compiled and prepared to provide the necessary service information for workshop, fitter, technical staff and individual owner, wishing to carry out basic maintenance and repair work on the TRIUMPH TRIDENT 750 c.c. MODEL T150R. and T150RV.

GENERAL DATA for all models within the above range is provided in ready reference form, and a separate section covering Service Tools is fully illustrated at the end of this manual.

The manual is divided into sections dealing with major assemblies, throughout the machine, each section sub-divided into sequence order corresponding to normal operations of strip down, examination and rebuilding procedure.

ENGINE AND FRAME NUMBERS

Note: The engine number is located on the left side of the engine, immediately below the cylinder barrel flange. The number is stamped onto a raised pad.

On later models the system of numbering is changed, and a prefix is added indicating the month and year of manufacture.

The first letter indicates the month of manufacture as follows:—

    A January
    B February
    C March
    D April
    E May
    G June
    H July
    J August
    K September
    N October
    P November
    X December

The second letter indicates the season year of manufacture as follows:—

    C 1969
    D 1970
    E 1971
    G 1972
    H 1973
    J 1974
    K 1975
    N 1976
    P 1977
    X 1978
    A 1979
    B 1980

The third Section is a numerical block of five figures which commence with engine number 00100.
The fourth Section indicates the model.

Example   Month   Year   Number   Model
                 N   C   00100   T150

The frame number is stamped on the left side of the frame, on the front engine mounting lug. Both the engine and frame numbers should coincide.

GUARANTEE

Please refer to your local dealer or distributor where required for the latest terms of guarantee.

EASTERN U.S.A. DISTRIBUTORS

TRIUMPH MOTORCYCLE CORPORATION,
P.O. BOX 6790, TOWSON, BALTIMORE 4,
MARYLAND 21204.
Cables: Triumph Baltimore.
Telex: 87728.

WESTERN U.S.A. DISTRIBUTORS

TRIUMPH MOTORCYCLE CORPORATION,
P.O. BOX 275,
EAST HUNTINGTON DRIVE,
DUARTE,
CALIFORNIA 91010.
Telex: 675469.

FACTORY SERVICE ARRANGEMENTS

UNITED KINGDOM ONLY

CORRESPONDENCE

Technical Advice, Guarantee Claims and Repairs

Communications dealing with any of these subjects should be addressed to **SERVICE DEPARTMENT.**

> In all communications the full engine number complete with all prefix letters and figures should be stated. This number will be found on the L.H. side of the crankcase just below the cylinder flange.

TECHNICAL ADVICE

It will be appreciated how very difficult it is to diagnose trouble by correspondence and this is made impossible in many cases because the information sent to us is so scanty. Every possible point which may have some bearing on the matter should be stated so that we can send a useful and detailed reply.

REPLACEMENT PARTS

Replacement parts are no longer supplied direct from the factory to the individual owner. They should be obtained from the nearest local Triumph dealer.

There is a nation-wide network of stockists, a list of which is available from the factory on request.

REPAIRS

Before a motorcycle is sent to our Works an appointment must be made by the retailer. This can be done by letter or telephone. When an owner wishes to return his machine for guarantee repairs, he should consult his Dealer as we do not accept machines in our Repair Shop direct from private owners. This avoids the machine being out of use for some days when it could be on the road. Where parts such as cylinders, petrol tanks, etc., are forwarded for repair, they should be packed securely so as to avoid damage in transit. The dealer's name and address should be enclosed together with full instructions. In the case of complete motorcycles, a label showing the dealer's name and address should always be attached and all accessories such as tools, inflator, handlebar mirrors and other parts removed.

SERVICE EXCHANGE RECONDITIONED UNITS

A range of service exchange reconditioned units is available from the Factory Service Department. This list includes petrol tanks, front forks, front and rear frames, clutch plates, brake shoes, etc., which are supplied after the return of the original equipment for inspection and acceptance. Operation of this scheme is maintained solely through the Dealer network.

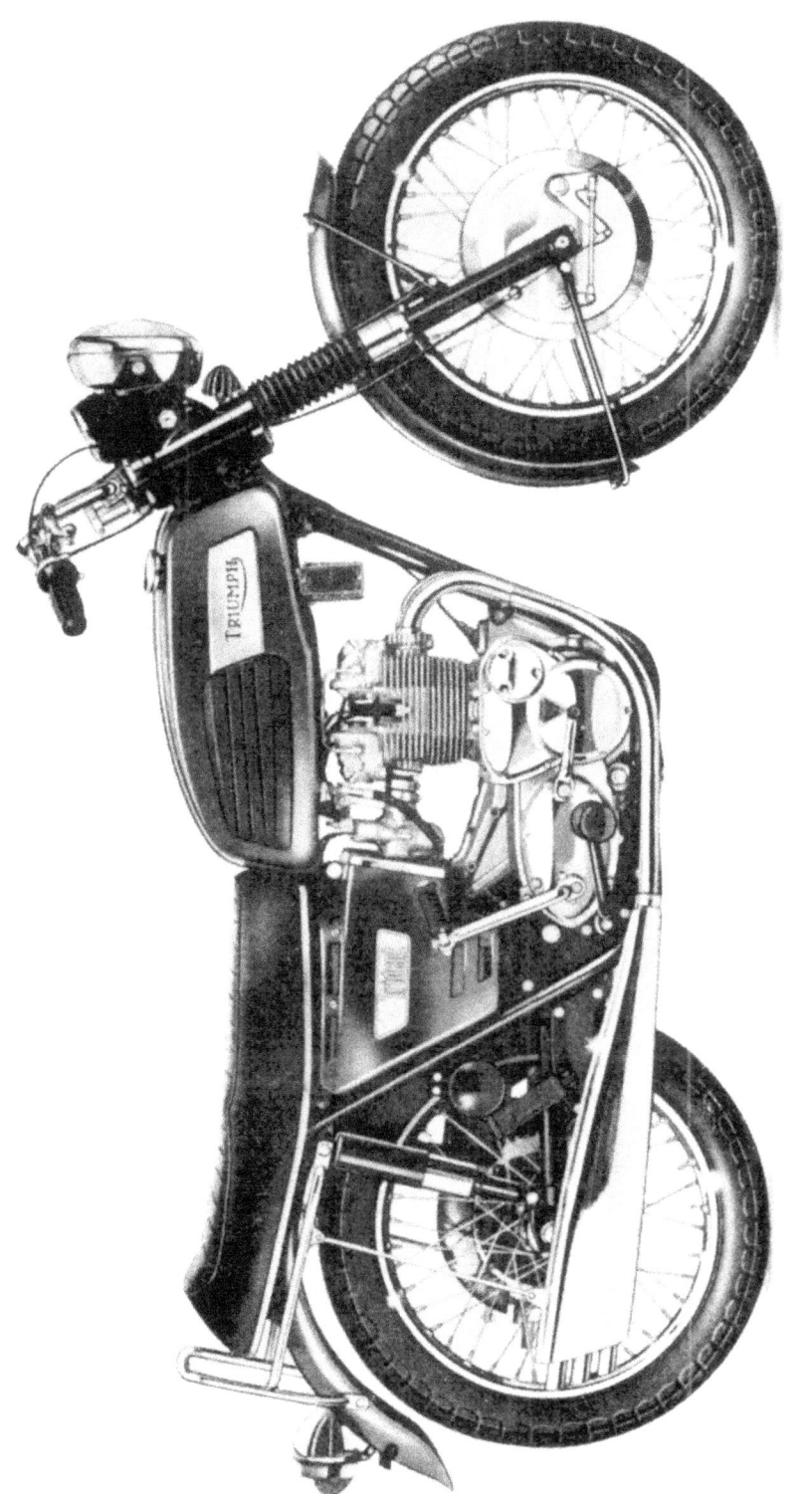

1969 **750 c.c. (45 cu. in.) three cylinder TRIDENT (T150).**

1971 750 c.c. (45 cu. in.) three cylinder TRIDENT

1973 750cc. THREE CYLINDER (45 cu. in.) TRIDENT T150V. U.S.A.

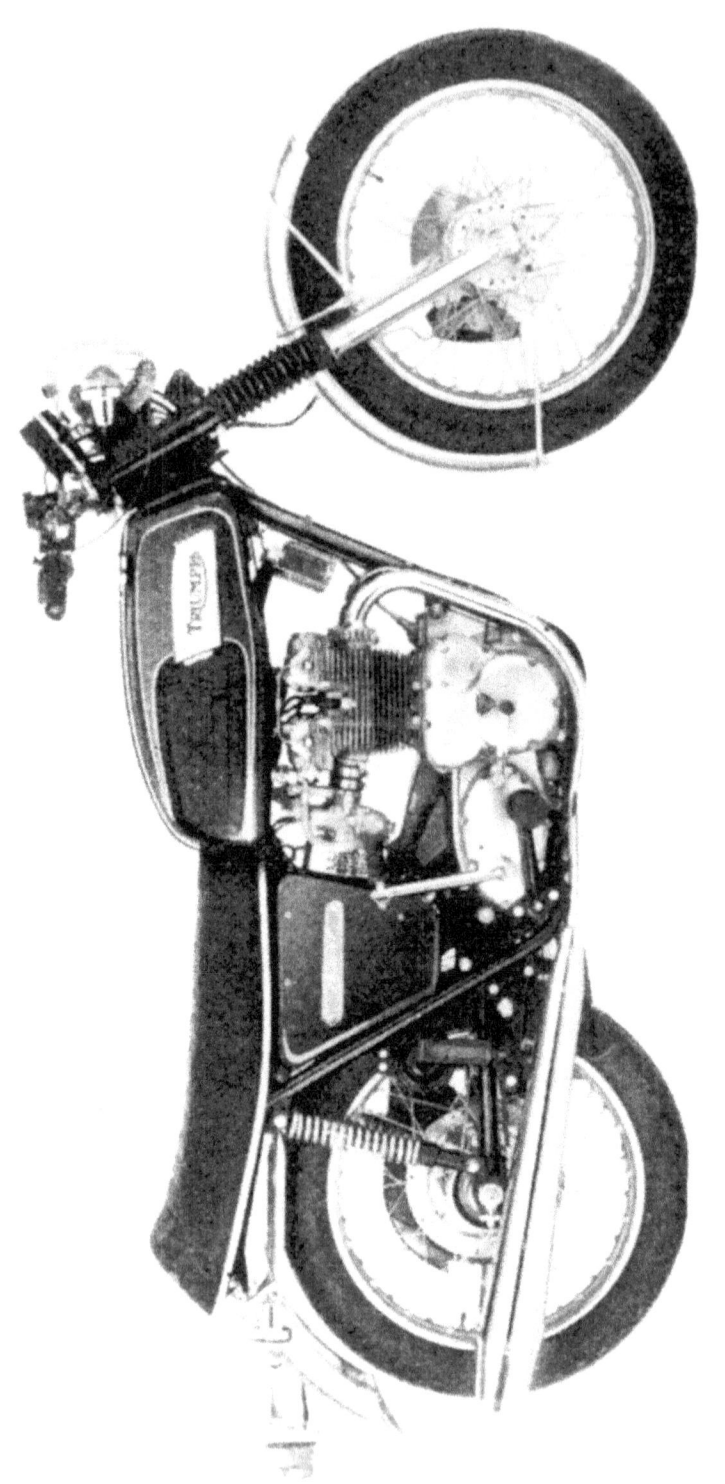

1973 750cc. THREE CYLINDER (45 cu. in.) TRIDENT T150V. HOME AND GENERAL EXPORT

GENERAL DATA

1969
TRIDENT
THREE CYLINDER MODEL T150

750 cc. (45 cu. ins.)

GENERAL DATA
MODEL T150 TRIDENT
LUBRICATION SYSTEM

OIL PUMP
- Body material ... Cast iron
- Bore diameters ... ·3438/·3433 in. (8·7325/8·7198 mm.)
- Scavenge gear—bore diameter ... ·3438/·3448 in. (8·7325/8·7579 mm.)
- Feed gear—bore diameter ... ·3438/·3448 in. (8·7325/8·7579 mm.)
- Spindle diameter ... ·3433/·3428 in. (8·7198/8·70712 mm.)
- Cover plate bore diameters: Spindle ... ·3433/·3438 in. (8·7198/8·7325 mm.)
- Drive scavenge gear ... ·4375/·4370 in. (11·1125/11·0998 mm.)
- Pump drive ratio ... 1·9 : 1 (engine to pump)

OIL PUMP DRIVE
- Intermediate gear—Bore diameter ... ·5625/·5620 in. (14·287/14·2748 mm.)
- Bush—Bore ... ·4387/·4382 in. (11·143/11·1302 mm.)
- —Length ... ·755/·745 in. (19·177/18·923 mm.)
- Spindle—Diameter ... ·4360/·4355 in. (11·0744/11·0617 mm.)

OIL PRESSURE RELEASE VALVE
- Piston diameter ... ·5605/·5610 in. (14·2367/14·2494 mm.)
- Working clearance ... ·001/·002 in. (0·0254/0·0508 mm.)
- Pressure release operates ... 90 lb./sq. in. (6·328 kg./sq. cm.)
- Spring length (Free) ... 1⅜ in. (34·925 mm.)
- Load at 1 3/16 in. ... 8 lbs. (3·632 kgm.)
- Rate ... 42·3 lbs. (19·2042 kgm.)

OIL PRESSURE
- Normal running ... 75–85 lb./sq. in. (5·273–5·624 kg./sq. cm.)
- Idling ... 20–25 lb./sq. in. (1·406–1·758 kg./sq. cm.)
- Oil pressure switch: Working range ... 7–11 lbs. (3·178/4·994 kgm.)

ENGINE

BASIC DETAILS
- Bore and stroke ... 67 × 70 mm.
- Cubic capacity ... 741 c.c. (45 cu. in.)
- Compression ratio ... 9 : 1
- Power out (B.H.P. @ R.P.M.) ... 58 @ 7,500 r.p.m.

CRANKSHAFT
- Crankshaft type ... EN16B hardened and tempered stamping-one piece
- Main bearing (drive side) size and type ... 1⅛ × 2 13/16 × 13/16 in. (caged ball) (28·58 × 71·43 × 20·63 mm.)
- Main bearing (centre) running clearance ... ·0005/·0022 in. (·0127/·05588 mm.)
- Main bearing (timing side) size and type ... 1⅛ × 2 13/16 × 13/16 in. (roller) (28·58 × 71·43 × 20·62 mm.)
- Right main bearing housing diameter ... 2·8110/2·8095 in. (71·3994/71·3613 mm.)
- Right main bearing journal diameter ... 1·1248/1·1245 in. (28·5699/28·5623 mm.)
- Centre main bearing housing diameter ... 2·0630/2·0625 in. (52·4002/52·3875 mm.)
- Centre main bearing journal diameter ... 1·9170/1·9175 in. (48·6918/48·7045 mm.)
- Left main bearing housing diameter ... 2·0447/2·0457 in. (51·9344/51·9608 mm.)
- Left main bearing journal diameter ... 0·9843/0·9840 in. (25·0012/24·9936 mm.)
- Big end journal diameter ... 1·6240/1·6235 in. (41·2496/41·2369 mm.)
- Min. regrind diameter ... 1·6200/1·6185 in. (41·148/41·1099 mm.)
- Crankshaft end float ... ·0015/·0145 in. (·038/·368 mm.)

CONNECTING RODS
- Material ... Alloy 'H' Section RR.56
- Length (centres) ... 5·751/5·749 in. (14·6075/14·6024 mm.)
- Big end bearings type ... Steel backed white metal
- Conn rod side clearance ... 0·013/0·019 in. (0·3302/0·4826 mm.)
- Bearing diametral clearance ... ·0005/·0020 in. minimum (·0127/·0508 mm.)

GUDGEON PIN (WRIST PIN)
- Material ... High tensile steel
- Fit in small end ... ·0005/·0011 in. (·0127/·0279 mm.)
- Diameter ... ·6883/·6885 in. (17·4828/17·4880 mm.)
- Length ... 2·250/2·235 in. (57·150/56·769 mm.)

GENERAL DATA

CYLINDER BLOCK
- Material ... Austenitic steel liner Aluminium Alloy
- Bore size ... 2·6368/2·6363 in. (66·9747/66·962 mm.)
- Maximum oversize ... +·040 in. (1·016 mm.)
- Tappet guide block housing diameter ... 1·1562/1·1557 in. (29·3675/29·3548 mm.)

CYLINDER HEAD
- Material ... Alum alloy die casting
- Inlet port size ... 1 in. dia. (25·4 mm.)
- Exhaust port size ... 1¼ in. dia. (31·75 mm.)
- Valve seatings:
  - Type ... Cast-in
  - Material ... Cast iron

VALVES
- Stem diameter: Inlet ... ·3100/·3095 in. (7·8740/7·8613 mm.)
-     Exhaust ... ·3095/·3090 in. (7·8613/7·8495 mm.)
- Head diameter: Inlet ... 1·534/1·528 in. (38·9636/38·812 mm.)
-     Exhaust ... 1·315/1·309 in. (33·401/33·2486 mm.)
- Exhaust valve material ... 21/4 'N' heat treated

VALVE GUIDES
- Material ... Hidural 5
- Bore diameter (Inlet and exhaust) ... ·3115/·3110 in. (7·9121/7·8994 mm.)
- Outside diameter (Inlet and exhaust) ... ·5005/·5010 in. (12·7127/12·7254 mm.)
- Length: Inlet ... 1·875 in. (47·625 mm.)
-     Exhaust ... 1·875 in. (47·625 mm.)

VALVE SPRINGS (RED AND WHITE)
- Free length: Inner ... 1·468 in. (37·2872 mm.)
-     Outer ... 1·600 in. (40·64 mm.)
- Total number of coils: Inner ... 6
-     Outer ... 5½
- Total fitted load
  - Valve open: Inner ... 82 lbs. (37·228 kgm.)
  -     Outer ... 115 lbs. (51·31 kgm.)
  - Valve closed: Inner ... 37–40 lbs. (16·798–18·144 kgm.)
  -     Outer ... 43–53 lbs. (21·792–24·062 kgm.)

VALVE TIMING
- Set all tappet clearances @ nil for checking ... Valve lift: Inlet 0·152 in. (3·86 mm.)
- Measure valve lift at T.B.C. with cold engine ... Exhaust 0·146 in. (3·71 mm.)

ROCKERS
- Material ... NI. CH. Steel stamping (EN33)
- Bore diameter ... ·5002/·5012 in. (12·7051/12·7305 mm.)
- Rocker spindle diameter ... ·4990/·4995 in. (12·6746/12·6873 mm.)
- Tappet clearance (cold): Inlet ... ·006 in. (0·1524 mm.)
-     Exhaust ... ·008 in. (0·2032 mm.)

CAMSHAFTS
- Journal diameters ... 1·0615/1·0605 in. (26·9621/26·9367 mm.)
- Diametral clearances ... ·0005/·0020 in. (·0127/·0508 mm.)
- End float ... ·007/·014 in. (·178/·356 mm.)
- Cam lift: Inlet and exhaust ... ·3045 in. (7·7343 mm.)
- Base circle diameter ... ·812 in. dia. (20·6248 mm.)

TAPPETS
- Material ... EN32B (Stellite tip)
- Tip radius ... 1·125 in. (28·575 mm.)
- Tappet diameter ... ·3115/·3110 in. (7·9121/7·8994 mm.)
- Clearance in guide block ... ·0005/·0015 in. (·0127/·0381 mm.)

TAPPET GUIDE BLOCK
- Diameter of bores ... ·3125/·3120 in. (7·9375/7·9248 mm.)
- Outside diameter ... 1·153/1·148 in. (29·2862/29·1592 mm.)
- Interference fit in cylinder block ... ·0027/·0082 in. (·06858/·20828 mm.)

ROCKER SPINDLE BUSHES
- Bush D/S: Bore diameter ... ·497/·498 in. (12·624/12·649 mm.)
-     Outside diameter ... ·6260/·6265 in. (15·9004/15·913 mm.)
- Bush T/S: Bore diameter ... ·375/·374 in. (9·525/9·4996 mm.)
-     Outside diameter ... ·501/·502 in. (12·725/12·751 mm.)

IGNITION TIMING
- Crankshaft position (B.T.D.C.) F.A. ... 38°
- Piston position (B.T.D.C.) F.A. ... ·357 in. (9·0678 mm.)
- Advance range:
  - Contact breaker ... 12°
  - Crankshaft ... 24°

GD

GENERAL DATA

TIMING GEARS
    Inlet and exhaust camshaft pinions:
        No. of teeth ... 50
        Interference fit on camshaft ... ·000/·001 in. (·000/·0254 mm.)
    Intermediate timing gear
        No. of teeth ... 42
        Bore diameter ... ·5618/·5625 in. (14·2697/14·2875 mm.)
    Intermediate timing gear needle roller ... $\frac{11}{16} \times \frac{7}{8} \times \frac{5}{8}$ in. (17·46 × 22·225 × 15·87 mm.)
    Intermediate wheel spindle
        Diameter ... ·6888/·6885 in. (17·4955/17·4879 mm.)
    Crankcase pinion:
        No. of teeth ... 25
        Fit on crankcase ... +·0003 in. (+·00762 mm.)
                                −·0005 in. (−·0127 mm.)

CONTACT BREAKER (7CA)
    Gap setting ... ·014–·016 in. (·35–·40 mm.)
    Advance range ... 12° (24° crankshaft)
    Fully advanced at ... 2,000 r.p.m.

PISTONS
    Material ... Aluminium Alloy—diecasting
    Clearance: Top of skirt ... ·0056/·0035 in. (·42/·089 mm.)
            Bottom of skirt ... ·0033/·0018 in. (·084/·0457 mm.)
    Gudgeon pin hole dia. ... ·6885/·6883 in. (17·9879/17·4828 mm.)

PISTON RINGS
    Material ... Cast iron HG10
    Compression rings (tapered):
        Width ... 2·729/2·577 mm.
        Thickness ... ·0625/·0615 in. (1·5875/1·5621 mm.)
        Fitted gap ... ·009/·013 in. (·2286/·3302 mm.)
        Clearance in groove ... ·0035/·0015 in. (·89/·038 mm.)
    Oil control ring:
        Width ... 2·729/2·577 mm.
        Thickness ... ·125/·124 in. (3·175/3·1496 mm.)
        Fitted gap ... ·010/·040 in. (·254/1·016 mm.)
        Clearance in groove ... ·0105/·0065 in. (·266/·165 mm.)

FUEL SYSTEM
    Triple carburetters ... Concentric
    Amal type ... 626
    Main jet size ... 150
    Needle jet size ... ·106
    Needle type ... STD
    Needle position ... 2
    Throttle valve:
        Type ... $2\frac{1}{2}$
    Carburetter nominal bore size ... 27 mm.
    Air cleaner element ... Filter cloth and wire guaze

TRANSMISSION

CLUTCH DETAILS
    Single diaphragm spring—clutch spring rate ... 1,000 lb. (approx.) (453·6 kgm.)
    Minimum travel to disengage ... ·035 in. (·889 mm.)
    Minimum wear of friction plate ... ·06 in. (1·524 mm.)
    Bearing—Outer thrust plate—Size and type ... $\frac{1}{2} \times 1\frac{1}{8} \times \frac{1}{4}$ in. (12·7 × 28·575 × 6·35 mm.)
    Needle race—Size and type ... (2 off) $1\frac{3}{8} \times 1\frac{5}{8} \times \frac{1}{2}$ in. (34·93 × 41·28 × 12·7 mm.)
    Thrust race—Size and type ... $1\frac{3}{8} \times 2\frac{1}{16} \times \frac{5}{64}$ in. (34·93 × 52·39 × 1·984 mm.)

THROTTLE OPERATING MECHANISM
    Spindle—Diameter ... ·3115/·3106 in.

GEARBOX

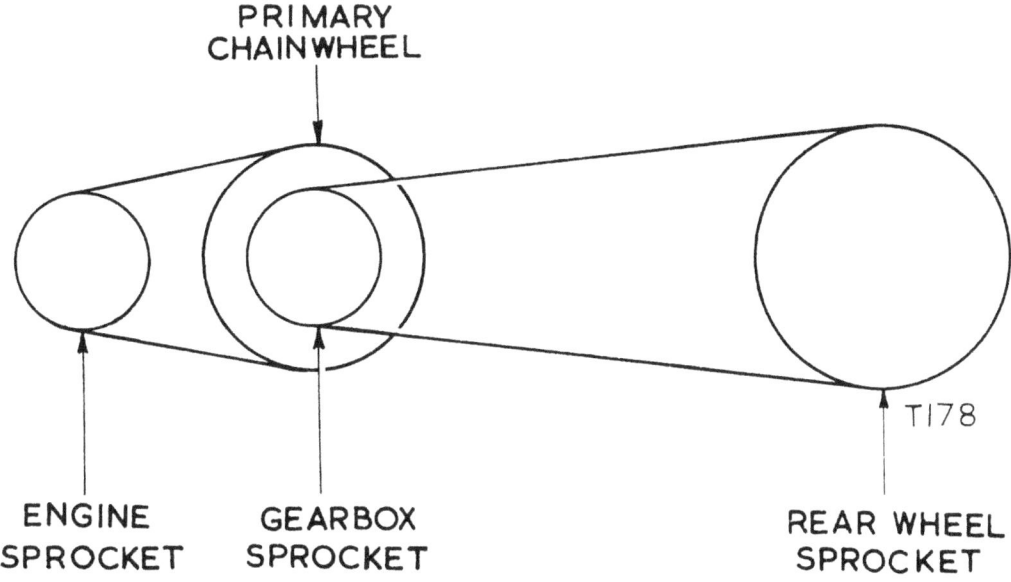

To find the gear ratios of a machine, calculate the top gear as follows:—

Divide the number of teeth on the primary chainwheel by the number of teeth on the engine sprocket and multiply the result by the number of teeth on the rear wheel sprocket, divided by the number of teeth on the gearbox sprocket, as example:—

$$\frac{\text{clutch sprocket (50)}}{\text{engine sprocket (28)}} \times \frac{\text{rear wheel sprocket (52)}}{\text{gearbox sprocket (18)}} = \frac{2600}{504} = 5{\cdot}156$$

To find the intermediate gear ratio, multiply the overall top gear by the internal gear ratio concerned, as example:—

top gear 4·891 or 4·9 × bottom gear internal ratio 2·44 = 11·95 bottom gear overall ratio

$$\text{Gearbox internal ratio} = \frac{\text{layshaft gear}}{\text{mainshaft gear}} \times \frac{\text{mainshaft top gear}}{\text{layshaft top gear}}$$

as example:—

$$\frac{\text{(layshaft 3rd) 22T}}{\text{(mainshaft 3rd) 24T}} \times \frac{\text{(mainshaft top) 26T}}{\text{(layshaft top) 20T}} = 1{\cdot}191$$

GD — GENERAL DATA

RATIOS
Internal ratios (Std.) 4th (Top) ... 1·00 : 1
                          3rd ... 1·19 : 1
                          2nd ... 1·69 : 1
                          1st (Bottom) ... 2·44 : 1

Overall ratios: 4th (Top) ... 4·89
                 3rd ... 5·83
                 2nd ... 8·3
                 1st (Bottom) ... 11·95

Engine R.P.M. @ 10 M.P.H. in 4th (Top) gear ... 655 r.p.m.
Gearbox sprocket teeth ... 18

GEAR DETAILS
Mainshaft high gear:
  Bore diameter (bush fitted) ... ·8135/·8145 in. (20·6629/20·6883 mm.)
  Working clearance on shaft ... ·0032/·0047 in. (·08128/·1194 mm.)
  Bush length ... 2¼ in. (57·15 mm.)

Layshaft low gear:
  Bore diameter (bush fitted) ... ·8135/·8145 in. (20·6629/20·6883 mm.)
  Working clearance on shaft ... ·0025/·0045 in. (0·0635/0·127 mm.)

GEARBOX SHAFTS
Mainshaft:
  Left end diameter ... ·8098/·8103 in. (20·5689/20·5816 mm.)
  Right end diameter ... ·7494/·7498 in. (19·0348/19·044 mm.)
  Length ... 10$\frac{21}{64}$ in. (262·3337 mm.)

Layshaft:
  Left end diameter ... ·6845/·6850 in. (17·4063/17·419 mm.)
  Right end diameter ... ·6845/·6850 in. (17·4063/17·419 mm.)
  Length ... 6$\frac{41}{64}$ in. (168·6941 mm.)

Camplate plunger spring:
  Free length ... 2$\frac{21}{32}$ in. (67·4675 mm.)
  No. of working coils ... 27
  Spring rate ... 9 lbs./in. (·633 kg./sq. cm.)
  Working range ... 7·5 to 11·5 lbs. (3·405 kgm./5·221 kgm.)

BEARINGS
High gear bearing ... 1¼ × 2½ × ⅝ in. Ball Journal (31·75 × 63·5 × 15·875 mm.)
Mainshaft bearing ... ¾ × 1⅞ × $\frac{9}{16}$ in. Ball Journal (19·05 × 47·625 × 14·282 mm.)
Layshaft bearing (left) ... $\frac{11}{16}$ × ⅞ × ¾ in. Needle Roller (17·463 × 22·227 × 19·05 mm.)
Layshaft bearing (right) ... $\frac{11}{16}$ × ⅞ × ¾ in. Needle Roller (17·463 × 22·227 × 19·05 mm.)

KICKSTART OPERATING MECHANISM
Bush bore diameter ... ·751/·752 in. (19·0754/19·1008 mm.)
Spindle working clearance in bush ... ·003/·005 in. (·0762/·127 mm.)
Ratchet spring free length ... ½ in. (12·7 mm.)

GEARCHANGE MECHANISM
Plungers:
  Outer diameters ... ·4315/·4320 in. (10·9601/10·9728 mm.)
  Working clearance in bore ... ·0005/·0015 in. (0·0127/·0381 mm.)

Plunger springs:
  No. of working coils ... 12
  Free length ... 1¼ in. (31·75 mm.)

Inner bush bore diameter ... ·6245/·6255 in. (15·7423/15·8877 mm.)
  Clearance on shaft ... ·0007/·0032 in. (·01778/·08128 mm.)
Outer bush bore diameter ... ·7495/·7505 in. (19·0373/19·0627 mm.)
  Clearance on shaft ... ·0005/·0025 in. (·0127/·0635 mm.)

Quadrant return springs:
  No. of working coils ... 9½
  Free length ... 1¾ in. (44·45 mm.)

FRAME AND ATTACHMENT DETAILS

HEAD RACES
No. of balls: Top ... 20
               Bottom ... 20
Ball diameter ... ¼ in. (6·35 mm.)

SWINGING FORK
Bush type ... Pre-sized steel-backed—phosphor bronze
Bush bore diameter ... 1·4460/1·4470 in. (36·7284/36·7538 mm.)
Sleeve diameter ... 1·4445/1·4450 in. (36·6903/36·702 mm.)
Distance between fork ends ... 7½ in. (190·5 mm.)

GENERAL DATA

REAR SUSPENSION
- Type ... Swinging fork controlled by combined coil spring/hydraulic damper units
- Colour code ... Black
- Extended distance between centre ... 12·875 in. (32·66 mm.)
- Compressed distance between centre ... 10·375 in. (23·36 mm.)

WHEELS, BRAKES AND TYRES

WHEELS
- Rim size: Front and rear ... WM2-19 Front WM3-19 rear
- Type: Front ... Spoke—single cross lacing
- Rear ... Spoke—double cross lacing
- Spoke details: Front: Left side ... 20 off 8/10 SWG butted 5⅝ in. U.H. straight (219·075 mm.)
  - Right side ... 10 off 8/10 SWG butted 4 11/16 in. U.H. 95° head (118·0625 mm.)
  - Right side ... 10 off 8/10 SWG butted 4 11/16 in. U.H. 80° head (118·0625 mm.)
- Rear: Left side ... 20 off 8/10 SWG butted 8 in. U.H. 90° head (203·2 mm.)
  - Right side ... 20 off 8/10 SWG butted 8⅜ in. U.H. 90° head (212·725 mm.)

WHEEL BEARINGS
- Front and rear, dimensions and type ... 20 × 47 × 14 mm.—Ball Journal
- Front and rear, spindle diameter (at bearing journals) ... ·7862/·7867 in. (19·9695 × 19·9822 mm.)

STANDARD REAR WHEEL
- Bolt size for detachable sprocket ... 5/16 in. dia. ¾ in. U.H. × 26 C.E.I. (7·9324 dia. 19·05 mm.)
- Number of bolts ... 8

REAR WHEEL DRIVE
- Gearbox sprocket ... See "Gearbox"
- Rear wheel sprocket teeth ... 52
- Chain details:
  - No. of links: Solo ... 107
  - Pitch ... ⅝ in. (15·875 mm.)
  - Width ... ⅜ in. (9·525 mm.)
- Speedometer drive gearbox ratio ... 2 : 1
- Speedometer cable length ... 68 in. (1·7272 mm.)

BRAKES
- Type ... Internal expanding 2 leading shoe
- Drum Diameter: Front ... 8 in. ± ·002 in. (203·2 mm.) ± ·0508 mm.
  - Rear ... 7 in. ± ·002 in. (177·8 mm.) ± ·0508 mm.
- Lining thickness: Front ... ·181/·188 in.
  - Rear ... ·165/·175 in.
- Lining area: Front ... 23·4 sq. in. (150·967 sq. cm.)
  - Rear ... 14·6 sq. in. (94·193 sq. cm.)

TYRES
- Size: Front ... 3·50 × 19 in.
  - Rear ... 4·10 × 19 in.
- Tyre pressure: Front ... 24 lb./sq. in. (1·685 kg./sq. cm.)
  - Rear ... 28 lb./sq. in. (1·97 kg./sq. cm.)

FRONT FORKS

TELESCOPIC FORK
- Type ... Telescopic—Oil damping
- Spring details:
  - Free length ... 9·688/9·812 in. (246·075/249·225 mm.)
  - No. working coils ... 15½
  - Spring rate ... 32½ lb. in. (4·485 kg. m.)
  - Gauge ... 5 swg.
  - Colour code ... Yellow/green
- Damper sleeve
  - Length ... 2⅛ in. (53·975 mm.)
  - Internal diameter ... 1·387/1·393 in. (35·2298/35·3822 mm.)
- Bush details: Material ... Sintered bronze

	Top bush	Bottom bush
Length	1 in. (25·4 mm.)	·870/·875 in. (22·098/22·225 mm.)
Outer diameter	1·498/1·499 in. (38·0492/38·0746 mm.)	1·4935/1·4945 in. (37·945/37·960 mm.)
Inner diameter	1·3065/1·3075 in. (33·185/33·2105 mm.)	1·2485/1·2495 in. (31·712/31·7373 mm.)
Stanchion diameter	1·3025/1·3030 in. (33·0835/33·0962 mm.)	
Working clearance in top bush	·0035/·0050 in. (·0889/·127 mm.)	
Fork leg bore diameter	1·498/1·500 in. (38·049/38·1 mm.)	
Working clearance of bottom bush	·0035/·0065 in. (·0889/·165 mm.)	

GD — GENERAL DATA

ELECTRICAL SYSTEM

ELECTRICAL EQUIPMENT
- Battery type (12v.) ... PUZ 5A
- Rectifier type ... 54048008 (Lucas)
- Alternator type ... RM20
- Horn type (12v.): R.H. ... P201
- L.H. ... P101

Bulbs:

	No.	Type
Headlight (L/H dip)	446	50/40 watts—pre-focus
Parking light	989	6 watts—MCC
Stop and tail light	380	6/21 watts—offset pin
Speedometer light	987	2·2 watts—MES
Ignition warning light	281	2 watts (BA 7S)
High beam indicator light	283	2 watts (BA 7S)

- Zener diode type ... ZD 715
- Coil type (2 off) ... SIBA 32000 3 off
- Contact breaker type ... Lucas 7CA (12°)
- Fuse rating ... 35 amperes
- Oil warning light ... 281 | 2 watts (BA 7S)

SPARKING PLUGS
- Type ... Champion N3
- Plug gap settings ... ·020 in. (·50 mm.)
- Thread size ... 14 mm. × ¾ in. reach (×19·05 mm.)

CAPACITIES
- Fuel tank ... 4·25 gall (5·12 U.S. galls)
- Oil tank ... 6 pints (3·41 litres)
- Gearbox ... 1¼ pints approx. (·710 litres)
- Primary chaincase ... Automatic level
- Telescopic fork legs ... 200 c.c.

BASIC DIMENSIONS
- Wheel base ... 56·25 in. (142·875 cm.)
- Overall length ... 86 in. (218·44 cm.)
- Overall width ... 32·5 in. (82·55 cm.)
- Overall height ... 43·5 in. (110·49 cm.)
- Ground clearance ... 6·5 in. (unladen) (16·51 cm.)
- Seat height ... 32 in. (81·28 cm.)

WEIGHTS
- Unladen weight ... 470 lbs. (213·4 kg.)
- Engine unit (dry) ... 180 lbs. (81·72 kg.)

TORQUE WRENCH SETTINGS (DRY)
- Conn. rod bolts ... 18 lb./ft. (2·489 kg./m.)
- Crankcase junction bolts ... 12 lb./ft. (1·659 kg./m.)
- Crankcase junction studs ... 15 lb./ft. (2·074 kg./m.)
- Cylinder block nuts ... 20/22 lb./ft. (2·765/3·042 kg./m.)
- Cylinder head bolts ... 18 lb./ft. (2·489 kg./m.)
- Rocker box nuts ... 6 lb./ft. (·691 kg./m.)
- Rocker box bolts ... 6 lb./ft. (·691 kg./m.)
- Rocker spindle domed nuts ... 22 lb./ft. (3·042 kg./m.)
- Kickstart ratchet pinion nut ... 40/45 lb./ft. (5·530/6·221 kg./m.)
- Rotor fixing nut ... 50 lb./ft. (6·913 kg./m.)
- Stator fixing nuts ... 8 lb./ft. (1·106 kg./m.)
- Headlamp pivot bolts ... 10 lb./ft. (1·383 kg./m.)
- Headrace sleeve nut pinch bolt ... 15 lb./ft. (2·074 kg./m.)
- Stanchion pinch bolts ... 25 lb./ft. (3·456 kg./m.)
- Front wheel spindle cap bolts ... 25 lb./ft. (3·456 kg./m.)
- Brake cam spindle nuts ... 20 lb./ft. (2·765 kg./m.)
- Zener diode fixing nut ... 2/2·3 lb./ft. (·277/·3174 kg./m.)
- Fork cap nut ... 80 lb./ft. (11·06 kg./m.)
- Clutch centre nut ... 60 lb./ft. (8·295 kg./m.)
- Gearbox sprocket—Lock nut ... 58 lb./ft. (8·019 kg./m.)
- Shock absorber nut ... 75/80 lb./ft. (10·369/11·06 kg./m.)
- Centre bearing nuts ... 18 lb./ft. (2·489 kg./m.)

GENERAL DATA
1971
TRIDENT
THREE CYLINDER MODEL T150 AND T150V

750 c.c. (45 cu. ins.)

GENERAL DATA
MODEL T150 TRIDENT
LUBRICATION SYSTEM

OIL PUMP
- Body material ... Cast iron
- Bore diameters ... ·3438/·3433 in. (8·7325/8·7198 mm.)
- Scavenge gear—bore diameter ... ·3438/·3448 in. (8·7325/8·7579 mm.)
- Feed gear—bore diameter ... ·3438/·3448 in. (8·7325/8·7579 mm.)
- Spindle diameter ... ·3433/·3428 in. (8·7198/8·70712 mm.)
- Cover plate bore diameters: Spindle ... ·3433/·3438 in. (8·7198/8·7325 mm.)
- Drive scavenge gear ... ·4375/·4370 in. (11·1125/11·0998 mm.)
- Pump drive ratio ... 1·9 : 1 (engine to pump)

OIL PUMP DRIVE
- Intermediate gear—Bore diameter ... ·5625/·5620 in. (14·287/14·2748 mm.)
- Bush—Bore ... ·4387/·4382 in. (11·143/11·1302 mm.)
- —Length ... ·755/·745 in. (19·177/18·923 mm.)
- Spindle—Diameter ... ·4360/·4355 in. (11·0744/11·0617 mm.)

OIL PRESSURE RELEASE VALVE
- Piston diameter ... ·5605/·5610 in. (14·2367/14·2494 mm.)
- Working clearance ... ·001/·002 in. (0·0254/0·0508 mm.)
- Pressure release operates ... 90 lb./sq. in. (6·328 kg./sq. cm.)
- Spring length (Free) ... $1\frac{3}{8}$ in. (34·925 mm.)
- Load at $1\frac{3}{16}$ in. ... 8 lbs. (3·632 kgm.)
- Rate ... 42·3 lbs. (19·2042 kgm.)

OIL PRESSURE
- Normal running ... 75–85 lb./sq. in. (5·273–5·624 kg./sq. cm.)
- Idling ... 20–25 lb./sq. in. (1·406–1·758 kg./sq. cm.)
- Oil pressure switch: Working range ... 7–11 lbs. (3·178/4·994 kgm.)

ENGINE

BASIC DETAILS
- Bore and stroke ... 67 × 70 mm.
- Cubic capacity ... 741 c.c. (45 cu. in.)
- Compression ratio ... 9·5 : 1

CRANKSHAFT
- Crankshaft type ... EN16B hardened and tempered stamping-one piece
- Main bearing (drive side) size and type ... $1\frac{1}{8} \times 2\frac{13}{16} \times \frac{13}{16}$ in. (caged ball) (28·58 × 71·43 × 20·63 mm.)
- Main bearing (centre) running clearance ... ·0005/·0022 in. (·0127/·05588 mm.)
- Main bearing (timing side) size and type ... $1\frac{1}{8} \times 2\frac{13}{16} \times \frac{13}{16}$ in. (roller) (28·58 × 71·43 × 20·62 mm.)
- Right main bearing housing diameter ... 2·8110/2·8095 in. (71·3994/71·3613 mm.)
- Right main bearing journal diameter ... 1·1248/1·1245 in. (28·5699/28·5623 mm.)
- Centre main bearing housing diameter ... 2·0630/2·0625 in. (52·4002/52·3875 mm.)
- Centre main bearing journal diameter ... 1·9170/1·9175 in. (48·6918/48·7045 mm.)
- Left main bearing housing diameter ... 2·0447/2·0457 in. (51·9344/51·9608 mm.)
- Left main bearing journal diameter ... 0·9843/0·9840 in. (25·0012/24·9936 mm.)
- Big end journal diameter ... 1·6240/1·6235 in. (41·2496/41·2369 mm.)
- Min. regrind diameter ... 1·6200/1·6185 in. (41·148/41·1099 mm.)
- Crankshaft end float ... ·0015/·0145 in. (·038/·368 mm.)

CONNECTING RODS
- Material ... Alloy 'H' Section RR.56
- Length (centres) ... 5·751/5·749 in. (14·6075/14·6024 mm.)
- Big end bearings type ... Steel backed white metal
- Conn rod side clearance ... 0·013/0·019 in. (0·3302/0·4826 mm.)
- Bearing diametral clearance ... ·0005/·0020 in. minimum (·0127/·0508 mm.)

GUDGEON PIN (WRIST PIN)
- Material ... High tensile steel
- Fit in small end ... ·0005/·0011 in. (·0127/·0279 mm.)
- Diameter ... ·6883/·6885 in. (17·4828/17·4880 mm.)
- Length ... 2·250/2·235 in. (57·150/56·769 mm.)

GENERAL DATA

CYLINDER BLOCK
- Material ... Austenitic steel liner Aluminium Alloy
- Bore size ... 2·6368/2·6363 in. (66·9747/66·962 mm.)
- Maximum oversize ... +·040 in. (1·016 mm.)
- Tappet guide block housing diameter ... 1·1562/1·1557 in. (29·3675/29·3548 mm.)

CYLINDER HEAD
- Material ... Alum alloy die casting
- Inlet port size ... 1 in. dia. (25·4 mm.)
- Exhaust port size ... 1¼ in. dia. (31·75 mm.)
- Valve seatings:
  - Type ... Cast-in
  - Material ... Cast iron

VALVES
- Stem diameter: Inlet ... ·3100/·3095 in. (7·8740/7·8613 mm.)
  - Exhaust ... ·3095/·3090 in. (7·8613/7·8495 mm.)
- Head diameter: Inlet ... 1·534/1·528 in. (38·9636/38·812 mm.)
  - Exhaust ... 1·315/1·309 in. (33·401/33·2486 mm.)
- Exhaust valve material ... 21/4 'N' heat treated

VALVE GUIDES
- Material ... Hidural 5
- Bore diameter (Inlet and exhaust) ... ·3115/·3110 in. (7·9121/7·8994 mm.)
- Outside diameter (Inlet and exhaust) ... ·5005/·5010 in. (12·7127/12·7254 mm.)
- Length: Inlet ... 1·875 in. (47·625 mm.)
  - Exhaust ... 1·875 in. (47·625 mm.)

VALVE SPRINGS (RED AND WHITE)
- Free length: Inner ... 1·468 in. (37·2872 mm.)
  - Outer ... 1·600 in. (40·64 mm.)
- Total number of coils: Inner ... 6
  - Outer ... 5½
- Total fitted load
  - Valve open: Inner ... 82 lbs. (37·228 kgm.)
    - Outer ... 115 lbs. (51·31 kgm.)
  - Valve closed: Inner ... 37–40 lbs. (16·798–18·144 kgm.)
    - Outer ... 43–53 lbs. (21·792–24·062 kgm.)

VALVE TIMING

Set all tappet clearances @ 0·020 in. (0·50 mm.) for checking ...
$\begin{cases} 50 \\ 64 \\ 67 \\ 47 \end{cases}$

ROCKERS
- Material ... NI. CH. Steel stamping (EN33)
- Bore diameter ... ·5002/·5012 in. (12·7051/12·7305 mm.)
- Rocker spindle diameter ... ·4990/·4995 in. (12·6746/12·6873 mm.)
- Tappet clearance (cold): Inlet ... ·006 in. (0·1524 mm.)
  - Exhaust ... ·008 in. (0·2032 mm.)

CAMSHAFTS
- Journal diameters ... 1·0615/1·0605 in. (26·9621/26·9367 mm.)
- Diametral clearances ... ·0005/·0020 in. (·0127/·0508 mm.)
- End float ... ·007/·014 in. (·178/·356 mm.)
- Cam lift: Inlet and exhaust ... ·3045 in. (7·7343 mm.)
- Base circle diameter ... ·812 in. dia. (20·6248 mm.)

TAPPETS
- Material ... EN32B (Stellite tip)
- Tip radius ... 1·125 in. (28·575 mm.)
- Tappet diameter ... ·3115/·3110 in. (7·9121/7·8994 mm.)
- Clearance in guide block ... ·0005/·0015 in. (·0127/·0381 mm.)

TAPPET GUIDE BLOCK
- Diameter of bores ... ·3125/·3120 in. (7·9375/7·9248 mm.)
- Outside diameter ... 1·153/1·148 in. (29·2862/29·1592 mm.)
- Interference fit in cylinder block ... ·0027/·0082 in. (·06858/·20828 mm.)

ROCKER SPINDLE BUSHES
- Bush D/S: Bore diameter ... ·497/·498 in. (12·624/12·649 mm.)
  - Outside diameter ... ·6260/·6265 in. (15·9004/15·913 mm.)
- Bush T/S: Bore diameter ... ·375/·374 in. (9·525/9·4996 mm.)
  - Outside diameter ... ·501/·502 in. (12·725/12·751 mm.)

IGNITION TIMING
- Crankshaft position (B.T.D.C.) F.A. ... 38°
- Piston position (B.T.D.C.) F.A. ... ·357 in. (9·0678 mm.)
- Advance range:
  - Contact breaker ... 12°
  - Crankshaft ... 24°

GD   GENERAL DATA

TIMING GEARS
- Inlet and exhaust camshaft pinions:
  - No. of teeth ... 50
  - Interference fit on camshaft ... ·000/·001 in. (·000/·0254 mm.)
- Intermediate timing gear
  - No. of teeth ... 42
  - Bore diameter ... ·5618/·5625 in. (14·2697/14·2875 mm.)
- Intermediate timing gear needle roller ... $\tfrac{11}{16} \times \tfrac{7}{8} \times \tfrac{5}{8}$ in. (17·46 × 22·225 × 15·87 mm.)
- Intermediate wheel spindle
  - Diameter ... ·6888/·6885 in. (17·4955/17·4879 mm.)
- Crankcase pinion:
  - No. of teeth ... 25
  - Fit on crankcase ... +·0003 in. (+·00762 mm.)
  -                 −·0005 in. (−·0127 mm.)

CONTACT BREAKER (7CA)
- Gap setting ... ·014–·016 in. (·35–·40 mm.)
- Advance range ... 12° (24° crankshaft)
- Fully advanced at ... 2,000 r.p.m.

PISTONS
- Material ... Aluminium Alloy—diecasting
- Clearance: Top of skirt ... ·0056/·0035 in. (·42/·089 mm.)
-           Bottom of skirt ... ·0033/·0018 in. (·084/·0457 mm.)
- Gudgeon pin hole dia. ... ·6885/·6883 in. (17·9879/17·4828 mm.)

PISTON RINGS
- Material ... Cast iron HG10
- Compression rings (tapered):
  - Width ... 2·729/2·577 mm.
  - Thickness ... ·0625/·0615 in. (1·5875/1·5621 mm.)
  - Fitted gap ... ·009/·013 in. (·2286/·3302 mm.)
  - Clearance in groove ... ·0035/·0015 in. (·89/·038 mm.)
- Oil control ring:
  - Width ... 2·729/2·577 mm.
  - Thickness ... ·125/·124 in. (3·175/3·1496 mm.)
  - Fitted gap ... ·010/·040 in. (·254/1·016 mm.)
  - Clearance in groove ... ·0105/·0065 in. (·266/·165 mm.)

FUEL SYSTEM
- Triple carburetters ... Concentric
- Amal type ... 626
- Main jet size ... 150
- Needle jet size ... ·106
- Needle type ... STD
- Needle position ... 2
- Throttle valve:
  - Type ... $3\tfrac{1}{2}$
- Carburetter nominal bore size ... 27 mm.
- Air cleaner element ... Filter cloth and wire gauze

TRANSMISSION

CLUTCH DETAILS
- Single diaphragm spring—clutch spring rate ... 1,000 lb. (approx.) (453·6 kgm.)
- Minimum travel to disengage ... ·035 in. (·889 mm.)
- Minimum wear of friction plate ... ·06 in. (1·524 mm.)
- Bearing—Outer thrust plate—Size and type ... $\tfrac{1}{2} \times 1\tfrac{1}{8} \times \tfrac{1}{4}$ in. (12·7 × 28·575 × 6·35 mm.)
- Needle race—Size and type ... (2 off) $1\tfrac{3}{8} \times 1\tfrac{5}{8} \times \tfrac{1}{2}$ in. (34·93 × 41·28 × 12·7 mm.)
- Thrust race—Size and type ... $1\tfrac{3}{8} \times 2\tfrac{1}{16} \times \tfrac{5}{64}$ in. (34·93 × 52·39 × 1·984 mm.)

THROTTLE OPERATING MECHANISM
- Spindle—Diameter ... ·3115/·3106 in.

GENERAL DATA

GEARBOX

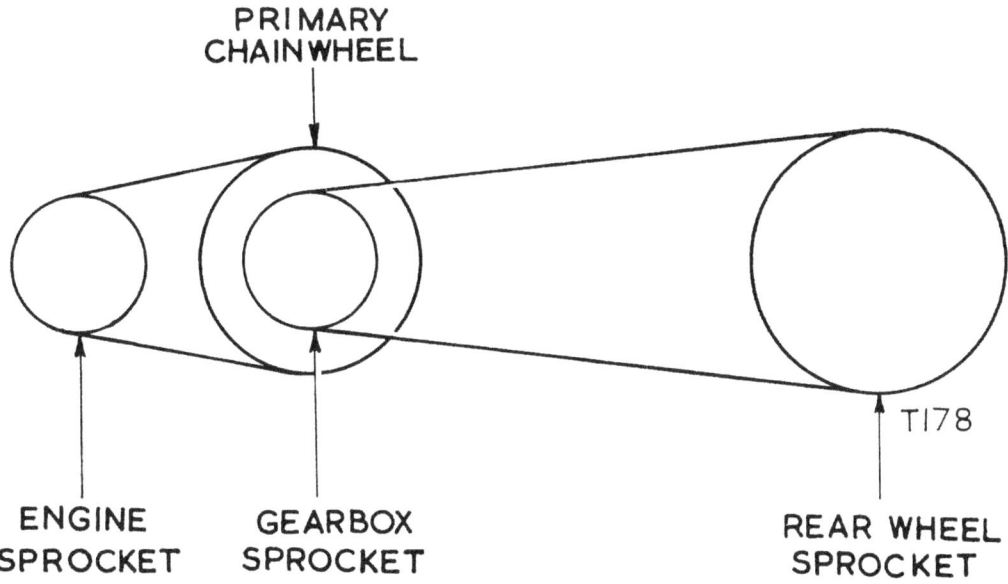

To find the gear ratios of a machine, calculate the top gear as follows:—

Divide the number of teeth on the primary chainwheel by the number of teeth on the engine sprocket and multiply the result by the number of teeth on the rear wheel sprocket, divided by the number of teeth on the gearbox sprocket, as example:—

$$\frac{clutch\ sprocket\ (50)}{engine\ sprocket\ (28)} \times \frac{rear\ wheel\ sprocket\ (53)}{gearbox\ sprocket\ (18)} = \frac{2650}{504} = 5\cdot26$$

To find the intermediate gear ratio, multiply the overall top gear by the internal gear ratio concerned, as example:—

$$top\ gear\ 5\cdot26 \times bottom\ gear\ internal\ ratio\ 2\cdot47 = 13\cdot00\ bottom\ gear\ overall\ ratio$$

$$Gearbox\ internal\ ratio = \frac{layshaft\ gear}{mainshaft\ gear} \times \frac{mainshaft\ top\ gear}{layshaft\ top\ gear}$$

as example:—

$$\frac{(layshaft\ 3rd)\ 22T}{(mainshaft\ 3rd)\ 24T} \times \frac{(mainshaft\ top)\ 25T}{(layshaft\ top)\ 19T} = 1\cdot26$$

GD — GENERAL DATA

RATIOS
Internal ratios (Std.) 4th (Top) ... 1·00 : 1
    3rd ... 1·26 : 1
    2nd ... 1·71 : 1
    1st (Bottom) ... 2·47 : 1

Overall ratios: 4th (Top) ... 5·26
    3rd ... 6·64
    2nd ... 9·00
    1st (Bottom) ... 13·00
Engine R.P.M. @ 10 M.P.H. in 4th (Top) gear ... 706 r.p.m.
Gearbox sprocket teeth ... 18

GEAR DETAILS
Mainshaft high gear:
  Bore diameter (bush fitted) ... ·8135/·8145 in. (20·6629/20·6883 mm.)
  Working clearance on shaft ... ·0032/·0047 in. (·08128/·1194 mm.)
  Bush length ... $2\frac{1}{4}$ in. (57·15 mm.)

Layshaft low gear:
  Bore diameter (bush fitted) ... ·8135/·8145 in. (20·6629/20·6883 mm.)
  Working clearance on shaft ... ·0025/·0045 in. (0·0635/0·127 mm.)

GEARBOX SHAFTS
Mainshaft:
  Left end diameter ... ·8098/·8103 in. (20·5689/20·5816 mm.)
  Right end diameter ... ·7494/·7498 in. (19·0348/19·044 mm.)
  Length ... $10\frac{21}{64}$ in. (262·3337 mm.)

Layshaft:
  Left end diameter ... ·6845/·6850 in. (17·4063/17·419 mm.)
  Right end diameter ... ·6845/·6850 in. (17·4063/17·419 mm.)
  Length ... $6\frac{41}{64}$ in. (168·6941 mm.)

BEARINGS
High gear bearing ... $1\frac{1}{4} \times 2\frac{1}{2} \times \frac{5}{8}$ in. Ball Journal (31·75 × 63·5 × 15·875 mm.)
Mainshaft bearing ... $\frac{3}{4} \times 1\frac{7}{8} \times \frac{9}{16}$ in. Ball Journal (19·05 × 47·625 × 14·282 mm.)
Layshaft bearing (left) ... $\frac{11}{16} \times \frac{7}{8} \times \frac{3}{4}$ in. Needle Roller (17·463 × 22·227 × 19·05 mm.)
Layshaft bearing (right) ... $\frac{11}{16} \times \frac{7}{8} \times \frac{3}{4}$ in. Needle Roller (17·463 × 22·227 × 19·05 mm.)

KICKSTART OPERATING MECHANISM
Bush bore diameter ... ·751/·752 in. (19·0754/19·1008 mm.)
Spindle working clearance in bush ... ·003/·005 in. (·0762/·127 mm.)
Ratchet spring free length ... $\frac{1}{2}$ in. (12·7 mm.)

GEARCHANGE MECHANISM
Plungers:
  Outer diameters ... ·4315/·4320 in. (10·9601/10·9728 mm.)
  Working clearance in bore ... ·0005/·0015 in. (0·0127/·0381 mm.)

Plunger springs:
  No. of working coils ... 12
  Free length ... $1\frac{1}{4}$ in. (31·75 mm.)
Inner bush bore diameter ... ·6245/·6255 in. (15·7423/15·8877 mm.)
  Clearance on shaft ... ·0007/·0032 in. (·01778/·08128 mm.)
Outer bush bore diameter ... ·7495/·7505 in. (19·0373/19·0627 mm.)
  Clearance on shaft ... ·0005/·0025 in. (·0127/·0635 mm.)

Quadrant return springs:
  No. of working coils ... $9\frac{1}{2}$
  Free length ... $1\frac{3}{4}$ in. (44·45 mm.)

Camplate plunger spring:
  Free length ... 2·28 in. (58 mm.)
  No. of working coils ... 21
  Spring rate ... 8·80 lbf/in.

GENERAL DATA

FRAME AND ATTACHMENT DETAILS

HEAD RACES
Caged ball type (top and bottom) .. Hoffman 9607

SWINGING FORK
Bush type .. Pre-sized steel-backed—phosphor bronze
Bush bore diameter .. 1·4460/1·4470 in. (36·7284/36·7538 mm.)
Sleeve diameter .. 1·4445/1·4450 in. (36·6903/36·702 mm.)
Distance between fork ends .. 7½ in. (190·5 mm.)

REAR SUSPENSION
Type .. Swinging fork controlled by combined coil spring/hydraulic damper units
Fitted length .. 8 in. (203·2 mm.) at mid position
Free length .. 8·810 in. (223·8 mm.)
Spring rate .. 110 lbs./in.
Mean coil diameter .. 1·98 in. (50·29 mm.)

WHEELS, BRAKES AND TYRES

WHEELS
Rim size: Front .. WM2-19
Rear .. WM3-19
Spoke details: Front: Left side .. 20 off 10 SWG 7·2 in. (mean length) 134° head
Right side (outer) .. 10 off 10 SWG 5·1 in. (overhaul length) 76° head
Right side (inner) .. 10 off 10 SWG 5·0 in. (mean length) 97° head
Rear: Left side (outer) .. 10 off 10 SWG 6·3 in. (mean length) 90° head
Left side (inner) .. 10 off 10 SWG 6·1 in. (mean length) 101° head
Right side .. 20 off 10 SWG 7·5 in. (mean length) 134° head

WHEEL BEARINGS
Front and rear, dimensions and type .. 20 × 47 × 14 mm.—Ball journal
Front and rear, spindle diameter (at bearing journals) .. ·7862/·7867 in. (19·9695 × 19·9822 mm.)

STANDARD REAR WHEEL
Bolt size for detachable sprocket .. ¼ in. dia. 2 in. U.H. × 28 UNF (6·35 mm. dia. × 50·8 mm.U.H.)
Number of bolts .. 5

REAR WHEEL DRIVE
Gearbox sprocket .. See "Gearbox"
Rear wheel sprocket teeth .. 53 (alternative 50)
Chain details:
No. of links: Solo .. 108
Pitch .. ⅝ in. (15·875 mm.)
Width .. ⅜ in. (9·525 mm.)
Speedometer drive gearbox ratio .. 1·25 : 1
Speedometer cable length .. 68 in. (1·7272 mm.)

BRAKES
Type .. Internal expanding twin leading shoes
Drum Diameter: Front .. 8 in. ± ·002 in.
Rear .. 7 in. ± ·002 in.
Lining front .. Lockheed 4523-166
Lining rear: thickness .. ·187/·197 in. (4·75/5 mm.)
Area (total) .. 14·2 sq. in.

TYRES
Size: Front .. 4·10 × 19 in.
Rear .. 4·10 × 19 in.
Tyre pressure: Front .. 26 lb./sq. in. (1·828 kg./sq. cm.)
Rear .. 28 lb./sq. in. (1·97 kg./sq. cm.)

FRONT FORKS

TELESCOPIC FORK
Type .. Telescopic—Oil damping
Spring details:
Free length .. 19·50 in. (495·3 mm.)
No. working coils .. 63
Spring rate .. 32½ lb./in. (4·485 kg./m.)
Gauge .. 7 s.w.g.
Colour code .. Orange
Stanchion diameter: (top) .. 1·355/1·350 in. (34·4/34·3 mm.)
(bottom) .. 1·3610/1·3605 in. (33·04/33·03 mm.)
Outer member bore diameter .. 1·365/1·363 in. (33·15/33·1 mm.)

GD7A

GD GENERAL DATA

GEARBOX (5 SPEED—MODEL T150V)

RATIOS
Internal ratios: 5th (Top) .. 1·00 : 1
 4th .. 1·19 : 1
 3rd .. 1·40 : 1
 2nd .. 1·837 : 1
 1st (Bottom) .. 2·585 : 1
Overall ratios: 5th (Top) .. 5·258
 4th .. 6·256
 3rd .. 7·360
 2nd .. 9·661
 1st (Bottom) .. 13·590
Engine R.P.M. @ 10 M.P.H. in 5th (Top) gear .. 706
Gearbox sprocket teeth .. 18

GEAR DETAILS
Mainshaft high gear:
 Bearing type .. Needle roller (torrington B1314)
 Bearing length .. ·875/·865 in. (22·23/21·97 mm.)
 Spigot diameter (high gear) .. 1·5077/1·5072 in. (38·36/38·28 mm.)

GEARBOX SHAFTS
Mainshaft:
 Left end diameter .. ·8103/·8098 in. (20·58/20·57 mm.)
 Right end diameter .. ·7494/·7498 in. (19·044/19·054 mm.)
 Length .. 10·33 in. (262·3 mm.)
Layshaft:
 Left end diameter .. ·6875/·6870 in. (17·46/17·404 mm.)
 Right end diameter .. ·6875/·6870 in. (17·46/17·404 mm.)
 Length .. 6·47 in. (164·33 mm.)

BEARINGS
Mainshaft bearing (left) .. $1\frac{1}{2} \times 2\frac{1}{2} \times \frac{5}{8}$ in. Roller bearing (38·1 mm./63·5 mm./15·875 mm.)
Mainshaft bearing (right) .. $\frac{3}{4} \times 1\frac{7}{8} \times \frac{9}{16}$ in. Ball Journal (19·05 mm./47·625 mm./14·288 mm.)
Layshaft bearing (left) .. $\frac{11}{16} \times \frac{7}{8} \times \frac{3}{4}$ in. Needle roller (17·463 mm./22·225 mm./19·05 mm.)
Layshaft bearing (right) .. $\frac{11}{16} \times \frac{7}{8} \times \frac{3}{4}$ in. Needle roller (17·463 mm./22·225 mm./19·05 mm.)
Layshaft 1st gear bush:
 Bore diameter .. ·800/·795 in. (20·32/20·203 mm.)
 Shaft diameter .. ·8075/·8070 in. (20·511/20·498 mm.)
Layshaft 2nd gear bush:
 Bore diameter .. ·800/·795 in. (20·32/20·203 mm.)
 Shaft diameter .. ·8075/·8070 in. (20·511/20·498 mm.)

ELECTRICAL EQUIPMENT
Battery .. Lucas PUZSA
Coil .. Lucas 17 M 12
Contact breaker unit .. Lucas 7CA
Generator .. Lucas RM20/21
Horn .. Clearhooter HF 80. High/Low
Horn Relay .. Lucas 6RA
Rectifier .. Lucas 2DS.506
Zener Diode .. Lucas ZD.715
Bulbs—headlamp (main) .. Lucas 370. 45/40 watt
 —headlamp (pilot) .. Lucas 989. 6 watt
 —warning lamps .. Lucas 281. 2 watt
 —stop-tail lamp .. Lucas 380. 21/6 watt
Speedometer/tachometer illumination .. Lucas 643. 2.2 watt
Direction indicators .. Lucas 382. 21 watt
Condenser .. Lucas 2CP
Capacitor .. Lucas 2MC
Flasher unit .. Lucas 8FL
Headlamp .. Lucas MCH 69
Handlebar switch (right) .. Lucas 169 SA
Handlebar switch (left) .. Lucas 169 SA
Ignition switch .. Lucas 149 SA
Rear stop switch .. Lucas 118 SA
Fuse rating .. 35 amperes
Sparking Plugs
 Type .. Champion N3
 —Plug gap settings .. ·020 in. (·50 mm.)
 —Thread size .. 14 mm. × $\frac{3}{4}$ in. reach (×19·05 mm.)

GENERAL DATA

CAPACITIES
Fuel tank	4·2 U.S. galls. (3½ Imp. galls.)(15·94 litres)
Oil tank	7·2 U.S. pints (6 Imp. pints)(3·8 litres)
Gearbox	1½ U.S. pints (1¼ Imp. pints)(750 c.c.)
Primary chaincase	¾ U.S. pints (⅝ Imp. pints)(350 c.c.)
Front forks (each leg)	230 c.c.

BASIC DIMENSIONS
Wheel base	56·25 in. (142·875 cm.)
Overall length	86 in. (218·44 cm.)
Overall width	32·5 in. (82·55 cm.) 33 in. (84 cm.)
Overall height	43·5 in. (110·49 cm.)
Ground clearance	6·5 in. (unladen) (16·51 cm.)
Seat height	32 in. (81·28 cm.)
Unladen weight	460 lbs. (208·8 kgs.)
Engine unit (dry)	180 lbs. (81·72 kgs.)

TORQUE WRENCH SETTINGS (DRY)
Conn. rod bolts	18 lb./ft. (2·489 kg./m.)
Crankcase junction bolts	12 lb./ft. (1·659 kg./m.)
Crankcase junction studs	15 lb./ft. (2·074 kg./m.)
Cylinder block nuts	20/22 lb./ft. (2·765/3·042 kg./m.)
Cylinder head bolts	18 lb./ft. (2·489 kg./m.)
Rocker box nuts	6 lb./ft. (·691 kg./m.)
Rocker box bolts	6 lb./ft. (·691 kg./m.)
Rocker spindle domed nuts	22 lb./ft. (3·042 kg./m.)
Kickstart ratchet pinion nut	40/45 lb./ft. (5·530/6·221 kg./m.)
Rotor fixing nut	50 lb./ft. (6·913 kg./m.)
Stator fixing nuts	8 lb./ft. (1·106 kg./m.)
Head race sleeve nut pinch bolt	25 lb./ft. (3·456 kg./m.)
Stanchion pinch bolts	25 lb./ft. (3·456 kg./m.)
Front wheel spindle cap bolts	15 lb./ft. (2·074 kg./m.)
Brake cam spindle nuts	20 lb./ft. (2·765 kg./m.)
Zener diode fixing nut	2/2·3 lb./ft. (·277/·3174 kg./m.)
Fork cap nut	80 lb./ft. (11·06 kg./m.)
Clutch centre nut	60 lb./ft. (8·295 kg./m.)
Gearbox sprocket—Lock nut	58 lb./ft. (8·019 kg./m.)
Shock absorber nut	75/80 lb./ft. (10·369/11·06 kg./m.)
Centre bearing nuts	18 lb./ft. (2·489 kg./m.)
Engine sprocket nut	60 lb./ft. (8·295 kg./m.)
Camshaft pinion nut	75 lb./ft. (10·369 kg./m.)

GENERAL DATA

1973
TRIDENT
THREE CYLINDER MODEL T150V

ENGINE

MAIN BEARING (RIGHT SIZE) SIDE AND TYPE ... 25 mm. × 52 mm. × 15 mm.
    Right main bearing housing diameter ... 2·0447/2·0457 in. (51·934/51·961 mm.)
    Right main bearing journal diameter ... 0·9843/0·9840 in. (25·0012/24·9936 mm.)
    Left main bearing housing diameter ... 2·8110/2·8095 in. (71·3994/71·3613 mm.)
    Left main bearing journal diameter ... 1·1248/1·1245 in. (28·5699/28·563 mm.)
    Minimum regrind diameter ... 1·5840/1·5833 in. (40·234/40·221 mm.)

CONNECTING RODS
    Big end bearings material ... Lead/bronze.

CYLINDER HEAD
    Inlet port size ... $1\frac{1}{16}$ in. (27 mm.)

CAMSHAFTS
    Cam lift-Inlet and Exhaust ... ·329. in. (8·356 mm.).

GEARBOX

RATIOS (Home & General Export Only)
    5th Top ... 4·95
    4th Fourth ... 5·88
    3rd Third ... 6·93
    2nd Second ... 9·1
    1st Bottom ... 12·8
    Engine R.P.M. @ 10 m.p.h. Top Gear ... 664

SPROCKETS (Home & General Export Only)
    Rear Wheel - No. of teeth ... 50

CHAINS (Home & General Export Only)
    Secondary $\frac{5}{8}$ in. pitch × $\frac{3}{8}$ in. wide, links ... 105

BRAKES & WHEELS

BRAKES
    Front type ... Hydraulicaly operated disc
    Disc diameter ... 10 in. (254 mm.)
    Friction pads type ... MINTEX M64
    Lining thickness ... ·25 in. (6·35 mm.)
    Hydraulic fluid ... LOCKHEED 329 or equivalent

WHEELS
    Spoke details-front:—
        Spoke (Inner) R.H. & L.H. ... 20 off 10 swg 7·75 in. (Mean length) 96° head.
        Spoke (Outer) R.H. & L.H. ... 20 off 10 swg 7·85 in. (Mean length) 80° head.

WEIGHTS
    Unladen weight ... 471 lbs (212 kg.)

TORQUE WRENCH SETTINGS (DRY)
    Front Brake disc retaining bolts ... 20 lb. ft. (2·8 kg. m.)

SECTION A

LUBRICATION SYSTEM

	Section
ROUTINE MAINTENANCE	A1
TABLE OF RECOMMENDED LUBRICANTS	A2
ENGINE LUBRICATION SYSTEM	A3
CHANGING THE ENGINE OIL AND CLEANING THE OIL FILTERS	A4
OIL PRESSURE	A5
STRIPPING AND REASSEMBLING THE OIL PRESSURE RELEASE VALVE	A6
REMOVING AND REPLACING THE OIL PUMP	A7
REMOVING AND REPLACING THE OIL COOLER	A8
REMOVING AND REPLACING THE ROCKER OIL FEED PIPE	A9
ANTI-DRAIN VALVE	A10
CONTACT BREAKER LUBRICATION	A11
GEARBOX LUBRICATION	A12
PRIMARY CHAINCASE LUBRICATION	A13
REAR CHAIN LUBRICATION AND MAINTENANCE	A14
GREASING THE STEERING HEAD RACES	A15
WHEEL BEARING LUBRICATION	A16
TELESCOPIC FORK LUBRICATION	A17
LUBRICATION NIPPLES	A18
LUBRICATING THE CONTROL CABLES	A19
SPEEDOMETER CABLE LUBRICATION	A20
REAR BRAKE SPINDLE LUBRICATION	A21

LUBRICATION SYSTEM

SECTION A1

ROUTINE MAINTENANCE

	Section
Every 250 miles (400 Kms.)	
Check level in oil tank	A4
Every 1,000 miles (1,600 Kms.)	
Lubricate control cables	A19
Grease swinging fork pivot	A18
Remove rear chain for cleaning and greasing	A14
Every 3,000 miles (3,800 Kms.)	
Check gearbox oil level	A12
Check front forks for external oil leakage	A17
Grease brake pedal spindle	A21
Every 4,000 miles (6,400 Kms.)	
Change oil in engine and chaincase	A4
Change disposable filter element	A4
Every 6,000 miles (9,600 Kms.)	
Change oil in gearbox	A12
Change oil in front forks	A17
Every 12,000 miles (19,200 Kms.)	
Grease wheel bearings	A16
Grease steering head bearings	A15

LUBRICATION SYSTEM   A

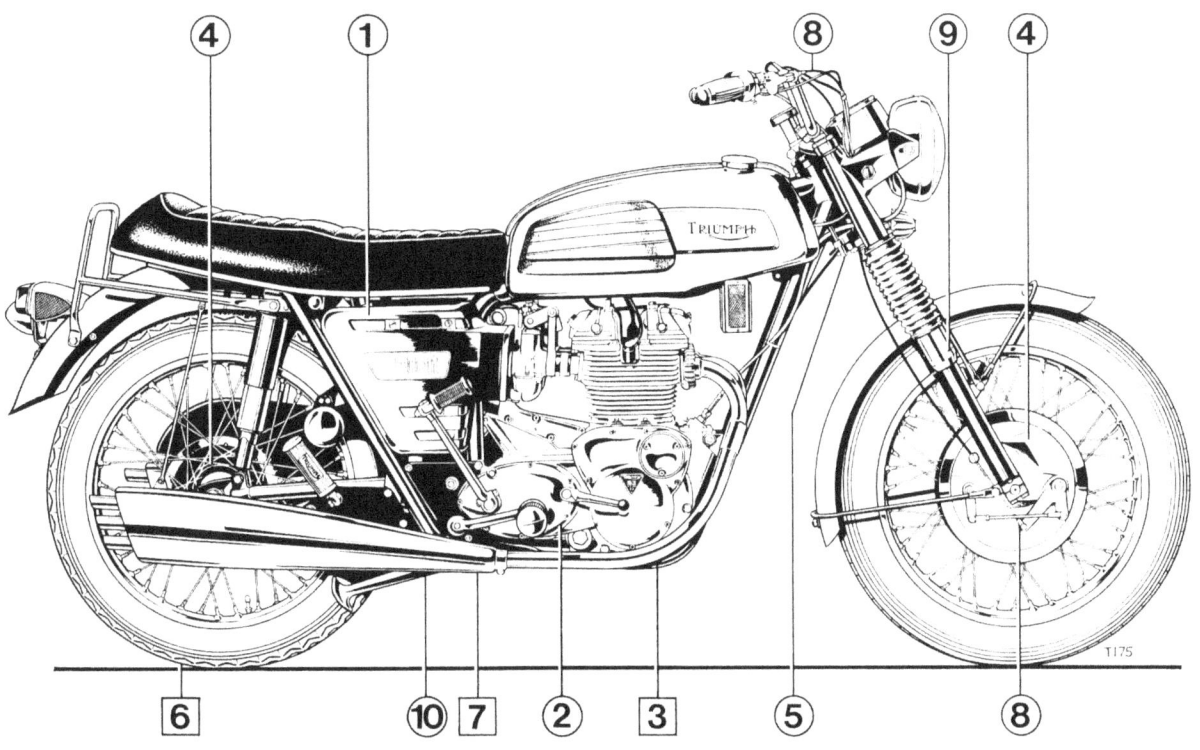

Fig. A1. LUBRICATION CHART

Numbers in circles refer to right side of machine
Numbers in squares refer to left side of machine

GUIDE TO LUBRICATION POINTS

Illustration No.	Description	SAE Oil grade
1	Engine oil tank	20W/50
2	Gearbox	90
3	primary chaincase	As engine
4	Wheel hubs	Grease
5	Steering head	Grease
6	Brake cam spindle	Grease
7	Brake pedal spindle	Grease
8	Exposed cables	20
9	Telescopic fork	20
10	Swinging fork pivot	Grease
—	All brake rod joints and pins	20

LUBRICATION SYSTEM

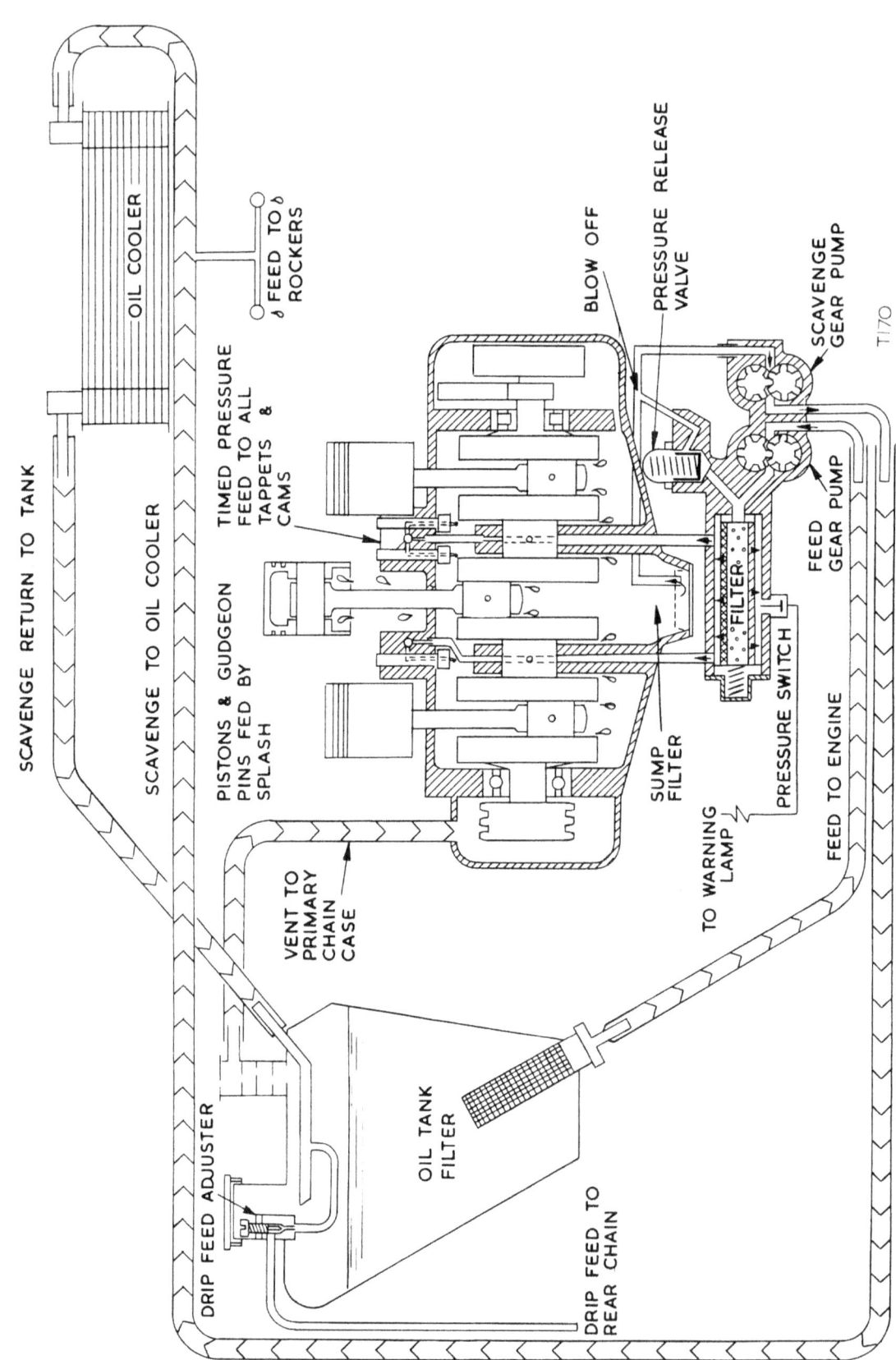

Fig. A2. Engine lubrication diagram

LUBRICATION SYSTEM

SECTION A2
RECOMMENDED LUBRICANTS

UNIT	MOBIL	B.P.	CASTROL	ESSO	SHELL	REGENT/TEXACO
Recommended Engine—Summer	Mobiloil Super 10W/50	Super Visco-Static 20W/50 or 10W/40	Castrol GTX	Uniflo	Shell Super 100 or Shell Super 101	Havoline 20W/50
—Winter			Castrolite			
Approved Engine—Summer	Mobiloil Special 20W/50		Castrol XL	Esso Extra Motor Oil 20W/50		URSA Oil Extra Duty 20W/40
—Winter			Castrolite			
OVERSEAS						
UNIT	MOBIL	B.P.	CASTROL	ESSO	SHELL	TEXACO
Recommended Engine—Summer	Mobiloil Super 10W/50	Super Visco-Static 20W/50 or 10W/40	Castrol GTX or Castrol XL	Uniflo	Shell Super 100 or Shell Super 101	Havoline 20W/50 20W/50
—Winter			Castrolite			
Approved Engine—Summer	Mobiloil Special 10W/30		Castrol XL	Esso Extra Motor Oil 20W/40		URSA Oil Extra Duty 20W/40
—Winter			Castrolite			
U.S.A. ONLY						
UNIT	MOBIL	B.P.	CASTROL	ESSO	SHELL	TEXACO
Recommended Engine—Summer	Mobiloil Super 10W/50	Super Visco-Static 20W/50 or 10W/40	Castrol XLR	Uniflo	Shell Super 100 or Shell Super 101	Havoline 20W/**50** or Havoline 20W/**20**
—Winter			Castrolite			
Approved Engine—Summer	Mobiloil Special 10W/30		Castrol XL	Esso Extra Motor Oil 20W/40		URSA Oil Extra Duty 20W/40
—Winter			Castrolite			
UNITED KINGDOM AND OVERSEAS						
Gearbox	Mobilube GX90	B.P. Gear Oil 90 E.P.	Castrol Hypoy 90 E.P.	Esso Gear Oil GX 90/140 or GX90	Shell Spirax 90 E.P.	Multigear Lubricant E.P.90
Primary Chaincase	USE SAME LUBRICANT AS ENGINE OWING TO ENGINE BREATHING SYSTEM					
Telescopic Forks	Mobiloil Super	Super Visco-Static 20W/50 or 10W/40	Castrolite	Uniflo or Esso Extra Motor Oil 20W/40	Shell Super 100 or Shell Super 101	Havoline 20/20W
Wheel Bearings and Swinging Fork	Mobilgrease M.P. or Mobilgrease Special	Energrease L2	Castrol L.M. Grease	Multipurpose Grease H	Shell Retinax A	Marfak All Purpose
Easing Rusted Parts	Mobil Handy Oil	Energol Penetrating Oil	Castrol Penetrating Oil	Esso Penetrating Oil	Shell Donax P	Graphited Penetrating Oil
U.S.A.						
Gearbox	Mobilube GX90	B.P. Gear Oil 90 E.P.	Castrol Hypoy 90 E.P.	Esso Gear Oil GX90	Shell Spirax 90 E.P.	Multigear Lubricant E.P. 90
Primary Chaincase	USE SAME LUBRICANT AS ENGINE OWING TO ENGINE BREATHING SYSTEM					
Telescopic Forks	Mobiloil Super	Super Visco-Static 20W/50 10W/40	Castrolite	Uniflo or Esso Extra Motor Oil 20W/40	Shell Super 100 or Shell Super 101	Havoline 20/20W
Wheel Bearings and Swinging Fork	Mobilgrease M.P. or Mobilgrease Special	Energrease L.2	Castrol M.P. Grease	Multipurpose Grease H	Shell Retinax A	Marfak All Purpose
Easing Rusted Parts	Mobil Handy Oil	Energol Penetrating Oil	Castrol Penetrating Oil	Esso Penetrating Oil	Shell Donax P	Graphited Penetrating Oil

SECTION A3

ENGINE LUBRICATION SYSTEM

The engine lubrication system is of the dry sump type. The oil is fed by gravity from the oil tank to the oil pump, the oil under pressure from the pump, is forced via a cartridge type oil filter through drillings to the inner main bearings and crankshaft big ends, where it escapes and lubricates the cylinder walls, roller journal outer main bearings and other internal engine parts. Oil is prevented from draining into the crankcase when the engine is not running by means of an anti-drain valve situated behind the oil pump.

The oil pressure between the oil pump and the crankshaft is controlled by the oil pressure release valve.

After lubricating the engine and primary transmission oil is forced to the sump, where it is scavenged through the sump filter and returned, via the oil cooler to the oil tank through the action of the oil pump scavene gears. The oil pump has been designed so that the scavenge gears have a greater pumping capacity than the feed gears, thus ensuring that the sump does not become flooded.

The valve operating mechanism oil feed is taken from the point between the scavenge side of the pump and the oil cooler. After travelling through the rocker spindle, the oil is fed into the rocker boxes by way of notches in the rocker arms, afterwards it falls by gravity down the push rod cover tubes. The oil then passes through holes in the tappet guide blocks and into the sump, where it is subsequently scavenged. The idler pinion needle roller bearing is lubricated by oil draining through a drilling in the right side crankcase.

A positive oil feed in provided for the tappets. The lubricant is pressure fed through two pipes, one from each inner main bearing cap to their respective exhaust tappets. The lubricant passes through the crankcase and cylinder block base flange drillings to an anular groove machined in each tappet guide block. Two holes are provided in each groove to mate with the oil holes in the tappets, which provide a channel for the lubricant to the tappets and camshaft working faces. (See Fig. A4 and A5).

SECTION A4

CHANGING THE ENGINE OIL AND CLEANING THE FILTERS

The oil in new and reconditioned engines should be changed at 250, 500 and 1,000 mile (400, 800 and 1,500 kms) intervals during the running-in period, and thereafter as stated in Section A1.

It is advisable to drain the oil when the engine is warm as it will flow more readily.

When the oil has been drained it is essential that the wire gauze filters are washed in paraffin (kerosene) and the cartridge filter is replaced.

Remove six nuts and locking washers which secure the sump plate, and remove the plate, two gaskets and wire gauze filter (see Fig. A3). Allow the sump to drain for approximately ten minutes. Clean the filter, and replace the gaskets. A gasket is fitted either side of the filter. Refit the sump plate, ensuring that the pocketed end is towards the rear of the engine.

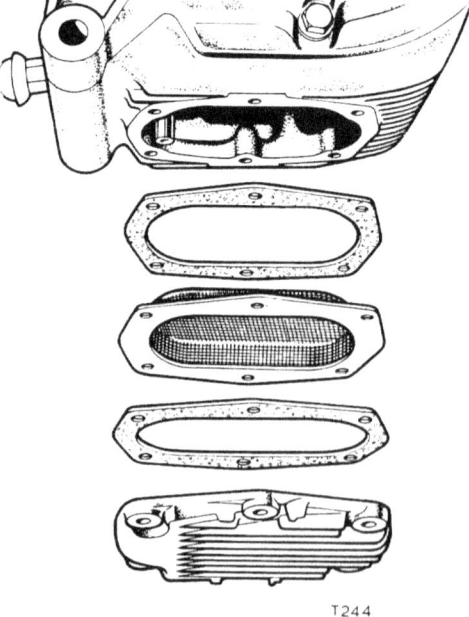

Fig. A3. Crankcase sump filter

LUBRICATION SYSTEM

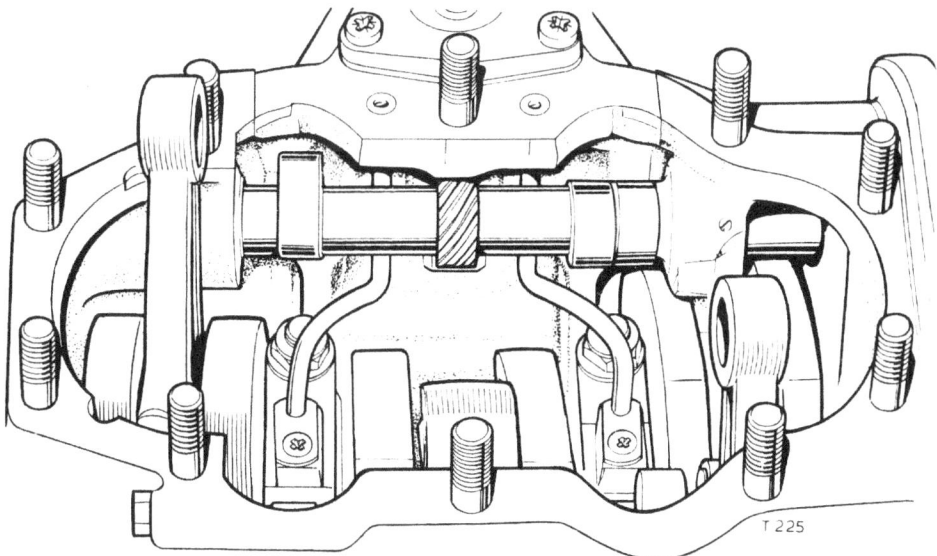

Fig. A4. Tappet oil feed from central main bearings

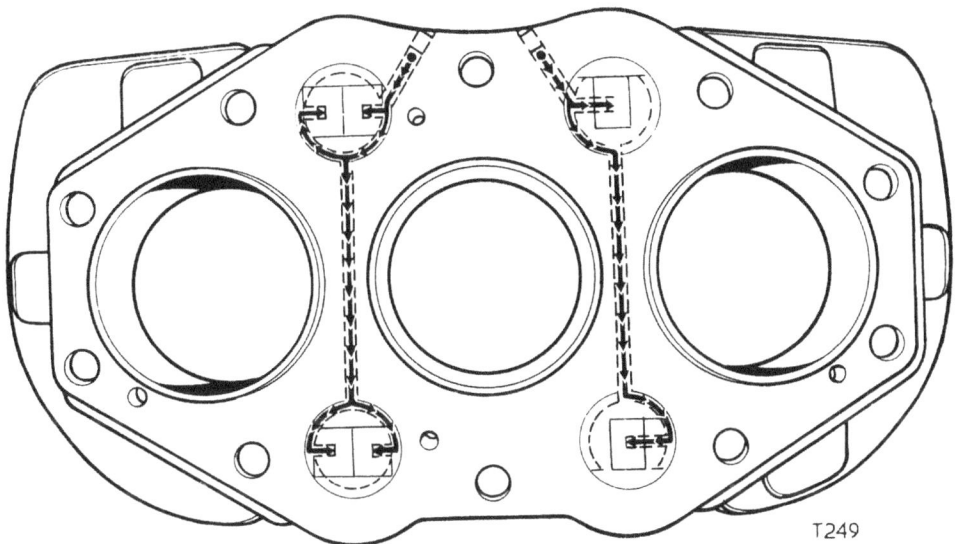

Fig. A5. Tappet oil feed through cylinder block

Remove the oil tank filler cap, and remove three Pozidriv screws securing the right side panel. Withdraw the panel and place a drain tray below the oil tank drain plug. Remove the drain plug and allow the oil approximately ten minutes to drain. Unscrew the large hexagonal headed oil tank filter and wash it thoroughly.

It is advisable to flush out the oil tank with flushing oil (obtainable from most garages) or, if this is not available, paraffin (kerosene) will do. However, if this is used ensure that all traces are removed from the outside of the oil tank prior to re-filling with oil. (For the correct grade of oil see Section A2).

NOTE: The level in the oil tank should be up to the top line on the dipstick. Further addition of oil will cause excessive venting through the oil tank breather pipe due to lack of air space.

The main feed oil filter is of the disposable type. This should be renewed every 4,000 miles (6,400 Km) when the oil is changed.

To remove the element remove the large diameter hexagonally headed cap from below the forward end of the gearbox outer cover, and remove the spring. Withdraw the element using a pair of long nosed pliers.

LUBRICATION SYSTEM

THE ELEMENT MUST BE FITTED WITH THE HOLE INWARDS, OTHERWISE THE OIL SUPPLY WILL BE CUT OFF.

A rubber sealing ring is attached to the end of the element. Ensure that this does not become detached. Replace the spring and cap, ensuring that the 'O' ring seal and fibre washer are in good order. Re-fill the oil tank and if for any reason the oil cooler has been removed, re-check and if necessary refill the tank after approximately five miles.

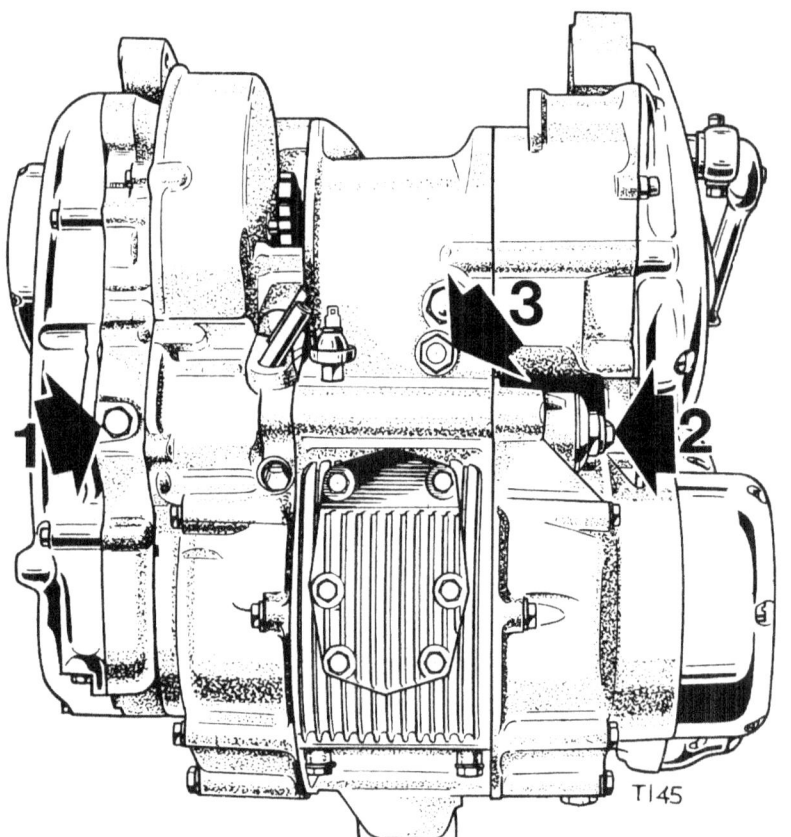

1. Primary chaincase drain plug
2. Cartridge oil filter housing cap
3. Gearbox drain and level plugs

Fig. A6. Underside view of eninge/gearbox unit

SECTION A5

OIL PRESSURE

The oil pressure is controlled by means of the release valve situated at the rear of the centre crankcase, on the left side. When the engine is stationary there will be no oil pressure. When the engine is started from cold, pressure may be as high as 90 lbs. p.s.i., reducing when hot to the normal running figure of 75/90 lbs. p.s.i. at three thousand r.p.m.

The pressure can only be checked with an oil gauge connected to an adaptor replacing one of the blanking plugs on the front of the centre crankcase (see Fig. B34).

If satisfactory readings are not obtained, check the following:—

(1) That the oil pressure relief valve is clean and the

LUBRICATION SYSTEM

piston has the correct working clearance in the valve body (see GENERAL DATA).

(2) That the oil tank level is not below the minimum and that oil is being returned to the tank.

(3) That the sump filter, crankcase filter and oil tank filter are clean and not blocked, and that the crankcase filter is not fitted in reverse.

(4) That the oil pump is functioning properly and that there is a supply of oil to the pump. Refer to Section A7 for checking the oil pump.

(5) That the drillings in the crankcase connecting the oil pipes to the oil pump are clear.

(6) That the big ends and centre plain main bearings are not badly worn. Should the bearings not have the correct working clearance, oil will escape more readily, particularly when the oil is warm and is more fluid, thus giving a drop in pressure.

(7) That the rubber sealing rings fitted at either end of the main bearing to tappet guide block oil pipes are not allowing an oil leakage, and thus a drop in pressure.

Excessive periods of slow running (such as in heavy traffic), or unnecessary use of the air control, can cause dilution in the oil tank and an overall drop in lubricating pressure due to the lower viscosity of the diluted oil.

Most lubrication and oil pressure troubles can be avoided by regular attention to the recommended oil changes.

SECTION A6

STRIPPING AND RE-ASSEMBLING THE OIL PRESSURE RELEASE VALVE

The oil pressure release valve is very reliable and should require no maintenance other than cleaning. It is situated on the underside of the engine to the rear of the oil pump housing. Oil pressure is governed by the single spring situated within the release valve body. When the spring is removed it can be checked for compressive strength by measuring the length. Compare this figure with that given in GENERAL DATA.

Unless a special tool is available, access to the release valve assembly can only be gained by stripping the primary transmission (Section C). Service tool D-2135 can be obtained to remove the release valve after the oil feed and scavenge pipes have been disconnected at the crankcase.

To prevent the loss of oil from the oil cooler and oil tank the ends of the pipes should be checked as they are disconnected.

When the valve has been removed the hexagonal domed cap can be unscrewed from the main body, thus releasing the piston which should be withdrawn.

Thoroughly clean all parts in paraffin (kerosene) and inspect for wear. The piston should be checked for possible scoring and the springs for signs of fracture

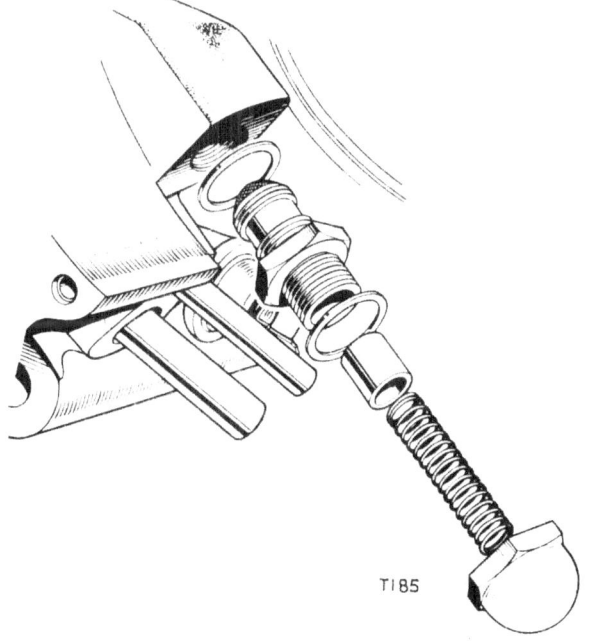

Fig. A7. Exploded oil pressure release valve

and also length. To reassemble the release valve unit offer the piston into the valve body and screw on the valve cap with new fibre washers. Similarly, when screwing the release valve unit into the crankcase, fit a new fibre washer between the release valve body and the crankcase. (Figure A7).

SECTION A7

REMOVING AND REPLACING THE OIL PUMP

The oil pump is mounted in the drive side crankcase protruding through the inner primary chaincase. The oil pump is driven by a train of gears from the crankshaft. Due to the moving part continually operating in oil, the degree of wear would be very slight, though after considerable mileage the driving and driven gears both of the feed and scavenge sides of the pump will require inspection for possible wear.

To gain access to the oil pump, remove the outer primary chaincase (Section C5) and the inner primary chaincase (Section C8). This will, of course, include removal of the oil pump drive gear. Remove the four Pozidriv screws holding the oil pump to the crankcase and the pump can be lifted clear. The remaining two slot headed screws serve to hold together the three portions of the oil pump body. These should be removed.

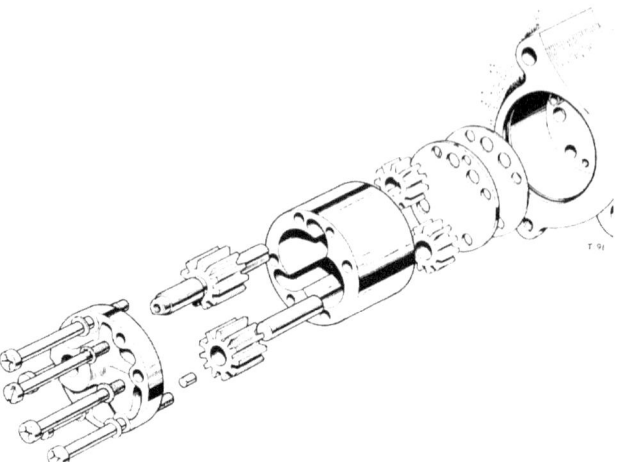

Fig. A8. Exploded oil pump

Using a thin soft alloy drift, from the in-board side of the pump the two spindles can be tapped gently through, releasing the gears. Wash all the parts thoroughly in paraffin (kerosene). Check the spindles and spindle bores both in the gears and portions of the body, comparing the dimensions with those given in the GENERAL DATA. Examine the gear teeth for scuffing and indentations.

Upon reassembly insure that a new gasket is fitted between the oil pump and crankcase, and the oil pump is properly located over the dowl in the crankcase recess and that the slot headed body screws (with serrated washers) are sufficiently tight. (Fig. A8).

Having fitted the pump do not over-tighten the Pozidriv screws which are of small diameter, threaded into alloy. Fit a new 'O' ring seal into the chaincase facing recess surrounding the pump body.

Replace the transmission and chaincases as in Sections C5 and C9.

Do not forget when fitting the oil pump gear to apply Loctite compound to the securing screw threads.

SECTION A8

REMOVING AND REFITTING THE OIL COOLER

To gain access to the oil cooler, oil pipe clips and to fixings, the petrol tank should be removed (Section E1).

Unscrew both oil pipe clips and note that the left hand pipe from the cooler leads to the rocker feed pipe. After removal of the pipes, ensure that the cooler is not tilted as it contains over half a pint of oil.

Slacken two support bracket top bolts sufficiently to allow eight corner packings to be removed (Fig. A9).

Whilst supporting the cooler, remove the support bracket bolts, nuts and washers, and collect four spigotted rubber washers.

LUBRICATION SYSTEM

The cooler is now free of the frame and should be removed and drained by inverting above a suitable container.

Do not attempt to flush out the inside of the cooler, as little or no foreign matter is collected. However, it is advisable to wash the outside with a soft brush and paraffin (kerosene).

To refit, assemble the support brackets as shown (Fig. A9), and note that the large oil pipe unions on the top of the cooler face rearwards. Suspend the cooler on the frame using spigotted rubbers and bolts as shown (Fig. A9).

Secure both brackets to the frame, and replace both large diameter oil pipes. The left side union connects to the scavenge pipe, i.e. the pipe which connects to the metal rocker feed pipe union. Tighten the union clips ensuring that the pipes are not damaged by over tightening.

Refit the petrol tank as in Section E1.

Note that the reflector rubbers are attached to the oil cooler by a suitable rubber adhesive.

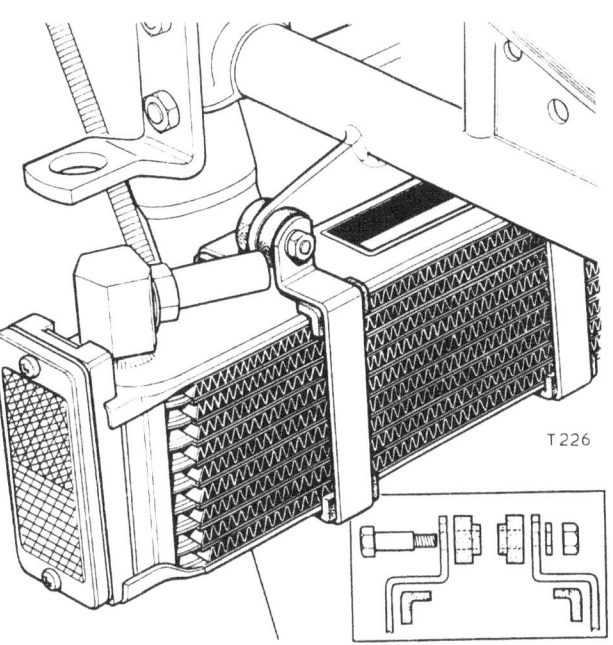

Fig. A9. Oil cooler mountings

SECTION A9

REMOVING AND REPLACING THE ROCKER OIL FEED PIPE

To disconnect the rocker oil feed pipe for removal, the two domed nuts should be removed from the ends of the rocker spindle, and the banjos withdrawn.

Disconnect the rocker oil feed pipe from the scavenge oil cooler pipe. Drain the pipe into an oil tray.

Care should be taken that the pipe is not bent excessively as this might ultimately result in a fracture. When removed, the rocker oil feed pipe should be thoroughly cleaned in paraffin (kerosene) and checked for blockage by sealing the first banjo with the thumb and first finger, whilst blowing through the other. Repeat this procedure for the other banjo.

When refitting the rocker oil feed pipe it is advisable to use new copper washers, but if the old ones are annealed they should give an effective oil seal. Annealing is achieved by heating to cherry red heat and quenching in water. Any scale that is formed on the washers should be removed prior to re-fitting them.

LUBRICATION SYSTEM

SECTION A10

ANTI-DRAIN VALVE

The anti-drain valve is situated in the crankcase centre section adjacent to the oil pump housing. The purpose of the valve is to prevent oil draining through from the feed side of the pump such as with the engine stationary overnight, or when the pump has suffered a great deal of wear. Should the crankcase fill with oil whilst the machine is standing, it must be assumed that the ball of this valve is sticking or being held off its seating by some means. To clean the ball and spring hold the cupped hand beneath the valve, remove the plug from the crankcase and collect the ball and springs. (Fig. A10). Wash these carefully in paraffin (kerosene) and replace.

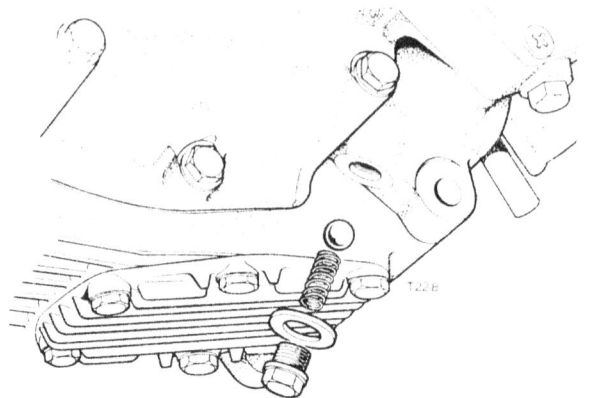

Fig. A10. Anti-drain valve

SECTION A11

CONTACT BREAKER LUBRICATION

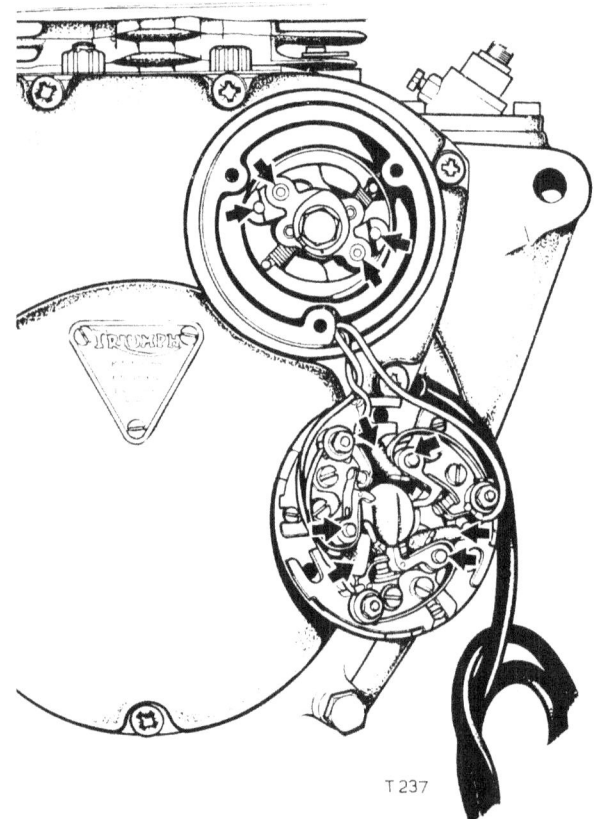

The contact breaker is situated in the timing cover and it is imperative that no oil from the engine lubrication system reaches the contact breaker chamber. For this purpose there is an oil seal at the back of the contact breaker unit, pressed into the timing cover. However, slight lubrication of the cam and auto advance pivots is necessary. **It is imperative that no liquid lubricant is introduced into the auto advance spindle as this has a self lubricating bearing. If oil comes into contact with the bearing it is possible that the shaft will seize.**

On initial assembly the three felt lubricating wicks and are impregnated with Shell Retinax "A" grease, and at intervals of 2,000 miles three drops of clean engine oil should be applied to each wick, in order to lubricate the cam and nylon heels. If this operation is not carried out, premature wear will occur on each of the nylon heels.

Fig. A11. Contact breaker lubrication points

LUBRICATION SYSTEM

SECTION A12

GEARBOX LUBRICATION

The gearbox is lubricated by means of an oil bath. Splash oil is fed to all gearbox components including the enclosed gearchange and kickstarter mechanisms. The oil in the gearbox should be drained and the gearbox flushed out after the initial 500 miles (800 Km) running in period. Thereafter, the oil should be changed as stated in Section A1.

The oil can be drained from the gearbox by means of the oil drain plug located underneath the gearbox (Figure A6. Ref. No. 3). Oil should be drained whilst the engine is warm, as the oil will flow more readily.

The gearbox oil filler plug is situated on top of the gearbox inner cover. When replenishing the oil, the oil drain plug should be replaced omitting the smaller oil level plug which screws into it. Oil should be poured into the gearbox until it is seen to drip out through the oil level plug hole.

(Fig. A12). The correct level has then been obtained, and the level plug should be replaced. (Section A2 for recommended lubricant).

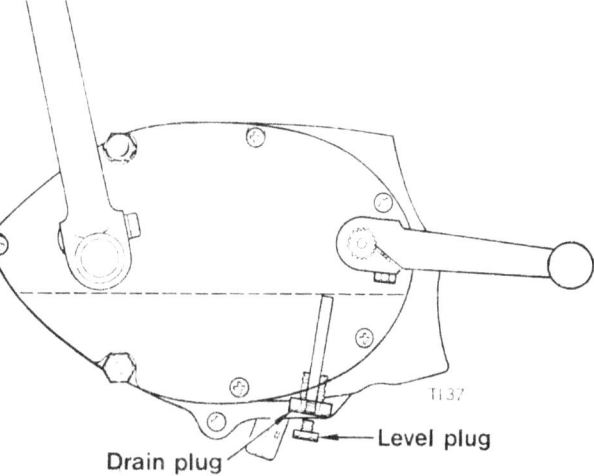

Fig. A12. Gearbox drain and level plugs

SECTION A13

PRIMARY CHAINCASE LUBRICATION

The primary chaincase is lubricated by means of an oil bath. The oil bath is filled initially through the inspection cap (Fig. A13) and thereafter the level is maintained by the engine lubrication system which "breathes" through the right side main bearing into the chaincase. The chaincase can be drained using the plug beneath the centre of the inner chaincase. Allow approximately ten minutes for draining and then replace the plug ensuring that the 'O' ring seal is serviceable. For initial filling a half pint of the correct grade of oil (see Section A2 for recommended grade) should be used.

The primary chain is lubricated by means of a collection chamber and an oil feed pipe built into the primary chaincase. The oil feed pipe directs a continuous supply of oil to a point on the bottom run on the tensioner blade. Periodically check that the feed pipe is clear. To do so requires the removal of the pipe securing clip. An air line can then be used to clear the feed. When the pipe is replaced be sure that the lower end passes through the drilled chaincase boss and that it just clears the chain.

LUBRICATION SYSTEM

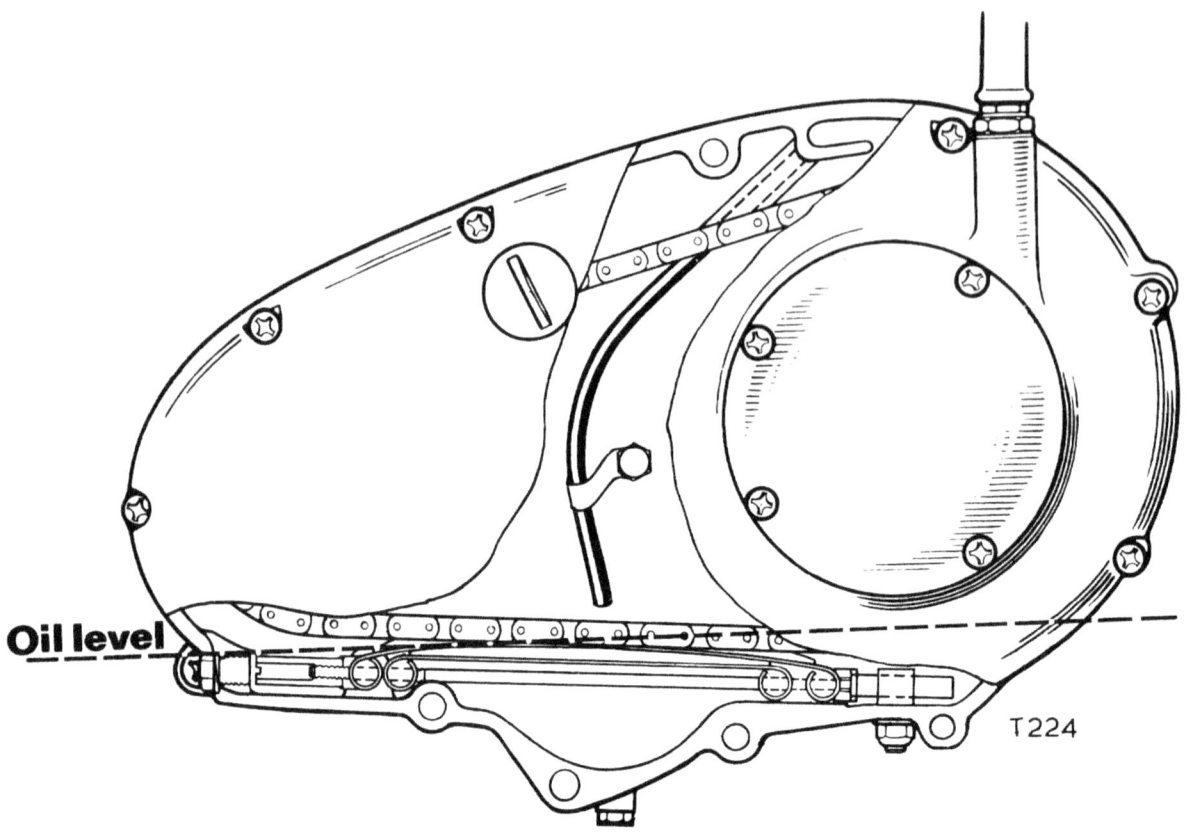

Fig. A13. Section through the primary chaincase

SECTION A14

REAR CHAIN LUBRICATION AND MAINTENANCE

The rear chain feed is taken from an oil junction block situated in the neck of the oil tank (see Fig. A14). The rate of flow of oil to the chain can be controlled by a threaded tapered screw provided in the oil junction block. The screw should be turned clockwise to reduce the flow and anti-clockwise to increase it.

Disconnect the connecting link and remove the chain. If available, connect an old chain to the end of the chain being removed and draw it onto the gearbox sprocket until the chain to be cleaned is clear of the machine and can be disconnected.

Remove all deposits of road dust etc. by means of a wire brush. Clean thoroughly in paraffin or kerosene and allow to drain.

Inspect the chain for excessive wear of the rollers and pivot pins and check that the elongation does not exceed $1\frac{1}{2}\%$. To do this first scribe two marks on a flat table exactly $12\frac{1}{2}$ inches (31,75 cm.) apart, place the chain opposite the two marks. When the chain is compressed to its minimum free length the marks should coincide with two pivot pins 20 links apart. When the chain is stretched to its maximum free length, the extension should not exceed $\frac{1}{4}$ in. (6,25 mm.). If it is required to remove a faulty link, or shorten the chain, reference should be made to Section C13.

To lubricate the chain, immerse it into MELTED grease (melt over a low flame, or, more safely, over a pan of boiling water) and allow it to remain in the grease for approximately 15 minutes, moving the

LUBRICATION SYSTEM

chain occasionally to ensure penetration of the grease into the chain bearings. Allow the grease to cool, remove the chain from the bath and wipe off the surplus grease.

The chain is now ready for refitting to the machine.

NOTE: The connecting link retaining clip must be fitted with the nose-end facing in the direction of motion of the chain.

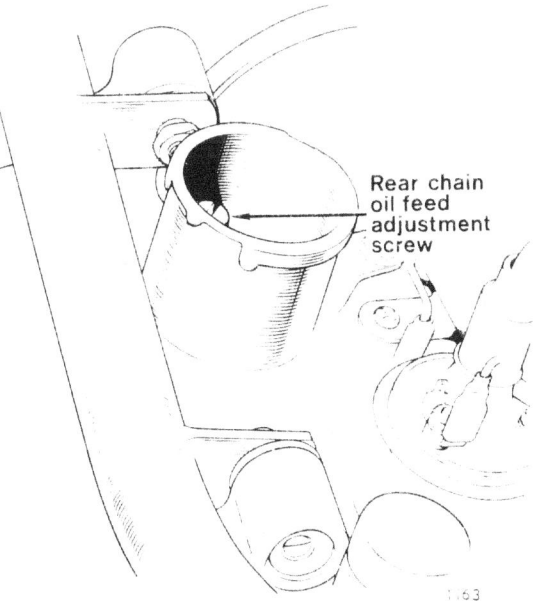

Fig. A14. Rear chain oil feed adjustment

SECTION A15

GREASING THE STEERING HEAD BALL RACES

The steering head races are packed with grease on assembly and require re-packing with the correct grade of grease at the interval stated in Section A1.

Removal and replacement of the ball bearings is comprehensively covered in the front fork section.

When the balls are removed they should be cleaned in paraffin (kerosene), also, the cups fitted to the frame head lug and the cones fitted to the middle lug stem should be cleaned thoroughly by means of a paraffin (kerosene) soaked rag, then inspected for wear, cracking or pocketing.

The fresh supply of grease should be utilised to hold the balls in position in the cups whilst the fork is assembled.

SECTION A16

WHEEL BEARING LUBRICATION

The wheel bearings are packed with grease on assembly but require re-packing with the correct grade of grease at the interval stated in Section A1.

The bearings on both the front wheel and rear wheel should be removed, cleaned in paraffin (kerosene) and assembled with the hubs well packed with the correct grade of grease. For details concerning the grade of grease to be used (which is the same for both wheels), see Section A2.

Removing and replacing the bearings for the front and rear wheels is comprehensively covered in Section F7.

SECTION A17

TELESCOPIC FORK LUBRICATION

The oil contained in the front fork has the dual purpose of lubricating the stanchion bearing bushes and also acting as the suspension damping medium. Therefore it is imperative that the fork legs have an equal amount of oil in them. On the shuttle valve fork it is important that only SAE 20 oil is used for lubrication purposes.

Oil leakage at the junction between the stanchion and bottom fork leg is prevented by means of an oil seal. If there is excessive oil leakage at this junction it may be necessary to renew the oil seal (see Section G6), but before undertaking this work, the fork should be checked to ensure that there is $\frac{1}{3}$ of a pint of oil in each leg.

Particular attention should be given to the oil change period. The fork should be drained and refilled with the correct grade of oil at the mileage stated in Section A1.

To drain the oil from the fork legs remove the two small hexagonal drain plugs adjacent to the left and right ends of the front wheel spindle.

Oil can be expelled at a greater rate by compressing the fork two or three times.

To refill the fork legs, the fork hexagonal cap nuts must be unscrewed and withdrawn, and the correct amount of oil poured into each fork leg. This will necessitate removal of the handlebar (Section A1).

SECTION A18

LUBRICATION NIPPLES

Both the brake operating cams and the swinging fork pivot bearings should be lubricated by means of the lubrication nipples.

The brake cams have integral lubrication nipples. Care should be taken that the surface of the nipple is not damaged. Slight distortion may be removed with a fine grade file.

The front and rear wheel brake cam and spindle bearing surfaces should be sparingly lubricated with the correct grade of grease (Section A2). This can be done by giving the lubrication nipples on the ends of the cams one stroke each from a grease gun. However, if the grease does not penetrate, the brake cams should be removed and cleaned thoroughly in paraffin (kerosene). Cam bearing surfaces should then be greased on reassembly.

SWINGING FORK PIVOT

The greasing nipple is situated centrally underneath the swinging fork and should be given several strokes with a high pressure grease gun until grease is forced through each end of the pivot bearings.

If the grease does not penetrate then the pivot must be removed to ensure adequate lubrication. Removal of the swinging fork is detailed in Section E9. When the fork is removed the sleeves and distance tube should be withdrawn and all parts should be thoroughly cleaned out in paraffin (kerosene) and allowed to drain.

Reassembly is a reversal of the above instructions. The space surrounding the distance tube should be carefully packed with the correct grade of grease, and the sleeves should be well greased on their bearing surfaces.

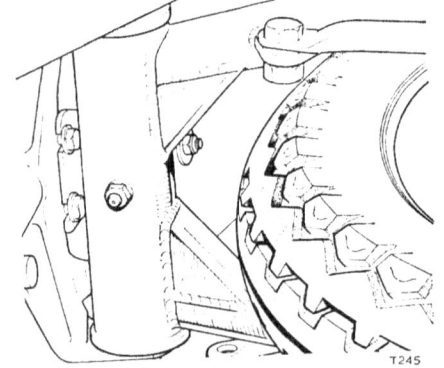

Fig. A15. Swinging fork pivot lubrication nipple

LUBRICATION SYSTEM

SECTION A19

LUBRICATING THE CONTROL CABLES

The control cables can be periodically lubricated at the exposed joint with a thin grade of oil (see Section A2).

A more thorough method of lubrication is that of feeding oil into one end of the cable by means of a reservoir. For this, the cable can be either disconnected at the handlebar end only, or completely removed.

The disconnected end of the cable should be threaded through a thin rubber stopper and the stopper pressed into a suitable narrow neck can with a hole in its base. If the can is then inverted and the lubricating oil poured into it through the hole, the oil will trickle down between the outer and inner cables. It is best to leave the cable in this position overnight to ensure adequate lubrication.

SECTION A20

SPEEDOMETER AND TACHOMETER CABLE LUBRICATION

The speedometer and tachometer cables should be lubricated by means of grease (see Section A2 for correct grade). It is not necessary to completely remove the cables but only to disconnect them from the instruments and withdraw the inner cables. Unscrew the union nuts at the base of both speedometer and tachometer, withdraw, the inner cables and clean in paraffin (kerosene). Smear the surfaces with grease except for six inches (15 cm) nearest to the speedometer and tachometer heads. The cables are now ready to be offered into the outer casings and excess grease wiped off. Care should be taken that both "squared" ends of the inner cables are located in their respective "square" drive housings before the union nuts are tightened.

SECTION A21

BRAKE PEDAL SPINDLE LUBRICATION

The brake pedal spindle is bolted to the left rear engine mounting plate. The spindle should be covered with a fresh supply of grease occasionally otherwise corrosion and inefficient operation may result.

To gain access to the spindle, slacken off the rear brake rod adjustment, unscrew the brake pedal retaining nut and withdraw the pedal.

Remove any rust from the spindle with fine emery. Clean the bore of the pedal and smear the spindle with grease (see Section A2) prior to refitting.

Do not forget to replace the spring washer between the retaining nut and brake pedal.

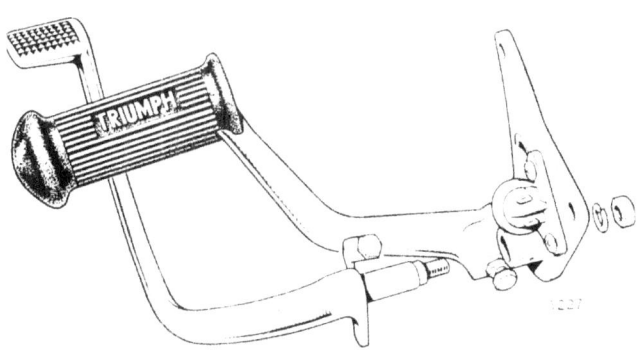

Fig. A16. Brake pedal spindle lubrication

NOTES

SECTION AA

LUBRICATION SYSTEM

	Section
ROUTINE MAINTENANCE	AA1
ENGINE LUBRICATION POINTS	AA2

SECTION AA1

ROUTINE MAINTENANCE

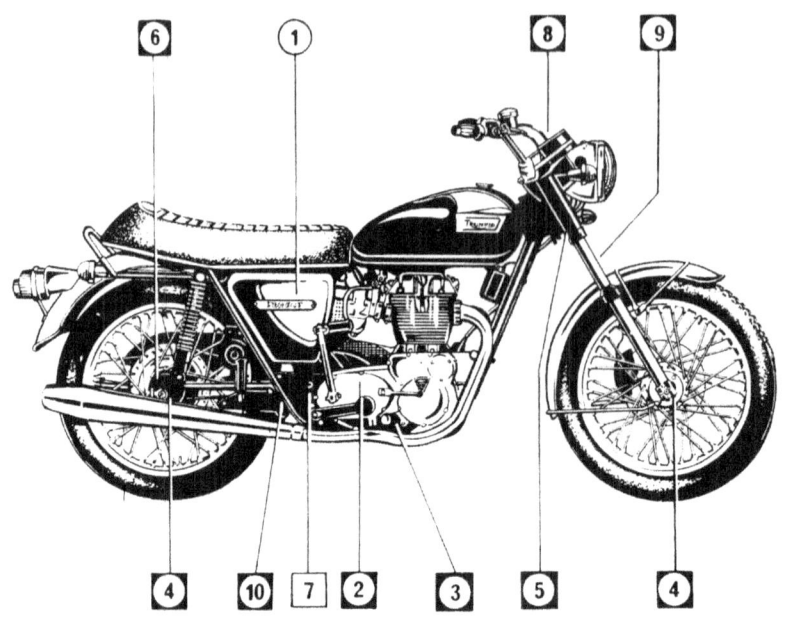

Fig. AA1. LUBRICATION CHART
Numbers in circles refer to right side of machine
Numbers in squares refer to left side of machine

GUIDE TO LUBRICATION POINTS

Illustration No.	Description	SAE Oil grade
1	Engine oil tank and primary chaincase	20/50
2	Gearbox	90 E.P.
3	Oil Filter Compartment	20/50
4	Wheel hubs	Grease
5	Steering head	Grease
6	Brake cam spindle	Grease
7	Brake pedal spindle	Grease
8	Exposed cables	10/30
9	Telescopic fork	Auto. trans. fluid
10	Swinging fork pivot	Grease
—	All brake rod joints and pins	10/30

SECTION AA2

ENGINE LUBRICATION POINTS

The engine lubrication system is of the dry sump type. The oil is fed by gravity from the oil tank to the oil pump, the oil under pressure from the sump, is forced via a cartridge type oil filter through drillings to the inner main bearings and crankshaft big ends, where it escapes and lubricates the cylinder walls, roller journal outer main bearings and other internal engine parts. Oil is prevented from draining into the crankcase when the engine is not running by means of an anti-drain valve situated behind the oil pump.

The oil pressure between the oil pump and the crankshaft is controlled by the oil pressure release valve.

After lubricating the engine and primary transmission oil is forced to the sump, where it is scavenged through the sump filter and returned, via the oil tank cooler to the oil tank through the action of the oil pump scavenge gears. The oil pump has been designed so that the scavenge gears have a greater pumping capacity than the feed gears, thus ensuring that the sump does not become flooded.

The valve operating mechanism oil feed is taken from the point between the scavenge side of the pump and the oil cooler. After travelling through the rocker spindle, the oil is fed into the rocker boxes by way of notches in the rocker arms. Afterwards it falls by gravity down the push rod cover tubes to lubricate the tappets and camshafts and finally into the sump where it is subsequently scavenged. The idler pinion needle roller bearing is lubricated by oil draining through a drilling in the right side crankcase.

Note:— From early 1972 engines are not fitted with pressure oil feed to the tappets.

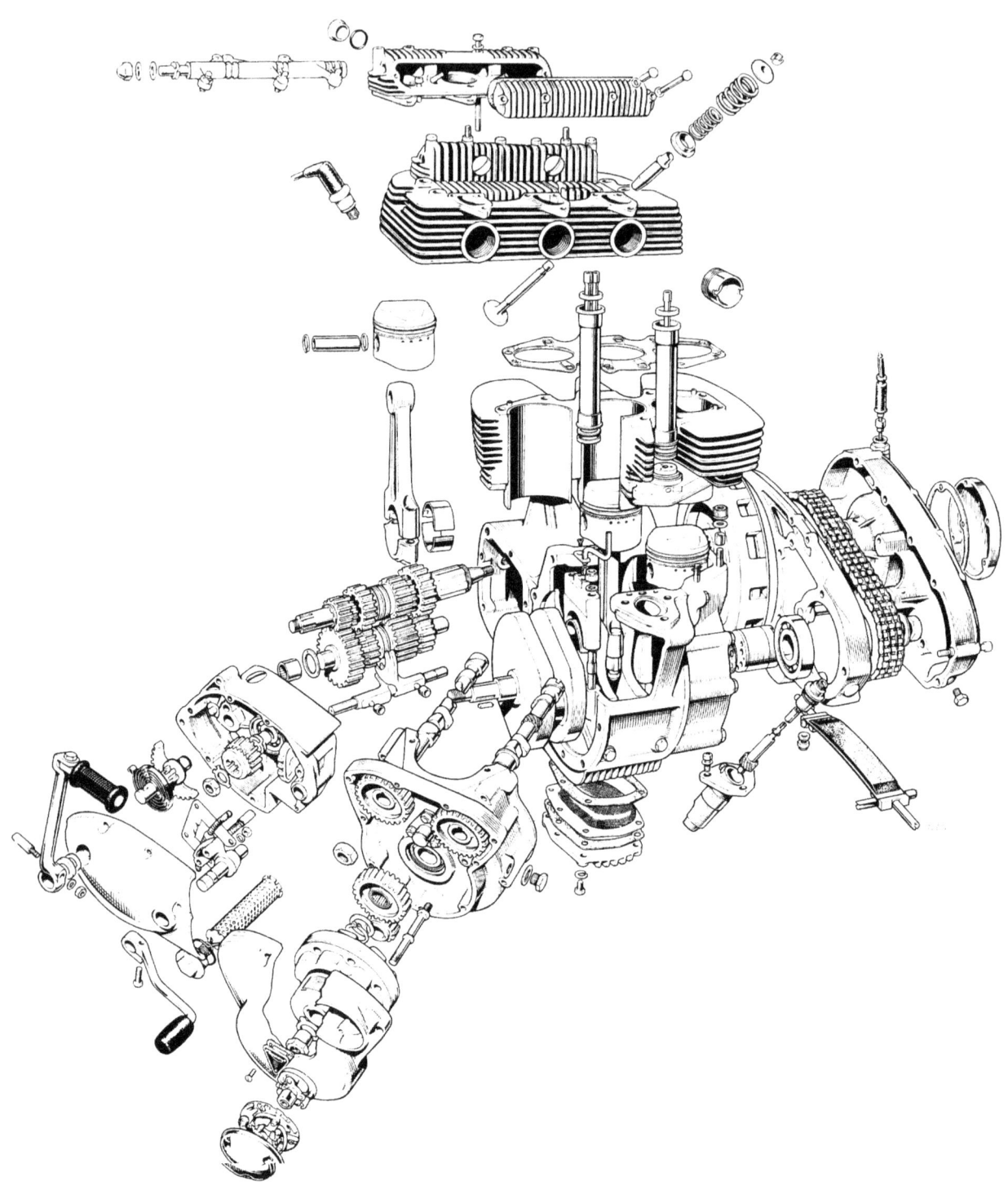

Exploded view of 750 c.c. engine/gearbox unit T150 4 Speed.

SECTION B
ENGINE

DESCRIPTION	Section
REMOVING AND REPLACING THE ENGINE UNIT	B1
REMOVING AND REPLACING THE ROCKER BOXES	B2
INSPECTING THE PUSH RODS	B3
STRIPPING AND REASSEMBLING THE ROCKER BOXES	B4
ADJUSTING THE VALVE ROCKER CLEARANCES	B5
REMOVING AND REPLACING THE AIR CLEANER	B6
CARBURETTER—DESCRIPTION	B7
REMOVING AND REPLACING THE CARBURETTERS	B8
STRIPPING AND REASSEMBLING THE CARBURETTERS	B9
INSPECTING THE CARBURETTER COMPONENTS	B10
RESETTING THE CARBURETTERS	B11
REMOVING AND REFITTING THE CYLINDER HEAD ASSEMBLY	B12
REMOVING AND REPLACING THE VALVES	B13
RENEWING THE VALVE GUIDES	B14
DECARBONISING	B15
RE-SEATING THE VALVES	B16
REMOVING AND REPLACING THE CYLINDER BLOCK AND TAPPETS	B17
INSPECTING THE CAM FOLLOWERS	B18
INSPECTING THE TAPPET GUIDE BLOCKS	B19
REMOVING AND REFITTING THE PISTONS	B20
REMOVING AND REPLACING THE PISTON RINGS	B21
INSPECTING THE PISTONS AND CYLINDER BORES	B22
TABLE OF SUITABLE REBORE SIZES	B23
REMOVING AND REPLACING THE CONTACT BREAKER	B24
ADJUSTING THE CONTACT BREAKER POINTS	B25
IGNITION TIMING—STATIC	B26
IGNITION TIMING BY STROBOSCOPE	B27
REMOVING AND REPLACING THE TIMING COVER	B28
EXTRACTING AND REFITTING THE VALVE TIMING PINIONS	B29
VALVE TIMING	B30
DISMANTLING AND REASSEMBLING THE CRANKCASE ASSEMBLY	B31
SERVICING THE CRANKSHAFT	B32
REFITTING THE CONNECTING RODS	B33
INSPECTING THE CRANKCASE COMPONENTS	B34
RENEWING THE MAIN BEARINGS	B35
REMOVING AND REFITTING TACHOMETER DRIVE	B36

ENGINE

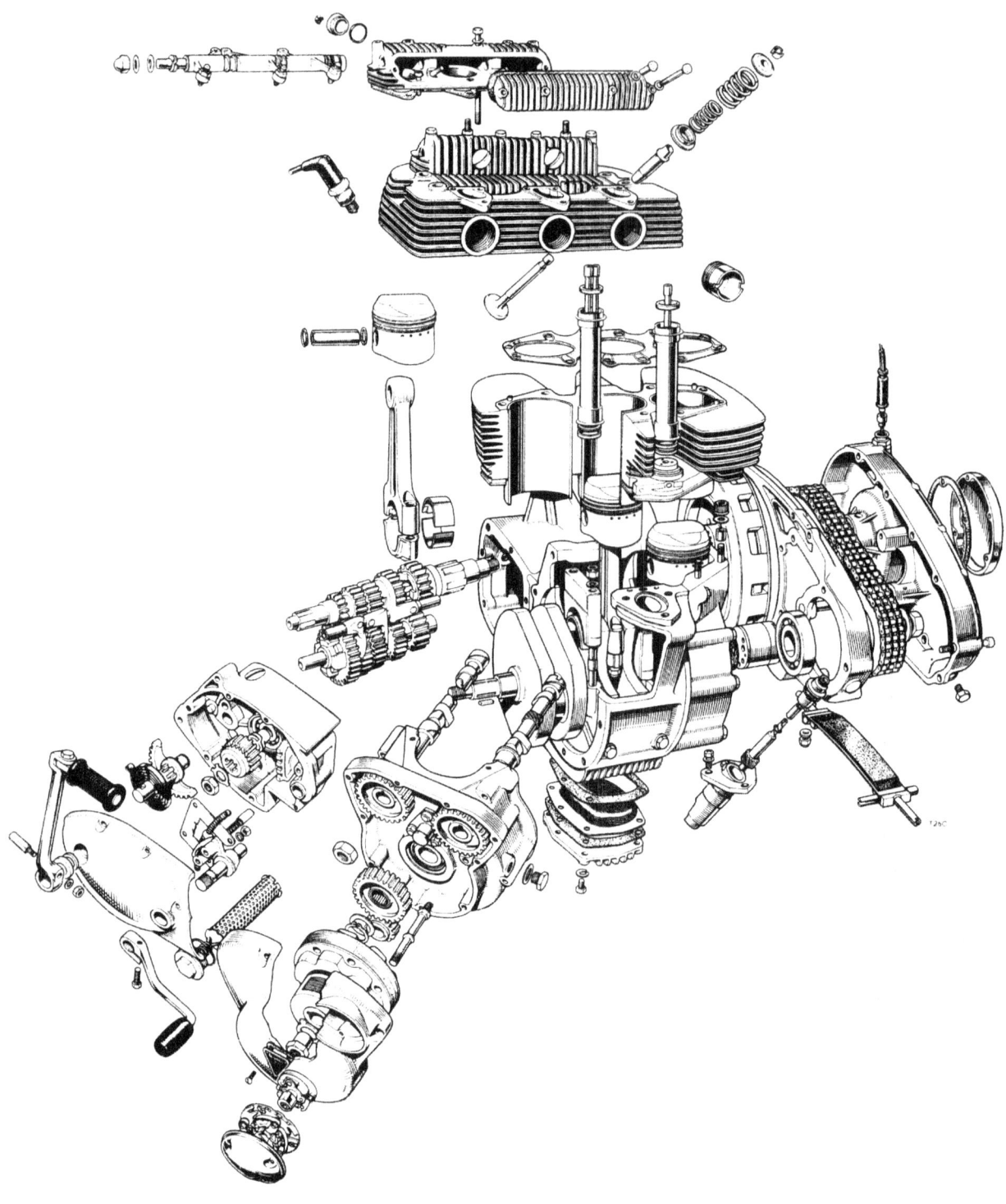

Fig. B1. Exploded view of 750c.c. engine/gearbox unit. T150 V.

ENGINE B

DESCRIPTION

The engine is of unit construction, having three cylinders, a 120 degree crankshaft, and three aluminium alloy mating crankcase sections. The gearbox housing is an integral part of the centre crankcase, and the clutch and primary transmission are housed in separate cases, bolted onto the main crankcase sections.

The aluminium alloy cylinder head has cast in Austenitic valve seat inserts, and houses the overhead valves which are operated by rocker arms housed in detachable alloy rocker boxes. Six aluminium push rods operate the rocker arms, which are each fitted with adjusters, accessible when the rocker box covers are removed.

The aluminium alloy die cast pistons each have two compression rings and one oil scraper ring. The connecting rods are of H Section RR56 alloy, with detachable end caps. These incorporate steel backed renewable "shell" type bearings. Each of the connecting rod caps are machined from a steel stamping and held in position by means of two high tensile steel bolts, which are tightened to a predetermined extension figure to give the correct working clearance for the bearing on the crankshaft journals.

The inlet and exhaust camshafts are fitted transversely in the upper part of the crankcase, and are driven by a train of timing gears from the right side of the crankshaft. The exhaust camshaft drives the adjustable contact breaker which is fitted with an automatic advance and retard mechanism, and the tachometer drive.

The three-throw one piece crankshaft is supported by two "shell" type bearings a roller bearing at the right side, and a ball bearing at the left side. The two plain inner main bearings are each retained by an alloy cap held by studs and self locking nuts, which are tightened to a predetermined torque setting.

The big end bearings and the two inner main bearings are lubricated at pressure with oil which travels along drillings in the crankcase and crankshaft, from the double gear oil pump. Oil pressure in the lubrication system is governed by means of the oil pressure release valve, which is situated at at the rear of the engine behind the inner primary chaincase cover.

The aluminium alloy cylinder barrel has Austenitic casting cylinder liners, and houses the pressed in aluminium alloy tappet guide blocks. Power from the engine is transmitted through the engine sprocket and primary chain to the shock absorber unit, diaphragm clutch and four speed constant mesh gearbox. Primary chain tension is given by an adjustable rubber pad chain tensioner which is immersed in the primary chain oil bath.

The electrical generator set consists of a rotor which is fitted to the right end of the crankshaft and a six coil stator which is mounted on three pillar bolts inside the timing cover. Carburation is by three Amal type 600 concentric carburetters with a common linkage.

SECTION B1

REMOVING AND REPLACING THE ENGINE UNIT

Unscrew the plastic moulded screw securing the left side battery cover, and pull the panel off the two locating pegs on the rear frame. Disconnect the fuse holder which is fitted in the negative side of the battery, and remove the petrol tank (Section E1). Remove the oil cooler (Section A8), and disconnect the rocker feed pipe by removing two domed nuts from the right side of the rocker boxes. Slide the banjo connections over the rocker spindles, and collect four copper washers. It is advisable at this stage to remove the right side panel to prevent damage. This is held in position with three Pozidriv screws. Unscrew the oil tank drain plug, and allow the oil to drain into a suitable receptacle. Remove the oil cartridge filter end plug from beneath the front of the gearbox outer cover, and allow the compartment to drain. Unscrew two clips retaining the oil pipes to the crankcase stubs, and withdraw both pipes, allowing any oil to drain into a suitable container. The oil pipe stubs are situated beneath the left side of the centre crankcase section. Remove the gearbox drain plug complete with the level plug from below the centre crankcase section. Allow the oil to drain into a suitable container. Refer to Fig. A6 for the position of drain plugs. The chaincase drain plug should be removed, and the chaincase allowed to drain. The drain plug is situated below the centre of the inner chaincase.

Disconnect the tachometer cable from its drive box forward of the cylinder barrel. Slacken the left side footrest securing nut, and remove four Pozidriv screws from the clutch release mechanism inspection cover. The cover can now be removed and the cable detached from the mechanism. The most satisfactory method of disconnecting the clutch cable is to slacken the lock nut and adjuster on the centre clutch pull rod, thereby producing the required amount of slack in the cable. The nipple can then be removed from the slotted roller. Collect the cable abutment as the cable is withdrawn.

The carburetter and air cleaner assembly can be removed as one unit, after having removed the cylinder head torque stays. Disconnect the air control cable at the handlebar lever, and draw the cable through any retaining clips on the frame top rail. The throttle cable should be removed from carburetter linkage by first of all unscrewing the adjuster, and withdrawing the cable from the cable stop. The nipple can be removed from the throttle actuating lever by turning it through 90 degrees and sliding the cable and nipple out of the lever sideways. Slacken the six worm drive clips securing the inlet manifold connection hoses, and also remove one rubber buffer from the bottom air filter support lug. Remove the air filter to crankcase breather pipe, when the whole assembly can be pulled off the connection hoses, and withdrawn from the left side of the machine.

Disconnect the three stator snap connectors which are located at the rear of the engine unit, and also disconnect three contact breaker snap connectors which are situated at the top front of the oil tank beneath the twinseat. Remove the stator wire protection shield after having removed one small slotted screw, and the top front engine plate nut from the right side.

Remove both exhaust pipes, after having slackened the silencer to exhaust pipe clips, and also exhaust pipe to exhaust manifold pinch bolts. The exhaust pipes can be removed by tapping downwards with a rubber hammer. Three finned cooling rings should be slackened at the exhaust manifold, and the manifold removed by tapping forwards with a rubber hammer. Disconnect the oil pressure switch wire, which is situated to the right side of the oil pipe stubs beneath the crankcase. Disconnect two stop light wires from the left side rear engine plate, and remove the rear brake adjusting nut. Remove the rear chain split link, and withdraw the chain. Withdraw the oil tank breather pipe from its hollow stub on the chaincase vent chamber inspection cover.

To remove the right side rear engine plate, disconnect the oil feed pipe from beneath the front of the oil tank, to allow removal of the top front engine plate bolt. Remove the remaining self locking nuts and bolts, and the large centre nut, and withdraw the enginge plate. To remove the left side engine plate, remove the nut and spring washer from the brake pedal spindle which is situated behind the the engine plate, and withdraw the brake pedal leaving the actuating lever and rod in position. Remove all securing bolts from the engine plate, and withdraw the plate complete with footrest.

ENGINE **B**

To remove the long engine securing bolt from beneath the crankcase, remove the left side nut and spring washer, and withdraw the bolt from the right hand side. There is a spacer fitted between the crankcase lug and bottom frame tube at the right hand side. Remove one nut and spring washer from the front engine plate to crankcase stud, and withdraw this. It is only necessary to remove one bolt and spring washer, and slacken one bolt on the left hand side detachable engine plate, to allow the plate to swivel clear of the front engine lug.

The engine unit is now ready to be lifted from the frame, and owing to the weight of the unit (180 lbs. approximately) it is advisable to employ the use of two lifting bars which can be located one in the front engine mounting lug, and one in the top rear left side engine plate mounting lug (Fig. B2). This operation will require two people, situated at either side of the crankcase. The most satisfactory method of removing the engine is to raise it and turn the unit counter-clockwise while viewed from the top of the machine in order to clear the front crankcase lug. The unit will then lift out to the left side.

To replace the complete engine unit it should be lifted into the frame again utilising two lifting bars in the same positions, gearbox first from the left side. The front of the unit should then be swung round into position. Replace the bottom mounting stud, from the right hand side, ensuring that the spacer is fitted in the correct position between the crankcase lug and bottom frame tube, on the right hand side. Replace the nut and spring washer. Line the front detachable engine plate up with the crankcase lug, and replace the stud spring washer and nut. Replace the bolt and spring washer, and tighten the remaining bolt. Replace the left side rear engine plate, ensuring that the two spacers are refitted between the rear crankcase lugs and the engine plate. Refit the remaining bolts, washers and self locking nuts, and the large swinging arm lug bolt and thick plain washer. Replace the right hand side engine plate and secure this with the bolts, washers and self locking nuts and the large central collar nut. **Do not replace the nut on the top front engine plate bolt at this stage.** Replace the rear brake pedal, position the rear brake actuating lever over the squared end of the brake pedal spindle, and replace the nut and spring washer. Retighten the left hand side footrest. Slide the air filter to clutch cover rubber pipe over the crankcase sleeve, and connect both the stator and contact

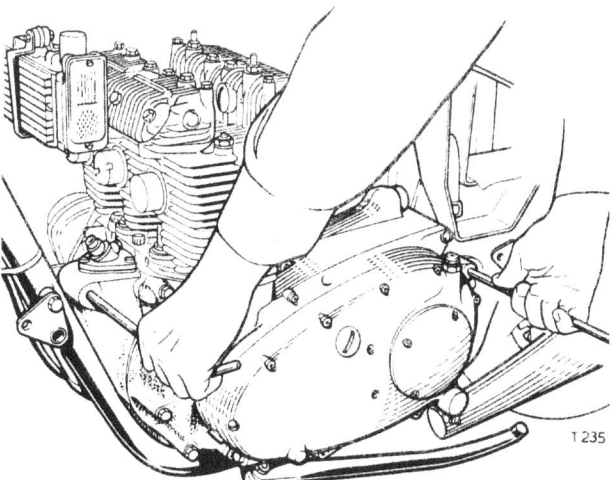

Fig. B2. Location of engine lifting bars

breaker leads (colour to colour). Position the stator lead shield over the top front right side engine plate bolt, and replace the self locking nut and slot headed screw.

Refit the rear chain over the gearbox sprocket and over the rear wheel sprocket. Fit the split link, ensuring that the closed end of the link is to the front of the machine when positioned on the top run of the chain. If any difficulty is experienced in refitting the chain, remove the rear wheel (Section F2), engage top gear, offer the chain to the top of the sprocket, and with the help of a second operator using the kickstart, slowly wind the chain over the sprocket. Reconnect the oil pipes beneath the engine, and tighten the securing clips. Ensure that the oil feed pipe from the bottom of the oil tank leads to the top small stub below the crankcase. The oil pipe from the larger bottom stub connects to the rocker feed pipe. The pipe from the front of the rocker feed connection leads to the left hand side of the oil cooler, and the right hand side pipe from the oil cooler connects to the return union at the top front of the oil tank.

From this point reassembly is completed as a reversal of the removal procedure but note the order of reconnecting the high tension leads:— Viewed from the right hand side of the machine, the top coil (Black/Yellow C.B. lead) connects to the left hand side cylinder. The bottom right coil (Red/Black C.B. lead) to the centre cylinder. Bottom left coil (Black/White C.B. lead) to the right hand side cylinder.

SECTION B2

REMOVING AND REPLACING ROCKER BOXES

Unscrew the plastic moulded securing screw from the left hand side panel, and withdraw the panel from two locating pegs. Disconnect the fuse from the negative side of the battery, turn both fuel taps off, and remove the fuel tank (Section E1). Remove two domed nuts securing the rocker feed pipe. Withdraw the rocker feed pipe from both rocker spindles, and collect four copper washers. Take off the cylinder head torque stays after having removed two nuts and spring washers from the rocker box studs and one bolt spring washer and nut from the stay to frame lug. Disconnect the three high tension leads, and to avoid possible damage at a later stage remove all three sparking plugs.

Remove four bolts and plain washers, from each rocker box inspection cover, and withdraw both covers. If any difficulty is experienced light taps from a hide faced mallet should effectively remove these covers. Remove three socket head screws from each rocker box, and the four rocker box end bolts. Loosen the eight rocker box bolts starting from the centre, and when all are slackened lift both rocker boxes away from the cylinder head. Remove the six push rods and four push rod cover tubes together with the cover tube bottom cups.

Remove nuts and bolts in the reverse order to Fig. B12, i.e. slacken the highest number first. Refit the bolts and nuts in the order shown.

When refitting ensure that the joint surfaces of both the rocker boxes and cylinder head are clean. Lightly grease the new rocker box gaskets, and position these on the cylinder head. Refit the four push rod tubes, ensuring that the cups are refitted the correct way up (see Fig. B3) and that new seals are fitted at both the top and bottom of each tube.

Refit the push rods, two in each right hand side tube, and one in each left hand side tube in the same position as they were originally fitted. Remove the

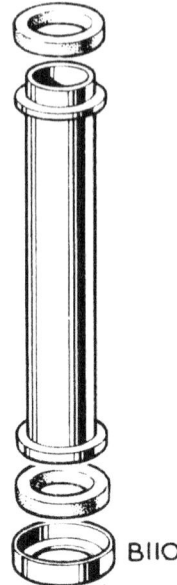

Fig. B3. Arrangement of push rod tube seals

two inspection covers from the inlet rocker box, and lower the rocker box onto the cylinder head. Each push rod can be located onto its respective rocker arm with the aid of a pair of thin nosed pliers. Ensure that the push rod tube and oil seal are positioned correctly in the rocker box recess.

Refit the four rocker box bolts and plain washers, ensuring that the two shorter bolts are fitted in the centremost holes. Lightly tighten these bolts, and refit three socket head screws, and two end bolts and plain washers.

Repeat this procedure for the exhaust rocker box and when assembled tighten the rocker box bolts and cylinder head bolts in the sequence shown (Fig. B12). The correct torque figure is given in GENERAL DATA.

Reassembly continues in the reverse order to the removal instructions. The valve rocker clearances should then be adjusted (Section B5).

SECTION B3

INSPECTING THE PUSHRODS

When the pushrods have been removed, examine them for worn, chipped or loose end-cups; also check that the push rod is true by rolling it slowly on a truly flat surface (such as piece of plate glass).

Bent pushrods are found to be the cause of excessive mechanical noise and loss of power and should be straightened if possible, or, preferably, renewed.

SECTION B4

STRIPPING AND REASSEMBLING THE ROCKER BOXES

Removal of the rocker spindles from the rocker boxes is best achieved by driving out, using a soft metal drift. When the spindles are removed the rocker arms and washers can be withdrawn. All parts should be thoroughly cleaned in paraffin (kerosene) and the oil drillings in the spindles should be cleaned with a jet of compressed air.

Remove the oil seals from the rocker spindles and renew them.

If it is required to renew the rocker ball pins, the old ones should be removed by means of a suitable drift. New ones should then be pressed in.

To ensure an oil-tight seal between the rocker box and cylinder head, in cases where an oil leak cannot be cured by fitting new gaskets, the joint surface of the rocker box should be linished to remove any irregularities.

An effective linish can be achieved by lightly rubbing the junction surface on a sheet of emery cloth mounted on a truly flat surface (such as a piece of plate glass).

The following method of assembly incorporates the use of a home made alignment bar, which can be made from a $\frac{7}{16}$ in. dia. bar x $9\frac{1}{2}$ in. long by grinding a taper at one end.

Smear the plain washers with grease and place them against the cast bosses or rocker arms as shown in Fig. B5.

Commencing from the left end of each rocker box (i.e. end with larger hole), fit the rocker arms. Compress each Thackery washer with thin nosed pliers and assemble these. Align each rocker in turn with the alignment bar. When all the arms and washers are correctly aligned, remove the bar.

Lubricate the spindle, and slide it, complete with oil seal, through the compressor D2221 (Fig. B4) and as far as possible into the rocker box. Finally tap it home with a hammer and soft metal drift.

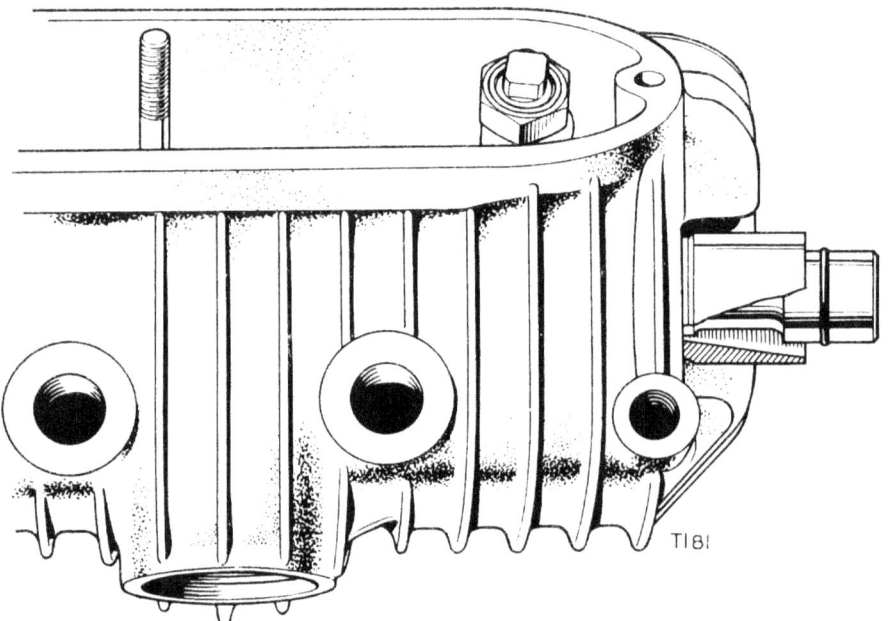

Fig. B4. Refitting rocker spindle using service tool D2221

ENGINE

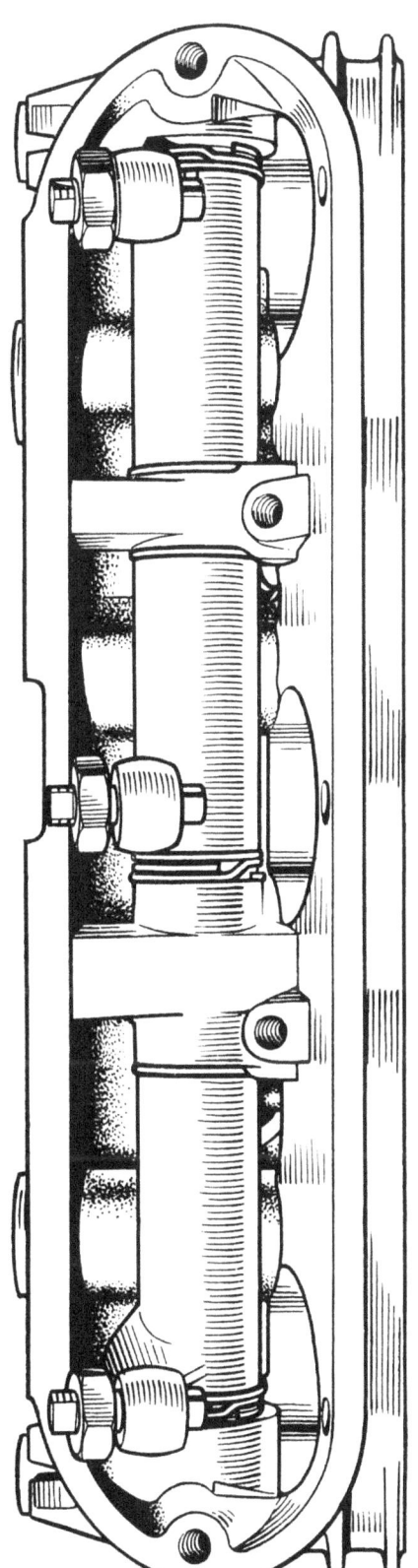
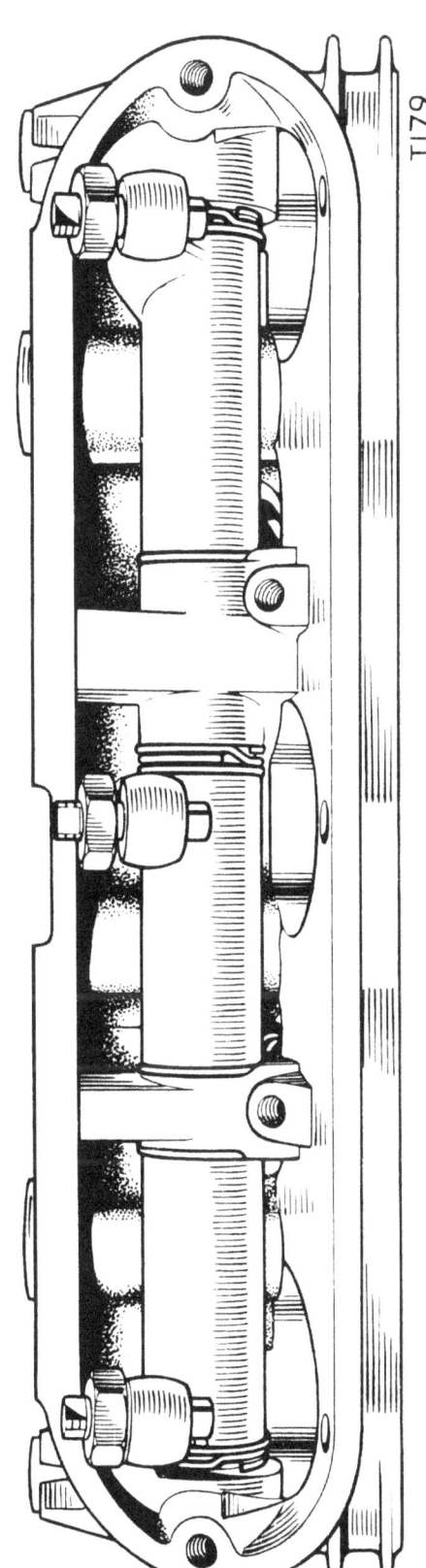

INLET

EXHAUST

Fig. B5. Arrangement of rocker arms and washers

SECTION B5

ADJUSTING THE VALVE ROCKER CLEARANCES

The valve rocker clearances should be checked and if necessary adjusted every 3,000 miles (4,800 Km). The correct clearance for the type of camshaft employed, ensures that a high valve operating efficiency is maintained, and that the valves attain their maximum useful lives.

NOTE: Adjustment should only be made when the engine is cold.

Access to the rocker arm adjuster screws and locknuts is gained by removing both the inlet and exhaust rocker inspection covers. These are retained by four bolts and plain washers.

Adjustment is aided by toolkit spanners D1907 (ring spanner) and D2020 (tappet key).

Disconnect the H.T. leads and remove the spark plugs. This will ease the compression, so enabling the engine to be turned more easily. Select top gear and position the crankshaft by turning the rear wheel.

Commencing with the inlet camshaft, turn the engine until any two rocker arms are "on the rock".

This is a condition whereby the two valves in question are open by equal amounts. In this case it will be approximately $\frac{1}{16}$ in. One valve is almost

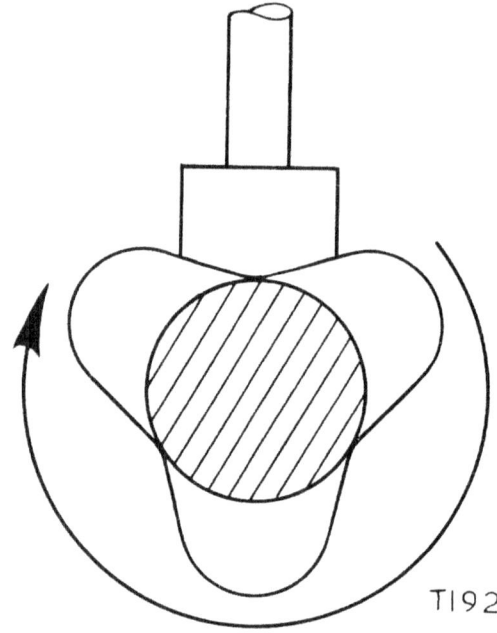

Fig. B7. Position of camshaft for valve setting

closed, and the other is just opening (see Fig. B7). At this stage the third valve is in the correct position for setting.

The correct rocker clearances are:

    Inlet   0.006 in.
    Exhaust 0.008 in.

Slacken the locknut, insert a feeler gauge of the correct thickness, between the rocker arm and valve stem, and rotate the adjuster pin either clockwise to decrease the clearance or anti-clockwise to increase it. The gauge should slide freely, without any apparent clearance (see Fig. B6).

Tighten the locknut ensuring that the adjuster does not move. Recheck the clearance, and if it has altered repeat this procedure.

Adjust the remaining clearances in a similar manner.

Replace the inspection covers, renewing the gaskets if any damage is evident, refit the spark plugs and the H.T. leads. (Each H.T. lead has a numbered plastic sleeve).

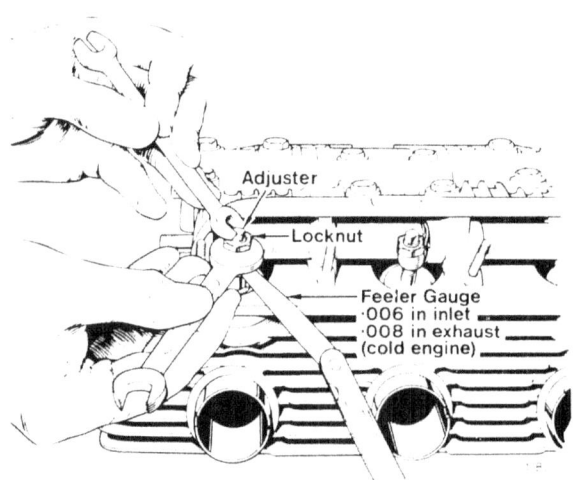

Fig. B6. Adjusting valve rocker clearances

SECTION B6

REMOVING AND REPLACING THE AIR CLEANER

A combined air cleaner assembly is fitted, having rubber grommets which fit over screwed rings at the carburetters. To remove the air filter it is necessary to remove both side panels. The air filter is held onto the carburetters by two bolts, and is not attached to the frame.

To dismantle the air filter, remove the breather pipe from the rear of the filter and remove the screw and claw holding the perforated band in position. Lift away the band and filter back plate. Collect the filter element for cleaning, by washing in petrol (gasolene). The element should be blown dry with an air line prior to refitting. To release the front plate of the filter from the carburetter assembly, two long bolts should be removed from the carburetter mounting flanges.

Reassembly is a reversal of the foregoing.

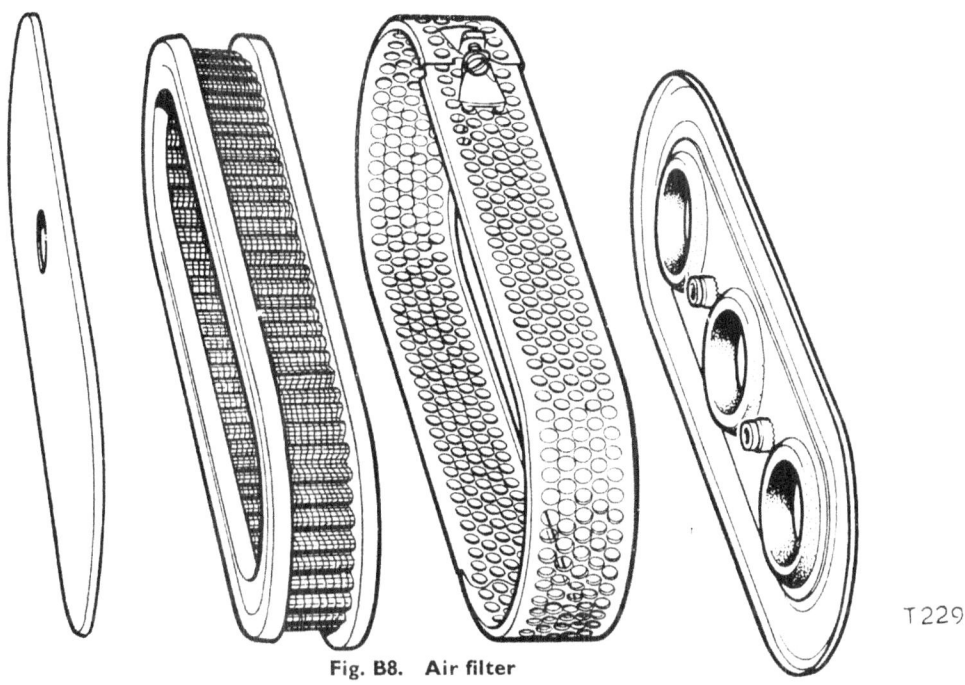

Fig. B8. Air filter

SECTION B7

CARBURETTER DESCRIPTION

The 600 series carburetter has the float concentric to the main jet. The float needle seating is integral with the float chamber and the chamber is secured by two Pozidriv screws. A captive tickler is used. Rubber "O" rings provide the necessary friction on the pilot air screw and throttle stop screws. The carburetter top is secured by two Pozidriv screws. The throttle slide has no conventional throttle spring, but is returned by a scissor spring on the external throttle linkage. Air slides are fitted, and controlled by a junction box from one handlebar lever. This primary air choke has a compensating action in conjunction with bleed holes in the needle jet, which serves the double purpose of air compensating the mixture from the needle jet, and allowing the fuel to provide a well, outside and around the needle jet, which is available for snap acceleration. The idling mixture is controlled by the pilot air screw which governs the amount of air that is allowed to mix with the fuel at tick-over speeds.

The throttle stop screw is used to adjust the slides so that they are kept open sufficiently to keep the engine running at a slow tick-over, when the twist grip is closed.

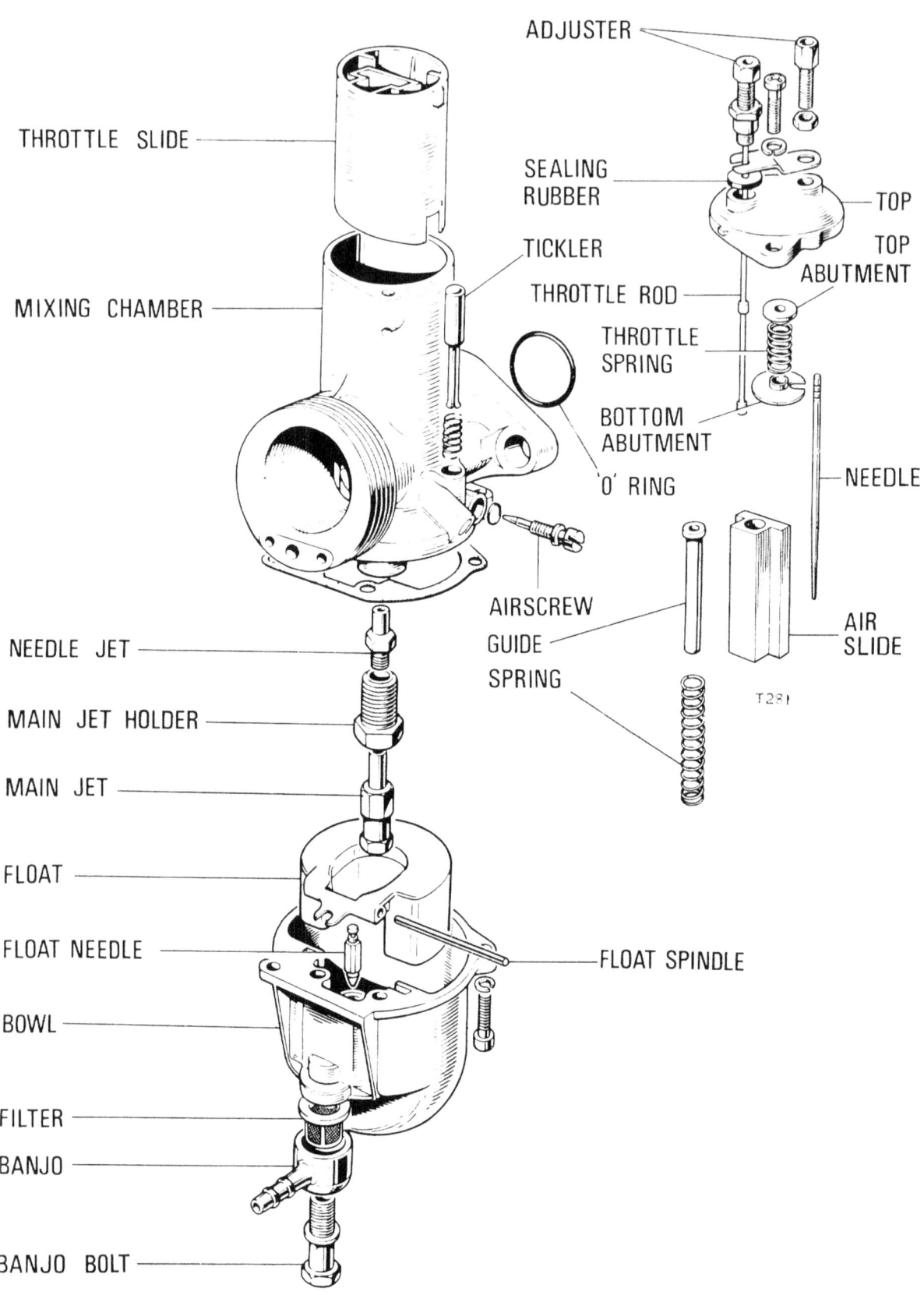

Fig. B9. Exploded view of carburetter

ENGINE

SECTION B8

REMOVING AND REPLACING THE CARBURETTERS

Remove the side panels (Section E2) and remove the petrol tank (Section E1). Disconnect the throttle cable from the throttle linkage, and disconnect the air control cable from the handlebar lever. Slacken off the worm drive clips at the carburetter end of the rubber sleeves, and if the air filter assembly is still in position, remove the rubber buffer from the air filter supporting bracket.

The carburetters, manifold and air filter can then be withdrawn to the left side of the machine.

Removal of each carburetter can be achieved merely by unscrewing two Pozidriv screws holding the carburetter top in position, and remove the two nuts from the holding studs. The carburetter is then drawn off the studs and downwards, leaving the air and throttle slides in position on the manifold assembly.

To disconnect the carburetter top from the manifold, disconnect the throttle slide from the throttle rod and the air slide from its cable. In the case of the throttle slide, remove the needle retaining spring clip and compress the throttle rod spring so that the top retaining plate can be extracted. Push the bottom nipple of the throttle rod downwards clear of the throttle slides. Removal of the air slide necessitates only compression of the spring whilst the cable nipple is pushed clear of the slide. Unscrew the air cable abutment to completely free the carburetter top.

Reassembly is a reversal of the aforegoing, but care must be taken to ensure that all six carburetter connection pipe clips are tightened. Refer to Fig. B10 for guidance.

Fig. B10. Inlet manifold assembly

SECTION B9

STRIPPING AND REASSEMBLING THE CARBURETTERS

Each carburetter will already be less the top, slides and needle with clip as removed from the machine.

Unscrew the two Pozidriv screws and remove the float chamber. Lift out the plastic float, float spindle and nylon float needle. The tickler cannot be removed. Unscrew the air screw, hold the main jet holder with one spanner whilst the main jet is unscrewed with another. Unscrew the main jet holder and remove the needle jet from this. Finally, unscrew the pilot jet with a screwdriver. Clean all parts thoroughly by washing in petrol (gasolene). Deposits on the carburetter body are most successfully removed with the use of a light grade wire brush.

It is advisable to wash the parts several times each in a quantity of clean petrol (gasolene) to avoid any particles of dirt remaining. Allow the parts to dry but if possible use a jet of compressed air from such as a hand pump or air line to clear all holes and drillings. Inspect all parts for wear and checks that the jets are in accordance with those recommended in GENERAL DATA.

Reassembly is a reversal of the aforegoing, referring to Fig. B9, for guidance.

During reassembly fit new "O" ring friction rings at the pilot air screw, and fit new fibre washers in replacement of any which may have deteriorated. Be careful to locate both ends of the float spindle in the float chamber recesses provided and note that the float needle fits pointed end downwards. When the mixing chamber body is offered up to the carburetter slide, air slide and carburetter top, take special care that the locating peg is lined up with the groove in the body.

SECTION B10

INSPECTING THE CARBURETTER COMPONENTS

The only parts liable to show wear after considerable mileage are the throttle valve slide, mixing chamber and the air slide.

(1) Inspect the throttle valve slide for excessive scoring to the front area and check the extent of wear on the rear slide face. If wear is apparent the slide should be renewed. In this case, be sure to replace the slide with the correct degree of cut-away (see "General Data").

(2) Examine the air valve for excessive wear and check that it is not actually worn through at any part. Check the fit of the air valve in the slide. Ensure that the air valve spring is serviceable by inspecting the coils for wear.

(3) Inspect the throttle return spring for efficiency, signs of cracking or breakage and loss of compressive strength.

(4) Check the needle jet for wear or possible scoring and carefully examine the tapered end of the needle for similar signs.

(5) Examine the float needle for efficiency by inserting it into the inverted float needle seating block, pouring a small amount of petrol (gasolene) into the aperture surrounding the needle and checking it for leakage.

(6) Ensure that the float does not leak by shaking it to see if it contains any fuel. Do not attempt to repair a damaged float. A new one can be purchased for a small cost.

(7) Check the petrol filter, which fits over the needle seating block, for any possible damage to the mesh thus enabling the petrol (gasolene) to by-pass it un-filtered.

ENGINE

SECTION B11

RESETTING THE CARBURETTERS

The carburetter assembly must be removed from the machine in order to synchronise the throttle slides. Refer to Section B8 for the removal procedure.

Arrange the carburetter and inlet manifold assembly, less air filter on a work bench. View the throttle slides through the engine side of the carburetters, and adjust the throttle stop screw until one slide is open approximately 0.010 inches. Compare the other two slides, and adjust the slide heights by screwing the individual adjusters (one on top of each carburetter) clockwise to lower the slides, and anti-clockwise to raise the slides. There is a locknut on each adjuster, and this should be tightened when the adjustment is completed.

The difference in slide heights is easily visible owing to the slide opening characteristics (see Fig. B11).

Turn each air screw fully in, and unscrew them $2\frac{1}{2}$ complete turns to obtain the approximate fuel/air ratio at idle. Turn the screw clockwise to enrichen the mixture and anti-clockwise to weaken it.

Refit the carburetter assembly to the machine (Section B8) and adjust the throttle stop screw to give an idle of approximately 500 r.p.m.

Adjust the throttle cable to remove any excessive slackness. The adjuster is situated at the carburetter end of the cable.

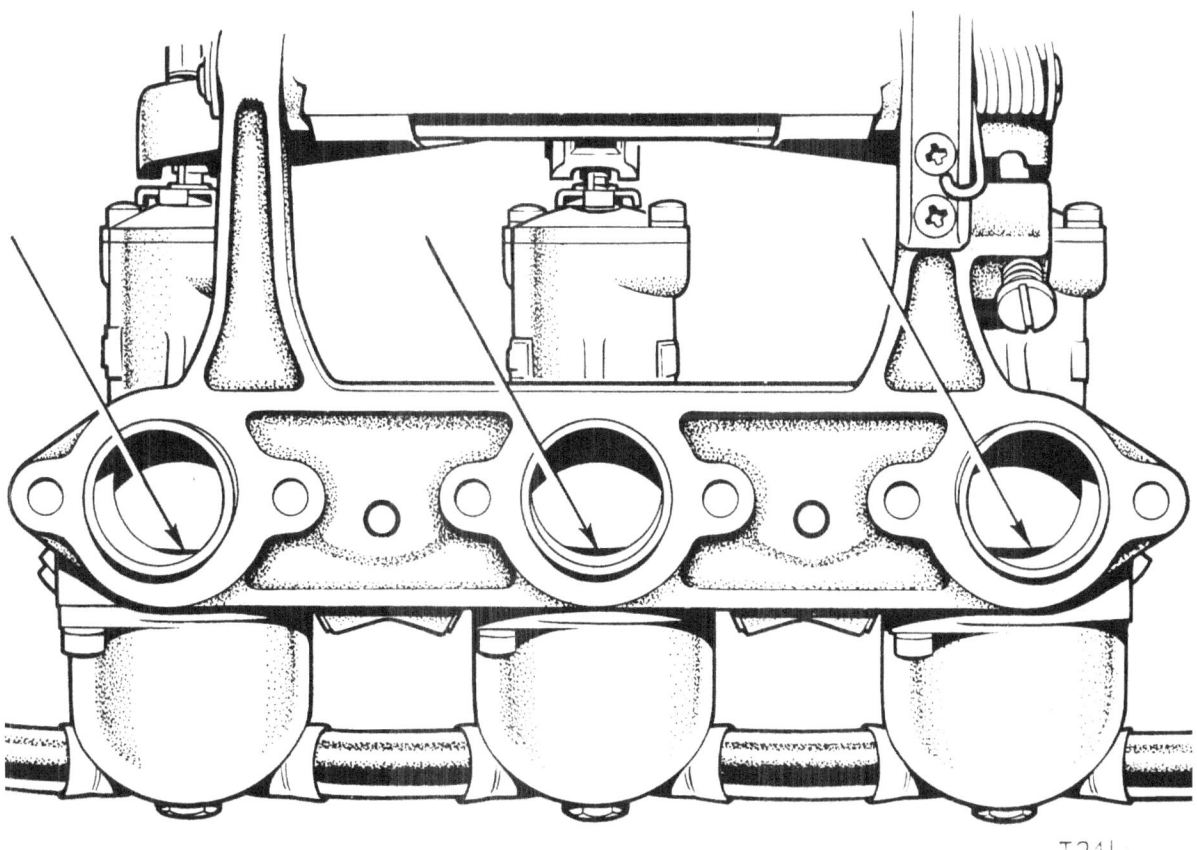

Fig. B11. Synchronising the throttle slides

SECTION B12

REMOVING AND REFITTING THE CYLINDER HEAD ASSEMBLY

Proceed as in Section B2, removing and replacing the rocker boxes.

Slacken the two exhaust pipe to silencer clip bolts, and the two exhaust pipe to exhaust manifold pinch bolts. Remove the exhaust pipes by tapping them downwards with a rubber mallet. Slacken the three manifold cooling rings, and remove the exhaust manifold by tapping it forwards off the exhaust stubs, with a rubber mallet.

Remove the carburetter and air cleaner assembly (Section B8), and remove the four remaining cylinder head securing nuts and plain washers, one turn at a time, until the load has been released. Lift the cylinder head off the locating studs, and remove the cylinder head gasket.

The steel cylinder head gasket should be renewed.

REFITTING THE CYLINDER HEAD

Ensure that the junction surfaces of the cylinder block, and head are clean. Lightly grease the gasket and place it in position over the cylinder barrel studs and dowels. Ensure that the corrugations face upwards.

Lower the cylinder head into position and fit the the four outer cylinder head nuts and plain washers finger tight. Continue as described in Section B2, refitting the rocker boxes.

Refit the exhaust manifold and pipes, ensuring that the three cooling ring clips are secure and also the manifold to exhaust pipe and exhaust pipe to silencer bolts are tight. Refit the carburetter and air cleaner assembly (Section B6 and B8).

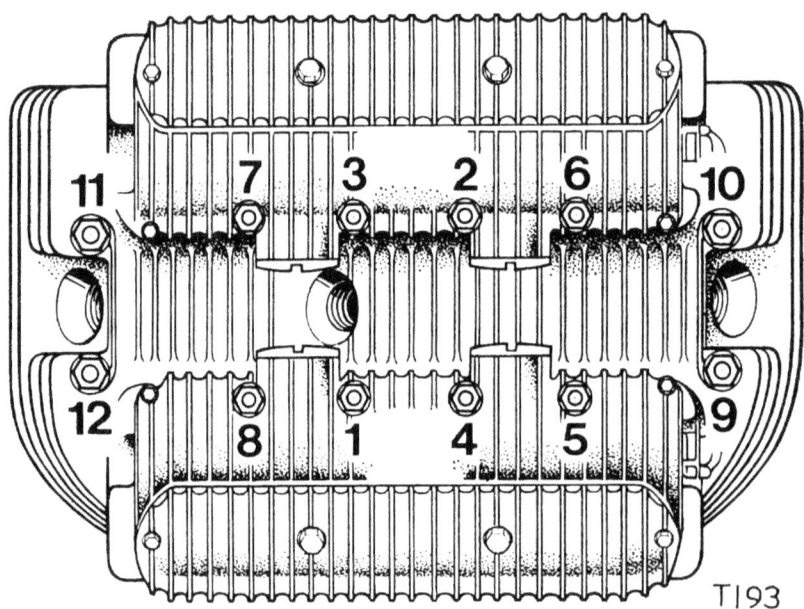

Fig. B12. Cylinder head bolt tightening sequence

SECTION B13

REMOVING AND REFITTING THE VALVES

Removal of the valves is facilitated by means of a "G" clamp type valve spring compressor. When the spring is compressed sufficiently, the split cotters can be removed with a narrow screwdriver, and the valve spring withdrawn when the compressor is released. As each valve is removed it should be marked so that it can be replaced in its original position.

NOTE: The inlet valves are marked "IN" and the exhaust valves "EX".

Fitting a new or reground valve necessitates seating by the grinding in process described in Section B16 but it does not necessitate recutting the cylinder head valve seat unless new valve guides have been fitted.

The valve springs should be inspected for fatigue and cracks, and checked for wear by comparing them with a new spring or the dimension given in GENERAL DATA.

All parts should be thoroughly cleaned in paraffin (kerosene) and allowed to drain before reassembling.

*Assemble the inner and outer springs and top and bottom cups over the valve guide, then slide the valve into position lubricating the stem with a small amount of graphited oil.

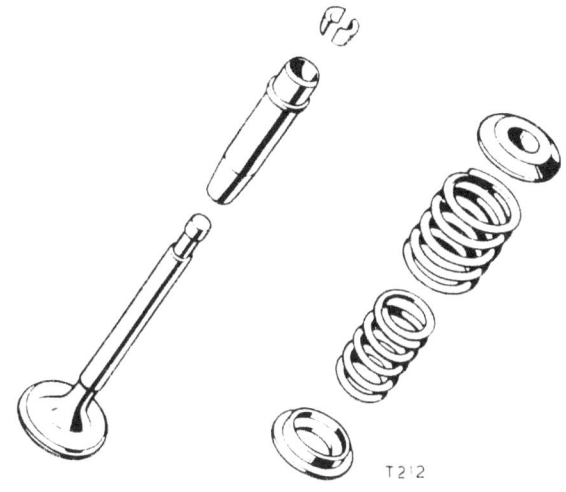

Fig. B13. Valve components

Compress the springs and slide the two halves of the split cotter into the exposed groove in the valve stem.

When assembled it is advisable to tap the cotter end of each valve with a hide faced mallet to ensure that the cotters are fitted securely.

* Each outer spring has a closed coil at one end. This end carries the colour code identification, and must be fitted towards the cylinder head.

SECTION B14

RENEWING THE VALVE GUIDES

The valve guides can be pressed out using service tool 61-6063 with the cylinder head inverted on the bench.

The same method may be employed to fit the new guide, although it is essential that 61-6063 replacement tool is used, to avoid causing damage to the knife edge of the guide.

In either case lightly grease the valve guide to assist assembly. Ensure that the guide is pressed in until the shoulder is flush with the cylinder head.

Where new valve guides have been fitted it is necessary to re-cut the valve seats in the cylinder head and grind in the valves (section B16).

ENGINE

SECTION B15

DECARBONISING

It is not normally advisable to remove the carbon deposits from the combustion chamber and exhaust ports until symptoms indicate that decarbonising is necessary.

Such symptoms as falling off in power, loss of compression, noisy operation and difficult starting are all indications that decarbonising may be necessary.

When the cylinder head is removed unscrew the sparking plugs and clean them in paraffin (kerosene), or preferably have them grit-blasted and checked. Before fitting the plugs, check that the gap setting is correct (see GENERAL DATA).

If special decarbonising equipment is not available then a blunt aluminium scraper or a piece of lead solder flattened at one end, should be used to remove the carbon deposits. Do not use a screwdriver or a steel implement of any kind on an aluminium surface.

When removing the deposits from the piston crown, a ring of carbon should be left round the periphery of the pistons to maintain the seal. Also the carbon ring round the top of the cylinder bore should not be disturbed. To facilitate this an old piston ring should be placed on top of the piston, level with the top surface of the cylinder block.

Remove the valves (Section B13) then remove the carbon deposits from the valve stems, combustion chamber and ports of the cylinder head. Remove all traces of carbon dust by means of a jet of compressed air or the vigorous use of a tyre pump, then thoroughly clean the cylinder head and valves in paraffin (kerosene). Finally, check the valves for pitting. If necessary, the valves can be ground-in as shown in Section B16.

SECTION B16

RE-SEATING THE VALVES

Where the valve guides have been renewed or the condition of a valve seat is doubtful, it is advisable to re-cut the cylinder head valve seat then grind in the valve, using a fine grade of grinding-in paste.

It is important that the cylinder head valve seat and the valve guide bore should be concentric. For the purpose of re-cutting the valve seats the following service tools are available.

    D1833   Inlet seat cutter (45°)
    D1832   Exhaust seat cutter (45°)
    D1835   Exhaust seat blender
    D1863   { Holder—seat cutters
             Pilot—seat cutters
             Tommy bar
             Tommy bar—cutter pilot

The valve seat cutting operation should be carried out with the greatest care, and only a minimum amount of metal should be removed.

After the seats have been re-cut, they should be blended to given an even seating of $\frac{3}{32}$ in. (2.4 mm.).

Examine the face of the valve to see if it is pitted, scored or damaged. If necessary, the face can be reground, but excessive re-grinding is not advisable for this adversely affects the heat transference properties of the valve and will ultimately result in critical pocketing.

The stem of the valve should be inspected for wear or scuffing and if either is pronounced, the valve should be renewed.

To grind in the valve use a fine grade carborundum grinding paste. Place a small amount evenly on the valve seat and place the valve in its guide with a holding tool attached.

Use a semi-rotary motion, occasionally lifting the valve and turning it through 180°. Continue this

ENGINE

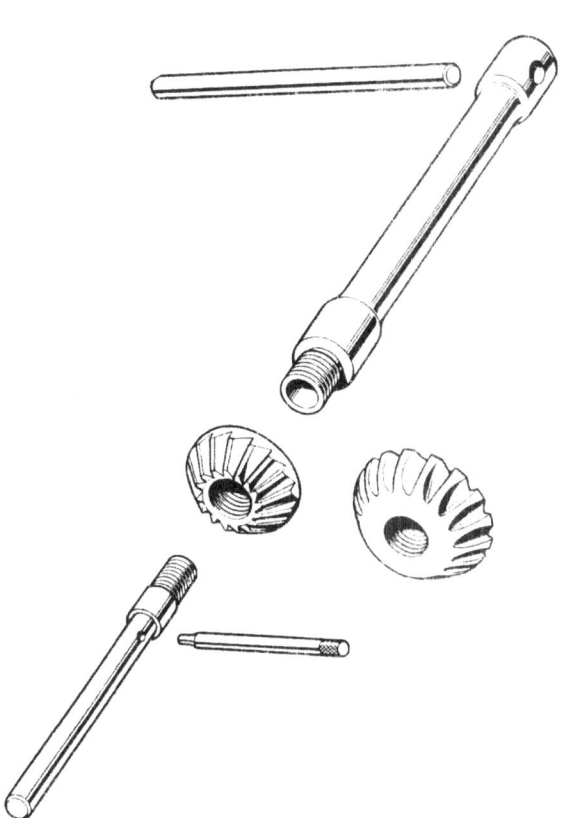

Fig. B14. Valve seating tools

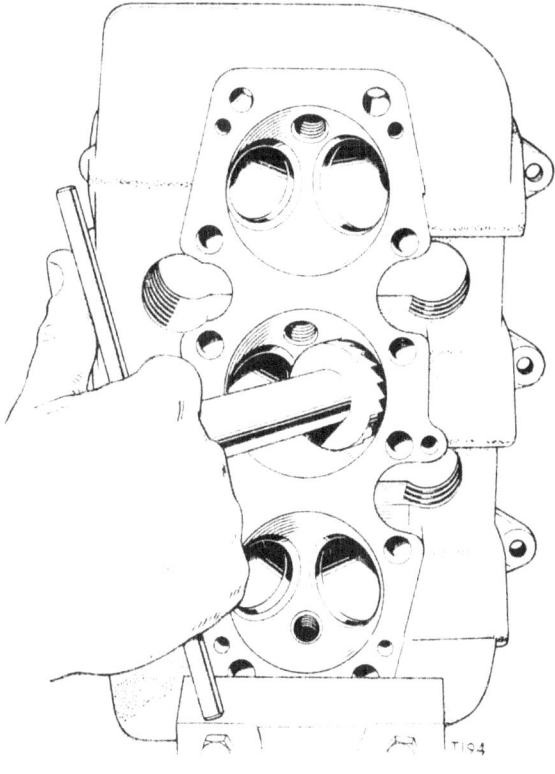

Fig. B15. Cutting a valve seat

process until a uniform seal results. Wash the parts in paraffin (kerosene) to remove the grinding paste. Apply a smear of "Engineer's" marking blue to the seat of the valve. Rotate the valve through one revolution and inspect both seats. Successful valve grinding will give an unbroken ring of blue on the valve seat.

Alternatively, assemble the springs and split cotters and pour a small amount of paraffin (kerosene) into the port. It should not penetrate the seating for at least 10 seconds if a good seal has been achieved.

Prior to reassembling the cylinder head, ensure that all traces of "Blue" or grinding paste are removed by thoroughly washing in paraffin (kerosene).

SECTION B17

REMOVING AND REPLACING THE CYLINDER BLOCK AND TAPPETS

Proceed as in Sections B2 and B12, remove and refit cylinder head and rocker boxes.

Remove ten $\frac{9}{16}$ in. A.F. twelve point cylinder base nuts, and plain washers. Release the tension on each nut before final removal, starting from the outer nuts and working in a diagonal pattern. Secure the six cam followers using rubber bands or "O" rings so that they will not drop into the crankcase mouth as the block is lifted. The tappet guide blocks will remain in the cylinder block. Gently lift the cylinder block over the three pistons, ensuring that as each piston is released, the connecting rod is protected from scratching or other possible damage. A scratch could initiate a fatigue failure. Sleeves made of sponge rubber taped together and fitted over the connecting rods will make ideal protectors. (See Fig. B16).

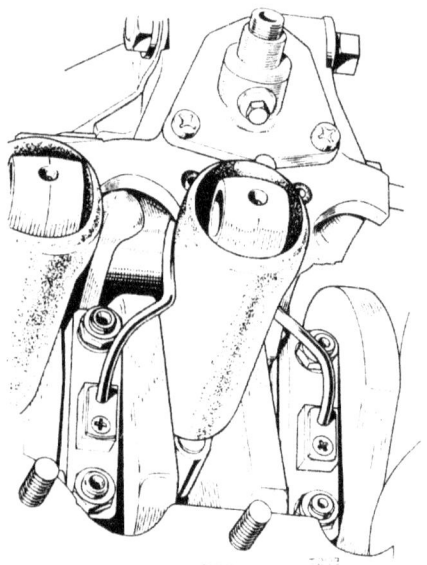

Fig. B16. Protecting the con. rods

When the cam followers are removed from the tappet guide blocks, ensure that they are stored in their correct order of removal, to ensure that they can be replaced in this order to avoid excessive cam and tappet wear. Wash all parts thoroughly in clean petrol (gasolene).

If it has been decided to fit new piston rings, then the bores must be lightly honed as described in Section B21.

To replace the block, assemble the cam followers into the tappet guide block, ensuring that they are fitted in the correct position. (See Fig. B17 for correct assembly). Ensure that the joint surfaces of both the cylinder block and crankcase are clean, and position a new gasket on the studs.

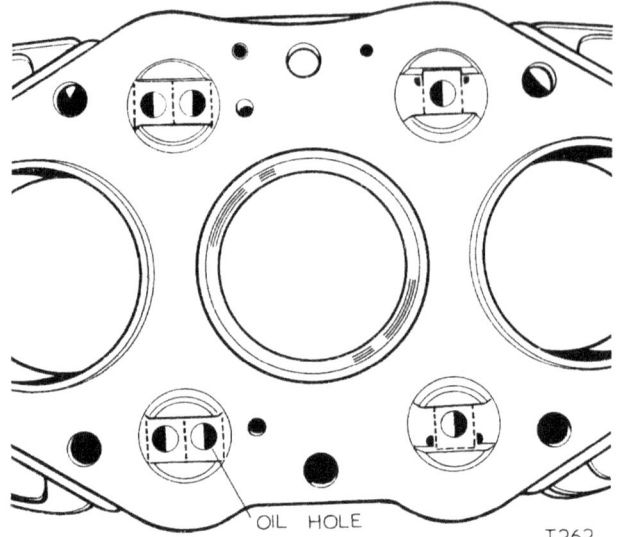

Fig. B17. Position of cam followers

There are two possible methods of replacing the cylinder block. Both methods are described in order that the operator may choose the method most satisfactory to himself.

METHOD 1

Position the crankshaft with the outboard pistons as near the top of their stroke as possible, with the centre piston at bottom dead centre. Support the outboard pistons with blocks of wood to prevent them tilting and being damaged on the cylinder base studs. Oil the bores and pistons lightly. Compress the piston rings on the outboard pistons with the use of toggle type piston ring clamps, part No. 61-6052. Fit the retaining rubbers to the cam followers to avoid the possibility of the cam followers falling into the crankcase, and offer the cylinder block to the two outboard pistons, ensuring that the square fins of the block are at the front of the engine. Push the cylinder block onto the pistons, and when all six piston rings have entered the bores, remove both toggle clamps and the wood blocks. Fit one toggle clamp over the centre piston rings, and slide the cylinder block over this. Remove

ENGINE

this toggle clamp from around the centre connecting rod. Push the cylinder block fully home onto the crankcase studs, and fit ten cylinder base plain washers and nuts and tighten down evenly working from the centre nuts outwards.

METHOD 2

Remove six bolts and plain washers which secure the sump plate to the centre crankcase section, and remove the plate, two gaskets and metal gauze filter.

Remove two locking nuts from the centre connecting rod bearing cap and withdraw the cap complete with one bearing shell. Note which way the cap is fitted as it is essential that it is replaced in this position.

Withdraw the centre connecting rod complete with piston from the crankcase mouth, oil the piston and cylinder bore, stagger the piston rings around the grooves and using a ring clamp 61-6052 enter the piston into the centre bore of the cylinder block.

The piston crown is stamped "front", and this should be towards the square fins of the block.

Position the two outer pistons so that they are level but as high as possible, and support them with wood blocks. Stagger the ring gaps, and oil the pistons and cylinder bores, using two piston ring clamps, lower the block over the pistons, remove the clamps and wood blocks, and lower the block over the studs. Refit ten plain washers and nuts.

Refit the bearing cap and two self locking nuts. Tighten these to the torque figure given in GENERAL DATA.

Refit the sump filter and plate using two new gaskets, and replace six bolts and plain washers.

Tighten the cylinder base nuts evenly commencing from the centre and working outwards.

Fig. B18. Refitting the cylinder block

SECTION B18

INSPECTING THE CAM FOLLOWERS

The base of the cam followers are fitted with a "stellite" tip. This material has good wear resisting qualities but the centre of the tips may show signs of slight indentation. If the width of the indentations exceed $\frac{3}{32}$ in. then the cam follower should be renewed.

SECTION B19

INSPECTING THE TAPPET GUIDE BLOCKS

The guide blocks fitted to this machine are pressed into the cylinder block, and are retained by pressed in aluminium alloy pegs.

No attempt should be made by the private owner to remove the guide blocks.

Wear in the guide block can be estimated by rocking a tappet whilst it is in position. It should be a sliding fit with little sideways movement (see GENERAL DATA for correct clearance).

If the guide blocks are in need of renewal, the cylinder block must be returned to a Triumph dealer.

SECTION B20

REMOVING AND REFITTING THE PISTONS

It is most important that the connecting rod protective rubbers are securely fitted at this stage.

Remove six circlips from the pistons with the aid of a pair of circlip pliers. Press out the gudgeon pins using a proprietary tool (Fig. B19).

Alternatively the pistons may be removed by driving out the gudgeon pin with a suitable drift. However, this is not a recommended practice, and may result in a damaged piston or distorted connecting rod. **The need for care cannot be over-stressed when using this method to remove the gudgeon pin.** When the pistons are removed they should be suitably scribed inside so that they can be refitted in their original positions. Each piston has "FRONT" stamped on the crown.

When refitting the pistons first place the inner circlip in position to act as a stop, then press the gudgeon pin into position using the proprietary tool.

It is advisable to renew the six circlips; this can be done for negligible cost.

If there is no alternative but to drive the gudgeon pin into position with a drift, the piston should be heated to 100 degrees centigrade (boiling water temperature) to assist assembly.

Finally, check that all the gudgeon pin retainer circlips are in position, and are correctly fitted. This is extremely important.

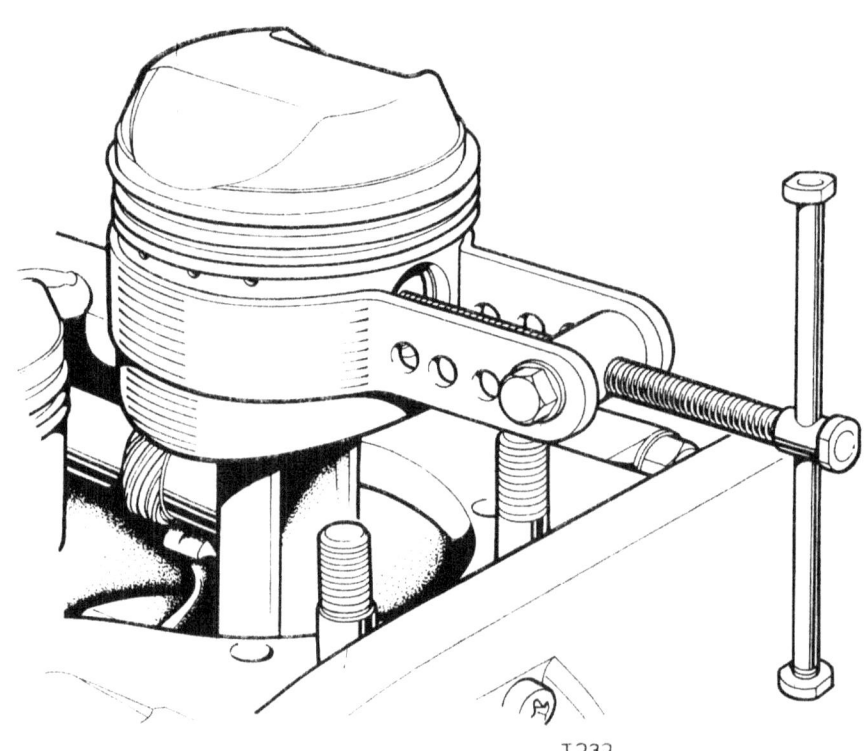

Fig. B19. Removing a piston

ENGINE

SECTION B21

REMOVING AND REPLACING THE PISTON RINGS

There should be little difficulty in removing piston rings, if the following procedure is adopted. Lift one end of the top piston ring out of the groove and insert a thin steel strip between the ring and piston. Move the strip round the piston, at the same time lifting the raised part of the ring upwards with slight pressure. The piston rings should always be lifted off and replaced over the top of the piston.

If the piston rings are to be refitted the carbon deposits on the inside surface of the rings must be removed and the carbon deposits in the piston ring grooves must also be removed.

When fitting new piston rings, the bores must be lightly honed with a fine-grade emery cloth so that the new piston rings can become bedded down properly. The honing should be carried out with an oscillatory motion up and down the bore until an even "criss-cross" pattern is achieved. The recommended grade of emery for this purpose is 300. Thoroughly wash the bores in paraffin (kerosene) and check that all traces of abrasives are removed.

Pistons and rings are available in ·010, ·020, and ·040 inches (·254, ·508 and 1·016 mm) oversizes. When fitting new rings the gap must be checked in the lowest part of the cylinder bore. The ring must lie square to the bore for checking purposes, and to ensure this, place the piston crown onto the ring and ease it down the bore. Check the gap with feeler gauges.

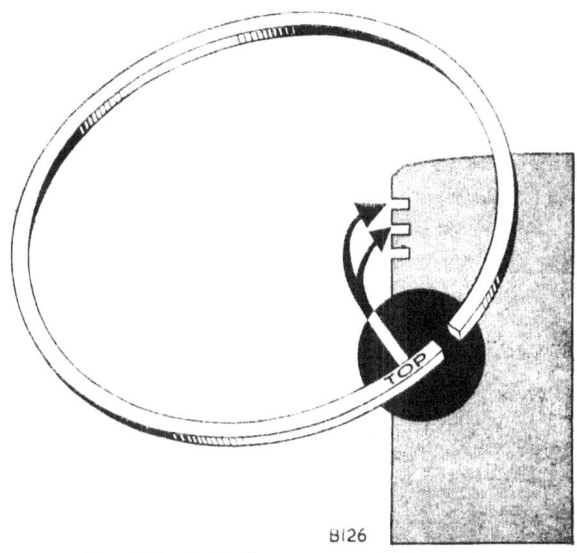

Fig. B20. Refitting a tapered piston ring

Piston rings, when new, should have the following gap clearances:

Compression ring gap: ·009/·013 in. (·2286/·3302 mm.)
Scraper ring gap:

Refitting the piston rings is straight forward, but check that the two compression rings are fitted the right way up.

The two taper compression rings are marked "TOP" to ensure correct assembly, and should be fitted with the "TOP" marking towards the cylinder head (see Fig. B20).

SECTION B22

INSPECTING THE PISTONS AND CYLINDER BORES

PISTONS

Check the thrust areas of the piston skirt for signs of seizure or scoring.

The piston skirt is of a special oval form and is designed to have limited working clearance within the bores. The clearances are given in GENERAL DATA.

Prior to inspection, ensure that both the cylinder bores and pistons are clean and free from dirt, etc. Any deposits of burnt oil round the piston skirt can be removed by using a petrol (gasolene) soaked cloth.

NOTE: The top lands on pistons have working clearances and thus allow the top piston ring to be viewed from above, and the piston to be rocked slightly. However, this is not critical; it is the skirt clearances that are all important.

CYLINDER BORES

The maximum wear occurs within the top half inch of the bore, whilst the portion below the piston ring working area remains relatively unworn. Compare the diameters, measured at right angles to the gudgeon pin, to obtain an accurate estimate of the wear. A difference between these figures in excess of ·005 in. (·13 mm.) indicates that a rebore is necessary. Compare the figures obtained with those given below so that an accurate figure for the actual wear can be determined.

An approximate method for determining the wear in a cylinder bore is that of measuring the piston ring gap at various depths in the bore and comparing with the gap when the ring is at the bottom of the cylinders. The difference between the figures obtained, when divided by three (an approximation of π) equals the wear on the diameters. As above, if the difference exceeds ·005 in. (·13 mm.), this indicates that a rebore is necessary.

SECTION B23

TABLE OF SUITABLE REBORE SIZES

Piston size ins. (mms.)	Bore ins.	Size mms.
Standard	2·6368	66·975
	2·6363	66·962
+0·010 (0·254 mm.)	2·6468	67·229
	2·6463	67·215
+0·020 (0·508 mm.)	2·6568	67·483
	2·6563	67·470
+0·040 (1·016 mm.)	2·6768	67·990
	2·6763	67·980

SECTION B24

REMOVING AND REPLACING THE CONTACT BREAKER

The contact breaker is housed in the timing cover on the right side of the engine, and is driven by the exhaust camshaft. It consists of three sets of points (one for each cylinder) and a fully automatic centrifugal type advance and retard mechanism. The working parts are protected by a circular cover and gasket. An oil seal is provided in the back of the housing to prevent the ingress of oil from the timing chest. The contact breaker plate is secured by three pillar bolts to the housing and the auto advance mechanism is a taper fit into the end of the exhaust camshaft.

To remove the contact breaker assembly, first disconnect the battery feed terminal at the fuse holder. Remove the three screws and withdraw the chromium plated cover and gasket. Remove the centre bolt and screw in service tool D782 until the auto advance cam is released from its locking taper in the camshaft. Unscrew the tool and remove three pillar bolts and plain washers from the contact breaker plate. Both the plate and auto advance can then be removed.

To detach the contact breaker completely it will be necessary to disconnect the three leads at the snap connectors terminals behind the gearbox so that the leads can be withdrawn through the grommet in the timing case.

ENGINE

Prior to refitting the cam unit it is advisable to add a small amount of oil to the pivot pins. (Refer to Section A11). The unit should be refitted into the camshaft taper, and the bolt refitted without tightening. The base plate should be repositioned so that the set of points with the Red/Black lead is rearmost. Replace the pillar bolts and plain washers.

Adjust the C.B. points (Section B25).

Reset the ignition timing (Section B26).

When the correct setting is achieved for all cylinders ensure that the contact breaker bolts are tight, then refit the cover and gasket.

IMPORTANT NOTE: "Run-out" on the contact breaker cam or misalignment of the secondary backplate centre hole can result in contact between the cam and backplate. This can result in the auto advance remaining retarded or the spark retarding. To check for "run-out" check the point gap with the contact nylon heel aligned with the cam scribe mark for each set of points. Should there be a discrepancy greater than 0·003 in. tap the outer edge of the cam with a brass drift with the cam securing bolt tight. In cases of misalignment of the secondary backplate hole, check the cam clearance in different positions and elongate the hole only where the backplate rubs the cam.

SECTION B25

ADJUSTING THE CONTACT BREAKER POINTS

The base plate should be assembled with the Red and Black lead rearmost.

To adjust the contact breaker gaps, turn the motor with the starter pedal until the scribe mark on the contact breaker cam aligns with the nylon heel of one set of points. Measure the gap using a 0·015 in. feeler gauge. The gauge should fit well with no apparent clearance, and without forcing the points apart. If the gap requires adjustment, slacken the contact locking screw and rotate the eccentric screw (see Fig. B21).

Retighten the locking screw, and recheck the gap.

Revolve the motor until the second nylon heel is in line with the scribed mark and proceed as before. Repeat this procedure for the third contact set.

NOTE: Setting the ignition timing is fully described in Sections B26 and B27.

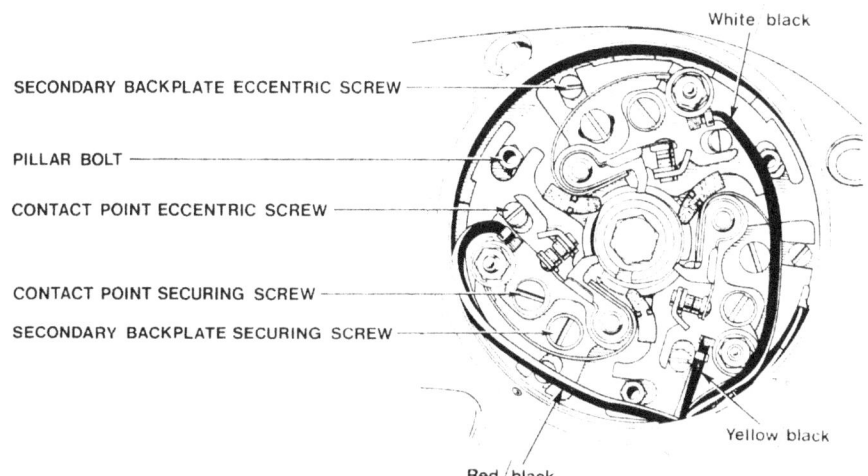

Fig. B21. Contact breaker, 7CA

SECTION B26

RE-SETTING THE IGNITION TIMING

STATIC TIMING

It should be noted that the firing order is one, three, two. The three leads as shown in Fig. B21 are coloured White and Black for number one cylinder (right hand side), Yellow and Black for number three cylinder (left hand side) and Red and Black for number two cylinder (centre).

Before the ignition timing is adjusted the contact breaker points must be checked and if not within the specified 0·014 in. to 0·016 in., they must be adjusted as described in Section B25.

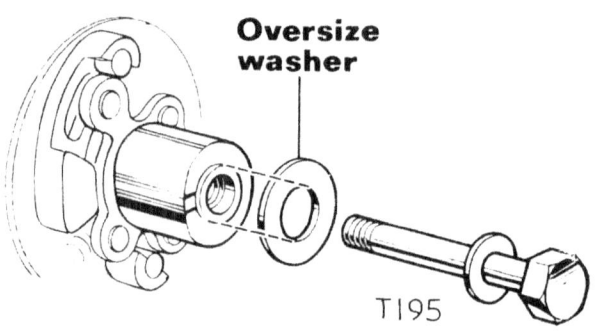

Fig. B23. Locking the auto advance mechanism

At the right front of the crankcase, slightly inboard of the timing cover, is the blanking plug for the 38 degree B.T.D.C. locating hole. This plug should be removed (Fig. B22).

Remove both rocker covers, three sparking plugs and engage second gear to allow the engine to be rotated with the rear wheel. Rotate the engine forwards until top dead centre (TDC) is located on number one cylinder, with both valves closed (i.e. clearance on both tappets). Screw the timing plunger and body D1858 into the crankcase, and apply light finger pressure to the plunger. Turn the rear wheel slowly backwards, whereupon the plunger will locate in the hole drilled in the crankshaft web. This is the 38 degree BTDC position. If the auto advance unit has been removed, it should only be assembled loosely. Slacken and remove the auto advance central bolt, and fit an oversized washer under the bolt (Fig. B23). This has the effect of locking the cam. The auto advance unit should be replaced in such a position that number one points (Black and White) are just opened (0·0015 ins.) when the auto advance is locked in the full advance, that is full clockwise motion, position.

Recheck this setting and if found incorrect, the secondary back plate securing screw should be slackened, and the eccentric screw turned to achieve the desired position. Retighten the securing screw, and recheck the point gap. If this is found to to be satisfactory, withdraw the timing locating plunger. Establish the TDC position on the compression stroke on number three cylinder. Rotate the engine backwards until the timing plunger is felt to locate. If the contact points do not commence to break with the auto advance unit still locked in the full advance position slacken the secondary back plate securing screw, and adjust the points on the eccentric screw. Retighten the securing screws, and withdraw the timing plunger. This procedure should be repeated for the centre cylinder (Red and Black lead).

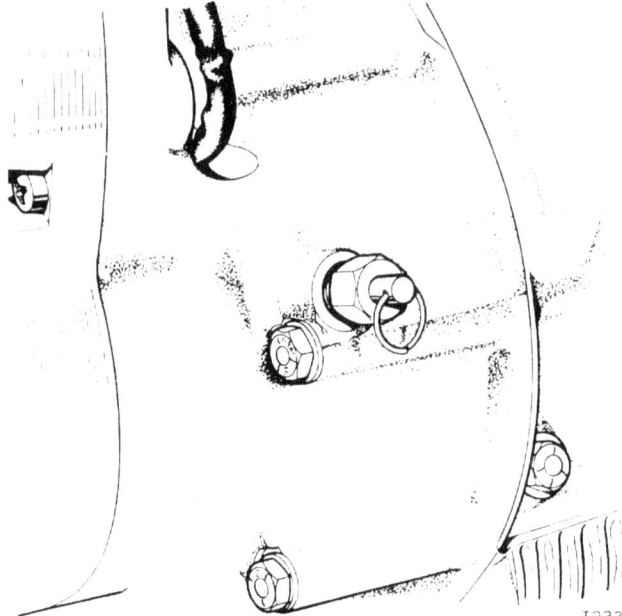

Fig. B22. Showing location tool in use

ENGINE

Remove the auto advance unit centre bolt, and remove the oversize washer. Care should be taken to ensure that the auto advance unit is not moved. Retighten the bolt.

The ignition timing will now be correct. Remove the timing plunger and body, and replace the blanking plug and fibre washer. Refit the sparking plugs and rocker covers and engage neutral position on the gear lever.

SECTION B27

IGNITION TIMING USING A STROBOSCOPE

Remove two upper screws and slacken the lower screw that secures the patent plate to the timing cover. There are three scribed lines on the rotor at 120° intervals, and the lower patent plate screw doubles as a pointer (Fig. B24).

A stroboscope should be connected to the right hand sparking plug and a power source.

NOTE: When using a stroboscope powered by a 12 volt battery as an external power source, do not use the machine's own battery. (A.C. pulses in the low tension wiring can trigger the stroboscope, and give false readings).

Remove the contact breaker cover plate and gasket, and ensure that the contact point gaps are correct (refer to Section B25 if necessary).

Start the motor and direct the stroboscope beam at the pointer and rotor mark. The motor should be revved at 2,000 r.p.m. or more, when the pointer and line should coincide. If these do not coincide, adjustment should be carried out on the Black/White contact point, by slackening the secondary bracket screws and adjusting the eccentric screw (Fig. B21). When an accurate setting has been obtained, retighten the secondary bracket.

Reconnect the stroboscope to the central spark plug, restart the motor and again direct the beam at the rotor mark. If adjustment is necessary, the Red/Black secondary bracket should be adjusted.

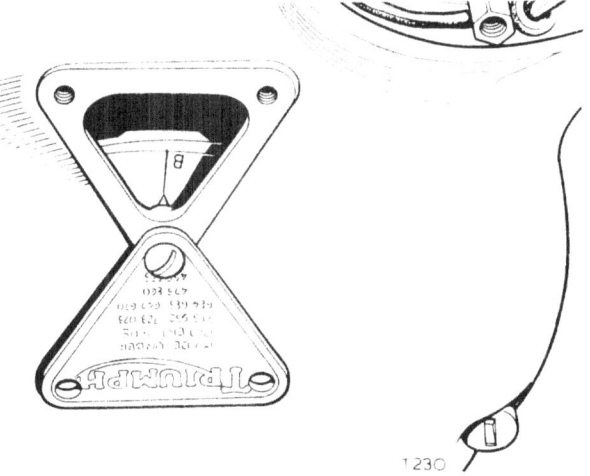

Fig. B24. Timing mark on the rotor

Repeat this procedure for the left hand cylinder, and carry out any necessary adjustment on the Yellow/Black secondary bracket.

Ensure that all contact breaker screws are tight, replace the gasket and cover, and disconnect the stroboscope.

From Engine No. PG 01603 a new crankshaft was introduced to meet emergency start requirements. Follow the procedure as shown in Section B27, but time the motor to the "B" position on the rotor. Note:— The rotor has two sets of timing marks as "A" and "B". The "A" marks are for the early crankshafts and the "B" marks for engines produced after PG01603.

SECTION B28

REMOVING AND REFITTING THE TIMING COVER

Remove the right exhaust pipe by slackening the exhaust pipe to exhaust manifold pinch bolt, and the exhaust pipe to silencer clip.

Remove three contact breaker cover screws and the cover. Check that the gasket is in good condition, in which case it can be reused. Remove the contact breaker assembly and auto advance unit as described in Section B24.

Remove nine Pozidriv screws from the timing cover, and note that three long screws are fitted to the lower holes. A sharp tap at the edge of the cover will break the joint and the cover can be lifted clear.

Before refitting the cover, clean off all traces of old jointing compound from both the timing cover and crankcase faces. Examine the contact breaker housing oil seal for signs of cracks or other damage. If necessary renew the seal by prising the old out with a screwdriver, and fitting a new seal spring side towards the engine. The seal must be tapped home with the spring side flush with the inner surface of the cover.

To refit the timing cover, fit the timing cover oil seal protector tool D1810 into the end of the camshaft. Apply jointing compound to the joint surface of the timing cover, and refit the cover over the protector tool and secure as a reversal of the dismantling procedure. The long screws (X) are shown in Fig. B25.
Adjust the C.B. points (Section B25).
Finally reset the ignition timing (Section B26).

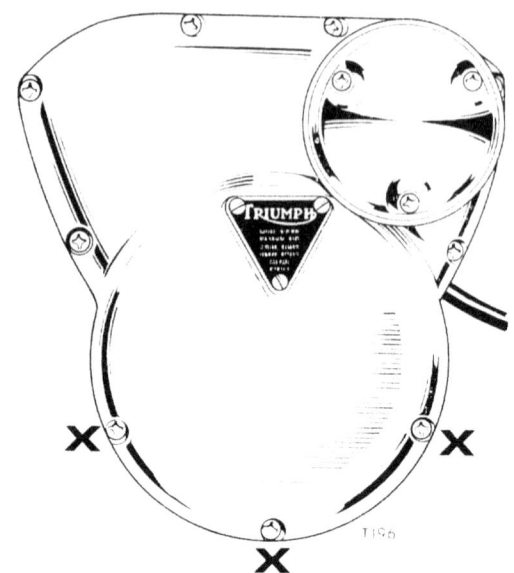

Fig. B25. Position of screws

SECTION B29

EXTRACTING AND REFITTING THE VALVE TIMING PINIONS

Before attempting to remove any of the valve timing gears, it is necessary to release the load on the camshafts caused by valve spring compression. This can be achieved by removing the rocker boxes (Section B2) or by slackening the valve rocker adjusters.

Remove the contact breaker (Section B24), the timing cover (Section B28) and the rotor and stator by removing three locking nuts and washers and the large crankshaft nut and tab washer.

Select fourth (top) gear and if possible obtain a second operator to apply the rear brake.

Remove the camwheel retaining nuts, bearing in mind that they have LEFT HAND threads.

Release the circlip which retains the intermediate pinion, and withdraw the thrust washer.

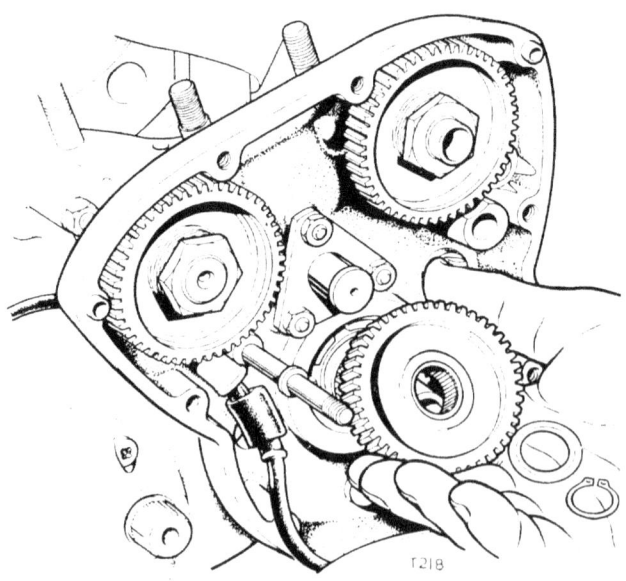

Fig. B26. Showing order of assembly of the intermediate pinion

ENGINE

CAMSHAFT PINIONS

To facilitate extraction and replacement of both the inlet and exhaust camshaft pinions, the extractor and replacer adaptor should be used in conjunction with the service tool, supplied under assembly number D2213.

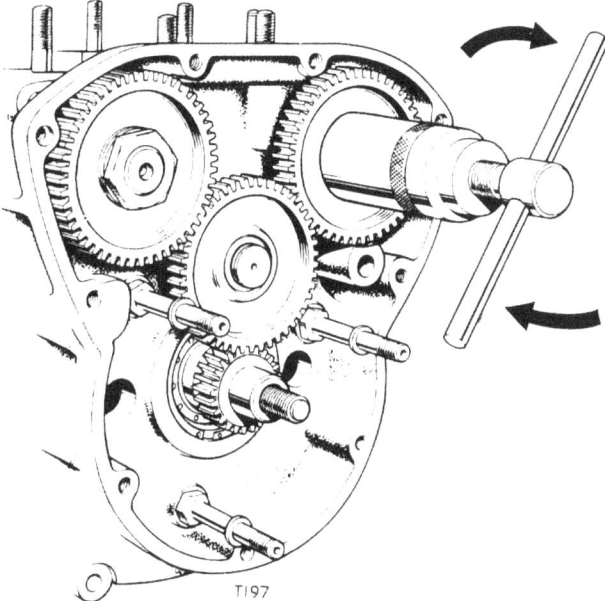

Fig. B27. Extracting camshaft pinion using D2213

To extract the inlet pinion, first screw on the extractor body, and then screw in the extractor bolt. The pinion will then be withdrawn from the camshaft (see Fig. B27).

In the case of the exhaust camshaft, the adaptor should be positioned on the end of the camshaft, to avoid damaging the contact breaker location taper.

The location keys in each camshaft are a tight fit, and may be left in position if it is not intended to remove the camshafts. The intermediate wheel can now be withdrawn. When replacing the pinion, ensure that the keys are correctly located, then screw the adaptor into the assembler bolt and onto the camshaft. The pinion should be lubricated to assist assembly, and the extractor body screwed onto it (remember that is a left hand thread). Slide the pinion and body over the replacer, align the key to the keyway opposite the timing mark, and screw on the replacer nut and washer (see Fig. B28).

CRANKSHAFT PINION

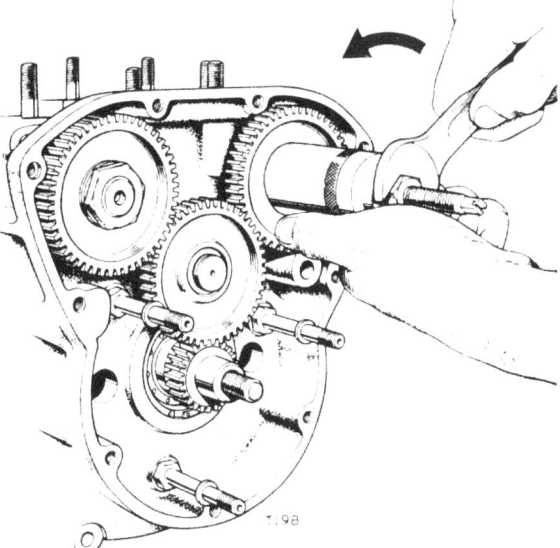

Fig. B28. Refitting the camshaft pinions

It is not necessary to extract the crankshaft pinion in order to dismantle the engine. Removal of the pinion is facilitated by service tool 61-6019 (see Fig. B29).

To extract the pinion unscrew the knurled collar on the extractor, at which point the feet will

Fig. B29. Extractor tool 61-6019

spread. Position the extractor ensuring that the feet are located in the pinion recess, and tighten the collar. Screw in the bolt until the pinion is free.

A spacing washer is fitted behind the pinion and if removed should be placed in safe-keeping.

Refitting the pinion is aided by service tool 61-6024 which consists of a tubular drift and guide, to ensure correct alignment.

If the spacing washer has been removed it should be replaced, and the key refitted to the shaft.

Fit the pinion with the chamfer and timing dot outwards.

Screw the guide onto the crankshaft, and slide the pinion over it, after having greased the pinion bore. Align the key and key way, and drive the pinion onto the crankshaft.

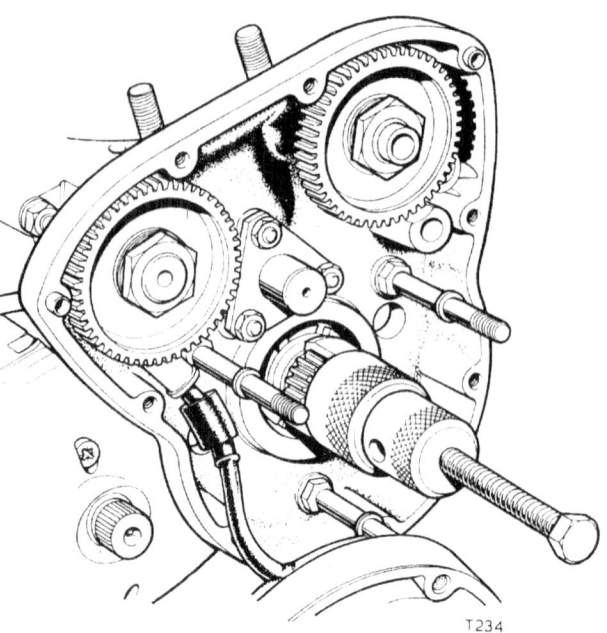

Fig. B30. Extracting the crankshaft pinion

SECTION B30

VALVE TIMING

Position the crankshaft and camshaft pinions so that the relevant timing marks are towards the intermediate pinion spindle. Assemble the intermediate wheel so that the timing marks coincide (see Fig. B31).

Due to the intermediate wheel having a prime number of teeth, the timing marks will only coincide every 94th revolution, thus there is no cause for alarm if the marks will not readily re-align.

When checking the valve timing against the figures given in GENERAL DATA, it should be noted that these are relative to a valve rocker clearance of nil for checking only.

Either camshaft can be advanced or retarded in steps of 15 degrees, which is equal to one tooth on the camshaft pinion, or 5 degrees by assembling the pinion on a different keyway.

Continue reassembly as a reversal of the dismantling procedure. The ignition timing procedure is fully described in Section B26.

ENGINE

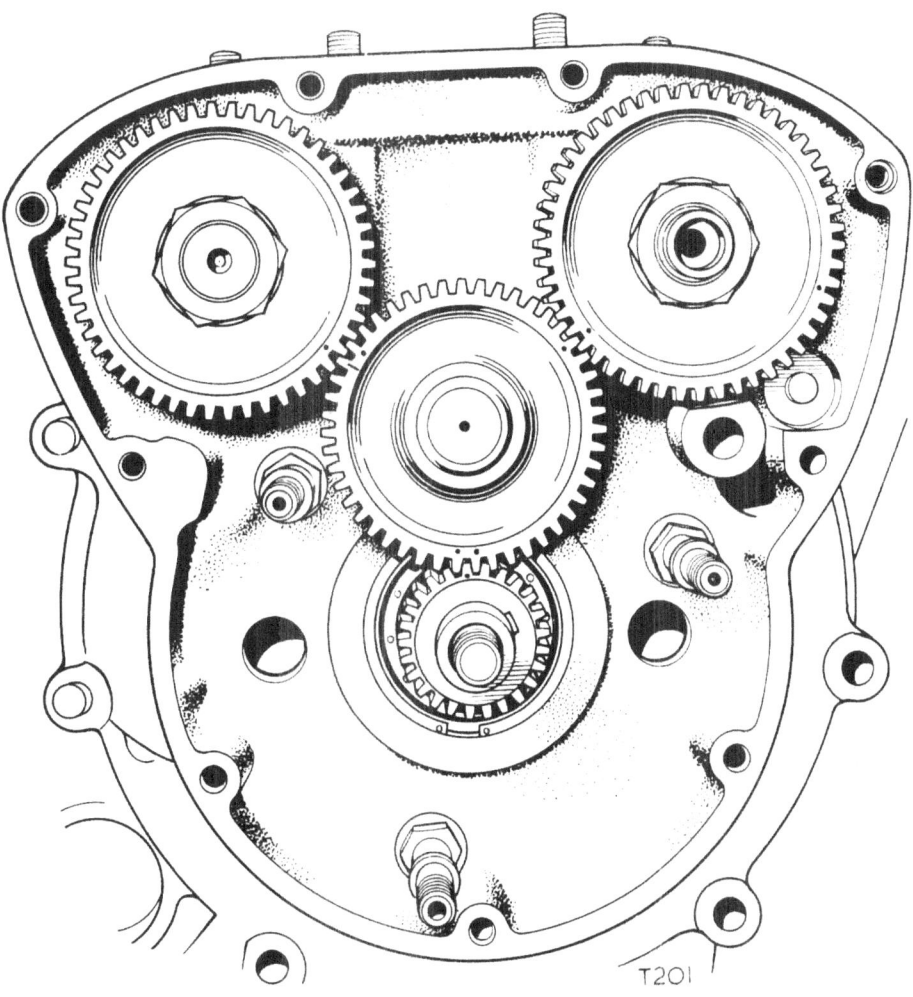

Fig. B31. Valve timing marks

SECTION B31

TO DISMANTLE AND REASSEMBLE THE CRANKCASE

(1) Remove the engine unit (Section B1).

(2) Remove the rocker boxes (Section B2).

(3) Remove the carburetters (Section B8).

(4) Remove the cylinder head (Section B12).

(5) Remove the cylinder block (Section B17).
DO NOT FORGET TO PROTECT THE CONNECTING RODS FROM MARKING.

(6) Remove the pistons (Section B20).

(7) Remove the primary chain, engine sprocket and shock absorber (Section C5-C7).

(8) Remove the clutch and housing (Section C7).

(9) Remove the oil pump (Section A7).

(10) Remove the gearbox outer cover (Section D2).

(11) Remove the gearbox inner cover and gear cluster (Section D7).

(12) Remove the timing cover (Section B28).

(13) Remove the rotor and stator.

To remove the right hand side crankcase section it is not necessary to remove the timing pinion and distance piece. If for any reason the pinion is removed, note that this is keyed to the crankshaft and will need the use of an extractor. The intermediate timing gear will have to be removed for valve timing purposes on reassembly, thus the circlip, thrust washer and intermediate gear complete with needle roller bearing must be removed. The right side case is located by dowels to the centre crankcase section and after removal of two nuts and plain washers, five bolts with plain washers and one socket head screw from within the timing cover, the crankcase section can be withdrawn with the aid of a light tap to break the sealed joint (see Fig. B32). To avoid any fouling caused by the cam lobes, the camshafts should be positioned so that the single lobes (i.e. those at the left hand end of the camshaft) point inwards.

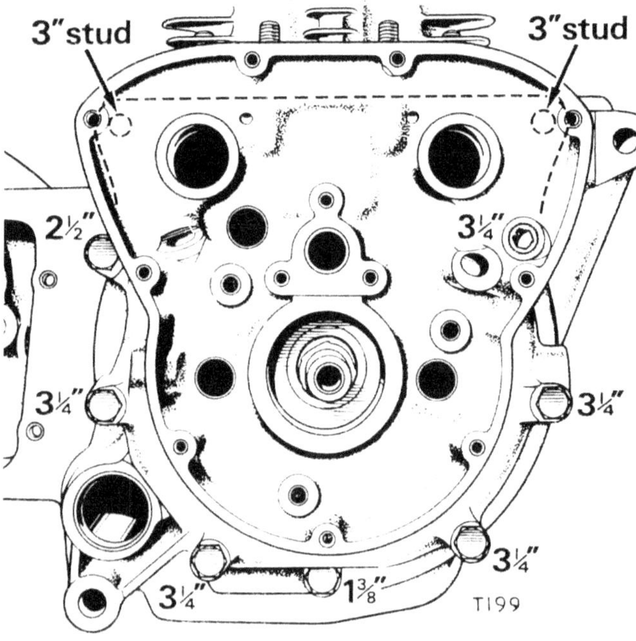

Fig. B32. Location of right side crankcase section

Remove eight bolts and plain washers securing the left side crankcase section, and lightly tap the section to break the sealed joint (see Fig. B33). It is adviseable at this stage to remove the oil pressure release valve (Section A6). The tachometer drive can now be removed from the crankcase centre section (Section B36).

Remove two countersunk screws holding the tappet oil feed pipes to their respective main bearing caps, and withdraw the pipes from the rubber seals at the main bearing caps and crankcase facings. Remove four self locking nuts and washers from the main bearing caps and as the caps are located on waisted studs the crank should be lifted to free them. Under no circumstances should the caps be prised off. After removing the crankshaft the connecting rods and big end shells can be

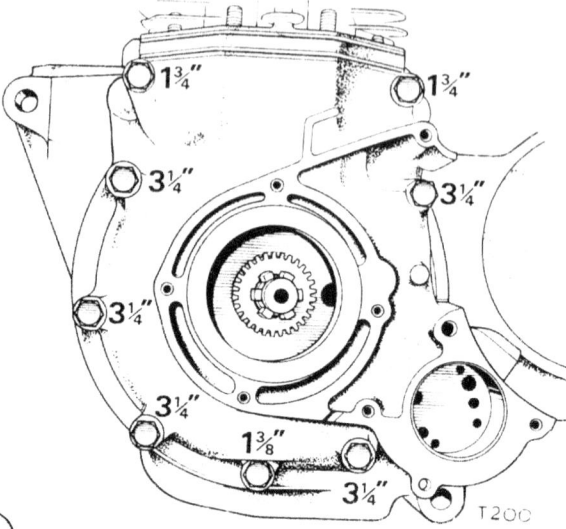

Fig. B33. Location of left side crankcase section

removed. The caps are retained by self locking nuts, and after removal of the connecting rods the caps should be refitted to them to ensure that they are reassembled to the corresponding connecting rods.

The gearbox sprocket and high gear should be removed (Sections D7, D11) in order to check the condition of the high gear bearing and oil seal. If these parts are worn they should be replaced.

Remove six bolts and plain washers securing the sump plate to the centre crankcase section, and remove the plate, two gaskets and the metal gauze filter. This filter should be cleaned thoroughly in petrol (gasolene). It is advisable at this stage to remove the anti-drain valve (Section A10) and also the two main bearing oil way plugs which are situated at the front of the centre crankcase, above the finned base. These oil ways should be blown through with an air line (See Fig. B34).

CRANKCASE REASSEMBLY

Prior to reassembly all parts should be thoroughly washed in paraffin (kerosene) and should be scrupulously clean. All traces of old jointing compound should be removed from the crankcase joint faces.

ENGINE

Replace the gearbox high gear and gearbox sprocket (Sections D7, D11), and the assembled tachometer drive assembly (Section B36).

Two tappet oil feed pipe sealing rubbers should be replaced in the crankcase at the cylinder barrel face rear of the tachometer drive. Assemble the lower main bearing shells into the crankcase, ensuring that the locking tab is to the rear on both shells. The top shell should be fitted into the main bearing caps, again ensuring that the locking tabs are to the rear of each shell.

When fitting the crankshaft to the centre crankcase, the connecting rods must be assembled to the crankshaft, and suitably protected from damage. The crankshaft should be fitted with the large diameter threaded end to the left hand side. Refit the main bearing caps complete with shells, and ensure that they are fitted in the same order as they were removed. Replace two plain washers and two self locking nuts on each cap, and tighten down to the torque figure given in GENERAL DATA. Check the crankshaft for rotation.

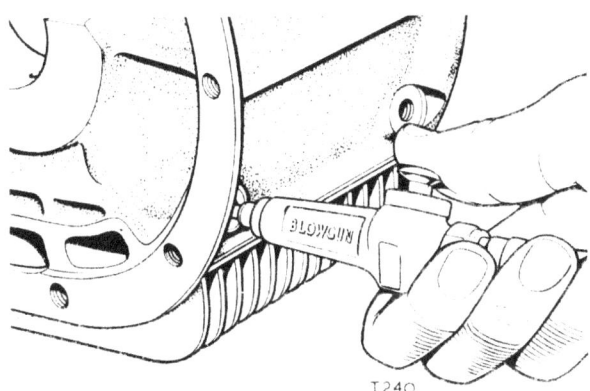

Fig. B34. Cleaning the crankcase oilways

Assemble one tappet oil feed pipe rubber sleeve into each main bearing cap, and fit the two oil pipes. The simplest method is by threading the pipes through the crankcase face rubbers first. If the rubbers appear damaged in any way, they should be renewed. Replace two countersunk Pozidriv screws, and secure these with Triumph LOCTITE.

Replace the oil pressure release valve (Section A6), the anti-drain valve (Section A10), and two oil way blanking plugs and fibre washers. Any suspect fibre washers should be renewed.

Assemble the sump plate, ensuring that two new gaskets are fitted, one above the gauze filter, and one below. The sump plate is fitted with the pocketed end towards the rear of the engine.

The remainder of the assembly procedure is a reversal of the dismantling procedure.

"O" ring seals are fitted in the recesses at either side of the oil filter housing on the centre crankcase section. If the seals appear damaged in any way they should be renewed.

Apply jointing compound to the joint surface of the left side crankcase section, lubricate the main bearing and camshaft supports and refit the section to the centre crankcase. Replace eight bolts and plain washers (see Fig. B33).

An "O" ring seal is fitted in a groove at the opening of the oil pump housing. If this seal appears damaged in any way it should be renewed.

Apply jointing compound to the joint surface of the right side crankcase, position the camshafts so that the left end lobes point inwards, and oil the camshaft journals and roller main bearing. Refit the crankcase section, and replace two nuts and plain washers, five bolts and plain washers and one socket head screw (see Fig. B32).

SECTION B32

SERVICING THE CRANKSHAFT

Three screwed plugs should be removed from the crankshaft webs, (Fig. B35) to enable the crankshaft oilways to be blown clear. Removal of the right hand plug will enable the right big end journal and right centre main bearing to be cleared, and the centre and left hand plug enable the centre and left hand big end journal and also the left hand centre main bearing to be cleared.

The crankshaft assembly should be thoroughly washed in paraffin (kerosene) and any deposits on the webbs removed with a wire brush. The complete assembly should be blown dry with an air line or vigorous use of a tyre pump, and the three oilway plugs replaced. These plugs should be secured with the aid of Triumph Loctite.

ENGINE

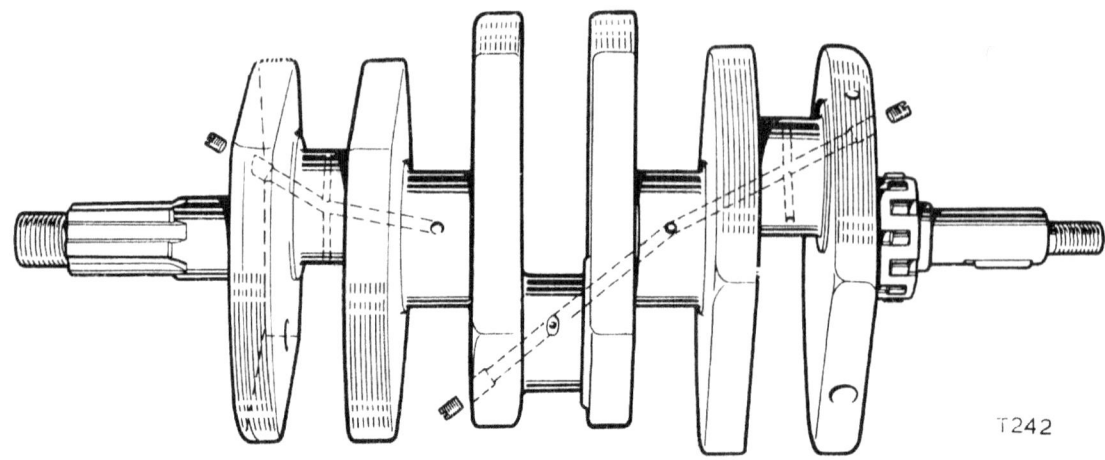

Fig. B35. Crankshaft oilways

SECTION B33

REFITTING THE CONNECTING RODS

First, ensure that the connecting rod and cap and both the front and rear of the bearing shells are scrupulously clean, then offer the shells to the rod and cap and locate the shell tabs into their respective slots. Smear the bearing surfaces with oil and refit the rod and cap to their original journals, ensuring that the tab location slots are adjacent (see Fig. B36).

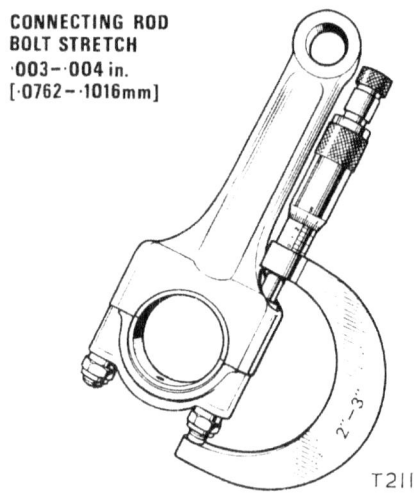

CONNECTING ROD BOLT STRETCH
·003–·004 in.
[·0762–·1016mm]

Fig. B37. Checking the bolt extension

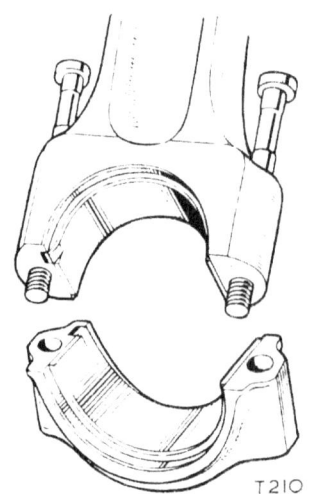

Fig. B36. Refitting a connecting rod

Refit the bolts and screw on the nuts, a turn at a time, until the centre punch marks on the rod and nut coincide. If new bolts or nuts are fitted then tighten them to the given torque figure, or, preferably, the bolt extension figure given (see Fig. B37).

SECTION B34

INSPECTING THE CRANKCASE COMPONENTS

In preparation for inspection, thoroughly clean the crankcase-halves, main bearings, crankshaft and connecting rods, etc., in paraffin (kerosene) and allow them to drain. If there is an air pump accessible, then dry the components with a jet of compressed air and examine them as follows:—

(1) **BID-END & CENTRE MAIN BEARINGS**

The extent of wear to the bearing journals can be determined by inspecting the bearing surfaces for scoring and by measuring the diameter of the journals. Light score marks can be reduced with smooth emery cloth but ensure that all parts are carefully washed after this operation.

Where a journal has been slightly scored the shell bearings should be renewed. If the scoring and wear is extensive the journals should be reground to a suitable size as given below.

NOTE: The replaceable white metal shell bearings are pre-finished to give the correct diametral clearance. Under no circumstances should the bearings be scraped or the end cap joint faces filed.

Service reground crankshafts are obtainable from a TRIUMPH dealer.

BIG-END BEARINGS

Shell bearing marking	Suitable crankshaft size	
	in.	mm.
Standard:—	1·6235	41·237
	1·6240	41·250
Undersize:—		
—·010	1·6135	40·983
	1·6140	40·996
—·020	1·6035	40·729
	1·6040	40·742
—·030	1·5935	40·475
	1·5940	40·488
—·040	1·5835	40·221
	1·5840	40·234

CENTRE MAIN BEARINGS

Shell bearing marking	Suitable crankshaft size	
	in.	mm.
Standard:—	1·9170	48·692
	1·9175	48·705
Undersize:—	1·9070	48·438
—·010	1·9075	48·451
—·020	1·8970	48·184
	1·8975	48·197
—·030	1·8870	47·930
	1·8875	47·943
—·040	1·8770	47·676
	1·8775	47·689

(2) **MAIN BEARINGS**

Clean the bearings thoroughly in paraffin (kerosene), then dry them with a jet of compressed air. Test the bearing for roughness by spinning. Check the centre race for side-play and inspect the balls and tracks for any signs of indentation and pocketing. Examine the main bearing diameters on the crankshaft for wear. The bearings should be a tight push fit on the crankshaft and a press fit in the crankcase. A loose fitting bearing would tend to cause crankcase "rumble". The correct diameters of the main bearing journals are given in "General Data".

(3) **CAMSHAFTS**

The camshaft journals normally show very little sign of wear. If however the journals are suspect, they should be measured with a micrometer and compared with the dimensions given in GENERAL DATA.

Wear on the cam form will be mainly centred on the opening flank of the cam and on the lobe of the cam. Particular attention should be given to these areas when examining the cam form for grooving. In a case where there is severe grooving the camshaft and tappet followers should be renewed.

ENGINE

A method of estimating the extent of wear on the cam form is that of measuring the over-all height of the cam and the base-circle diameter. The difference is the cam lift. If all other aspects of the camshaft are satisfactory and the wear on the cam form does not exceed 0·010 in., then the camshaft may be used for further service.

(4) CRANKCASE FACES AND DOWELS

Ensure that all faces are clean and free from burring. Any small scratches etc. can be removed with a fine file. Ensure that all dowels are in position and undamaged. Any suspect dowel should be replaced.

SECTION B35

RENEWING THE MAIN BEARINGS

To remove the left side ball bearing, remove both retaining circlips with the aid of a pair of circlip pliers. Heat the crankcase section to approximately 100°C. (boiling water) and drive the bearing out using service tool 61-6021.

To assemble the new bearing, ensure that the bearing housing is clean and grease free, and that the outside of the bearing is also grease free. Reheat the crankcase, and apply a small amount of Triumph Loctite to the bearing. Refit either one of the retaining circlips, and drive the bearing in from the opposite side, ensuring that it enters squarely. If possible use a press for this operation. When the bearing is correctly positioned replace the second circlip.

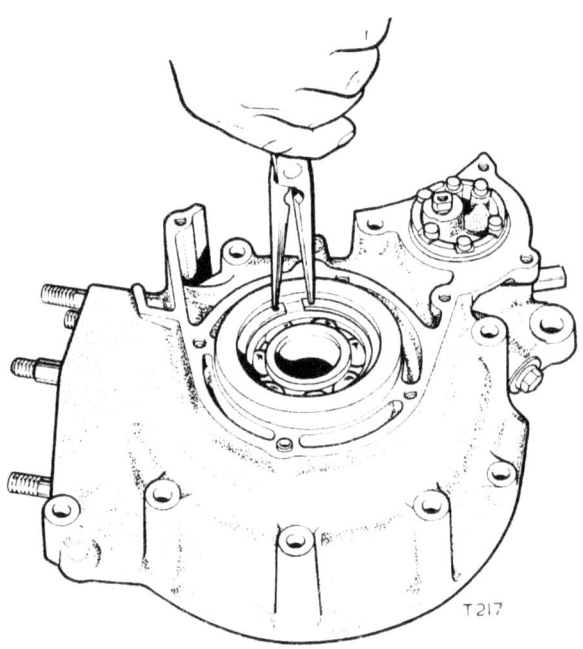

Fig. B39. Removing a circlip

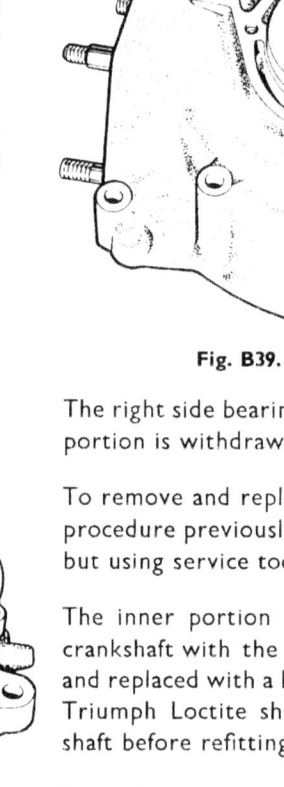

Fig. B38. Removing a bearing

The right side bearing is a roller type, and the inner portion is withdrawn with the crankshaft.

To remove and replace the outer race, employ the procedure previously described for the left bearing, but using service tool 61-6020.

The inner portion should be extracted from the crankshaft with the aid of service tool No. D3677 and replaced with a hollow drift. A small amount of Triumph Loctite should be applied to the crankshaft before refitting the inner portion.

To replace the centre bearing shells, they should be gently lifted away from either the bearing caps or crankcase supports. Use a small screwdriver, and lift each shell from beneath the locating tab. Ensure that each cap and support is clean, and refit the new shells, taking care to ensure that the tabs are located correctly in the machined slots.

SECTION B36

REMOVING AND REPLACING THE TACHOMETER DRIVE

The tachometer drive is situated on the top of the centre crankcase section forward of the cylinder barrel flange.

Remove three Pozidriv screws from the securing flange, and withdraw the complete drive assembly. Remove the gasket from the crankcase face.

To dismantle the drive assembly, remove the hexagonal headed locating peg, and withdraw the driven gear spindle housing. The driven gear can then be withdrawn from the drive housing.

Ensure that the gear teeth are not worn or damaged, and that the milled slot which engages with the drive cable thimble is in good condition. A bush is fitted in the gear spindle housing, and this should be checked for wear by inserting the gear spindle. If an excessive amount of sideways movement is apparent, then the bush should be renewed.

To remove this bush, it is advisable to screw a $\frac{5}{16}$ in. tap into the soft material, hold the tap securely in a vice, and withdraw the housing from the bush with the aid of a soft metal drift and hammer. The new bush should be pressed in with a shouldered drift.

An "O" ring seal is fitted to this housing, and should be replaced on reassembly.

Refit the gear and spindle into the drive body, gear first. Refit the spindle housing, ensuring that the grooved peg location hole lines up with that in the main body. Refit the screwed peg.

Fit a new gasket at the crankcase joint, and replace the complete drive box assembly. Secure this with the three Pozidriv screws.

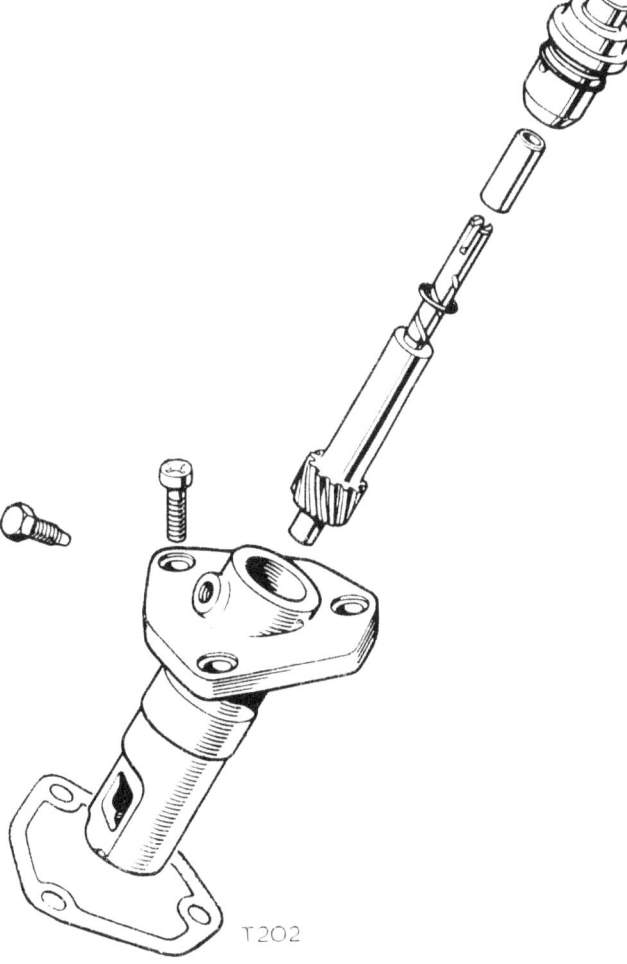

Fig. B40. Tachometer drive assembly

NOTES

SECTION C

TRANSMISSION

DESCRIPTION	Section
DESCRIPTION OF TRANSMISSION	C1
CLUTCH	C2
ADJUSTING CLUTCH OPERATING MECHANISM	C3
ADJUSTING PRIMARY CHAIN TENSION	C4
REMOVE AND REPLACING THE OUTER PRIMARY CHAINCASE COVER	C5
REFITTING THE CLUTCH COVER	C6
STRIPPING PRIMARY TRANSMISSION	C7
REASSEMBLING PRIMARY TRANSMISSION	C8
PRIMARY CHAIN ALIGNMENT	C9
REFITTING THE INNER PRIMARY CHAINCASE	C10
RENEWING SHOCK ABSORBER RUBBERS	C11
REMOVING AND REPLACING THE CHAINWHEEL AND ENGINE SPROCKET	C12
INSPECTION OF TRANSMISSION COMPONENTS	C13
REAR CHAIN ALTERATIONS AND REPAIRS	C14

SECTION C1
TRANSMISSION

The engine unit transmits its power output from the engine sprocket by a triple row primary chain to the clutch chainwheel, through the rubber, vane type shock absorber, to a single plate diaphragm spring clutch. From the clutch, power is transmitted through the gearbox to the high gear and gearbox final drive sprocket and, in turn by the heavy duty rear chain to the rear sprocket and wheel. The purpose of the clutch is to provide the means of separating the power train between the engine and rear wheel. It is not necessary to remove the engine unit to carry out work on the transmission.

SECTION C2
CLUTCH

CLUTCH DESCRIPTION

A cast iron drive ring bolted to a pressed steel cover encloses a driven plate, a cast iron pressure plate and a diaphragm spring. The diaphragm spring applies the clamping load to the pressure plate. The clutch is released by a pull rod acting on a ball bearing in the centre of the pressure plate. This separates the two friction surfaces and allows the driven plate to revolve freely between them. There is no need to free the clutch before starting the engine.

MAINTENANCE

The only maintenance necessary is adjustment of the clutch pull rod (Section C3). Whenever the primary chain is removed it may be advantageous to examine the clutch facings at the same time to ensure that undue wear has not occurred, as considerable work is otherwise entailed in gaining access to these parts. No attempt should be made to lubricate any part of the clutch unless it is completely dismantled, as there would be a risk of oil contaminating the facings. If clutch slip or clutch drag is noticed, first check that the pull rod is not binding. If no fault is revealed, it will be necessary to strip the clutch and make replacements. Should the motorcycle be driven under conditions of continued slip, the heat generated could cause considerable damage to the clutch unit.

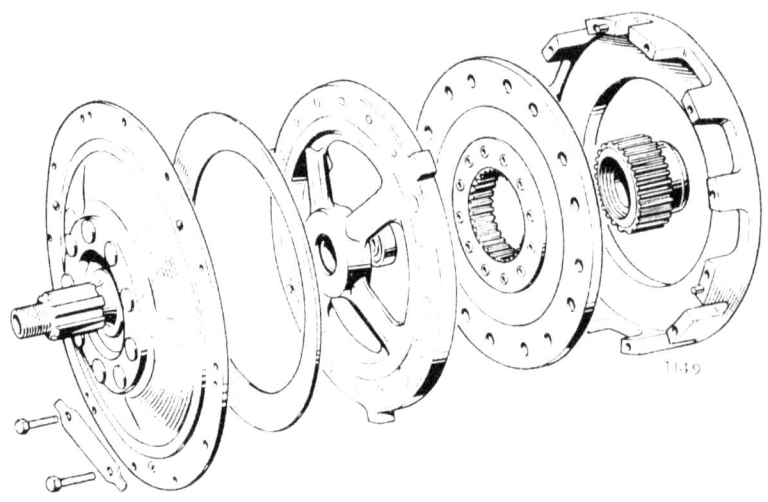

Fig. C1. Exploded view of clutch

SECTION C3
ADJUSTING THE CLUTCH OPERATING MECHANISM

Remove four Pozidriv screws which retain the inspection plate and gasket, to the rear of the outer primary chaincase, and remove the inspection plate to allow access to the clutch operating mechanism.

Very little movement is required in the clutch pull-rod to disengage the friction plate, so there must be a clearance of not less than .005 in. between the rear face of the large adjuster nut and the ball bearing in the actuating plate. If too much clearance is allowed then it may be found impossible to disengage the clutch. On the other hand, if insufficient clearance is present, the clutch friction plate will constantly slip and will eventually burn out.

Before adjusting the clutch, see that the cable adjusters on both the outer primary cover and the handlebar lever are completely slackened off.

Loosen the small locknut at the end of the pull-rod and turn the large adjuster nut to obtain the correct setting. A slot is provided in the end of the pull-rod to enable it to be held with a screwdriver and so prevent it from turning during adjustment. Tighten the small locknut and recheck the setting for accuracy.

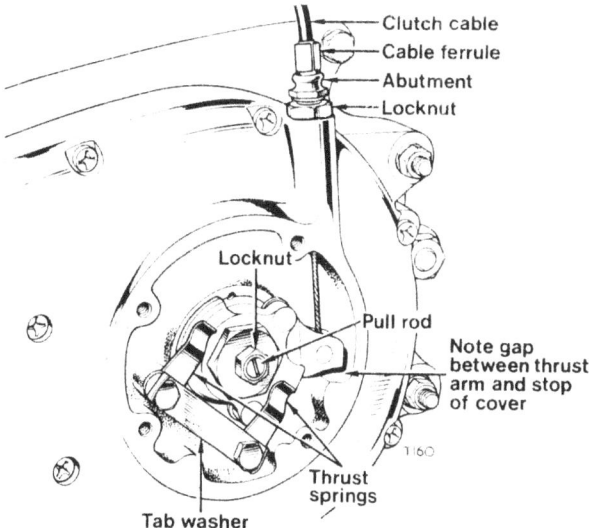

Fig. C2 Showing clutch adjustment

Finally, rotate the cable adjusters until there is just a small amount of free-play at the handlebar control lever and ensure that the control operates correctly.

Take the greatest care during cable adjustment at the handlebar that in the process the clutch is not partially freed.

SECTION C4
ADJUSTING THE PRIMARY CHAIN TENSION

The primary chain is of the triple row type, and is non-adjustable as the centres of the engine mainshaft and gearbox mainshaft are fixed. Provision for take-up of wear in the primary chain is made by means of a rubber faced tension slipper blade below the lower run of the chains. The free movement in the chain can be felt with the finger after removing the slotted inspection plug from the primary chaincase with the engine stopped.

The correct chain adjustment is ½ in. (12 mm.) free movement. To adjust the chain tension first place a drip tray beneath the front of the chaincase, and unscrew the hexagonal plug (A) from the front of the outer cover. Insert a screwdriver, and turn the slotted adjuster (B) clockwise to increase the chain tension and anti-clockwise to decrease the tension.

When adjustment is completed, replace the adjuster plug, and also the slotted inspection plug. It is not necessary to refill the chaincase with oil, as when the engine is started the chaincase will automatically be topped up to the correct level.

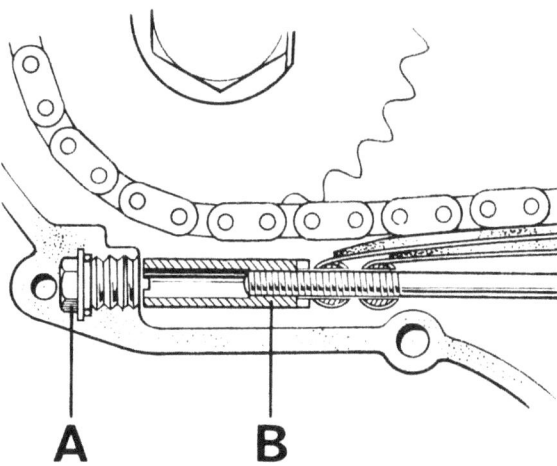

Fig. C3. Primary chain adjustment

SECTION C5

TO REMOVE AND REPLACE THE OUTER PRIMARY CHAINCASE COVER

Position a suitable receptacle beneath the centre of the outer chaincase, and drain the chaincase by removal of the oil drain plug from the lower centre of the inner chaincase. Remove the left footrest by removing the large nut and washer from behind the left side rear engine plate, and slacken the left exhaust pipe to manifold pinch bolt and silencer clamp. The exhaust pipe can be removed by delivering downward blows with a rubber mallet. Slacken the rear brake adjustment until the pedal can be positioned below the chaincase.

Remove four Pozidriv screws from the clutch mechanism inspection cover, and remove the cover complete with gasket. Remove the clutch pull rod adjuster lock nut, followed by the large nut. The clutch operating mechanism is not separated from the pull rod.

Slacken the clutch cable adjustment at both the handlebar and chaincase ends, and release the lower nipple from the operating mechanism.

Remove eleven Pozidriv screws, and three countersunk screws from the chaincase (See Fig. C4).

A-3 **C**-1¾ **E**-2 (countersunk)
B-2¼ **D**-1¼ **F**-¾ (countersunk)

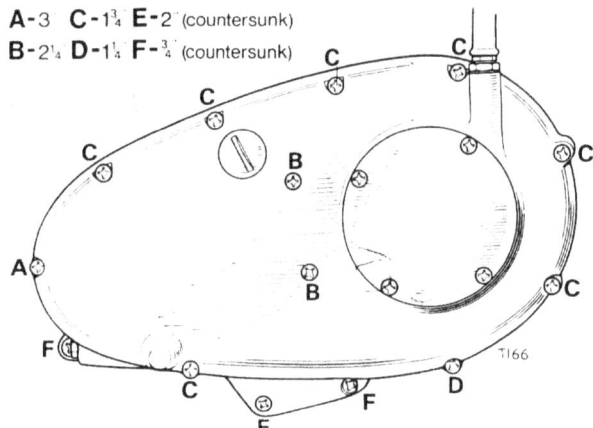

Fig. C4. Showing outer chaincase screw location
Underhead lengths of screws inset

Before the lower front countersunk screw can be removed, the tensioner plug must be removed (See Fig. C5).

The chaincase is now free to be removed, although it may require a light tap with a hide mallet to break the joint.

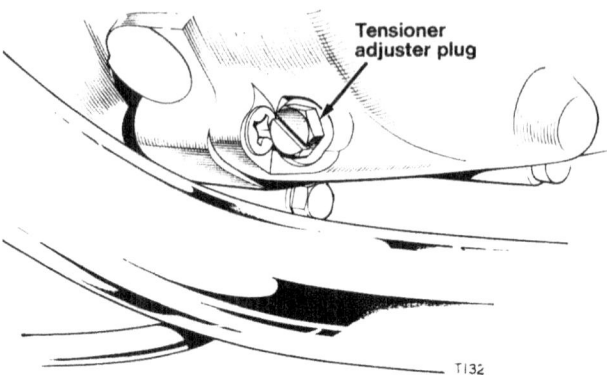

Fig. C5. Screw obscured by chain tensioner plug

The clutch operating mechanism is very robust and should not normally require attention. If however it is required to strip and reassemble the mechanism, the following procedure should be followed.

Bend back the tab washer from the two retaining bolts for the spring clips, remove both bolts and collect the tab washer, springs and spacers. Lift the clutch lever assembly clear, collecting the three ball bearings. The thrust plate is now free to be removed.

Examine the balls and tracks for pitting and corrosion, also checking the release bearing for wear. Replace parts as necessary.

To reassemble, place the thrust plate in position on the chaincase, noting that the notch must fit over the locating peg. Smear grease in the ramps and use this to stick the balls in position whilst the clutch lever complete with bearing is placed in position (with the cable trunnion at 3 o'clock). Using a new tab washer, refit the springs and fit and secure the bolts. Place the oil seal protector 61-6051 over the pull rod threads and then screw on the large adjuster nut with oil seal. Remove the oil seal protector and turn the clutch lever until the ball bearings are in their lowest positions in the ramps. It is only necessary then to adjust the mechanism as described in Section C3.

Prepare the chaincase for refitting by removing all traces of the joint washer, and ensure that both

TRANSMISSION

faces are clean and free from burrs. Ensure that both locating dowels are fitted into the two counter-bored screw holes on the inner chaincase grease the joint surface and position the gasket. Offer up the cover with care over the oil pump idler spindle, clutch pull rod, and locating dowels. Replace the two middle Pozidriv screws first, but do not fully tighten these. Refit the remaining nine Pozidriv screws and three countersunk screws, (See Fig. C4, for correct screw positions). Tighten the screws in a diagonal pattern to avoid distorting the chaincase.

Refer to Section C4 for adjusting the primary chain tension.

Refit the left side footrest, and replace the large washer and nut, and replace the left side exhaust pipe and tighten the manifold clamp bolt and silencer clamp bolt. Finally adjust the rear brake, and add $\frac{1}{2}$ pint of the recommended grade of lubricant, (See Section A2).

SECTION C6
REFITTING THE CLUTCH COVER

Check that the oil seal in the centre of the cover is not cut or otherwise damaged. If it is necessary to renew the seal, drive this out using a shouldered drift and tap the new seal into position, lip towards the gearbox and flush with the outboard boss of the cover. Ensure the joint surfaces are clean and with a hide hammer, tap the clutch cover gently home to the crankcase until the spigot locates. Fit and tighten up the three screws which are spaced 180° apart.

SECTION C7
STRIPPING THE PRIMARY TRANSMISSION
(To gain access to the Clutch)

Remove the outer primary chaincase and associated fittings (See Section C5) and collect the plain steel thrust washer and face needle roller bearing from the centre of the chainwheel (the order of bearings and washers is shown in Fig. C6). Tap the washer clear of the engine sprocket nut and remove the nut using a box spanner, tommy bar and hammer. There is no tab washer on the chainwheel nut but before attempting removal, fit the oil seal protector tool 61-6051 over the threads of the clutch pull rod. Remove the nut and both sprockets are then ready for removal as in Section C11. Note that the sprockets and primary chain must be removed as a set. For safety, collect the bronze thrust washer from the back of the chainwheel and any shims from behind the engine sprocket. Remove the screw holding the oil pump drive gear to the oil pump spindle. (This is secured with Loctite and

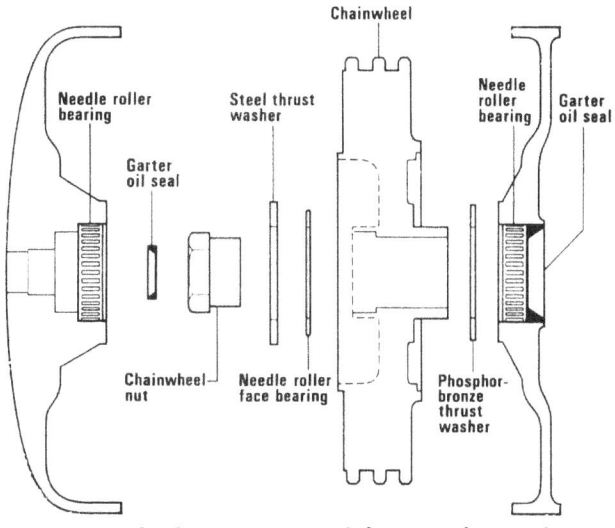

Fig. C6. Showing order of thrust washers and needle roller bearings

will be very tight). Remove this drive gear which merely pushes over a flat on the spindle. Do not disturb the oil pump driving pinion on the crankshaft, but lift the oil pump idler gear off its spindle.

Remove the long countersunk screw which passes through the top front of the breather duct cover from the other side of the machine. Remove all the screws indicated in Fig. C4 and the chaincase is free to be removed. The clutch is now exposed. This is a sliding fit on the splines of the clutch hub and can be lifted straight off, complete with pull rod. With the machine in gear, apply the back brakes fully.

The hub nut then requires removal with a box spanner, tommy bar and hammer. The clutch hub is keyed and tapered to the gearbox mainshaft and can only be removed using extractor D1860 which threads into the end of the splined hub. The clutch cover is secured by three screws only, after removal of which the cover can be lifted clear. The breather duct cover is secured to the clutch cover with three remaining countersunk screws.

SECTION C8
REASSEMBLING THE PRIMARY TRANSMISSION

Refit the clutch cover (see Section C6). Place the oil pump to crankcase gasket in the crankcase recess **taking care** not to blank off any hole. Fit the oil pump locating dowel in the top front hole of the crankcase recess. Fit the oil pump ready assembled and secure with the two lone slot headed screws. Fit the 'O' ring into the groove in the crankcase joint face around the oil pump.

Fit the oil pump drive gear onto the crankshaft shouldered side inwards and if necessary tap home as far as the main bearing inner race.

Fit the clutch splined hub shouldered side inwards, fit the tap washer and fit and tighten securely the nut using a box spanner, tommy bar and hammer. To prevent the shaft turning, engage gear (preferably bottom) and hold the rear brake fully on. The tab washer should then be peened over the nut on one or two flats. Grease the splines lightly and offer up the clutch assembly **complete with pull rod.** The clutch must be free to move to and fro on the splines.

Fit the distance ring over the clutch splined shaft, chamfered side outwards, and tap this home to the face of the clutch cover plate.

Fit the inner primary chaincase (see Section C10). Fit the oil pump gear over the flat on the pump spindle. Using Loctite on the threads fit the securing screw very tightly, lubricate and place the idler gear (boss outwards) over the spindle, meshing both with the crankshaft and oil pump gears.

Fit the cross-grooved bronze thrust washer over the rear boss of the clutch chainwheel.

Offer the chainwheel to the clutch shaft and the engine sprocket to the crankshaft, if necessary using a hammer and hollow drift to drive both fully home on the splines. See section C9 for primary chain alignment.

When alignment is correct, remove the sprockets leaving any shims in position and fit both sprockets into the primary chain. Offer the sprockets and primary chain as a set to the shafts, driving home on the splines if necessary. Fit the engine sprocket tab washer locating the internal tab into one of the sprocket splines. Fit the sprocket nut and tighten securely using a box spanner, tommy bar and hammer and lastly peen the locking tab onto the nut.

At the chainwheel the centre nut is fitted with a small garter oil seal which will be damaged unless extreme care is taken. Before fitting the nut and seal over the clutch pull rod, insert the oil seal protector and as the nut is pushed and screwed home the seal will not be damaged. Secure the centre nut. Oil lightly and fit the needle roller face bearing over the chainwheel centre boss, followed by the thick steel thrust washer.

SECTION C9

PRIMARY CHAIN ALIGNMENT

INTRODUCTION

It is essential that the primary chain misalignment on three cylinder machines does not exceed 0.010 in.

Owing to the design of the primary transmission, the engine and shock absorber sprockets cannot be accurately aligned with the customary use of a straight edge.

Normal manufacturing tolerances which apply to the inner and outer primary covers and all other components from which the shock absorber is constructed create a variation in the amount of shock absorber end float. Since the normal operating position of the shock absorber assembly is against the thrust race in the outer cover, the end float present in each particular engine unit must be determined.

If either of the primary covers or any component part of the shock absorber is changed for any reason, the amount of end float will almost certainly alter. It is also necessary to account for variations in the thickness of the primary cover gasket.

When the primary outer cover is removed, the shock absorber outrigger support bearing is also removed and the shock absorber moves from its normal running position. This again must be taken into account.

SHOCK ABSORBER MODIFICATIONS

It is necessary to remove the shock absorber, detach the end plate and withdraw the spider and rubbers to determine whether certain early faults are present.

(1) Ensure that no casting marks or numbers are standing proud in the shock absorber which could restrict the paddle movement.

(2) Measure the depth of the spider location (see Fig. C7). Later shock absorbers have a dimension of 0.7560/0.7535 in. This depth need not be modified. If the shock absorber is not within these dimensions, it is an early type and must be modified by removing 0.0095 in. from the shoulder (see Fig. C7). This ensures that the spider end float is controlled to within a 0.001/0.0054 in. tolerance.

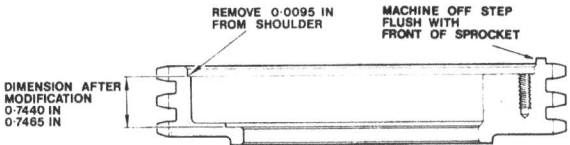

Fig. C7. Shock Absorber Modifications

(3) Several early shock absorbers have a lip on the front face (see Fig. C7). This serves no useful purpose and does not allow the use of service tool 61-6105 to check sprocket alignment without necessitating certain compensations. It is either necessary to remove this lip by machining flush with the front face of the sprocket (see Fig. C7), or to compensate for it as described in "Checking and Correcting Alignment".

(4) Replace the two needle roller bearings, part number T3643, which support each journal of the shock absorber with 0.0015 in. undersize bearings, part number T11805.

MEASURING SHOCK ABSORBER END FLOAT

Remove the primary outer cover and detach the clutch operating mechanism. Push the shock absorber inwards until it bears on its thrust washer in the primary inner cover. Replace the outer cover less clutch operating mechanism, ensuring that the joint gasket to be used during final assembly is fitted. Replace every second screw to retain the cover.

Screw service tool 61-6104 onto the clutch pull rod until the clutch becomes disengaged (see Fig. C8). Allow the tool to remain in this position.

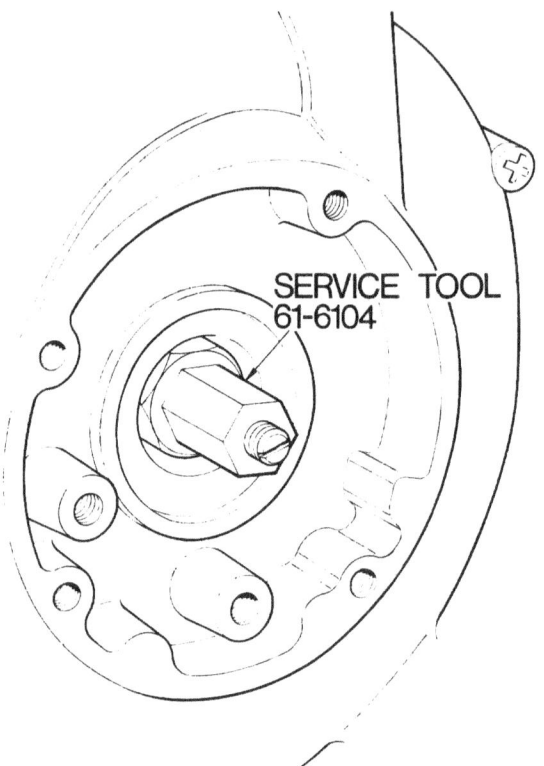

Fig. C8. Location of Service Tool 61-6104

Attach a dial indicator to the crankcase and position it such that the plunger is in contact with and perpendicular to the front face of the shock absorber nut (see Fig. C9). Zero the gauge.

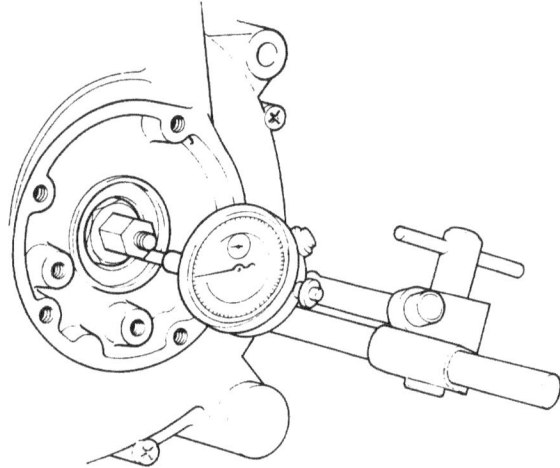

Fig. C9. Measuring Shock Absorber End Float

Pull the clutch pull rod outwards to bring the shock absorber assembly against the outer thrust race and note the reading on the gauge. This is the amount of end float on this particular engine. If it is necessary to re-check this figure, the shock absorber may be pushed back against the inner thrust race by inserting a thin screwdriver alongside the pull rod and nut.

Usually a reading of between 0.010 in. and 0.025 in. is achieved.

After having established the amount of end float, remove the dial indicator and the primary outer cover.

SETTING THE SHOCK ABSORBER TO THE NORMAL RUNNING POSITION

Select a feeler gauge or gauges of the same thickness as the measured end float and insert it behind the shock absorber so that it is trapped between this and the inner thrust race (see Fig. C10).

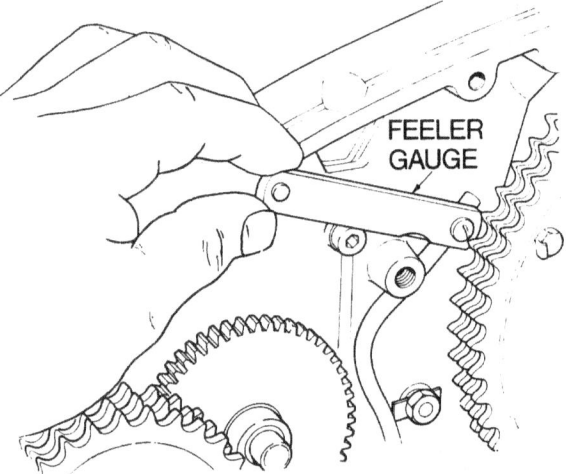

Fig. C10. Location of Feeler Gauge behind Shock Absorber

Assemble service tool 61-6103 to the primary inner cover passing the central boss over the clutch pull rod. Secure the tool with three outer cover screws (see Fig. C11). At this stage the shock absorber is in its normal running position.

CHECKING AND CORRECTING ALIGNMENT

Two types of shock absorber body have been used. The early type has a shoulder on the front face, whereas the later type does not (see Fig. C7). When alignment with service tool 61-6105 on the

TRANSMISSION

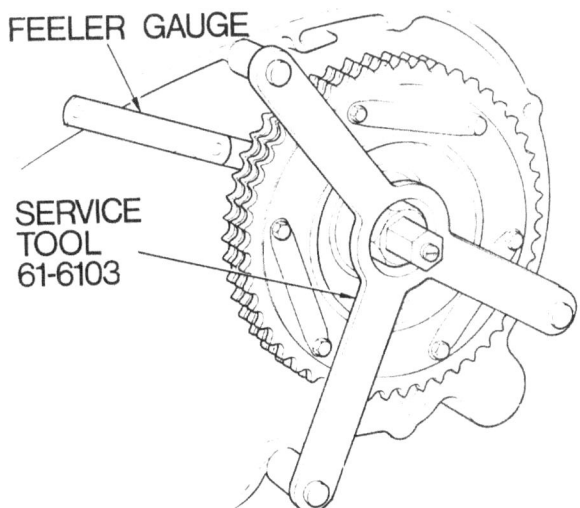

Fig. C11. Location of Service Tool 61-6103

shouldered sprocket the additional thickness of the lip must be taken into consideration either by machining as described in "Shock Absorber Modification", or by measuring the shoulder with a straight edge and feeler gauges and compensating whilst using the service tool. This is achieved either by adding the appropriate quantity of shims behind the engine sprocket or adding feeler gauges of the correct thickness between the ground face of the engine sprocket and the service tool.

Position service tool 61-6105 against the faces of the shock absorber and engine sprockets (see Fig. C7). If the sprockets are in line each of the four legs of the tool will touch the front and rear of each sprocket.

Mis-alignment may be caused by either of the following:—

(1) Engine sprocket positioned inboard of the shock absorber.

(2) Engine sprocket positioned outboard of the shock absorber.

Shims must be added or removed accordingly from behind the engine sprocket. They are available in 0.010 in. and 0.015 in. thickness under part numbers E9634 and E8039 respectively.

CONDITION I

This is indicated by clearance between the legs of the service tool and the ground face of the engine sprocket. Measure the amount of clearance present with feeler gauges and add the same quantity of shims behind the engine sprocket (see Fig. C12).

CONDITION II

This is indicated by clearance between the legs of the service tool and the face of the shock absorber sprocket. Again measure the amount of clearance present and subtract this quantity of shims from behind the engine sprocket (see Fig. C13).

At this stage the primary chain is aligned within the manufacturers tolerance, and the primary transmission should be re-assembled. Ensure that the feeler gauges are removed from behind the shock absorber sprocket.

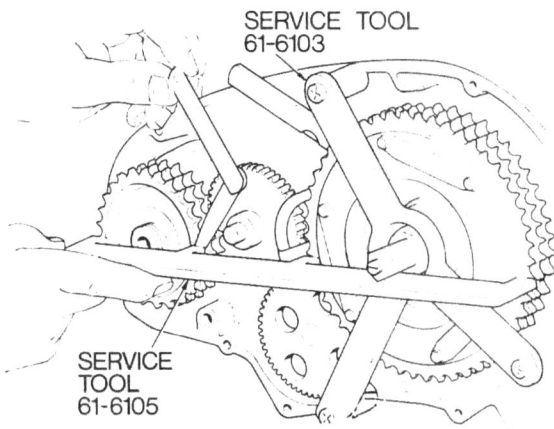

Fig. C12. Location of Service Tool 61-6105. Measuring clearance between engine sprocket and gauge

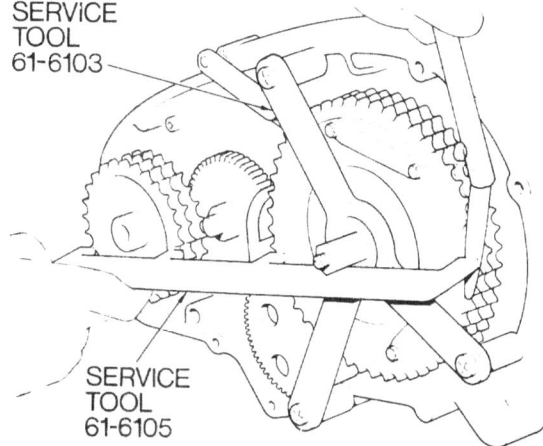

Fig. C13. Location of Service Tool 61-6105. Measuring clearance between shock absorber sprocket and gauge

SECTION C10

REFITTING THE INNER PRIMARY CHAINCASE

Removing the inner primary chaincase is covered in Section C7, but the additional following information is required during reassembly.

Clean all traces of old joint washer and jointing compound from both joint surfaces. Next examine the clutch shaft oil seal for cuts or other damage. The old seal can be prised out with a screwdriver—this of course destroys the seal. A new seal should then be fitted, lip away from the gearbox by tapping in level a little at a time with a light hammer. If the needle race needs replacing, use a shouldered drift to knock out both the race and seal together. Fit the new race, flush with the outer surface and tap in the seal from the back.

If the inner primary case is renewed, the P.V.C. oil pipe and pipe clip should be bolted into position and the oil pump idler spindle tapped gently into the face (blind end inwards) before the case is fitted. Ensure the front locating dowel is in position on the crankcase at the front chaincase screw hole. Fit a new gasket over the crankcase joint surface, greasing this lightly to retain it. Offer the inner primary chaincase over the front dowel, tapping the cover home, with a hide hammer till the spigot on the clutch cover locates to the back of the case. Fit and lock up the screws, bolts and nuts. See Fig. C14). Do not forget the top front countersunk screw through the breather duct cover.

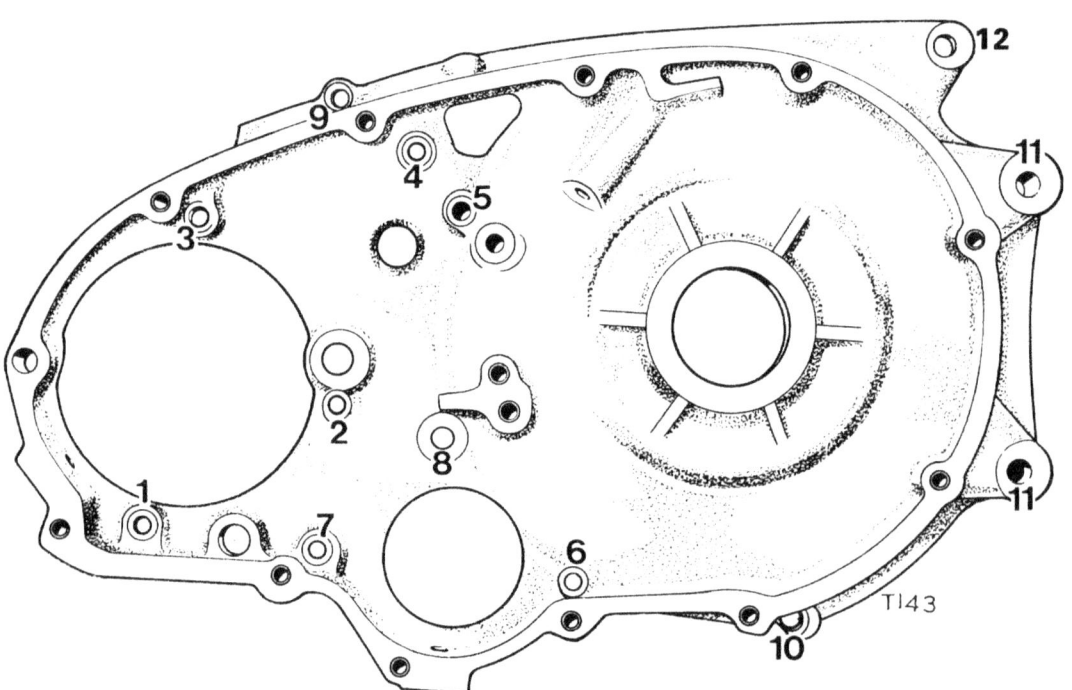

Fig. C14. Items 1-7 socket head screws, 8—hexagon headed bolt (4¼ in. UH), 9 and 10 cross-headed screws, 11—bolts to engine plate, 12—hexagon headed bolt (4½ in. UH)

SECTION C11

RENEWING SHOCK ABSORBER RUBBERS

When the outer primary chaincase is removed, access will be gained to the chainwheel and shock absorber assembly. If the shock absorber rubbers are to be renewed, it is recommended that the chainwheel assembly be removed completely and mounted on a special jig which can be held securely in a vice. This is shown in Fig. C16 together with the special leverage bar which will be essential for this task. We do not supply the jig and bar, since these can be made up locally quite simply to the dimensions shown, in Fig. C16.

On late models the chainwheel shock absorber retaining plate is secured with locking plates and bolts as shown in Fig. C18. On these models, tap the tabs clear before removing the bolts.

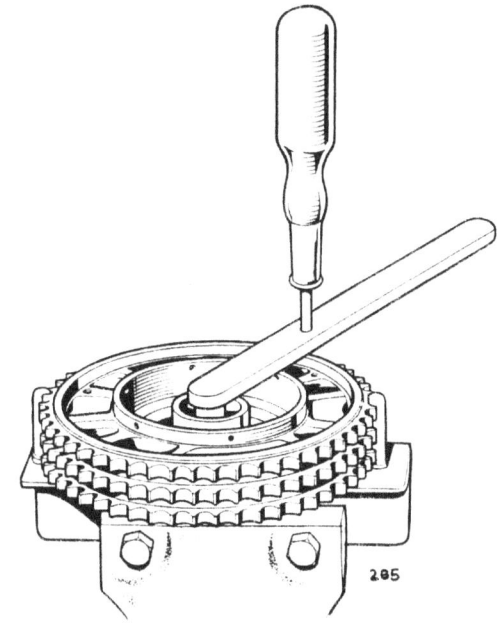

Fig. C15. Showing jig and bar in use

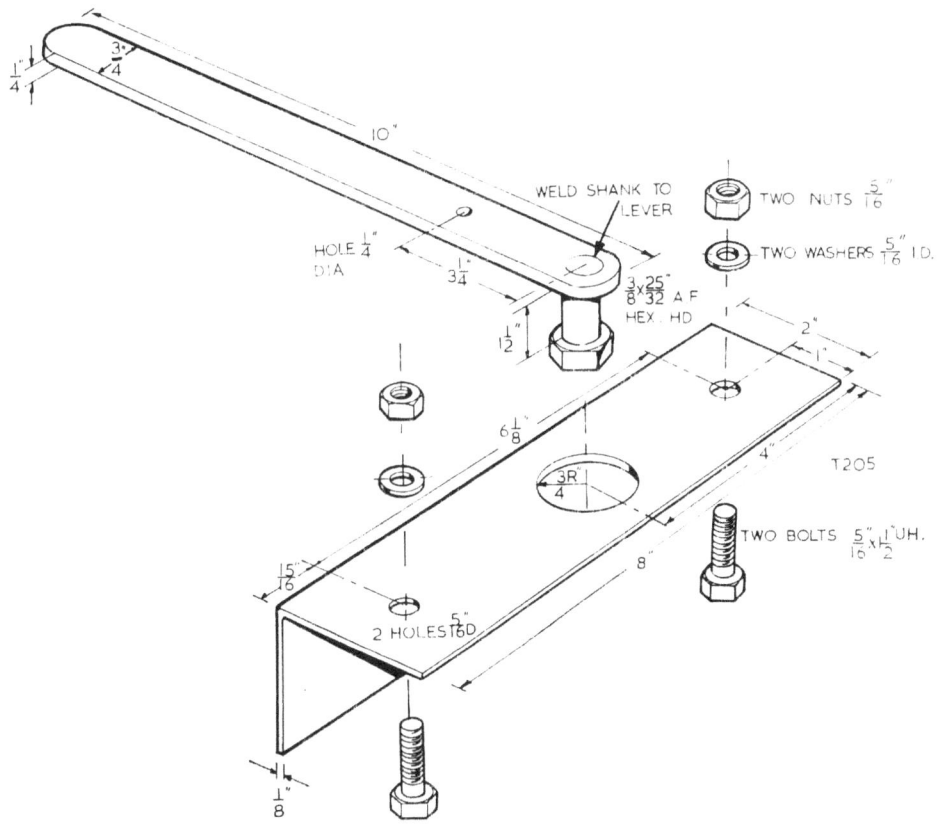

Fig. C16. Sketch of shock absorber mounting plate and leverage bar

TRANSMISSION

A number of machines were produced on which the outer retaining plate was secured with countersunk socket-headed screws, treated with Loctite sealant. The screws will be sufficiently tight that they will need to be heated with an acetylene torch to break the LOCTITE bond, prior to removal. Then, remove the six socket headed countersunk screws retaining the outer plate. After the screws are removed the plate can be lifted off and the rubber segments are exposed. At this stage the hexagon portion of the leverage bar should be placed in the splines of the shock absorber spider. A strong pull on the bar will then revolve the spider against one set of rubbers. The bar will be held in this position by inserting a screwdriver blade or tommy bar through the hole in the bar to engage with the sprocket teeth. The first set of rubbers can then be lifted out and with care, the bar held whilst the screwdriver blade is withdrawn. At this stage the second set of rubbers will be free for removal and the spider can be lifted out. To reassemble, offer the spider to the housing, boss downwards.

On early models large rubbers were used on the drive and small for the rebound side. Late models use only one type of rubber for both drive and rebound. See Figs. C17 and C18.

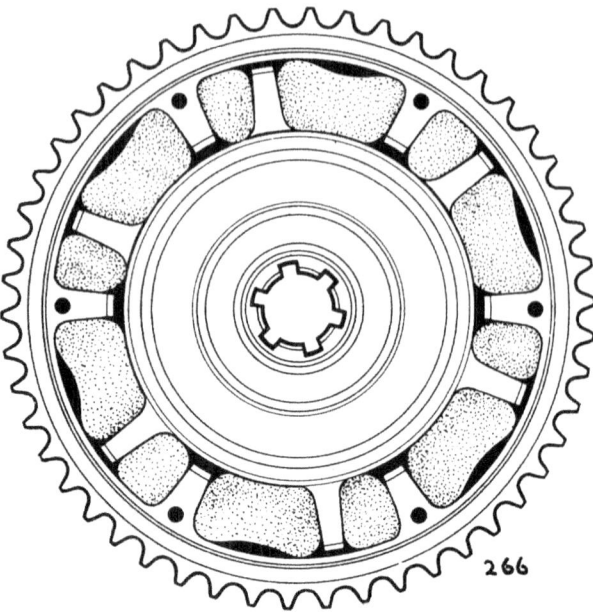

Fig. C17. Earlier shock absorber with two types of rubber in situ

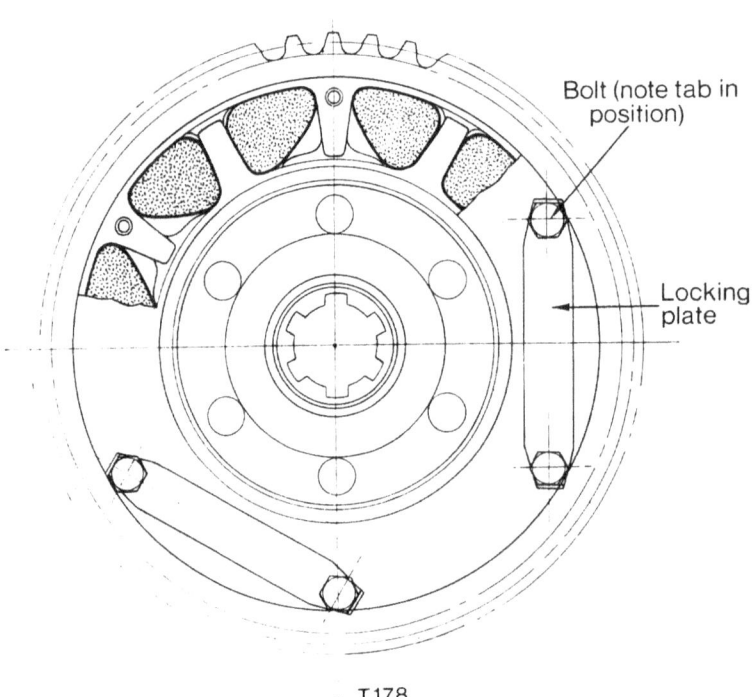

Fig. C18. Late type with common rubbers
(Showing also the later retaining plate fixing using locking plates and bolts)

TRANSMISSION

Drop the new rubbers into place as illustrated using the mounting jig and bar. There is no reason why the later set of rubbers should not be fitted to an earlier shock absorber. Where the shock absorber has previously had locking plates and bolts, merely fit the retaining plate, fit the tab washer and fit and secure the bolts. Tap the tab washers home last of all and the chainwheel is ready to refit. On assemblies which previously had countersunk screws, refit the retaining plate with the counter sinks inboard and replace the screws with 6 T3940 bolts and 3 T3941 locking plates.

SECTION C12

REMOVING AND REPLACING THE CHAINWHEEL AND ENGINE SPROCKET

Remove the outer primary chaincase as described in Section C5 and collect the steel thrust washer and face needle roller bearing. Lever the engine sprocket nut tab washer clear, remove the nut (a box spanner, tommy bar and hammer will be needed), and collect the tab washer. Using the oil seal protector 61-6051 over the clutch pull rod, remove the centre nut and plain washer from the centre of the chainwheel.

It will be necessary to extract the chainwheel and engine sprocket simultaneously from the splined shafts using extractor D1860 for the chainwheel and 61-6046 for the engine sprockets as shown in Figs. C19 and C20.

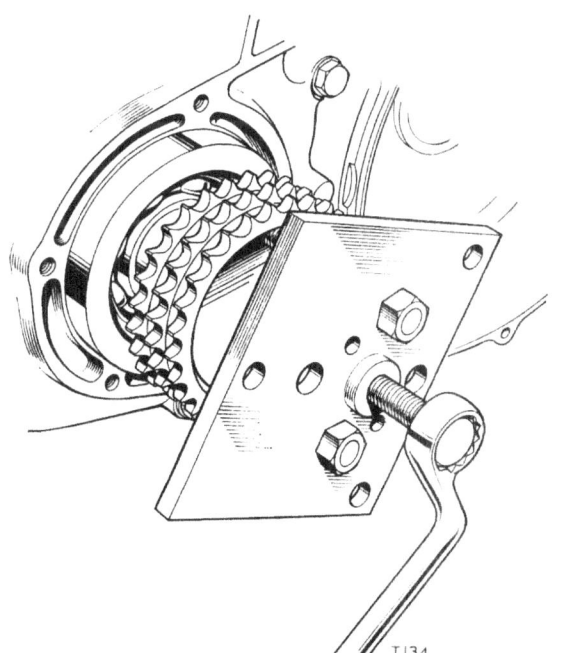

Fig. C19. Extracting the engine sprocket

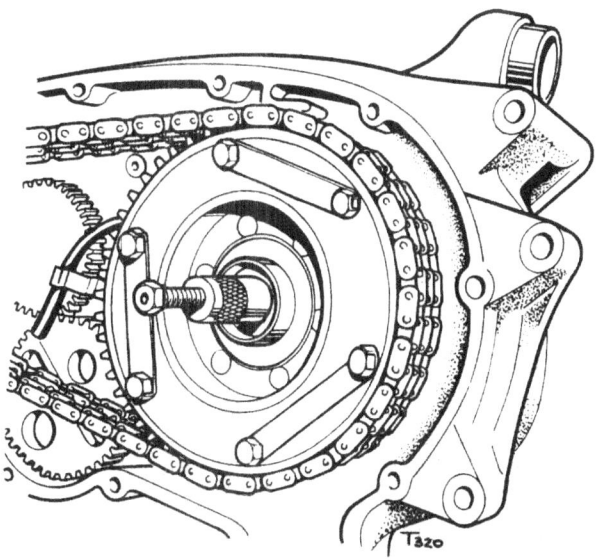

Fig. C20. Extracting the chainwheel

Screw the body of the chainwheel extractor into the centre until the maximum depth of thread is engaged, then tighten the centre bolt until the hub is released. When this is achieved, assemble the engine sprocket extractor 61-6014 and screw in the centre bolt to extract the engine sprocket.

The sprockets complete with chain can then be lifted clear as a set and the sprockets separated from the chain. Collect the phosphor bronze thrust washer. Thoroughly clean all the parts in paraffin (kerosene) and inspect them for wear or fatigue as shown in Section C12.

To reassemble, note that the engine sprocket fits with the boss towards the main bearing. It will be necessary to offer the chainwheel, engine sprocket and primary chain as a set, aligning the splines so that the set can be pushed home. If necessary, tap the sprockets home with a hide mallet and then fit the tab washer and nut at the engine sprocket, tapping the tab carefully into position after securing the nut. See Fig. C6 for the order of assembly of thrust washers etc. Fit the plain steel washer at the chainwheel centre, put the oil seal protector 61-6051 over the clutch pull rod threads and fit the securing nut, tightening this fully.

Oil lightly and fit the face needle roller bearing and large plain steel washer. The outer primary chaincase should now be refitted as in Section C5 and the clutch adjusted.

SECTION C13

INSPECTION OF TRANSMISSION COMPONENTS

(1) Inspect the primary chain for excessive wear of the rollers and pivot pins and check that the elongation does not exceed $1\frac{1}{2}\%$. To do this, first scribe two marks on a flat surface exactly 12 in. (30·5 cm.) apart, then after degreasing or washing the chain in paraffin (kerosene), place the chain opposite the two marks. When the chain is compressed to its minimum free length the marks should coincide with the centres of two pivot pins 32 links apart. When the chain is stretched to its maximum free length the extension should not exceed $\frac{1}{4}$ in. (6·25 mm.).

Inspect the condition of the sprocket teeth for signs of hooking and pitting.

A very good method of indicating whether the chain is badly worn or not is to wrap it round the clutch sprocket and attempt to lift the chain from its seating at various points around the sprocket. Little or no lift indicates that both the sprocket and chain are in good condition.

If either the spider or engine sprocket are tight fitting on the clutch hub and crankshaft respectively, there is no cause for concern as such a fit is to the best advantage.

(2) Check the fit between the shock absorber spider and the clutch shaft splines. The spider should be a push fit onto the clutch hub and there should not be any radial movement.

Similarly check the fit of the engine sprocket splines onto the crankshaft. Again, there should not be any radial movement.

(3) Check that the shock absorber spider is a good working fit in the inner and outer retaining plate and that the arms of the spider have not caused excessive score marks on the inner face of the housing. A good idea is to check the working clearance by assembling the shock absorber unit without the rubbers.

SECTION C14

REAR CHAIN ALTERATIONS AND REPAIRS

If the chains have been correctly serviced, very few repairs will be necessary. Should the occasion arise to repair, lengthen or shorten the chain, a rivet extractor, as shown in Fig. C22, and a few spare parts will cover all requirements.

To shorten a chain containing an even number of pitches, remove the dark parts shown in (1) and replace by crank double link and single connecting link as shown in (2).

To shorten a chain containing an odd number of pitches remove the dark parts shown in (3) and replace by a single connecting link and inner link as shown in (4).

To repair a chain with a broken roller or inside link, remove the dark parts shown in (5) and replace by two single connecting links and one inner link as shown in (6).

Fig. C21. Rear chain alterations

The rivet extractor can be used on all motorcycle chains up to $\frac{3}{4}$ in. pitch whether the chains are on or off the chain-wheels.

When using the extractor:—

(1) Turn screw anti-clockwise to permit the punch end to clear the chain rivet.

(2) Open the jaws by pressing down the lever (see below).

(3) Pass jaws over chain and release the lever. Jaws should rest on a chain roller free of chain link plates (see below).

(4) Turn the screw clockwise until the punch contacts and pushes out the rivet end through the chain outer link plate. Unscrew the punch, withdraw the extractor and repeat the complete operation on the adjacent rivet in the same chain outer link plate. The outer plate is then free and the two rivets can be withdrawn from opposite sides with the opposite plate in position. Do not use the removed part again.

When the alterations are finished the chain should be lubricated as shown in Section A2.

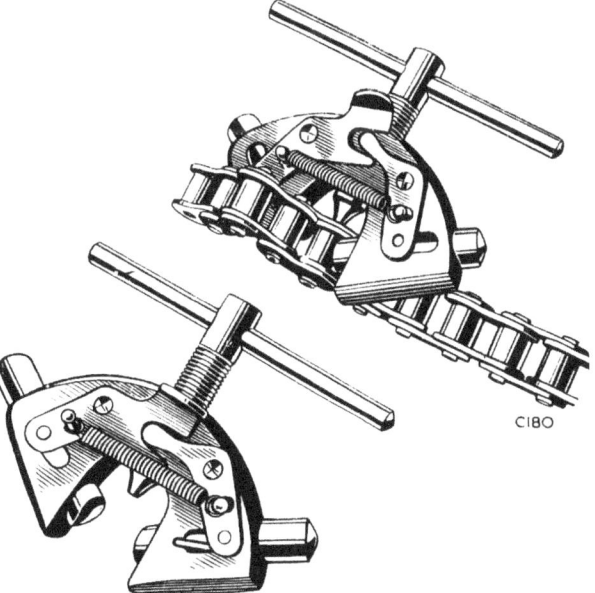

Fig. C22. Chain link rivet extractor, part number 167

NOTES

SECTION CC

TRANSMISSION

	Section
ADJUSTING THE PRIMARY CHAIN TENSION	CC5

SECTION CC5

ADJUSTING THE PRIMARY CHAIN TENSION

Latest machines employ a new type of tensioner mounted in the bottom of the outer primary cover. Remove the slotted inspection plug from the chaincase with the engine stopped. The correct chain adjustment is $\frac{1}{2}$ in (12 mm) free movement. To make the adjustment slacken the large locking nut at the bottom of the chaincase and using a screwdriver turn the slotted adjuster protruding from the nut clockwise to increase the chain tension and anti-clockwise to decrease the tension.

SECTION D
GEARBOX

DESCRIPTION	Section
SEQUENCE OF GEARCHANGING	D1
REMOVING AND REPLACING THE OUTER COVER ASSEMBLY	D2
DISMANTLING AND REASSEMBLING THE KICKSTART MECHANISM	D3
DISMANTLING AND REASSEMBLING THE GEARCHANGE MECHANISM	D4
INSPECTING THE GEARCHANGE AND KICKSTART COMPONENTS	D5
RENEWING KICKSTART AND GEARCHANGE SPINDLE BUSHES	D6
DISMANTLING THE GEARBOX	D7
INSPECTION OF THE GEARBOX COMPONENTS	D8
RENEWING MAINSHAFT AND LAYSHAFT BEARINGS	D9
REASSEMBLING THE GEARBOX	D10
CHANGING THE GEARBOX SPROCKET	D11

GEARBOX

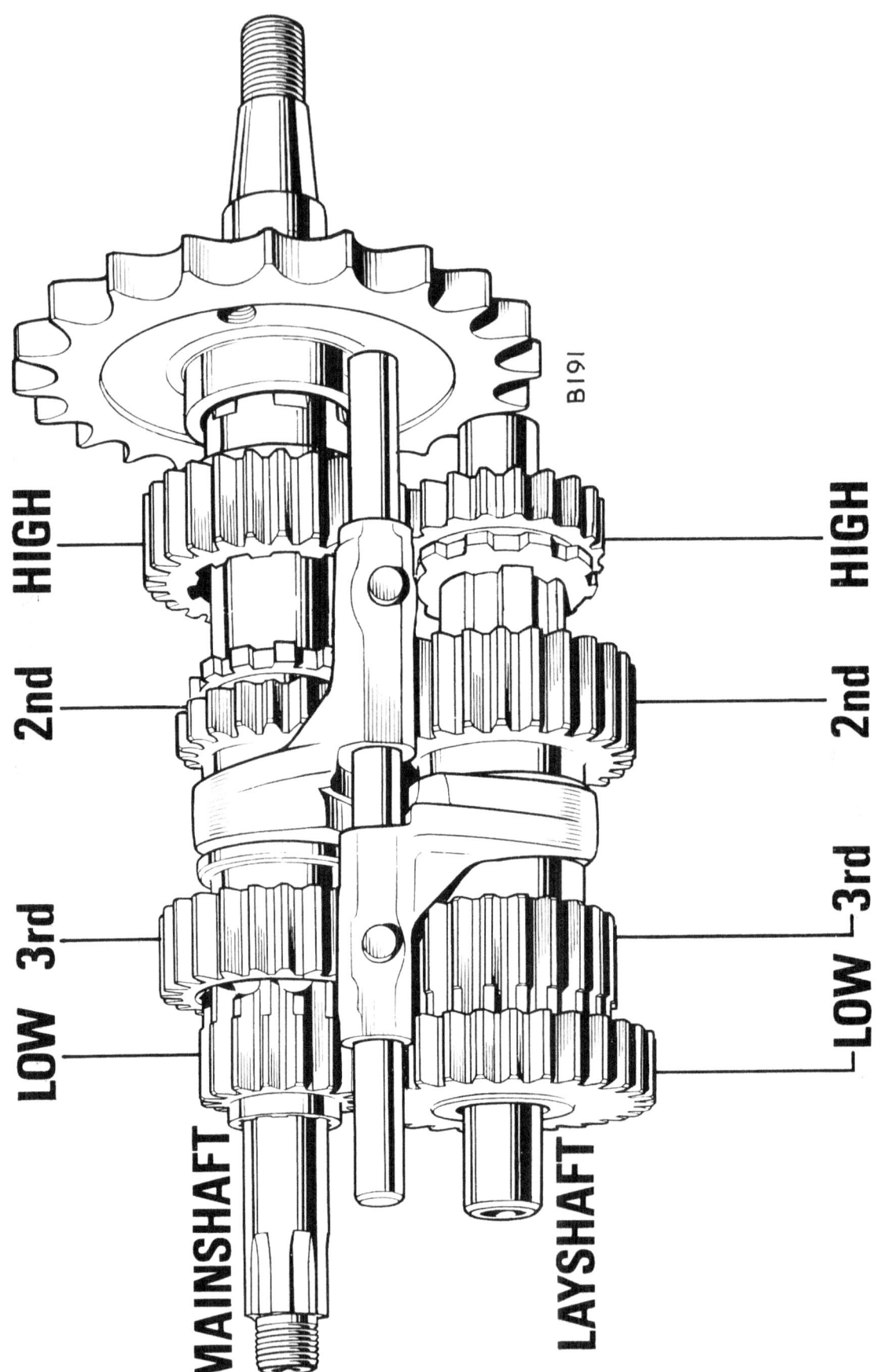

Fig. D1. Plan of Gearbox Components

GEARBOX

DESCRIPTION

The Trident is fitted with a four-speed gearbox which is an integral part of the right half crankcase. The gearbox inner and outer covers are made of aluminium alloy D.T.D. 424 which gives the utmost rigidity and strength. Gears are manufactured from high quality nickel steel and subsequently case hardened and are designed to withstand heavy loading.

The mainshaft is supported by heavy duty ball races at each end, and the layshaft by special needle roller bearings which are pressed into the casing and inner cover. Keyed to the left end of the gearbox mainshaft is a splined hub carrying the dry single plate diaphragm clutch.

The kickstarter quadrant and the gearchange quandrant are all housed in the gearbox outer cover.

SECTION D1
SEQUENCE OF GEARCHANGING

The gearbox is operated by the pedal on the right side of the machine, the pedal being splined to the gear change spindle and plunger housing. Two chamfered plungers with springs fit into the housing in such a way that as the gear pedal is moved up and down the plungers locate in the teeth at the outboard end of the quadrant. The quadrant is pivoted in the centre and the inboard end is formed to mate with the captive pinion of the camplate. See Fig. D2.

Figs. D3A to D3E illustrate the camplate with its locating plunger and spring. The four sliding pinions (the inboard pinions) are moved along the mainshaft and layshaft by the selector forks as the forks are moved together and apart against the track of the camplate. Note the arcs showing the selector roller position relative to the camplate spindle in each gear. The neutral positions of the camplate and gears are shown in Fig. D3A.

When the pedal is depressed to engage low gear (first) the camplate is turned clockwise moving the layshaft selector fork to mesh the layshaft sliding gear with the layshaft first gear. As second gear is selected by lifting the pedal, the camplate is moved anti-clockwise to move the layshaft sliding gear into mesh with the layshaft second gear.

Movement in the same direction will select third gear by moving both the selector forks, which in turn moves the layshaft sliding gear to a neutral position and the mainshaft sliding gear into mesh with the mainshaft third gear.

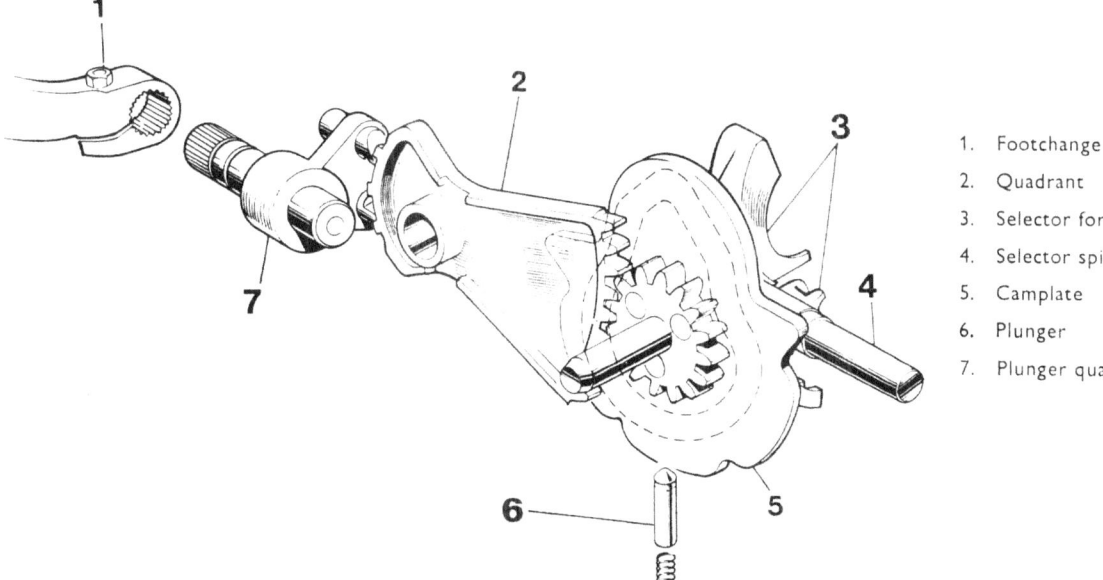

1. Footchange locknut
2. Quadrant
3. Selector forks
4. Selector spindle
5. Camplate
6. Plunger
7. Plunger quadrant

Fig. D2. Gear selection components

GEARBOX

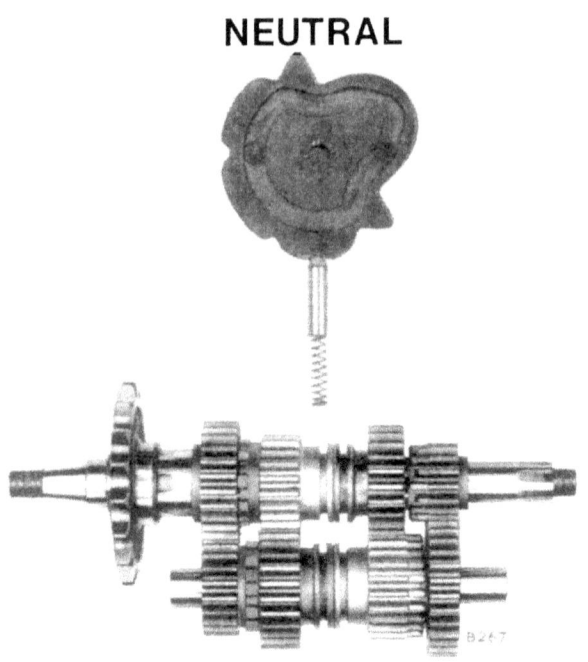

Fig. D3A. Gear camplate selector rollers and gear cluster in neutral position

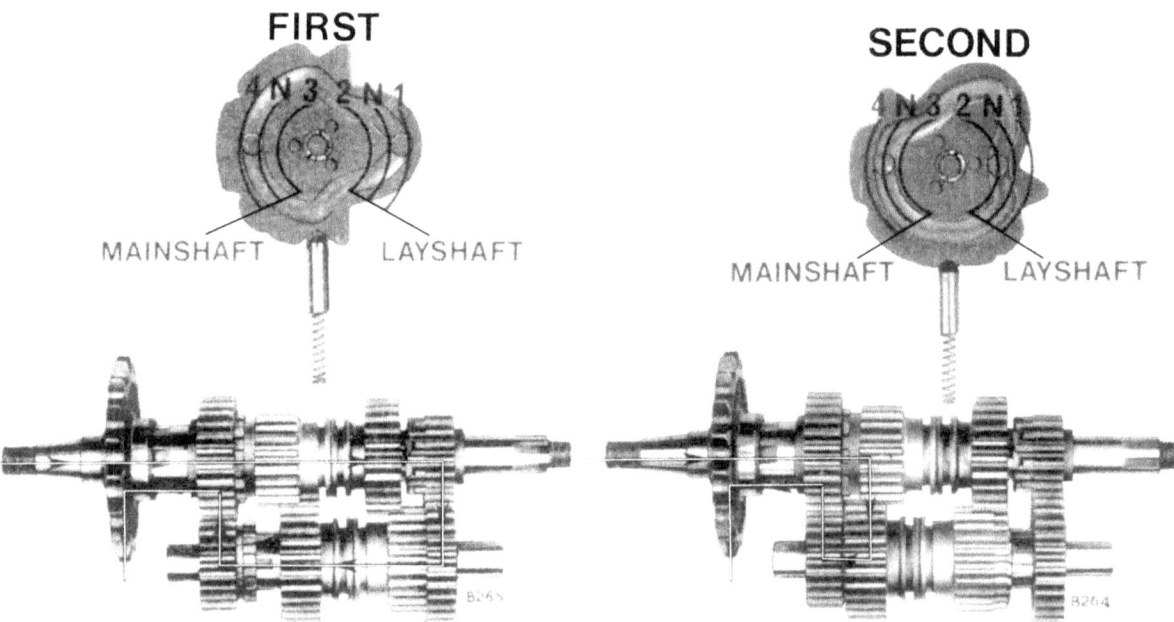

Fig. D3B. First gear selected (Note arrowed line showing power being transmitted through the gear cluster)

Fig. D3C. Second gear

The final movement into top gear (fourth) is in the same direction and moves the mainshaft sliding gear into mesh with the high gear, that is, the gear onto which is fitted the gearbox sprocket. It should be noted that throughout the range of gear pedal movements the gear pedal spindle and plunger housing return to the original position ready for the next selection.

GEARBOX

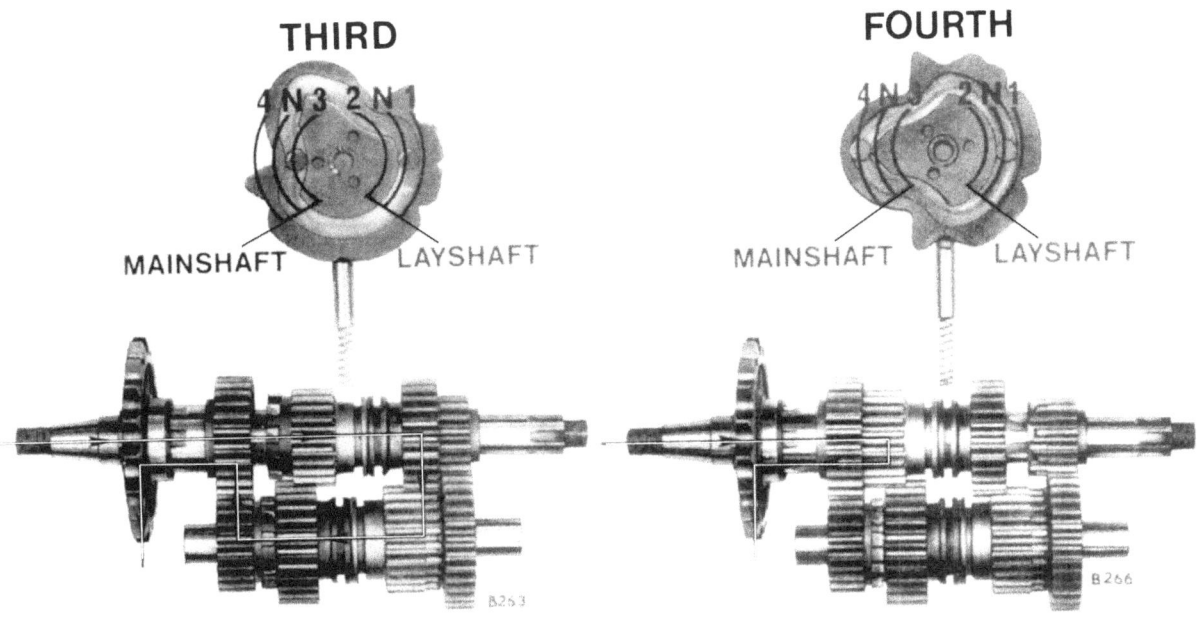

Fig. D3D. Third gear

Fig. D3E. Fourth gear

SECTION D2

REMOVING AND REPLACING THE GEARBOX OUTER COVER ASSEMBLY

Remove the right hand footrest, secured from the back of the rear engine plate with a single nut.

Place a drip tray underneath the gearbox and unscrew the gearbox filler plug and drain plug.

Engage 4th (top) gear. This will allow several otherwise difficult nuts to be unscrewed by subsequently applying the rear brake when required.

Unscrew the top and bottom hexagonal nut and the recess screws from the periphery of the gearbox cover. Depress the kickstart lever slightly and tap the cover until it is free.

When the cover is removed, the gear-change mechanism and kickstart mechanism will be accessible. The gearchange pedal should be carefully raised then depressed, to control the release of the plungers and springs from the gearchange quadrant.

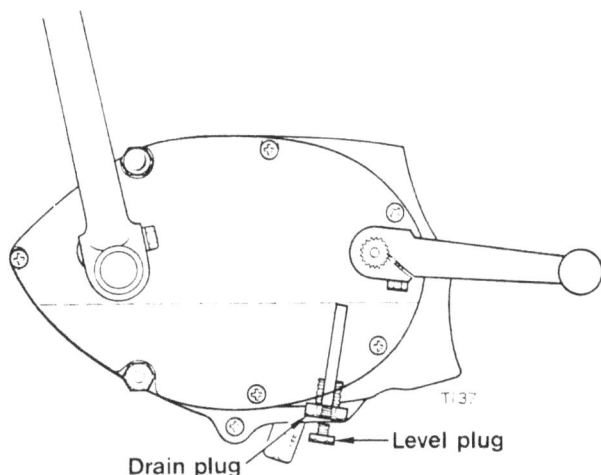

Fig. D4. Showing gearbox oil level and oil drain plugs

GEARBOX

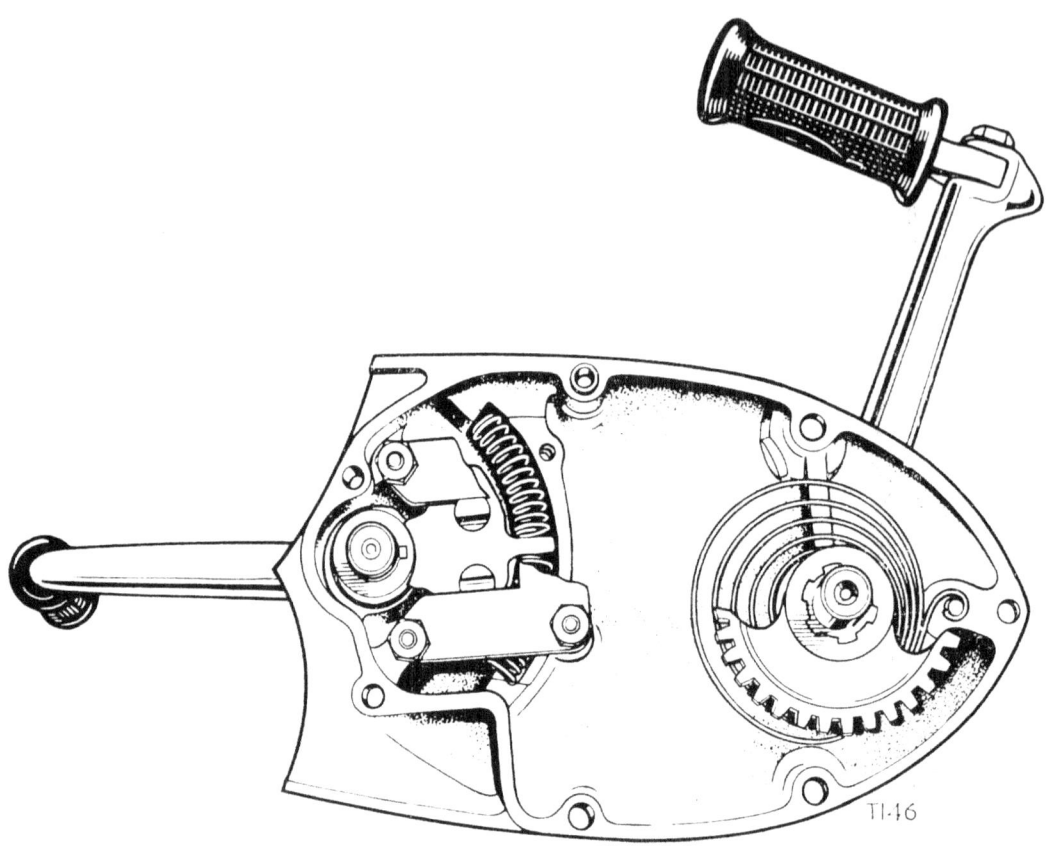

Fig. D5. Gearbox outer cover, showing gearchange mechanism, clutch operating mechanism and kick-start quadrant

Prior to refitting the outer cover ensure that the junction surface is clean and free from any deposits of old jointing compound, then thoroughly clean it in paraffin (kerosene). Apply a fresh coat of jointing compound to the junction surface and ensure that the two location dowels are in position

Turn the kickstart pedal until it is half way down its operational stroke and offer the cover to the gearbox. Check that the kickstart pedal returns to its normal fully-returned position. Reassembly then continues as a reversal of the above instructions. Finally, refill the gearbox to the correct level with the recommended grade of oil (see Section A2).

SECTION D3

DISMANTLING AND REASSEMBLING THE KICKSTART MECHANISM

Slacken the kickstarter crank cotter pin nut about two or three turns and release the cotter pin from its locking taper by using a hammer and a soft metal drift. Slide the pedal off the shaft and withdraw the quadrant and spring assembly. Apply the rear brake, bend back the tab on the lock washer and unscrew the kickstart ratchet pinion securing nut from the gearbox mainshaft. Withdraw the pinion, ratchet, spring and sleeve, then thoroughly clean all parts in paraffin (kerosene) and inspect them for wear etc., as shown in Section D5.

If the kickstarter quadrant is to be renewed the spindle should be driven out using a hammer or press and the gear quadrant pressed onto the spindle so that the kickstart crank location flat is positioned correctly relative to the quadrant (see Fig. D5).

GEARBOX

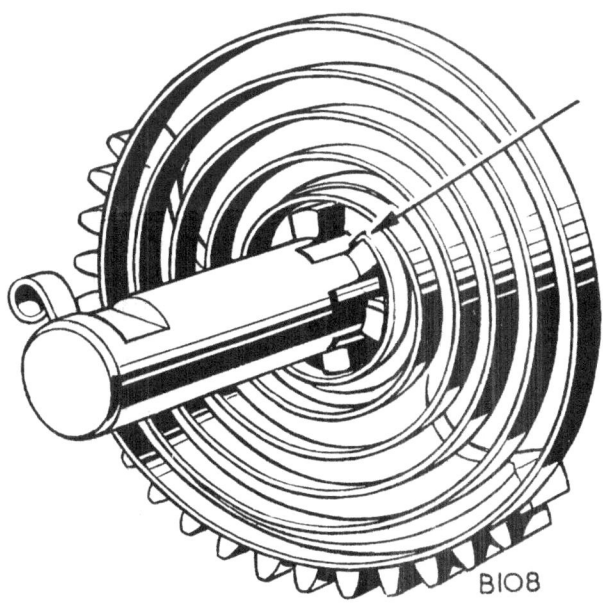

Fig. D6. Kickstart quadrant and spring. Arrow indicates correct spring location

To reassemble the mechanism, first refit the thin walled steel sleeve, spring, pinion and ratchet to the gearbox mainshaft and assemble the tab washer, then screw on the retaining nut to the torque figure given in "General Data". **Do not overtighten the retaining nut as this may result in failure of the thin walled inner steel sleeve.**

Fit the return spring to the kickstart quadrant as shown in Fig. D6. Offer the spindle into the kickstart bush and locate the return spring onto the anchor peg at the rear of the cover. Fit the oil seal over the spindle and assemble the kickstart crank, locking it into position with the cotter pin from the rear. Refit the outer cover as shown in Section D2. Do not forget to refit the oil seal. Refill the gearbox with the correct grade of lubricant (Section A2).

SECTION D4

DISMANTLING AND REASSEMBLING THE GEARCHANGE MECHANISM

Slacken off the gear change pedal locking bolt and withdraw the pedal from the serrated shaft. A little leverage between the pedal and the cover may be necessary. For this, choose a suitable tool to avoid damage to the cover.

Remove the four nuts and locking washers securing the guide plate. Withdraw the guide plate, plunger quadrant and curved return springs. Thoroughly clean the parts in paraffin (kerosene) and inspect them for wear etc., as shown in Section D5.

To reassemble the mechanism, first fit a **new** rubber "O" ring to the spindle and offer it to the outer cover bush using a smear of oil to assist assembly, then refit the two quadrant return springs and ensure that they locate correctly over the step in the cover. To facilitate assembly of the springs, first fit the gearchange pedal and clamp it in position, thus enabling the quadrant to be turned and the springs to be compressed (see Fig. D5).

Refit the retainer plate, not forgetting the locking washers which fit one under each of the four nuts. Finally, refit the springs and plungers, taking care that they are not suddenly ejected from their seats during assembly.

SECTION D5

INSPECTING THE GEARCHANGE AND KICKSTART COMPONENTS

GEARCHANGE:

(1) Inspect the gearchange plungers for wear and ensure that they are a clearance fit in the quadrant. Check the plunger springs by comparing their lengths with the figures given in "General Data".

(2) Examine the plunger guide plate for wear and grooving on the taper guide surfaces. Renew the plate if grooving has occurred.

(3) Inspect the footchange pedal return springs for fatigue and if they show signs of corrosion due to condensation, they should be renewed.

(4) Examine the gearchange quadrant bush for wear and possible ovality by inserting the quadrant into the bush and feeling the amount of play.

(5) Check the tips of the plungers and the teeth of the camplate operating quadrant for chipping and wear. To remove the camplate quadrant, first remove the inner cover as shown in Section D8, then remove the two split pins and withdraw the spindle.

KICKSTART:

(1) Examine the kickstart quadrant for chipped or broken teeth or looseness on the spindle and the kickstart return spring for fatigue cracks and signs of wear, particularly at the centre where it engages on the splines of the spindle.

(2) Examine the kickstart spindle bush for wear. If the required measuring instruments are not available, use the spindle as a gauge and feel the amount of play.

(3) Examine the kickstart ratchet mechanism for wear, giving particular attention to the ratchet teeth ensuring that they have not become chipped or rounded. Check that the thin walled steel bush is a clearance fit in the kickstart pinion and that the spring is not badly worn.

(4) Finally, check that the kickstart stop peg is firmly pressed into the inner cover and is not distorted.

SECTION D6
RENEWING KICKSTART AND GEARCHANGE SPINDLE BUSHES

If it is found necessary to renew the kickstart spindle bush this should be done by completely stripping the outer cover of its assembly parts and heating it to 100°C., then driving the bush out using a suitable shouldered drift. Press in the new bush while the cover is still hot.

Adopt a similar procedure for renewal of the outer cover gearchange spindle bush. The inner cover bush does not usually wear much, even after great mileage has been covered. However, if it is required to renew the bush, the inner cover should be removed (Section D8) and the camplate operating quadrant disconnected.

Using a suitable tap (e.g. $\frac{3}{4}$ in. dia. x 10 Whit.) cut a thread in the bush to a depth of $\frac{3}{4}$ in.; heat the cover to 100°C., then reinsert the tap, or, preferably, a suitable bolt. Grip the bolt (or tap) firmly in a vice, then drive the cover away using a hide mallet until the bush is free.

A press or suitably shouldered drift is required to drive in the new bush, which should be done whilst the cover is still hot.

SECTION D7
DISMANTLING THE GEARBOX

Remove the gearbox outer cover as shown in Section D2, leaving the gearbox with 4th (top) gear selected.

Remove the two short bolts, two long bolts and a centre nut which serves to retain the rear right engine mounting plate, then withdraw the plate.

Bend back the tags on the lock washer and unscrew the kickstart pinion ratchet retainer nut from the end of the gearbox mainshaft. This should be easily achieved with 4th (top) gear selected and the rear brake applied.

Remove the outer and inner primary covers and dismantle the transmission as in Sections C5, C7, finally remove the clutch (Section C7). Do not forget to remove the key from the gearbox mainshaft.

Unscrew the large extended hexagonal nut from underneath the gearbox and withdraw the camplate indexing plunger and spring.

The gearbox inner cover is retained by a socket screw, two Phillips recessed screws and a hexagonal bolt (See Fig. D8). When these are removed the cover can be released by tapping it outwards with a hide mallet. The gearbox mainshaft can be withdrawn easily after the selector fork spindle has been removed. The layshaft and remaining gears can then

GEARBOX

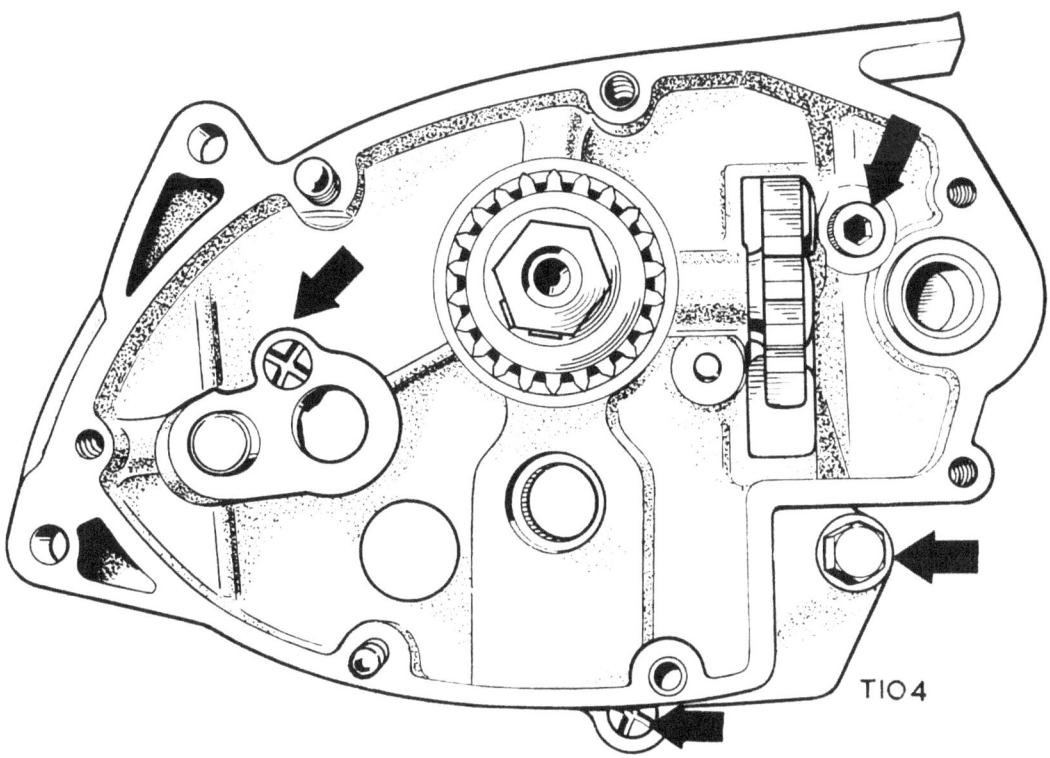

Fig. D7. Gearbox inner cover retaining screws

be withdrawn. Remove the camplate and spindle assembly, then remove the two brass thrust washers which locate over the needle roller bearings.

The mainshaft high gear, in which the gearbox mainshaft runs, is locked through the main bearing and gearbox sprocket. The oil is prevented from leaving the gearbox through the main bearing by an oil seal which runs on a ground boss on the gearbox sprocket. To remove the mainshaft high gear and renew the oil seal it will be necessary to remove the sprocket. This can be done by removing the circular plate from the primary inner cover at the rear of the clutch, tapping back the bent over portion of the locking plate and unscrewing the large hexagonal gearbox sprocket nut (1·66 in. across flats). To facilitate removal of the nut, spanner number 61-6061 is available.

When the nut is removed, drive the high gear through into the gearbox using a hammer with a soft metal drift.

To remove the sprocket, disconnect the rear chain and remove it from around the sprocket, which can then be easily withdrawn through the aperture. Drill to release the centre-pop of each screw holding the high gear bearing oil seal holder to the crankcase see Fig. D8. The oil seal can be driven out of the housing with care using a suitable shouldered drift.

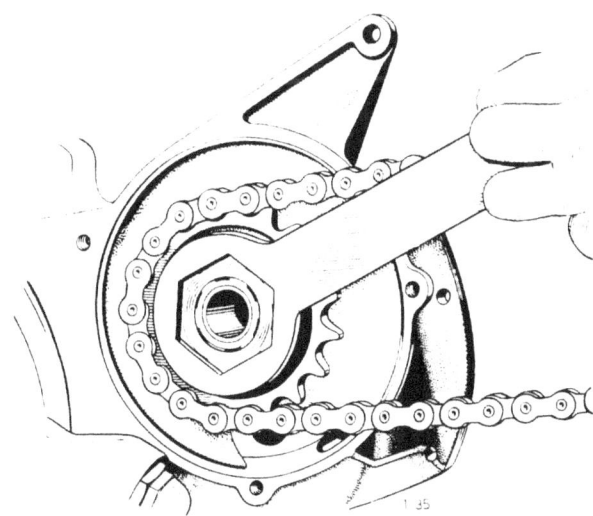

Fig. D8. Removing the gearbox sprocket nut with rear brake applied

SECTION D8

INSPECTION OF THE GEARBOX COMPONENTS

Thoroughly clean all parts in paraffin (kerosene) and check them for wear and fatigue, as follows:—

(1) Inspect the gearbox housing and inner cover for signs of cracking and damage to the joint faces. Check that the location dowels are in position correctly in the gearbox and inner cover (2 dowels each). In preparation for reassembly, clean the junction surfaces of the gearbox, inner cover and outer cover of any old deposits of jointing compound.

(2) Examine both the mainshaft and layshaft for signs of fatigue, damaged threads and badly worn splines. Check the extent of wear to the bearing diameters of both shafts by comparing them with the figures given in "General Data". Examine the shafts carefully for signs of seizure. Excessive friction resistance and seizure will be indicated by local colouring on the shaft.

(3) Check the layshaft needle roller bearing by inserting the layshaft and feeling the amount of play.

(4) Inspect the gearbox mainshaft ball bearing races for roughness due to pitting or indentation of the ball tracks. An estimate can be made of ball wear by feeling the amount of side play of the centre track. It should not be possible to detect any movement by hand if the bearing is in good condition. The mainshaft should be a hand press fit in the inner cover bearing. Similarly the mainshaft high gear should be a good hand press fit in the opposite bearing.

(5) Examine the gears thoroughly, for chipped, fractured or worn teeth. Check the internal splines and bushes. Make sure that the splines are free on their respective shafts with no tendency to bind, and the bushes in the mainshaft high gear and layshaft low gear are not loose or excessively worn. Again, reference should be made to the dimensions given in "General Data".

(6) Check that the selector fork rod is not grooved and that it is a good fit in the gearbox casing and the inner cover. Inspect the selector fork running faces for wear. This will only have occurred if the gearbox is being continually used with a badly worn mainshaft bearing. The camplate rollers which fit on the selector fork are of case hardened steel and consequently wear should be negligible.

(7) The gear selector camplate should be inspected for signs of wear in the selector tracks. Excessive wear will occur if the mainshaft main bearing has worn badly. Check the fit of the camplate spindle in its housing. Examine the camplate gear wheel for excessive wear. Difficulty will be encountered in gear selection, causing subsequent damage to the gears, if this gear is badly worn.

(8) Examine the mainshaft high gear bush for wear by inserting the mainshaft into it and feeling the amount of play. It is advisable to take micrometer readings of the mainshaft and compare them with caliper readings of the bush. If the clearance is excessively greater than the figure given in "General Data" the bush should be renewed as shown in Section D10.

(9) Ensure that the camplate plunger works freely in the housing and that the moving parts are free from corrosion. To check if the spring has become inefficient, measure its length and compare it with "General Data".

SECTION D9

RENEWING MAINSHAFT AND LAYSHAFT BEARINGS

MAINSHAFT

The mainshaft ball bearings are a press fit into their respective housings and are retained by spring circlips to prevent sideways movement due to end thrust. To remove the right bearing, first lever out the circlip, then heat the cover to approximately 100°C. and drive out the bearing using a suitably shouldered drift. The new bearing should be pressed or drifted in whilst the cover is still hot using a suitable tubular drift onto the outer race ($2\frac{1}{2}$ in. outside diameter x 6 in. long). Do not forget to refit the circlip.

To remove the high gear bearing on the left of the machine, first remove the screws and oil seal holder. Carefully heat the casing locally to approximately

GEARBOX

100°C. then drive out the bearing from the inside by means of a suitably shouldered drift. Whilst the casing is still hot, drive in the new bearing, using a suitable tubular drift onto the outer race, then refit the circlip and press in the new oil seal.

MAINSHAFT HIGH GEAR BUSH

If it is required to renew this bush, this can be done by pressing out the bush using a suitable drift, which can be made from a 5 in. x 7/8 in. diameter piece of bar by machining a 1 3/16 in. dia. x 3/4 in. long pilot at one end. The bush must be pressed out by inserting the drift at the teeth end of the gear. The new bush must be pressed in with the oil groove in the bore of the bush at the teeth end. It is most important that only the correct bush is used. On no account must the similar 'B' range bush be fitted since this has a different oil groove

Finally, ream the bush to size using service tool reamer 61-6010. The pressed-in bore size is given in "General Data".

LAYSHAFT

The right needle roller bearing should be removed by heating the cover to approximately 100°C. then pressing or drifting out the bearing using a tool similar to that shown in Fig. D9.

The new bearing should be pressed in, plain end first, whilst the cover is still hot, from the inside of the cover, until ·073/·078 in. of the bearing protrudes above the cover face (see Fig. D9).

The left needle roller bearing is of the closed-end type and is accessible from the left, through the sprocket cover plate aperture. The casing should be heated to approximately 100°C. and the bearing driven through into the gearbox using a soft metal drift, taking care not to damage the bore into which the bearing fits. The new bearing must be carefully pressed in whilst the casing is hot, until ·073/·078in. protrudes above the spot face surface inside the gearbox. Do not use excessive force or the needle roller outer case may become damaged, resulting in the roller seizing, or breaking up.

Finally, the outer portion of the bore into which the bearing fits, should be sealed with a suitable proprietary sealant.

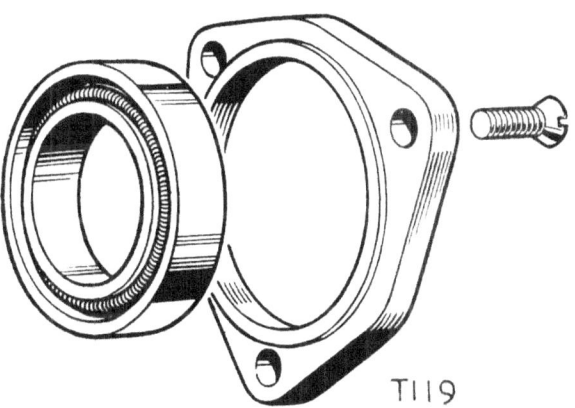

Fig. D9. High gear bearing oil seal and housing

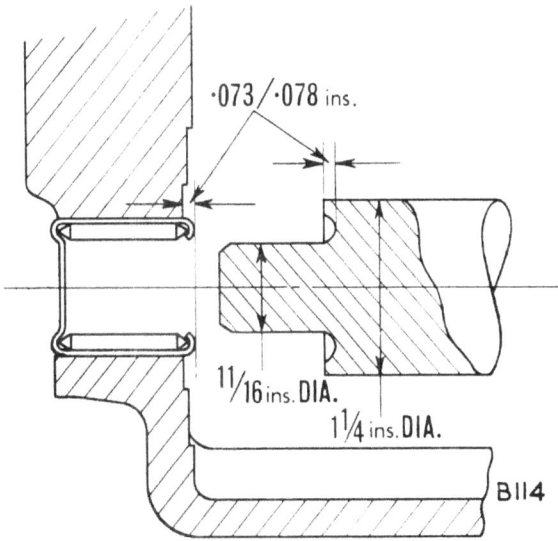

Fig. D10. Sketch of needle roller and drift

SECTION D10

REASSEMBLING THE GEARBOX

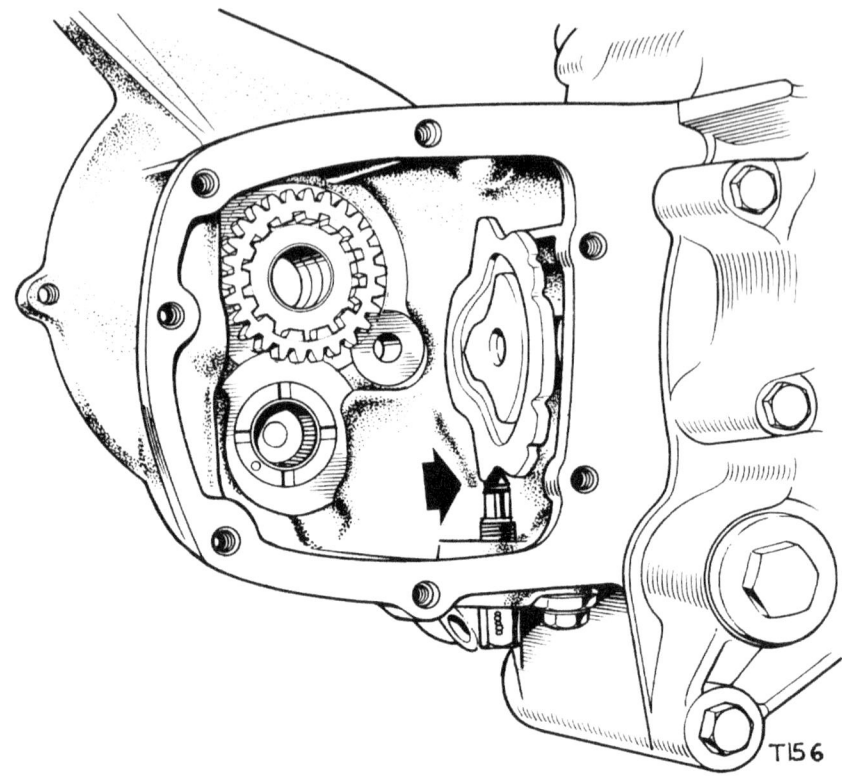

Fig. D11. Reassembling the gearbox. Arrow indicates camplate in the 4th gear position

Fit the high gear bearing oil seal in its triangular housing, the closed side flush with the outer face. (See Fig. D10). Press the high gear into the bearing. Lubricate the ground tapered boss of the sprocket with oil and slide it onto the high gear. Screw on the securing nut finger tight.

Re-mesh the rear chain with the sprockets and replace the connecting link. Apply the rear brake and tighten the sprocket securing nut as tight as possible using service tool 61-6061. (See Fig. D9.)

Lubricate the camplate spindle and offer it into the spindle housing within the gearbox. Assemble the camplate plunger and spring into the extended hexagonal plunger retaining nut and screw it into position underneath the gearbox, but do not forget the sealing washer. Set the camplate in the 4th gear position. See Fig. D11.

Locate the bronze thrust washer over the inner needle roller bearing. The thrust washer can be held in position by smearing its rear surface with grease. Note that the grooved surface of the thrust washer is towards the layshaft. (See Fig. D11).

Lubricate the mainshaft and layshaft captive gears, then assemble the mainshaft and layshaft gear clusters as shown in Fig. D12.

Position the selector forks in their respective grooves in the gears as shown in Fig. D12. (The fork with the smaller radius is for the mainshaft cluster). The assembly is now ready to be offered into the gearbox housing. As the mainshaft and layshaft are being located in their respective bearings, the gears should be slid into position and aligned so that the selector forks locate in the tracks in the camplate and the bores for the selector forks are approximately aligned. Smear the selector fork spindle with oil and slide it through the selector forks, shoulder end first, until it is fully engaged in the gearbox housing.

Do not force the spindle in too far so that it contacts and distorts the high gear bearing oil seal holder. The mainshaft selector fork will be noted in the innermost position.

GEARBOX   D

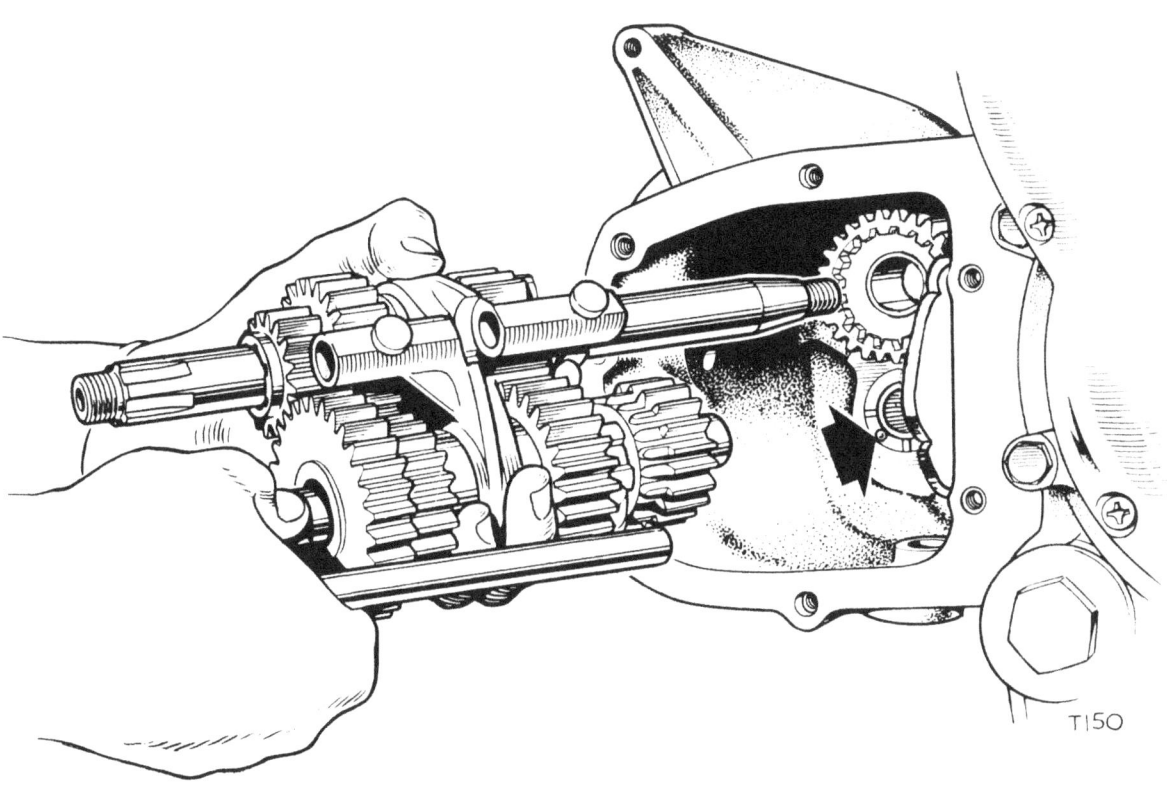

Fig. D12. Reassembling the gearbox components. Arrows indicate camplate rollers in position and thrust washer correctly located

Check the camplate operating quadrant is moving freely in the inner cover and position the bronze layshaft thrust washer over the needle roller bearing in the inner cover. Again, use grease to hold the thrust washer in position during assembly.

Using a pressure oil can, lubricate all the moving parts in the gearbox, then apply a fresh coat of jointing compound to the gearbox junction surface.

Ensure that the two location dowels are in position and offer the inner cover assembly to the gearbox. When the cover is approximately $\frac{1}{4}$ in. (6 mm.) away from the gearbox junction face, position the camplate quadrant in the 4th gear position. (See Fig. D13).

Screw in the socket screw, the two cross headed screws and the bolt, then temporarily assemble the outer cover and gearchange lever and check that the gearchanging sequence is correct by simultaneously operating the gearchange pedal and turning the rear wheel. In the event of any problem of selection it must be assumed that the quadrant teeth are not engaged accurately with the camplate pinion. To rectify this, remove the inner cover again and check that the camplate has been set as shown in Fig. D12. Offer up the inner cover again ensuring that the quadrant is as shown in Fig. D13.

When correct gearchanging is established, re-assemble the kickstart pinion and ratchet, replace the tab washer and screw on the securing nut to the torque figure given in "General Data". To facilitate this, the rear brake should be applied with fourth gear selected.

Refit the gearbox outer cover as shown in section D2 then reassemble the transmission, referring to section A2 for the correct quantities and grades of lubricant for the primary chaincase and gearbox.

GEARBOX

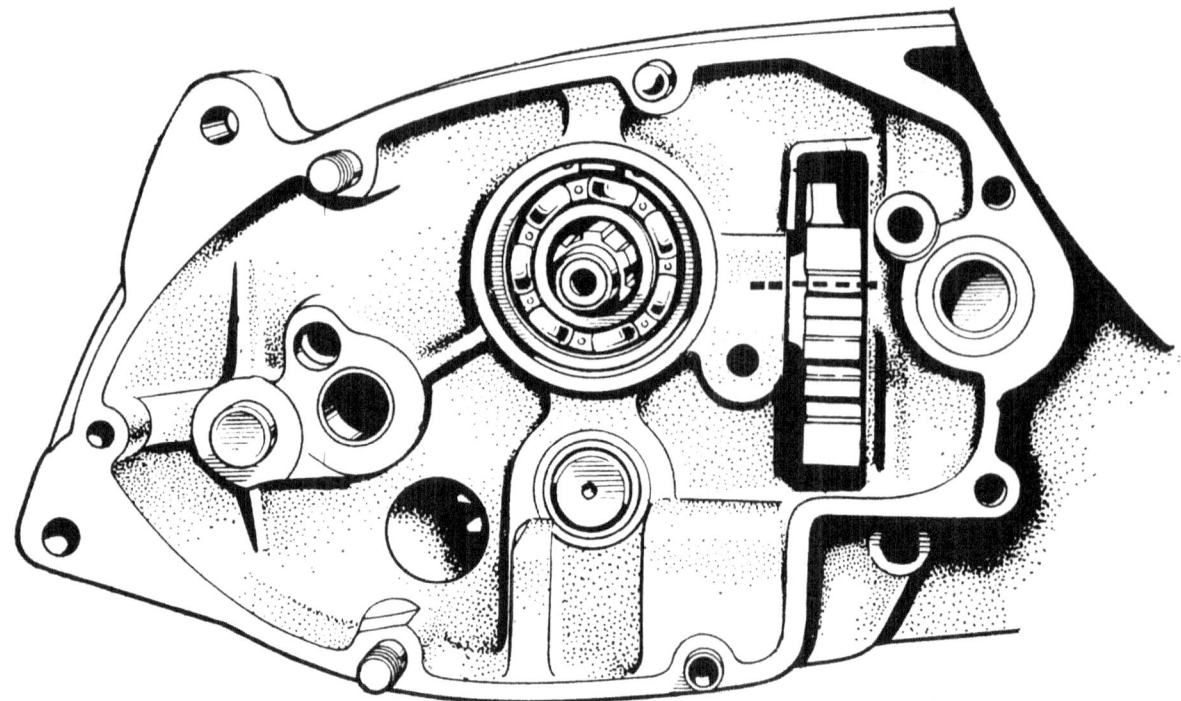

Fig. D13. Refitting the gearbox inner cover

SECTION D11
CHANGING THE GEARBOX SPROCKET

To gain the access to the gearbox sprocket, first remove the left exhaust pipe (one clamp bolt at the manifold and one clip at the silencer nose).

Detach one spade terminal from the stoplamp switch and remove the finger nut from the rear brake rod to allow the brake pedal to drop clear the chaincase.

Remove the left footrests (secured by one nut from the back).

Remove the clutch thrust inspection cover and release the cable from the thrust mechanism. Place a suitable container beneath the centre of the chaincase and remove the drain plug.

Allow a few minutes for the case to drain and then remove the outer chaincase (Section C5), the transmission (Section C7), the inner chaincase, the clutch and the clutch cover (Section C6).

Tap the tab washer clear of the gearbox sprocket retaining nut. Leave the chain *in situ* and unscrew the gearbox sprocket securing nut using service tool 61-6061. The rear chain may now be disconnected and the gearbox sprocket withdrawn. 'Hydroseal' is used on the splines and the sprocket will need to be removed using the extractor 61-6046.

Before fitting the new sprocket check that the gearbox oil seal in is good condition and that the rear chain is not excessively worn. Check the extension as shown in Section A14.

If the old chain is to be retained for further use it should be thoroughly cleaned in paraffin and lubricated in a grease bath. Lubricate the ground boss with oil, fit a new locking plate and slide the sprocket over the gearbox mainshaft and high gear. When the sprocket is located on the splines screw on the securing nut finger tight, then re-connect the chain.

With the rear brake applied tighten the nut until it is as tight as possible and tap over the lockplate.

SECTION DV

FIVE SPEED GEARBOX

DESCRIPTION	Section
SEQUENCE OF GEARCHANGING	... DV 1
REMOVING AND REPLACING THE OUTER COVER ASSEMBLY	... DV 2
DISMANTLING AND REASSEMBLING THE KICKSTART MECHANISM	... DV 3
DISMANTLING AND REASSEMBLING THE GEARCHANGE MECHANISM	... DV 4
INSPECTING THE GEARCHANGE AND KICKSTART COMPONENTS	... DV 5
RENEWING KICKSTART AND GEARCHANGE SPINDLE BUSHES	... DV 6
DISMANTLING THE GEARBOX	... DV 7
INSPECTION OF THE GEARBOX COMPONENTS	... DV 8
RENEWING MAINSHAFT AND LAYSHAFT BEARINGS	... DV 9
REASSEMBLING THE GEARBOX	... DV 10
CHANGING THE GEARBOX SPROCKET	... DV 11

GEARBOX

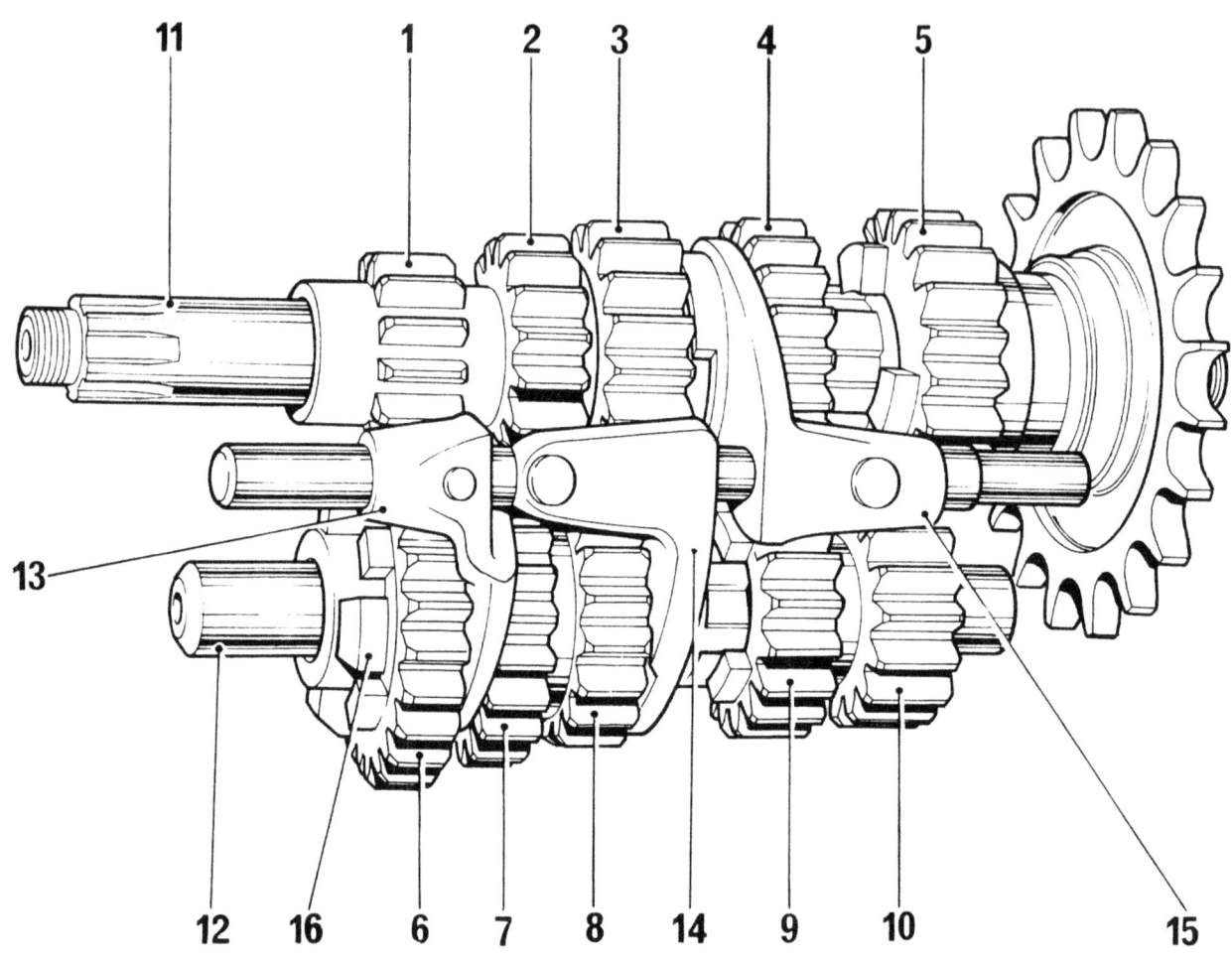

1. Low gear
2. Second gear
3. Third gear
4. Fourth gear
5. Fifth gear
6. Low gear
7. Second gear
8. Third gear
9. Fourth gear
10. Fifth gear
11. Mainshaft
12. Layshaft
13. First gear layshaft selector fork
14. Third gear layshaft selector fork
15. Mainshaft selector fork
16. Layshaft engaging dog

Fig. DV 1. Plan of Gear components

GEARBOX

SECTION DV 1

SEQUENCE OF GEARCHANGING

The gearbox is operated by the pedal on the right side of the machine, the pedal being splined to the gear change spindle and plunger housing. Two chamfered plungers with springs fit into the housing in such a way that as the gear pedal is moved up and down the plungers locate in the teeth at the outboard end of the quadrant. The quadrant is pivoted in the centre and the inboard end if formed to mate with the captive pinion of the camplate. See Fig. DV 2.

Figs. DV 3(i) to DV 3(vi) illustrate the camplate with its plunger and the engaging pins of the selector forks which can be seen in the camplate track. The three sliding pinions are moved along the mainshaft and layshaft by the selector forks. The neutral positions of the camplate and gears are shown in Fig. DV 3(ii).

When the pedal is depressed to engage low gear (first) the camplate is turned anti-clockwise moving the layshaft selector fork to mesh the sliding first gear with the dog-lock on the end of the layshaft. (The dog-lock is illustrated in Fig. DV 1).

As second gear is selected by lifting the pedal, the second layshaft selector fork brings the sliding third gear into mesh with the layshaft second gear, while the previous selector fork disengages first gear from the dog-lock.

Movement of the gear lever in the same direction will select third gear by moving the mainshaft sliding gear into mesh with the mainshaft third gear. At the same time the second layshaft selector disengages second gear.

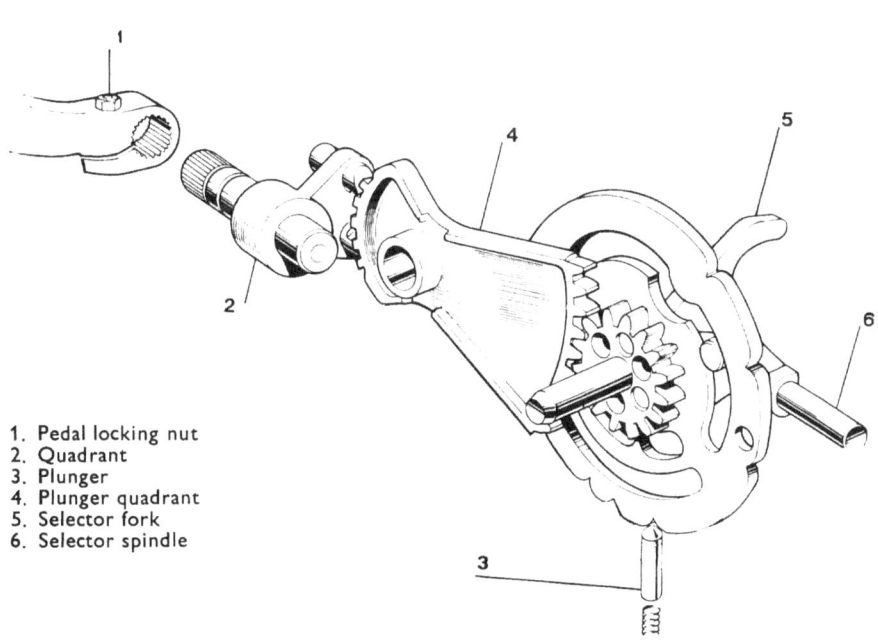

1. Pedal locking nut
2. Quadrant
3. Plunger
4. Plunger quadrant
5. Selector fork
6. Selector spindle

Fig. DV 2. Gear selection components

GEARBOX

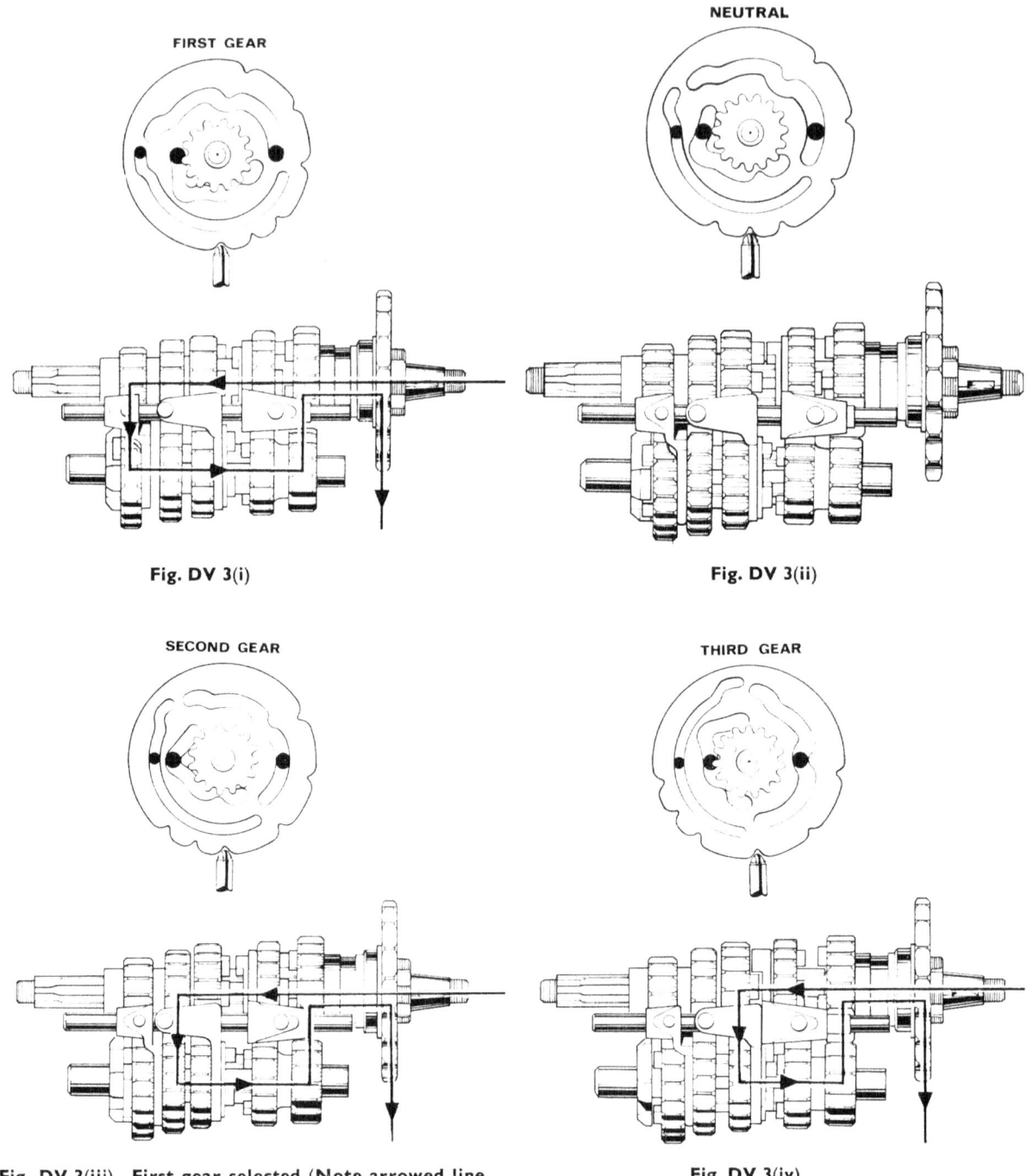

Fig. DV 3(i)

Fig. DV 3(ii)

Fig. DV 3(iii). First gear selected (Note arrowed line showing power being transmitted through the gear cluster)

Fig. DV 3(iv)

Further movement of the gear lever will select fourth gear by moving the sliding layshaft third gear into mesh with the layshaft fourth gear while the mainshaft fourth gear is moved into a neutral position.

Finally, fifth gear is obtained by a final movement of the lever in the same direction. The mainshaft selector fork will bring the mainshaft sliding gear (fourth gear) into mesh with the mainshaft fifth gear. At the same time the second layshaft sliding gear (third gear) is moved into a neutral position.

It should be noted that throughout the range of gear pedal movements the gear pedal spindle and plunger housing return to the original position ready for the next selection.

GEARBOX

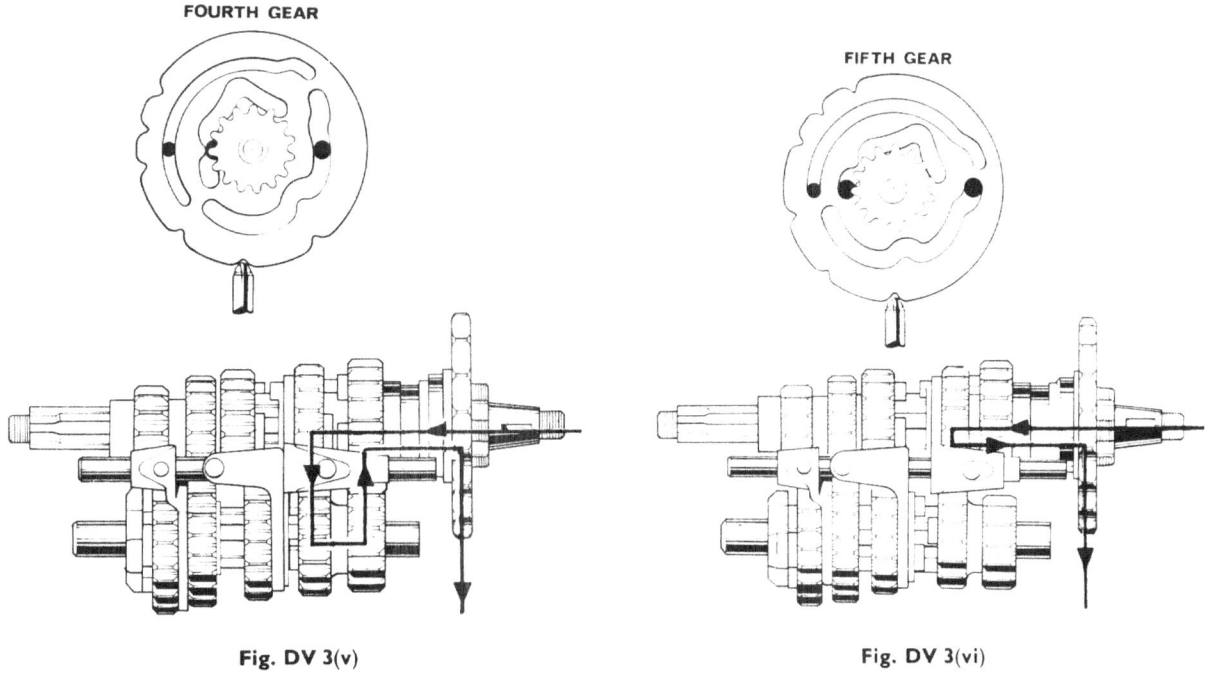

Fig. DV 3(v)

Fig. DV 3(vi)

SECTION DV 2

REMOVING AND REPLACING THE GEARBOX OUTER COVER ASSEMBLY

Remove the right hand footrest, secured from the back of the rear engine with a single nut.

Place a drip tray underneath the gearbox and unscrew the gearbox filler plug and drain plug.

Engage 4th (top) gear. This will allow several otherwise difficult nuts to be unscrewed by subsequently applying the rear brake when required.

Unscrew the top and bottom hexagonal nut and the recess screws from the periphery of the gearbox cover. Depress the kickstart lever slightly and tap the cover until it is free.

When the cover is removed, the gear-change mechanism and kickstart mechanism will be accessible. The gearchange pedal should be carefully raised then depressed, to control the release of the plungers and springs from the gearchange quadrant.

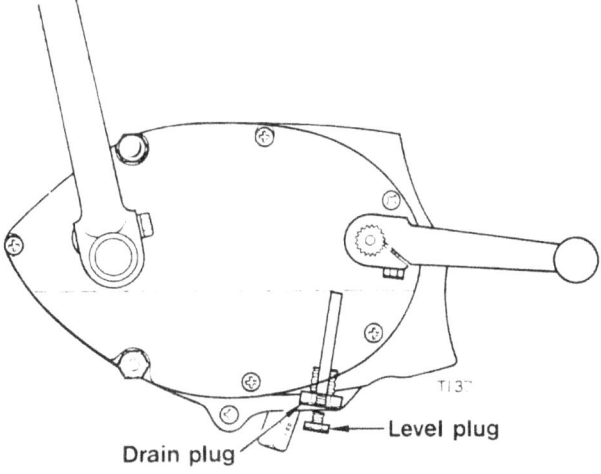

Fig. DV 4. Showing gearbox oil level and oil drain plugs

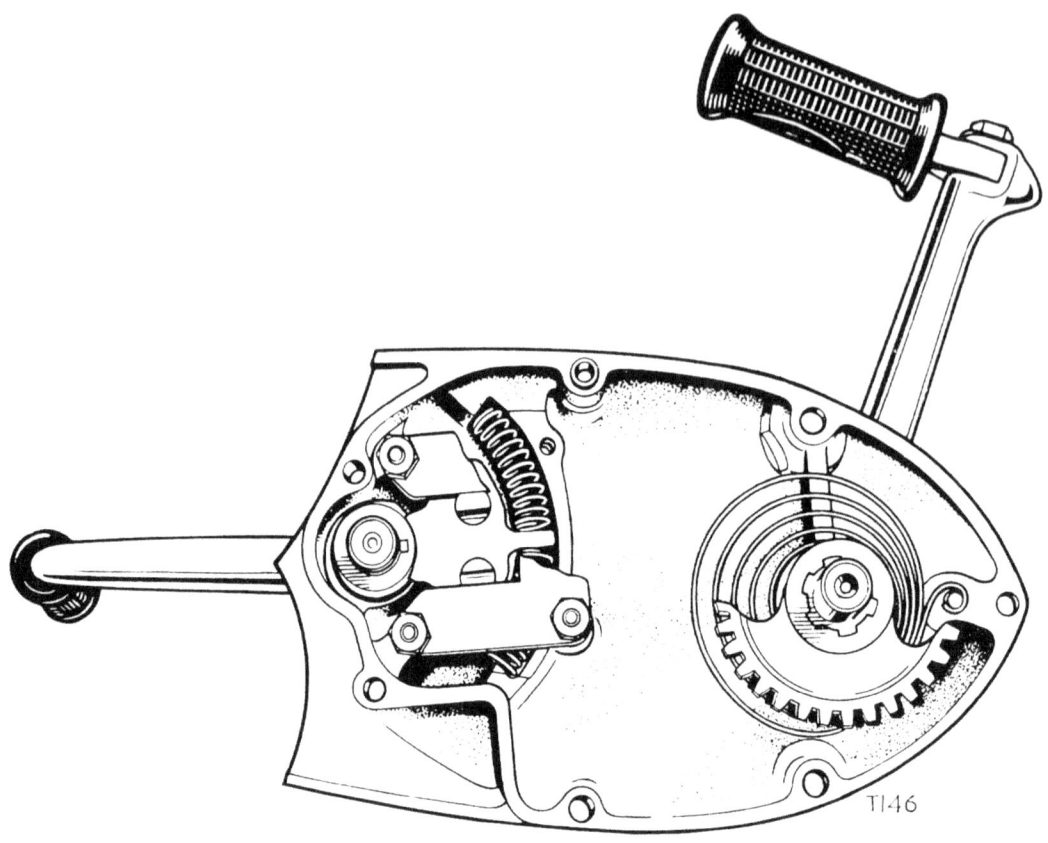

Fig. DV 5. Gearbox outer cover, showing gearchange mechanism, and kickstart quadrant

Prior to refitting the outer cover ensure that the junction surface is clean and free from any deposits of old jointing compound, then thoroughly clean it in paraffin (kerosene). Apply a fresh coat of jointing compound to the junction surface and ensure that the two location dowels are in position.

Turn the kickstart pedal until it is half way down its operational stroke and offer the cover to the gearbox. Check that the kickstart pedal returns to its normal fully-returned position. Reassembly then continues as a reversal of the above instructions. Finally, refill the gearbox to the correct level with the recommended grade of oil (see Section A2).

SECTION DV 3

DISMANTLING AND REASSEMBLING THE KICKSTART MECHANISM

Slacken the kickstarter crank cotter pin nut about two or three turns and release the cotter pin from its locking taper by using a hammer and a soft metal drift. Slide the pedal off the shaft and withdraw the quadrant and spring assembly. Apply the rear brake, bend back the tab on the lock washer and unscrew the kickstart ratchet pinion securing nut from the gearbox mainshaft. Withdraw the pinion, ratchet, spring and sleeve, then thoroughly clean all parts in paraffin (kerosene) and inspect them for wear etc., as shown in Section DV 5.

If the kickstarter quadrant is to be renewed the spindle should be driven out using a hammer or press and the gear quadrant pressed onto the spindle so that the kickstart crank location flat is positioned correctly relative to the quadrant (see Fig. DV 6).

GEARBOX

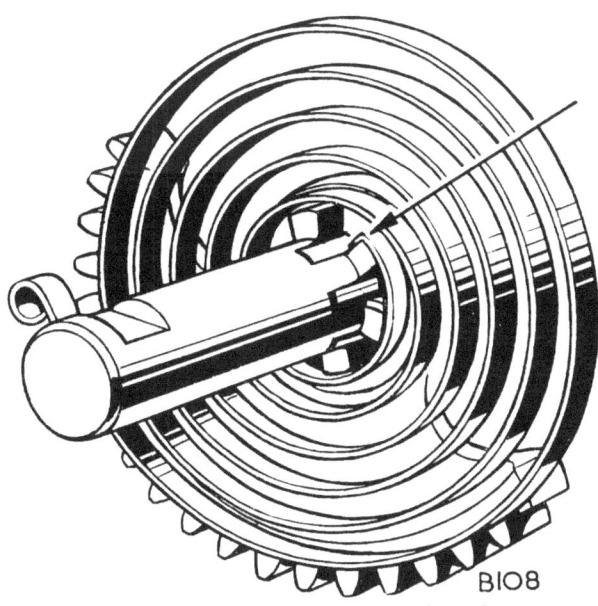

Fig. DV 6. Kickstart quadrant and spring. Arrow indicates correct spring location

To reassebmle the mechanism, first refit the thin walled steel sleeve, spring, pinion and ratchet to the gearbox mainshaft and assemble the tab washer, then screw on the retaining nut to the torque figure figure given in "General Data". **Do not overtighten the retaining nut as this may result in failure of the thin walled inner steel sleeve.**

Fit the return spring to the kickstart quadrant as shown in Fig. DV 6. Offer the spindle into the kickstart bush and locate the return spring onto the anchor peg at the rear of the cover. Fit the oil seal over the spindle and assemble the kickstart crank, locking it into position with the cotter pin from the rear. Refit the outer cover as shown in Section DV 2. Do not forget to refit the oil seal. Refill the gearbox with the correct grade of lubricant (Section A2).

SECTION DV 4

DISMANTLING AND REASSEMBLING THE GEARCHANGE MECHANISM

Slacken off the gear change pedal locking bolt and withdraw the pedal from the splined shaft. A little leverage between the pedal and the cover may be necessary. For this, choose a suitable tool to avoid damage to the cover.

Remove the four nuts and locking washers securing the guide plate. Withdraw the guide plate, plunger quadrant and curved return springs. Thoroughly clean the parts in Paraffin (kerosene) and inspect them for wear etc., as shown in Section DV 5.

To reassemble the mechanism, first fit a **new** rubber "O" ring to the spindle and offer it to the outer cover bush using a smear of oil to assist assembly, then refit the two quadrant return springs and ensure that they locate correctly over the step in the cover. To facilitate assembly of the springs, first fit the gearchange pedal and clamp it in position, thus enabling the quadrant to be turned and the springs to be compressed (see Fig. DV 5).

Refit the retainer plate, not forgetting the locking washers which fit one under each of the four nuts. Finally, refit the springs and plungers, taking care that they are not suddenly ejected from their seats during assembly.

SECTION DV 5

INSPECTING THE GEARCHANGE AND KICKSTART MECHANISM

GEARCHANGE:
(1) Inspect the gearchange plungers for wear and ensure that they are a clearance fit in the quadrant. Check the plunger springs by comparing their lengths with the figures given in "General Data".
(2) Examine the plunger guide plate for wear and grooving on the taper guide surfaces. Renew the plate if grooving has occurred.
(3) Inspect the footchange pedal return springs for fatigue and if they show signs of corrosion due to condensation, they should be renewed.
(4) Examine the gearchange quadrant bush for wear and possible ovality by inserting the quadrant into the bush and feeling the amount of play.

(5) Check the tips of the plungers and the teeth of the camplate operating quadrant for chipping and wear. To remove the camplate quadrant, first remove the inner cover as shown in Section DV 8, then remove the two split pins and withdraw the spindle.

KICKSTART:

(1) Examine the kickstart quadrant for chipped or broken teeth or looseness on the spindle and the kickstart return spring for fatigue cracks and signs of wear, particularly at the centre where it engages on the splines of the spindle.

(2) Examine the kickstart spindle bush for wear. If the required measuring instruments are not available, use the spindle as a gauge and feel the amount of play.

(3) Examine the kickstart ratchet mechanism for wear, giving particular attention to the ratchet teeth ensuring that they have not become chipped or rounded. Check that the thin walled steel bush is a clearance fit in the kickstart pinion and that the spring is not badly worn.

(4) Finally, check that the kickstart stop peg is firmly pressed into the inner cover and is not distorted.

SECTION DV 6

RENEWING KICKSTART AND GEARCHANGE SPINDLE BUSHES

If it is found necessary to renew the kickstart spindle bush this should be done by completely stripping the outer cover of its assembly parts and heating it to 100°C., then driving the bush out using a suitable shouldered drift. Press in the new bush while the cover is still hot.

Adopt a similar procedure for removal of the outer cover gearchange spindle bush. The inner cover bush does not usually wear much, even after great mileage has been covered. However, if it is required to renew the bush, the inner cover should be removed (Section DV 8), and the camplate operating quadrant disconnected.

Using a suitable tap (e.g. $\frac{3}{4}$ in. dia. $\times$ 10 Whit.) cut a thread in the bush to a depth of $\frac{3}{4}$ in.; heat the cover to 100°C., then reinsert the tap, or, preferably, a suitable bolt. Grip the bolt (or tap) firmly in a vice, then drive the cover away using a hide mallet until the bush is free.

A press or suitably shouldered drift is required to drive in the new bush, which should be donewhilst the cover is still hot.

SECTION DV 7

DISMANTLING THE GEARBOX

Remove the gearbox outer cover as shown in Section DV 2, leaving the gearbox with 5th (top) gear selected.

Remove the two short bolts, two long bolts and a centre nut which serves to retain the rear right engine mounting plate, then withdraw the plate.

Bend back the tags on the lock washer and unscrew the kickstart pinion ratchet retainer nut from the end of the gearbox mainshaft. This should be easily achieved with 5th (top) gear selected and the rear brake applied.

Remove the outer primary cover and dismantle the transmission as shown in Section C, not forgetting, finally, to remove the key from the gearbox mainshaft.

GEARBOX

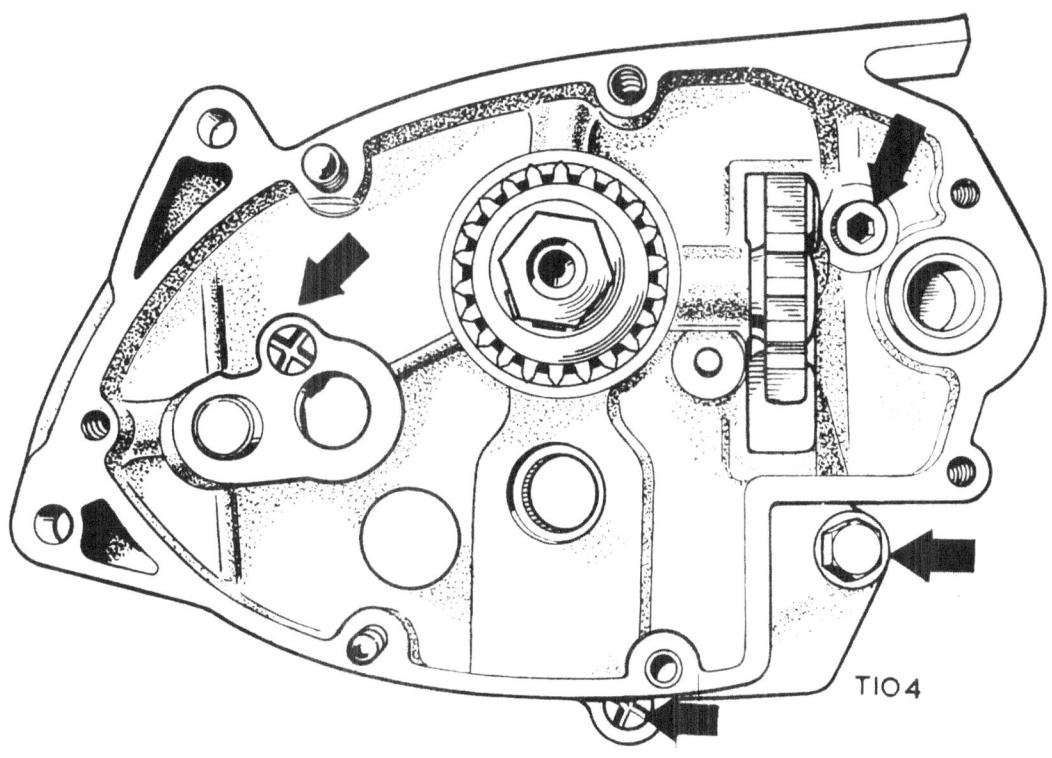

Fig. DV 7. Gearbox inner cover retaining screws

The gearbox inner cover is retained by a socket screw, two Phillips recessed screws and a hexagonal bolt (See Fig. DV 7). When these are removed the cover can be released by tapping it outwards with a hide mallet.

Withdraw the engaging dog from the layshaft. See Fig. DV 8, then remove the circlip from the end of the layshaft with a pair of circlip pliers. Pull the selector rod out and then remove the layshaft first gear with its selector fork. Withdraw the second gear from the layshaft and then remove the mainshaft complete with first, second and third gears in position. Remove the mainshaft fourth and layshaft third gears with their selector forks and then withdraw the layshaft with the fifth and fourth gears in position. Detach the two brass thrust washers which locate over the needle roller bearings. Before removal of the camplate, the mainshaft high gear will have to be detached from the gearbox sprocket and withdrawn from the crankcase. This can be done by removing the circular plate from the primary inner cover at the rear of the clutch, tapping back the bent-over portion of the locking plate and unscrewing the large hexagonal gearbox sprocket nut (1·875" across the flats). To facilitate removal of the nut, Workshop Tool number 60-6125 is available. When the nut has been removed, tap the high gear into the gearbox using a hide mallet or a soft metal drift. It is now possible to remove the camplate from its housing in the crankcase. To remove the gearbox sprocket, disconnect the rear chain and remove it from around the sprocket which can now be easily withdrawn through the aperture.

The oil is prevented from leaving the gearbox through the main bearing by an oil seal which runs on a ground boss on the gearbox sprocket. Check the oil seal for cracking and wear (see Section DV 9 for bearing and oil seal removal details).

DV GEARBOX

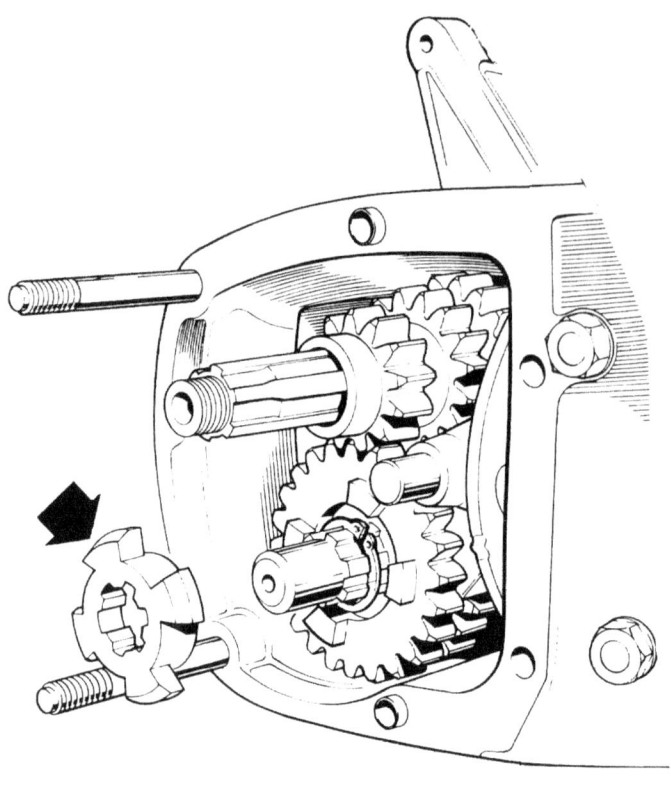

Fig. DV 8. Showing removal of engaging dog

SECTION DV8

INSPECTION OF THE GEARBOX COMPONENTS

Thoroughly clean all parts in paraffin (kerosene) and check them for wear and fatigue, as follows:—

(1) Inspect the gearbox housing and inner cover for signs of cracking and damage to the joint faces. Check that the location dowels are in position correctly in the gearbox and inner cover (2 dowels each). In preparation for re-assembly, clean the junction surfaces of the gearbox, inner cover and outer cover of any old deposits of jointing compound.

(2) Examine both the mainshaft and layshaft for signs of fatigue, damaged threads and badly worn splines. Check the extent of wear to the bearing diameters of both shafts by comparing them with the figures given in "General Data". Examine the shafts carefully for signs of seizure.

GEARBOX

Excessive friction resistance and seizure will be indicated by local colouring on the shaft.

(3) Check the layshaft needle roller bearing by inserting the layshaft and feeling the amount of play.

(4) Inspect the gearbox mainshaft bearings for roughness due to pitting or indentation of the ball/roller tracks. Note that the high gear bearing operates directly in a roller bearing pressed into the right hand side crankcase half. If wear is apparent at the high gear bearings (check general data for high gear spigot dimensions), it will be necessary to replace the roller bearing *and* the high gear. Under no circumstances should the bearing or the high gear be replaced independently.
Check the inner cover bearing by feeling the amount of side play of the centre track. It should not be possible to detect any movement by hand if the bearing is in good condition. The mainshaft should be a push fit into the inner cover bearing.

(5) Examine the gears thoroughly, for chipped, fractured or worn teeth. Check the internal splines, dogs and bushes. Make sure that the splines are free on their respective shafts with no tendency to bind, and the bushes in the mainshaft third gear, layshaft second gear and layshaft first gear are not loose or excessively worn. Again, reference should be made to the dimensions given in "General Data".

(6) Check that the selector fork rod is not grooved and that it is a good fit in the gearbox casing and the inner cover. Inspect the selector fork running faces for wear. This will only have occurred if the gearbox is being continually used with a badly worn mainshaft bearing.

(7) The gear selector camplate should be inspected for signs of werar in the selector tracks. Excessive wear will occur if the mainshaft main bearing has worn badly. Check the fit of the camplate spindle in its housing. Examine the camplate gear wheel for excessive wear. Difficulty will be encountered in gear selection, causing subsequent damage to the gears, if this gear is badly worn.

(8) Inspect the mainshaft high gear needle roller bearings for roughness or fracture. Check the mainshaft diameter with the "General Data" and check for surface pitting or damage due to scoring.

SECTION DV 9

RENEWING MAINSHAFT AND LAYSHAFT BEARINGS

MAINSHAFT

The mainshaft bearings are a press fit into their respective housings and are retained by spring circlips to prevent sideways movement due to end thrust. To remove the right bearing, first lever out the circlip, then heat the cover to approximately 100°C. and drive out the bearing using a suitably shouldered drift. The new bearing should be pressed or drifted in whilst the cover is still hot using a suitable tubular drift onto the outer race. Do not forget to refit the circlip.

To remove the high gear bearing on the left of the machine, first remove the screws and oil seal holder Carefully heat the casing locally to approximately 100°C., then drive out the bearing from the inside by means of a suitably shouldered drift. Whilst the casing is still hot, drive in the new bearing, using a suitable tubular drift onto the outer race, and press in the new oil seal into the holder.

MAINSHAFT HIGH GEAR BEARINGS

Two caged needle bearings are fitted into each end of the high gear and they can be both pressed out together using a drift of the following dimensions.

DV GEARBOX

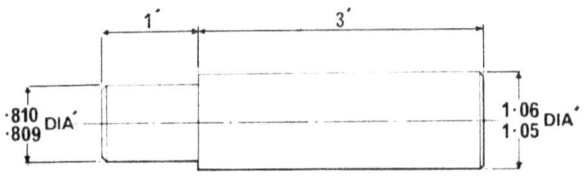

Fig. DV 9. Drift dimensions

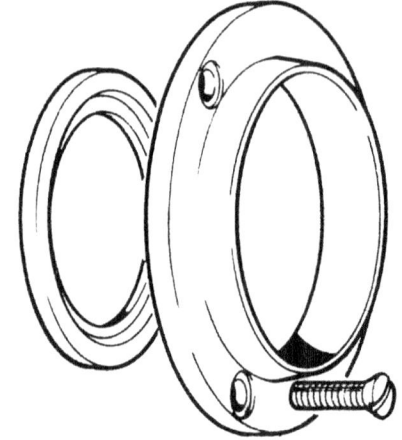

Fig. DV 10. High gear bearing oil and seal housing

LAYSHAFT

The right needle roller bearing should be removed by heating the cover to approximately 100°C., then pressing or drifting out the bearing using a tool similar to that shown in Fig. DV 11.

The new bearing should be pressed in, plain end first, whilst the cover is still hot, from the inside of the cover, until ·073/·078 in. of the bearing protrudes above the cover face (see Fig. DV 11).

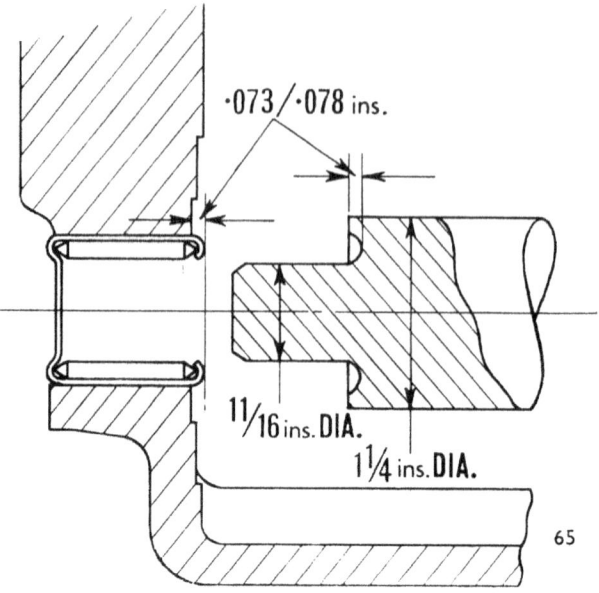

Fig. DV 11. Sketch of needle roller and drift

The left needle roller bearing is of the closed-end type and is accessible from the left, through the sprocket cover plate aperture. The casing should be heated to approximately 100°C. and the bearing driven through into the gearbox using a soft metal drift, taking care not to damage the bore into which the bearing fits. The new bearing must be carefully pressed in whilst the casing is hot, until ·073/·078 in. protrudes above the spot face surface inside the gearbox. Do not use excessive force or the needle roller outer case may become damaged, resulting in the rollers seizing, or breaking up.

Finally, the outer portion of the bore into which the bearing fits, should be sealed with a suitable proprietary sealant.

SECTION DV 10

REASSEMBLING THE GEARBOX

Lubricate the camplate and spindle and offer it into the spindle housing within the gearbox.

Fit the high gear bearing oil seal in its circular housing, the closed side flush with the outer face. (See Fig. D11). Press the high gear into the bearing. Lubricate the ground tapered boss of the sprocket with oil and slide it onto the high gear. Screw on the securing nut finger tight.

Re-mesh the rear chain with the sprockets and replace the connecting link. Apply the rear brake and tighten the sprocket securing nut as tight as possible using service tool 61-6061.

GEARBOX

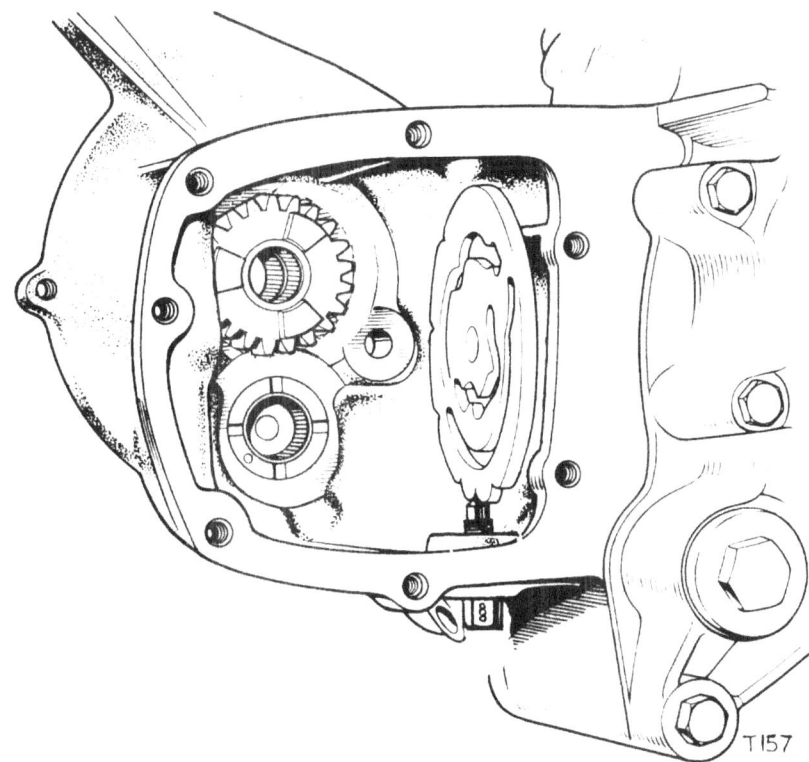

Fig. DV 12. Reassembling the gearbox. Arrow indicates camplate in the neutral gear position

Locate the bronze thrust washer over the inner needle roller bearing. The thrust washer can be held in position by smearing its rear surface with grease. Note that the grooved surface of the thrust washer is towards the layshaft. (See Fig. DV 13).

Set the camplate in the neutral gear position (See Fig. DV 12). Lubricate the needle roller bearings in the high gear (use oil recommended in Section A2) and layshaft bearing. Place the mainshaft fourth gear with its respective selector fork onto the mainshaft. See Fig. DV 1. This selector fork has a large engaging pin and no cuttaway on the housing. Assemble the shaft into the high gear using a heavy grease to retain the selector fork on the gear and in the camplate track. Replace the layshaft assembly with fifth and fourth gears into the gearbox and engage with the mainshaft fifth and fourth gears (note that with the gearbox in the neutral position none of the sliding dogs will be engaged).

Replace the layshaft third gear with its respective selector fork (See Fig. DV 1). This selector fork has a large engaging pin and a cuttaway on the selector housing. Then replace the mainshaft third gear and engage with the layshaft third. Replace the layshaft second gear after first lubricating the bush with oil. Replace the combined first and second gear onto the mainshaft. Replace the layshaft bottom gear with its selector fork (this selector fork has a small diameter engaging pin and a cuttaway to match the previous selector fork. See Fig. DV 1. Replace the selector rod. Fit the circlip onto the end of the layshaft and the engaging dog up against the circlip. Turn the camplate towards the inner cover from the top thereby placing the gearbox into the first gear position (note engaging dog on layshaft will be in mesh with the dogs on the layshaft first gear).

Check the camplate operating quadrant is moving freely in the inner cover and position the bronze layshaft thrust washer over the needle roller bearing in the inner cover. Again, use grease to hold the thrust washer in position during assembly.

DV 13

GEARBOX

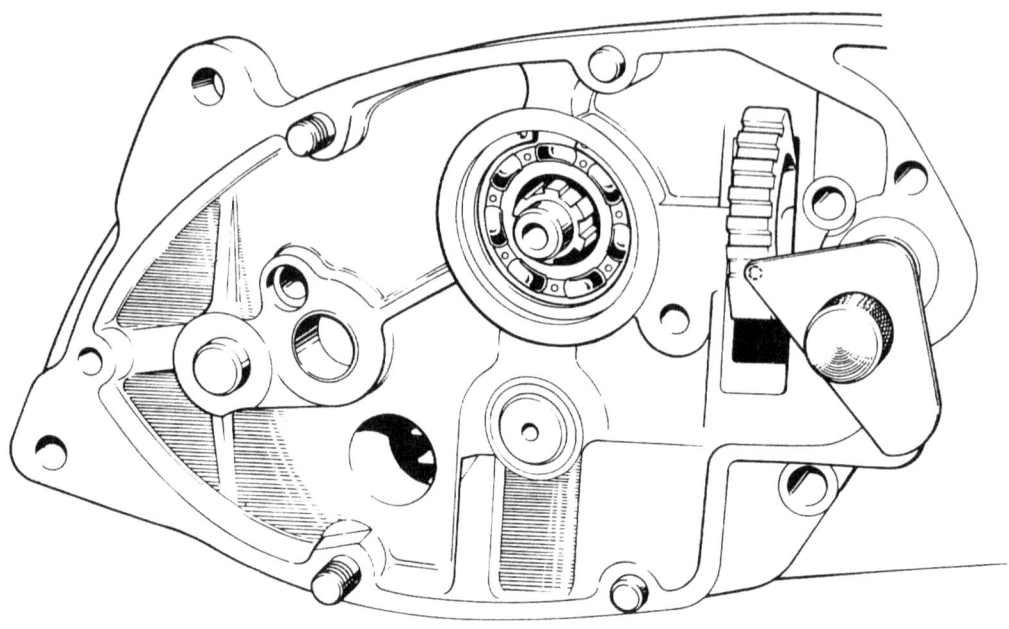

Fig. DV 13. Refitting the gearbox inner cover

Using a pressure oil can, lubricate all the moving parts in the gearbox, then apply a fresh coat of jointing compound to the gearbox junction surface.

Ensure that the two location dowels are in position and offer the inner cover assembly to the gearbox. When the cover is approximately $\frac{1}{4}$ in. (6 mm.) away from the gearbox junction face, position the camplate quadrant as detailed in Fig. DV 13 and position service tool 60-6128 as shown. If this tool is not available line up the top edge of the second tooth on the quadrant with the centre line passing through the footchange spindle housing.

Screw in the socket screw, recessed screws and the bolt, then temporarily assemble the outer cover and gearchange lever and check that the gearchanging sequence is correct by simultaneously operating the gearchange pedal and turning the rear wheel. In the event of any problem of selection it must be assumed that the quadrant teeth are not engaged accurately with the camplate pinion. To rectify this, remove the inner cover again and check that the camplate has been set in the first gear position. Offer up the inner cover and repeat as previous.

When correct gearchanging is established, re-assemble the kickstart pinion and ratchet, replace the tab washer and screw on the securing nut to the torque figure given in "General Data". To facilitate this, the rear brake should be applied with fourth gear selected.

Refit the gearbox outer cover as shown in section DV 2 then reassemble the transmission, referring to section A2 for the correct quantities and grades of lubricant for the primary chaincase and gearbox.

SECTION DV 11

CHANGING THE GEARBOX SPROCKET

To gain the acces to the gearbox sprocket, first remove the left exhaust pipe (one clamp bolt at the manifold and one clip at the silencer nose).

Detach one spade terminal from the stoplamp switch and remove the finger nut from the rear brake rod to allow the brake pedal to drop clear of the chaincase.

Remove the left footrests (secured by one nut from the back).

Remove the clutch thrust inspection cover and release the cable from the thrust mechanism. Place a suitable container beneath the centre of the chaincase and remove the drain plug.

Allow a few minutes for the case to drain and then remove the outer chaincase (Section C5), the transmission (Section C7), the inner chaincase, the clutch and the clutch cover (Section C6).

Tap the tab washer clear of the gearbox sprocket retaining nut. Leave the chain *in situ* and unscrew the gearbox sprocket securing nut using service tool 61-6061. The rear chain may now be disconnected and the gearbox sprocket withdrawn. 'Hydroseal' is used on the splines and the sprocket will need to be moved using the extractor 61-6046.

Before fitting the new sprocket check that the gearbox oil seal is in good condition and the the rear chain is not excessively worn. Check the extension as shown in Section A14.

If the old chain is to be retained for further use it should be thoroughly cleaned in paraffin and lubricated in the grease bath. Lubricate the ground boss with oil, fit a new locking plate and slide the sprocket over the gearbox mainshaft and high gear. When the sprocket is located on the splines screw on the securing nut finger tight, then re-connect the chain.

With the rear brake applied tighten the nut until it is as tight as possible and tap over the lockplate.

NOTES

SECTION E

FRAME AND ATTACHMENT DETAILS

	Section
REMOVING AND REFITTING THE FUEL TANK	E1
REMOVING AND REPLACING THE SIDE PANELS	E2
REMOVING AND REPLACING THE OIL TANK	E3
REMOVING AND REPLACING THE BATTERY CARRIER ASSEMBLY	E4
REMOVING AND REPLACING THE REAR MUDGUARD	E5
ADJUSTING THE REAR SUSPENSION	E6
REMOVING AND REFITTING THE REAR SUSPENSION UNITS	E7
STRIPPING AND REASSEMBLING THE SUSPENSION UNITS	E8
REMOVING AND REFITTING THE SWINGING FORK	E9
RENEWING THE SWINGING FORK BUSHES	E10
REMOVING AND REPLACING THE REAR FRAME	E11
FRAME ALIGNMENT	E12
FAIRING ATTACHMENT LUGS AND STEERING LOCK	E13
FITTING REPLACEMENT SEAT COVERS	E14
REPAIRS	E15
PAINTWORK REFINISHING	E16

FRAME

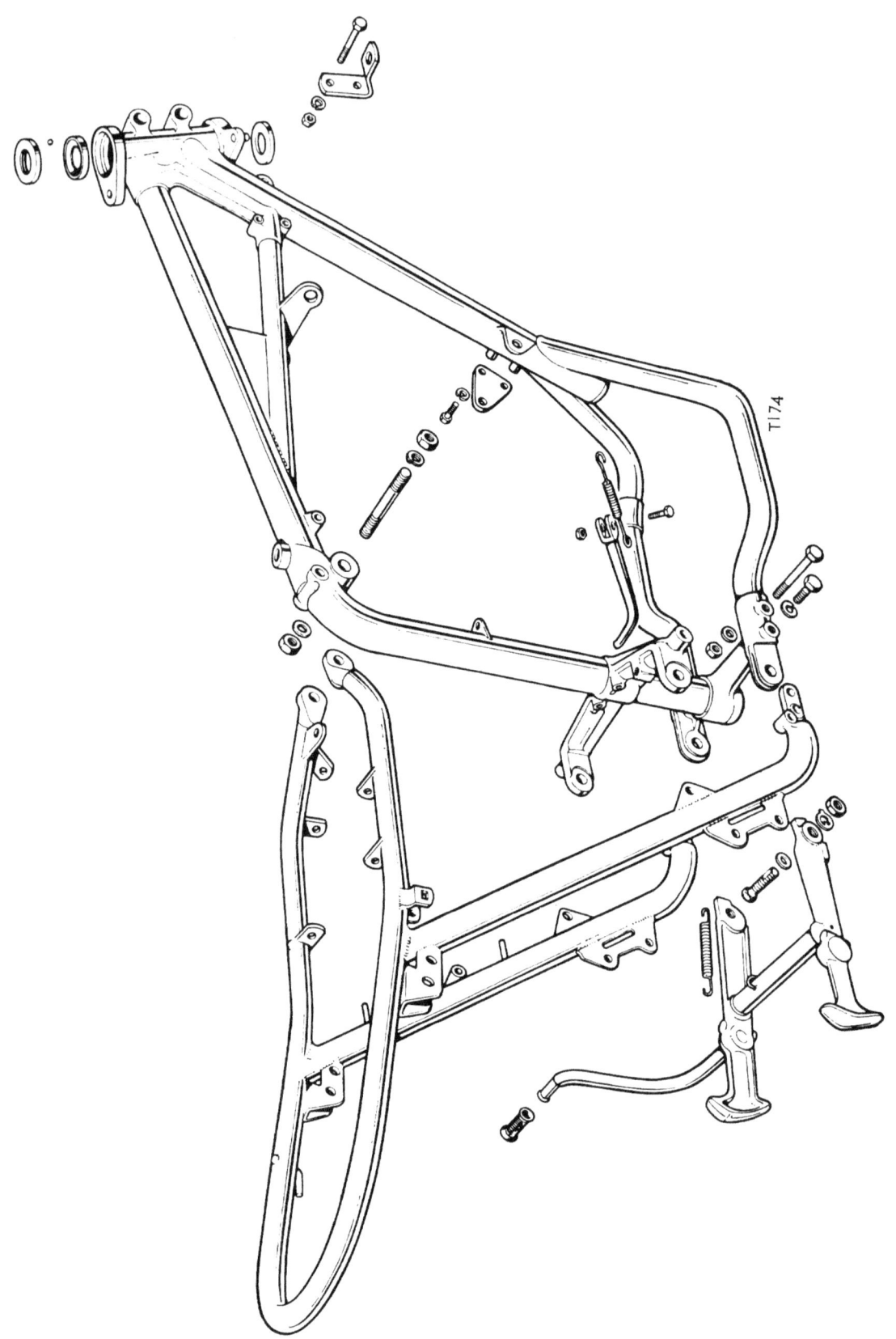

Fig. E1. General arrangement of front and rear frame assembly

FRAME

SECTION E1

REMOVING AND REPLACING THE FUEL TANK

Turn both fuel taps to the "off" position, then unscrew both unions and disconnect the feed pipes at the taps. Raise the twin seat, then unscrew the rear fuel tank securing bolt. Remove two clevelock nuts from the front mounting studs, and remove the petrol tank. Collect two thick rubber washers, two thin spigotted rubber washers and two cupped steel washers from the front mountings, and the thick spigotted rubber washer from the rear mounting.

Refitting the tank is a reversal of the above procedure, referring to Fig. E2 for the correct order of assembling the rubber washers.

A number of early machines were built with bolts securing the front of the fuel tank. Ensure that the bolts are securly wired together.

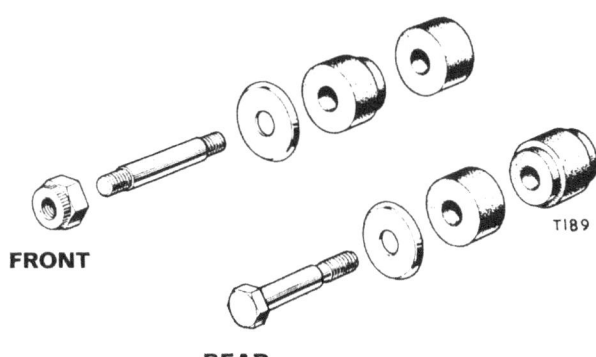

Fig. E2. Assembly order of fuel tank rubbers

SECTION E2

REMOVING AND REPLACING THE SIDE PANELS

To remove the right side panel, merely remove two "Posidriv" screws which secure the panel to the oil tank, and withdraw the panel.

To remove the left side panel, unscrew the plastic securing knob at the top front of the panel, and slide it forwards off the two spigotted rubber mounting bushes at the rear.

Refitting the panels is a direct reversal of the above.

SECTION E3

REMOVING AND REPLACING THE OIL TANK

Lift the twin seat, disconnect the breather pipe from the froth tower. Unfasten the securing clip and disconnect the pipe running from the front of the oil tank (this leads to the right side of the oil cooler). Remove the right-hand side panel after taking out the three "Posidriv" screws. With a drain tray beneath, disconnect the oil feed pipe union nut at the bottom front of the oil tank and allow several minutes whilst the oil tank completely drains. Remove the oil tank gauze filter (large hexagon head). Unfasten the front top mounting nut and push the slot headed peg clear of the spigotted rubber.

Unfasten the rear top mounting nut and washer, removing the seat retaining wire. Push the slotted peg through the spigotted rubber. Remove the air cleaner as described in Section B6.

Lift the oil tank off the bottom spigot and move the top inwards. The bottom can then be pulled outwards and down until the tank is clear of the frame.

To refit the oil tank, offer the top first, up behind the top rear frame rail. The tank which has a rubber sleeve at the bottom can then be positioned over the bottom mounting spigot.

FRAME

Refit the slot headed pegs through the top spigotted rubbers (see Fig. E3), and refit the nuts and washers, not forgetting to refit the twin seat check wire to the rear peg. Clean the oil tank gauze filter in paraffin (Kerosene), and replace the fibre washer if the old one appears in any way damaged. Refit the filter. Re-connect the breather, top return and bottom feed pipes to the tank. Refit the air filter and box and before refitting the right side panel, ensure that the air cleaner hose is correctly positioned in the filter box.

Refill the oil tank with the correct quantity and grade of oil (refer to Sections A1 and A2).

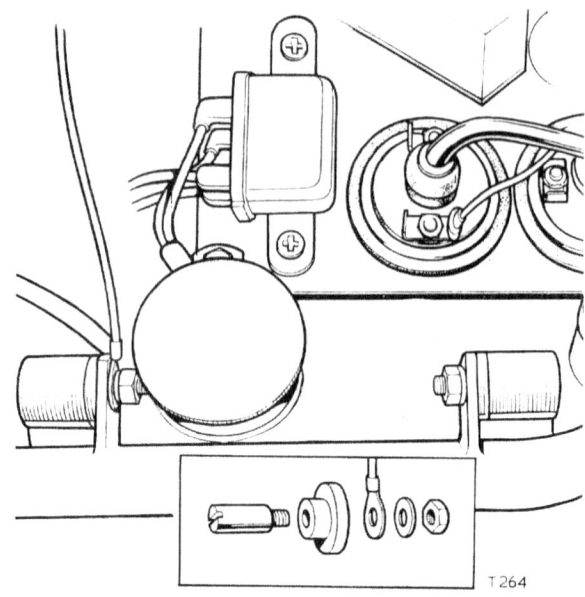

Fig. E3. Oil tank rubber mountings

SECTION E4

REMOVING AND REPLACING THE BATTERY CARRIER

Remove the left side panel, as in section E2. Disconnect the fuse holder on the brown/blue lead to the battery and keep the fuse safely for refitting. Unscrew the red (positive) lead from the battery. Pull down the rubber battery retaining strap to release the outer bottom buckle of the strap from the carrier. Lift the battery clear and remove the rubber tray.

Remove the nut and plain washer and long rear carrier to frame bolt. Remove the top carrier bolts, nuts, and washers and the battery carrier and fibre glass tool holder will be free of the frame.

To remove the tool carrier from the battery carrier, remove two cleveloc nuts, washers and bolts from the top front mounting, and the countersunk screw and nut from the base of the carrier.

Reassembly is a reversal of the fore-going, reference being made to Fig. E4 for the correct order of assembly of grommets etc.

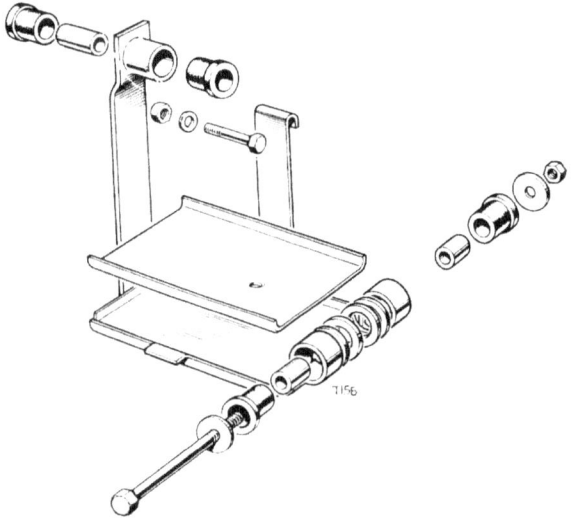

Fig. E4. Battery carrier mountings

FRAME

SECTION E5

REMOVING AND REFITTING THE REAR MUDGUARD

Remove the rear wheel (Section F2), and remove the bottom front bolt, nut and washer which hold the mudguard blade to the pivot lug bracket.

Release the silencer stays by removal of each top nut, bolt and washer, and remove two nuts, bolts and spring washers securing the hand rail to the rear mudguard. Remove two nuts, bolts and spring washers which hold the rear frame clip, wiring protector, and support strip. Remove the tail lamp housing top nut and plain washer to release the lower end of the wiring protector.

Disconnect the tail lamp wire connectors, which are situated beneath the twin seat, and pull the wires through the grommet in the mudguard. Remove two nuts, bolts and washers securing the bridge to the mudguard. The mudguard can then be drawn clear of the frame. If it is required to remove the complete tail lamp, and tail lamp housing, this can be released by removal of the two lower nuts and bolts which also secure the number plate support bracket.

Reassembly is a reversal of the afore-going, but do not overlook re-connection of the tail lamp leads.

SECTION E6

ADJUSTING THE REAR SUSPENSION

The movement is controlled by Girling combined coil spring and hydraulic damper units. The hydraulic damping mechanism is completely sealed but the static loading of the spring is adjustable.

There is a three position cam ring below the chromium plated dust cover and a "C" spanner is provided in the toolkit.

To increase the static loading of the spring place the machine on the stand so that there is least load on the spring and use the "C" spanner to turn the cam; both units must be on the same notch whichever may be chosen.

The standard lowest position, a is for solo riding, the second position, b is for heavier solo riders or when luggage is carried on the rear of the machine and the third or highest position, c is for use when a pillion passenger is being carried.

The later unit, d is adjusted by turning the ring in the direction of arrow 'A' to increase the loading.

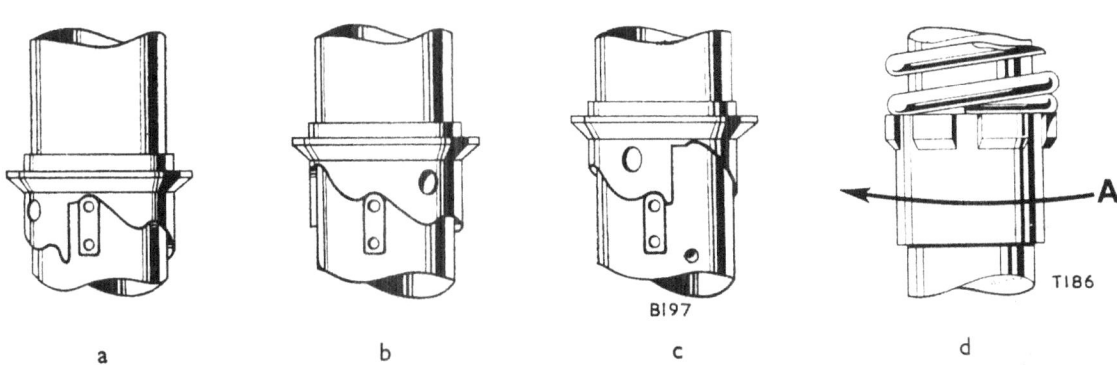

Fig. E5. Adjusting the rear suspension units

SECTION E7

REMOVING AND REFITTING THE REAR SUSPENSION UNITS

Removal of the suspension units is achieved by removing the top and bottom fixing bolts whilst the machine is suitably mounted, so that the rear wheel is off the ground.

The top suspension fixing bolts are fitted with their heads towards the outside of the machine, so that it is possible to remove the suspension units without dismantling the rear mudguard assembly etc.

These bolts also serve to retain the hand rail. When refitting the suspension unit, ensure that the hand rail is positioned outside the frame brackets. It may be necessary to use an alignment bar to assist in bringing the bolt holes into line.

SECTION E8

STRIPPING AND REASSEMBLING THE SUSPENSION UNITS

The suspension unit consists of a sealed hydraulic damper unit, outer coiled spring and dirt shields. The static loading on the spring is adjustable and should be set according to the type of conditions under which the machine is to be used (see Section E6).

To dismantle the suspension unit and remove the spring, it is required to compress the spring whilst the two semi-circular spring retainer plates are removed. To do this first turn the cam until it is in the "LIGHT-LOAD" position, then carefully grip the bottom lug in a vice. Take firm hold of the outer dirt shield and pull it until the spring is sufficiently compressed to allow the spring retainers to be removed.

The damper unit should be checked for leakage, bending of the plunger rod and damping action. Check the bonded pivot bushes for wear and ensure that the sleeve is not loose in the rubber bush.

The bushes can be easily renewed by driving out the old one and pressing in the new one using a smear of soapy water to assist assembly.

Squeaking coming from a suspension unit will probably be due to the spring rubbing on the bottom shield. To overcome this, smear some high-melting point grease on the inside of the shield. Under no circumstances should the plunger rod be lubricated.

Note.—For information concerning suspension units or spare parts, the local Girling agent should be consulted.

Reassembly is a reversal of dismantling. Check that the cam is in the light load position before compressing the spring.

FRAME

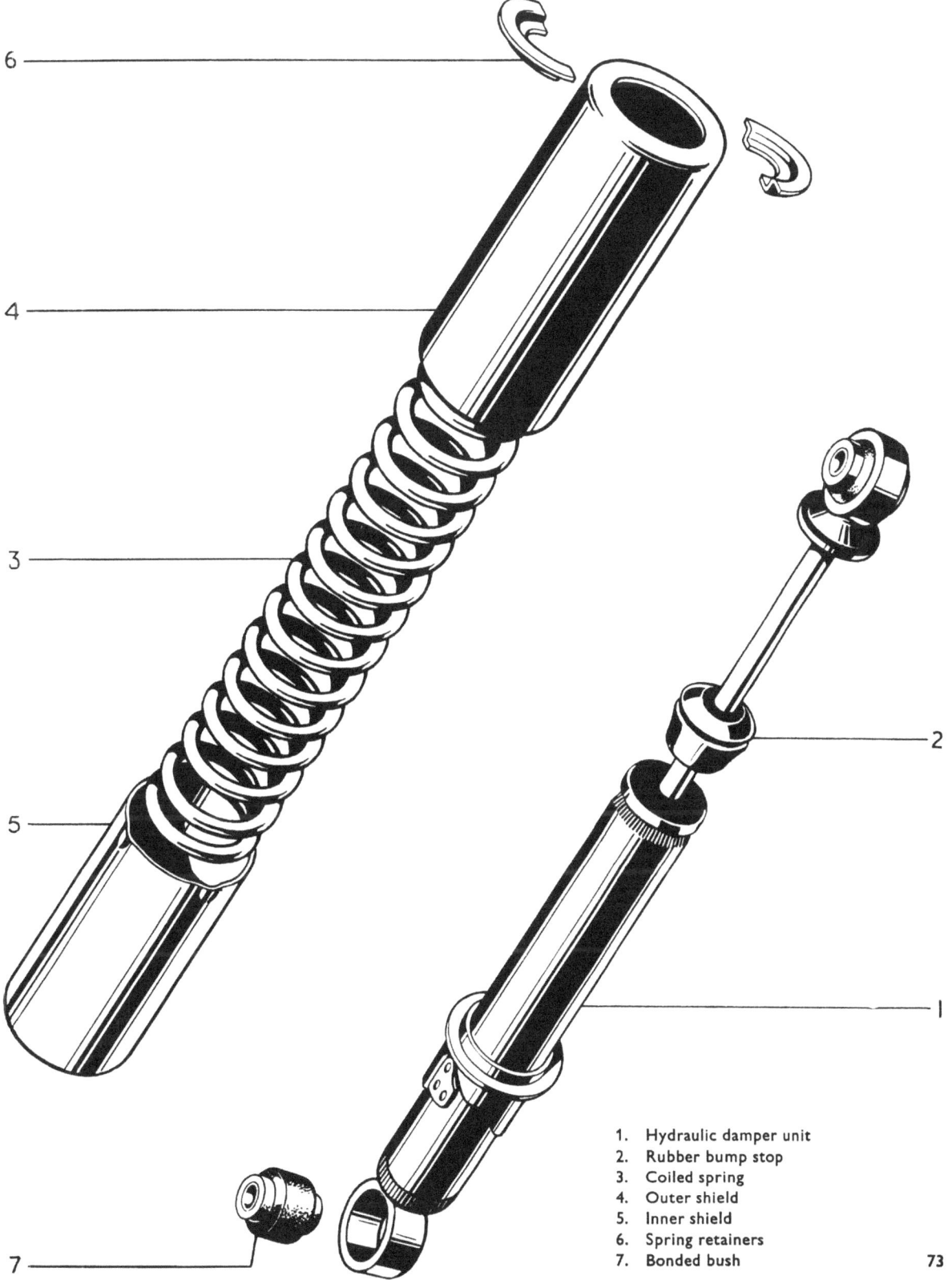

1. Hydraulic damper unit
2. Rubber bump stop
3. Coiled spring
4. Outer shield
5. Inner shield
6. Spring retainers
7. Bonded bush

Fig. E6. Exploded view of the rear suspension unit

SECTION E9

REMOVING AND REFITTING THE SWINGING FORK

Disconnect the chain and remove the front anchor stay securing bolt, then unscrew the brake operating rod adjuster nut and remove the speedo cable from the rear wheel drive. Slacken the wheel spindle nuts and withdraw the rear wheel.

The side panels must be removed (section E2).

Remove two long and two short bolts and the large central bolt from the left side and large nut from the right side engine mounting plates. Disconnect the stop lamp switch leads, and withdraw the plates.

Slacken off the rear chain guard bolt and remove the front chain guard securing bolt.

Remove the two bolts which secure the suspension units to the swinging forks, and disconnect the rear chain oiler pipe.

To remove the spindle, first bend back the tab washer, and unscrew the locking nut from the left hand side of the spindle. Unscrew the spindle until it is free to be withdrawn. The swinging fork can then be removed and the lipped end plates with "O" rings, outer sleeves and distance tube withdrawn.

All parts should be thoroughly cleaned in paraffin (Kerosene) and inspected for wear giving particular attention to the fit of the two outer sleeves in the swinging fork bushes. The working clearance between the sleeve and bush should not be excessive.

If excessive wear is in evidence, the bushes will require renewing, for details of this see section E10. The parts should be reassembled in the order shown (Fig. E8), with the addition of a sufficient quantity of the recommended grade of grease to fill the space surrounding the distance tube. Also, the sleeves and bushes should be well greased. The "O" rings should be inserted into the lipped end plates and pushed over the ends of the swinging fork cross tube whilst the swinging fork is offered to the pivot lug and the swinging arm bolt inserted from the right-hand side. The bolts should be tightened until the fork can just be moved upwards and downwards with little effort. The lock nut and tab washer should then be fitted and the nut tightened. Reassembly then continues as the reversal of the above instructions. To remove side play where the bushes are sound, it is necessary only to take out the distance tube and file one end to reduce the overall length.

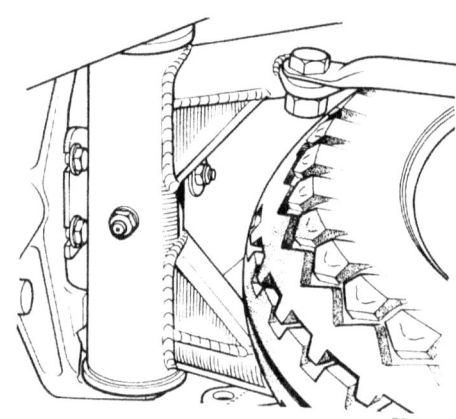

Fig. E7. Swinging fork grease nipple

FRAME

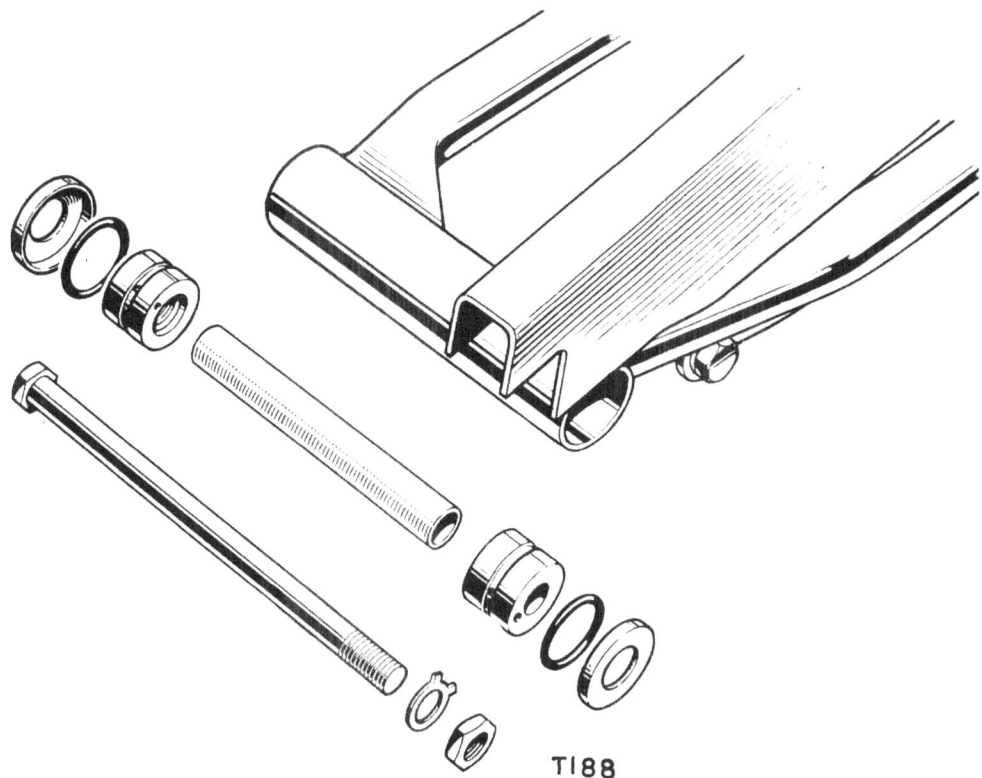

Fig. E8. Exploded view of swinging fork assembly

SECTION E10

RENEWING THE SWINGING FORK BUSHES

If the swinging fork bushes require renewing they should be removed by means of a suitable soft metal drift inserted in the tubular housing at an angle and located onto the far side bush. By dexterous use of a hammer and a drift moving it round the edge of the bush a little at a time the bush should be easily removed with no resultant damage to the bore of the housing (see Fig. E9).

New bushes are of the steel backed pre-sized type and when carefully pressed in, using a smear of grease to assist assembly, they will give the correct diametral working clearance. If a press is not available the bush can be fitted by using 61-6050 drift and a hammer. Ensure that the bush enters squarely and that no burr is set up due to misalignment. Bore sizes and working clearances are given in "General Data".

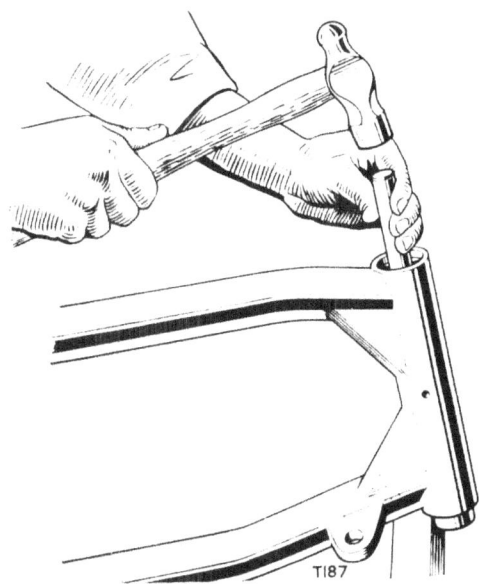

Fig. E9. Removing a swinging fork bush

SECTION E11

REMOVING AND REPLACING THE REAR FRAME

Remove the left and right side panels (Section E2), disconnect and remove both the battery and the battery carrier (Section E4). Lift the twin seat, disconnect the check wire at the seat pan, and remove two bolts and spring washers holding the front hinge to the twin seat pan. Slide the seat complete with rear hinge plate off the rear frame hinge pin. Disconnect the silencer stay bottom nuts and bolts, and the nuts and bolts securing the silencers to the pillion footrest support brackets. Slacken the exhaust pipe to exhaust manifold pinch bolts, and withdraw the exhaust system.

Remove the two nuts and bolts holding each horn to the frame, and disconnect the terminals.

Disconnect the "Lucar" connectors at the horn relay, condenser pack and three coils (see Fig. E10) Remove the nuts, bolts and plain washers which secure the coil mounting plate, and note that distance pieces are fitted beneath the plate. Withdraw the plate complete with the electrical components.

Remove the oil tank (Section E3).

Remove the rear wheel (Section F2).

Remove the rear suspension (Section E7).

Remove the rear chain guard and swinging arm (Section E9).

Remove the rear mudguard (Section E5).

Remove two short bolts, two long bolts, and the large central bolt from the left engine plate and a large central nut from the right engine plate, and disconnect the stop lamp switch wires. Withdraw both engine mounting plates complete with footrests.

Ensuring that the machine is supported securely on the centre stand, remove two bolts and two nuts and bolts holding the bottom of the rear frame to the front frame, and lastly remove the top stud and nuts (located just to the rear of the petrol tank) at which point the rear frame is free to be withdrawn. This is best achieved by lifting it vertically upwards over the swinging fork.

Replacement is the reversal of the afore-going, but refer to Fig. E10 when re-connecting the electrical units.

B = Black
W = White
R = Red
G = Green
Y = Yellow
N = Brown
U = Blue

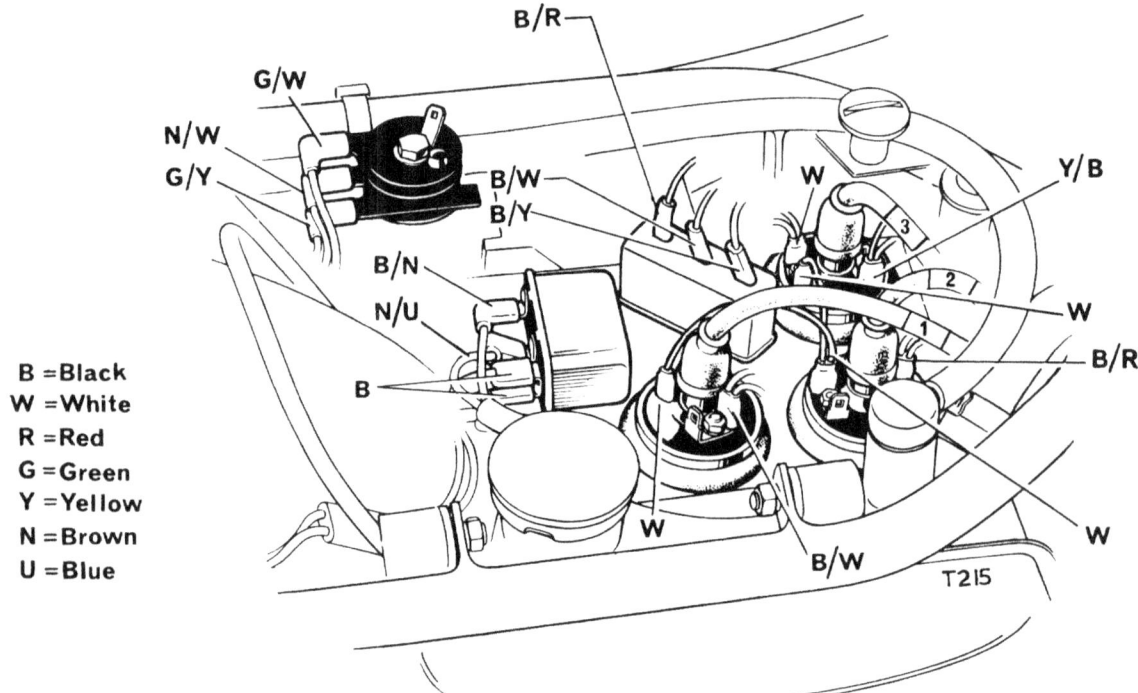

Fig. E10. Electrical connections underneath the twin seat

SECTION E12
FRAME ALIGNMENT

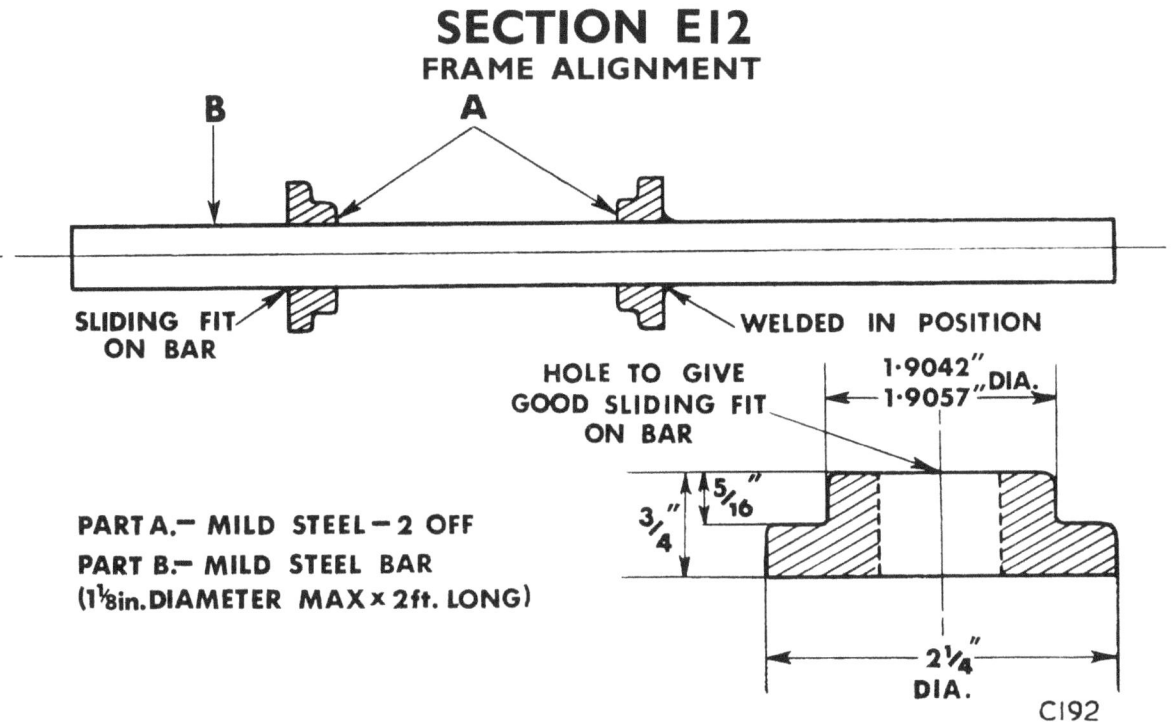

Fig. E11. Sketch of frame checking fixture

If the machine has been damaged in an accident the frame portions must be checked for correct alignment. In the following paragraph details are given of alignment checking for all parts of the frame (excepting the telescopic fork which is dealt with in Section G).

Basic requirements for alignment checking are a engineer's checking table (surface area approximately 3 feet × 5 feet), adjustable height gauge (Vernier type preferable) two suitable "V" blocks, several adjustable height pillars, a set-square and a suitable bar as shown in the sketch (Fig. E10).

FRONT FRAME

It is essential that after setting, or checking the front frame lug centre line is in a plane perpendicular to the plane of the swinging fork pivot lug centre line. It is also essential, that the remaining tubes and lugs are in their relative positions within the stated limits of accuracy.

The method of checking the front frame is that of securely fitting an adaptor spindle of the type shown in Fig. E11 to the head lug. It is then required to support the spindle and head lug on a plane parallel to, and approx. 6 ins. (15 cm.) from, the checking table surface. For this purpose two "V" blocks, packing pieces and two suitable "G" clamps will be required. At the other end of the frame (swinging fork and rear frame removed) an adjustable pillar should be placed under the down tube adjacent to the swinging fork pivot lug (see Fig. E12). The height of the pillar can be determined by measuring the diameter of the tube which is to rest on it, halving the diameter and then subtracting it from the dimension between the head lug centre line and table surface.

The frame centre line should now lie parallel to the checking table surface if the frame alignment is correct.

To verify this take height readings on the front down tube, top tube and rear down tube. See Figs. E12 and E13. Permissible maximum variation is $\frac{1}{32}$ in. (0·75 mm.).

Fit the swinging fork pivot spindle with the two outer sleeves and distance tube attached and check the pivot lug for squareness using a set square at the two location points as shown in Figs. E12 and E13.

Then, using a set square, check that the bottom tubes are aligned by bringing the set square to bear on them at the front and rear.

Using a steel rule or suitable instrument measure the hole centres and compare the figures obtained with those given in Fig. E14.

FRAME

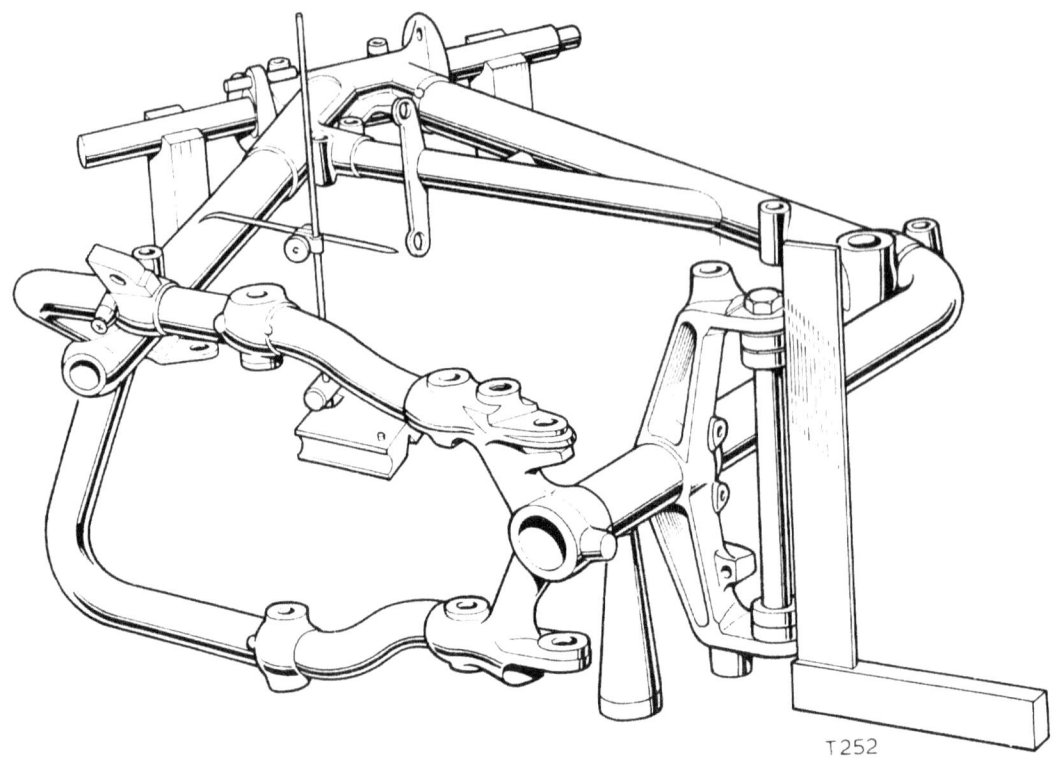

Fig. E12. Checking the front frame alignment

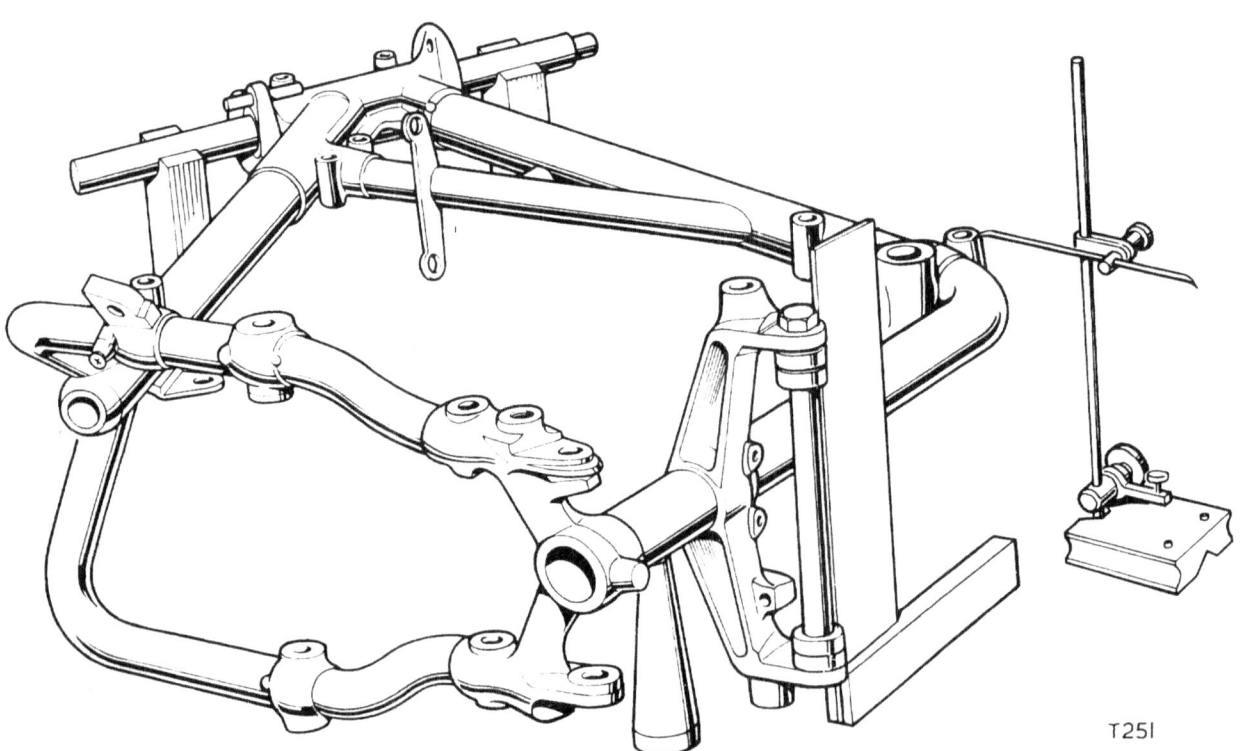

Fig. E13. Checking the front frame alignment

FRAME E

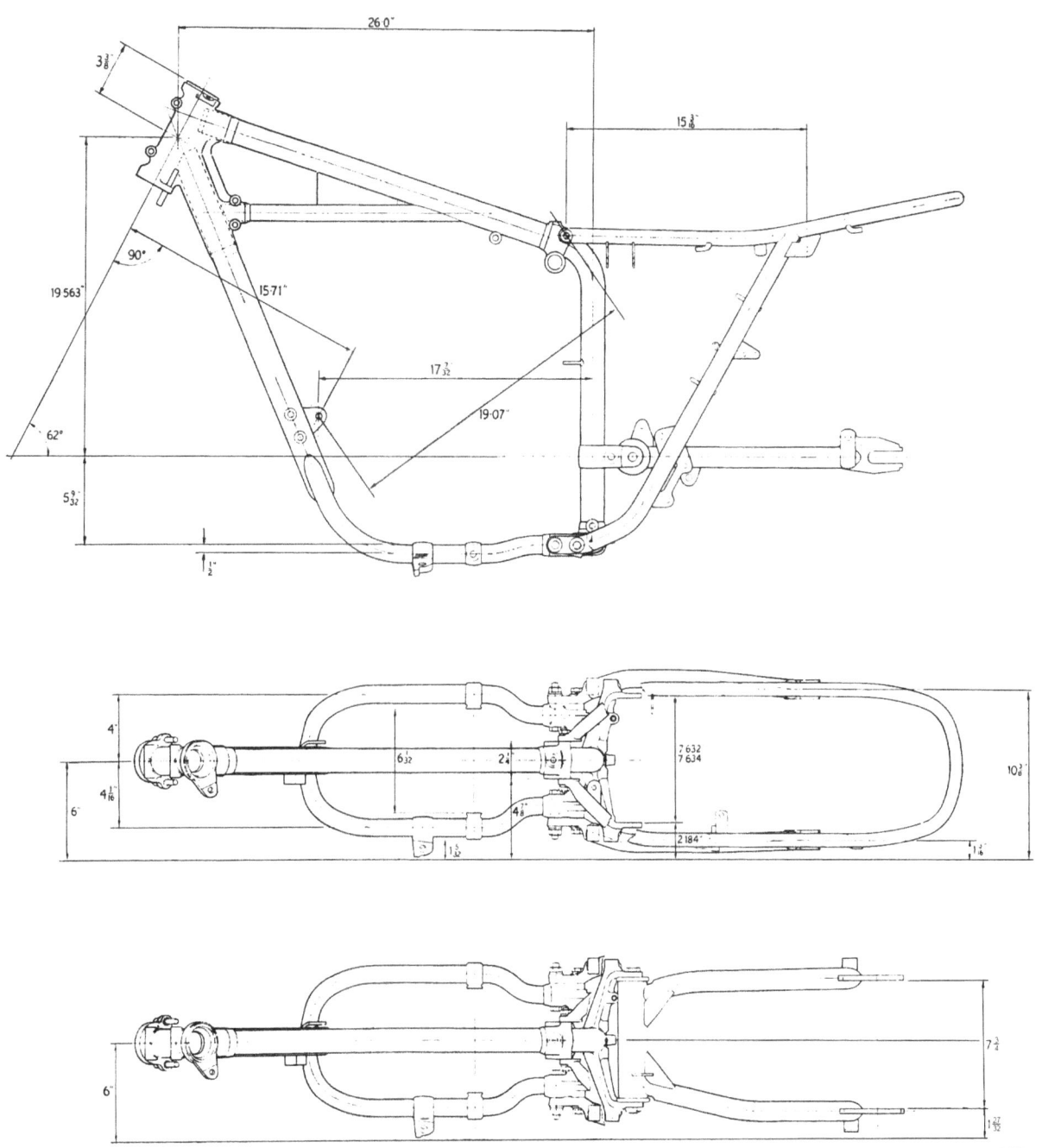

Fig. E13. Basic dimension of the frame assembly

REAR FRAME

The rear frame basically serves to mount the rear suspension units and twinseat etc., and it is only alignment between the top suspension unit support brackets with those on the swinging fork that is of most importance. The best means of checking rear frame alignment is that of fitting it to the front frame and taking readings as indicated in the following paragraph.

FRAME ASSEMBLY

Securely bolt the rear frame to the front frame and fit the swinging fork so that it can just be rotated by slight hand pressure. Mount the complete assembly horizontally on the checking table as described above, then take height readings at the swinging fork ends and top and bottom suspension unit mounting brackets, referring to Fig. E13 for dimensions. These brackets should not be more

E13

FRAME

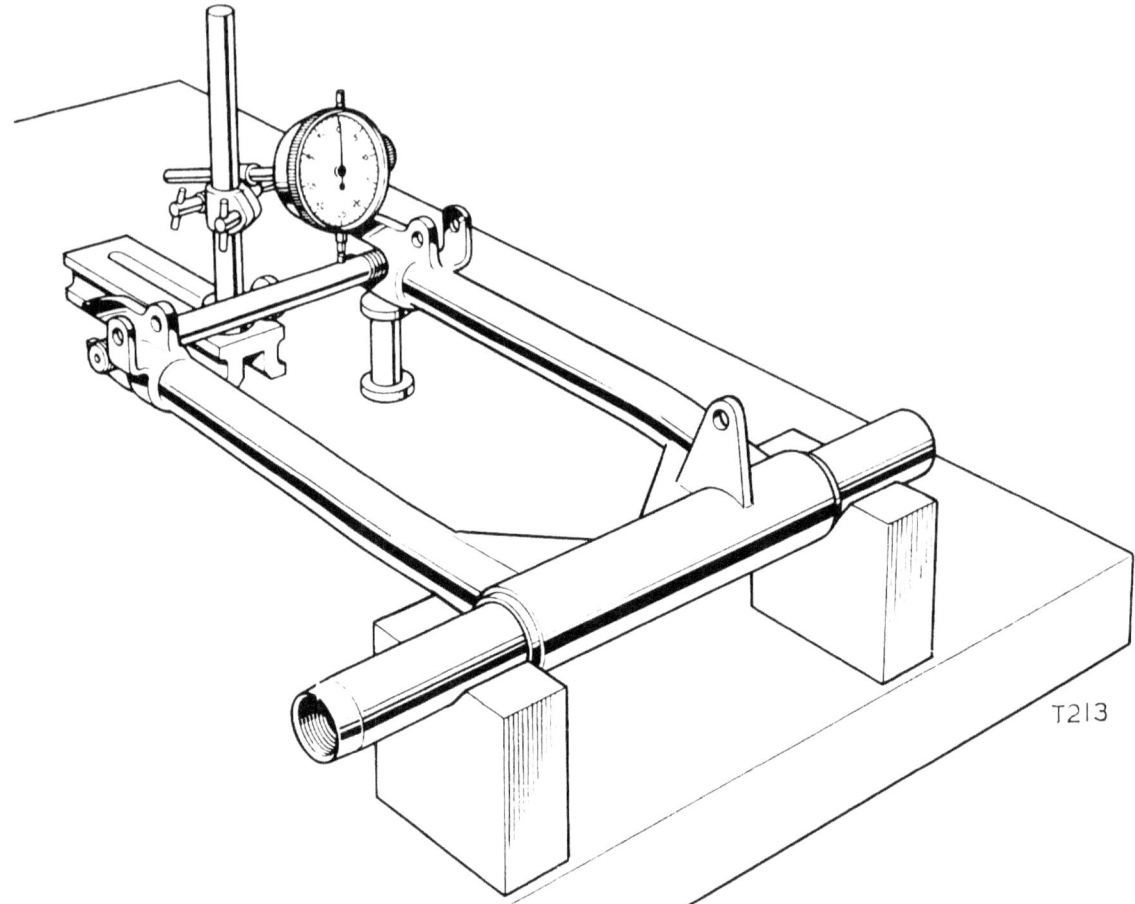

Fig. E14. Checking the swinging fork

than $\frac{1}{16}$ in. (1·5 mm.), out of line otherwise the suspension units will be working under excessive stress.

If, when frame alignment is completed, the amount of discrepancy is excessive and rectification is needed, then it is advisable to return the damaged part to the Service Department of Triumph Engineering Company. However, in the case of the swinging fork where the misalignment is not more than $\frac{1}{4}$ in. (6 mm.), measured at the tips of the fork ends, it may be possible to rectify this by the following means.

SWING FORK

It is required to check that the centre line of the pivot spindle is in the same plane as the centre line of the rear spindle. To do this, first place a tube or bar of suitable diameter into the swinging fork bearing bushes, then mount the swinging fork on two "V" blocks, one either side, and clamp it lightly to the edge of the checking tabel. Fit the rear wheel spindle into the fork end slots or, alternatively, use a straight bar of similar diameter, then support a fork end so that the swinging fork is approximately horizontal. Height readings should then be taken at both ends of the wheel spindle to establish any mis-alignment. (Fig. E14).

Next, check that the distance between the fork ends is as given in "General Data".

It is now necessary to lever the fork ends in the correcting direction until the wheel spindle can be inserted and found to be parallel with the pivot bush centre line. To do this, a bar of 4 ft. length by $1\frac{1}{4}$ in. diameter is required. It is now that great care is required. Insert the bar at the end of the swinging fork adjacent to the suspension unit mounting brackets so that it is over the "high" fork leg and under the "low" fork leg. Exert gentle pressure at the end of the bar then insert the spindle and re-check the alignment. Repeat this procedure using increased loads until the spindle height readings shows that the swinging arm is now misaligned in the opposite sense. A small leverage now applied from the other side will bring the wheel back to parallel.

Note: Apply the leverage bar as near as possible to the suspension unit brackets, otherwise the tubes may become damaged. DO NOT USE THE FORK ENDS.

FRAME

SECTION E13

FAIRING ATTACHMENT LUGS AND STEERING LOCK

FAIRING ATTACHMENT LUGS

The two lugs shown in Fig. E16 are fitted to facilitate mounting a fairing after the headlamp has been removed.

STEERING LOCK

A barrel type steering lock is fitted into the fork top lug. If for any reason the lock is to be removed, a grub screw (see Fig. E17) must be removed, and the lock can be lifted clear. Note, however, that a blanking slug is fitted into the lug over the grub screw and this will have to be prised out to gain access to the screw. The slug is of lead, hammered into the screw hole and should be renewed after re-fitting the lock.

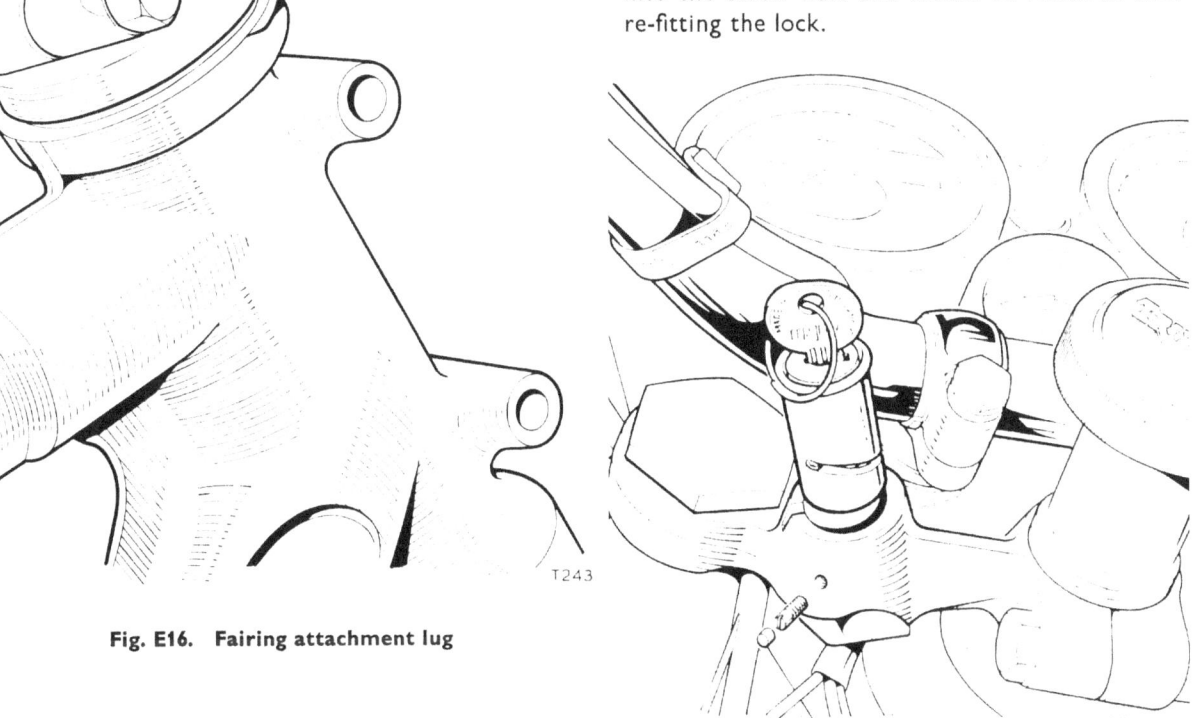

Fig. E16. Fairing attachment lug

Fig. E17. Steering lock

SECTION E14

FITTING REPLACEMENT SEAT COVERS

'Quiltop' twinseats have a cover retained by sprags which are part of the seat pan.

When fitting a replacement seat cover it is **very important** to first soak the complete cover assembly in hot water in order to soften the plastic so that it can easily be stretched into place. After soaking the cover in hot water, wring out the excess water and you will find that the cover can very easily be stretched into place to give a neat fit without any wrinkles. This job is very difficult if you do not follow this suggested method.

Ideally the seat should be allowed to dry out in a warm place before being put back into service.

SECTION E15

REPAIRS

Repairs covered in this section are simple operations requiring only a minimum of special tools. The type of repairs possible with these tools are those such as small dents to mudguards, caused by flying stones or slight grooves which have not affected a large area or torn the metal. The tools required are shown below in Fig. E18.

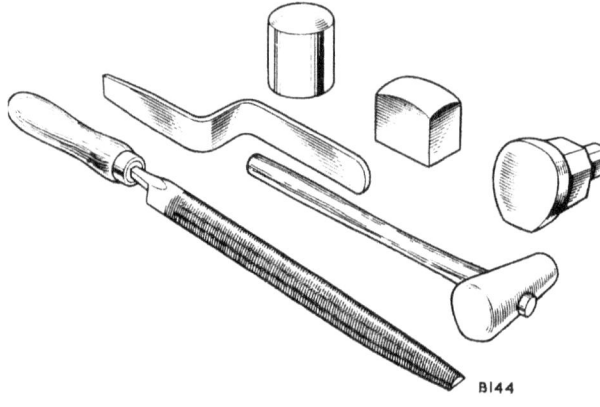

Fig. E18. Tools used for panel repairs

REMOVAL OF DENTS

To remove small dents a spoon and suitably shaped dolly block are required. A suitable spoon can be made from a file by removing the teeth and polishing the surface then cranking it as shown in Fig. E19.

Place the dolly block underneath the panel then hammer the dent(s) carefully with the spoon until something like the original contour is achieved. Lightly file the surface to show any high spots there may be and use the dolly and spoon to remove them.

Note.—Do not file more than is necessary to show up the high spots. Care should be taken to keep filing to a minimum otherwise serious thinning of the metal will occur.

Where denting has occured without resultant damage to the paint-work the dent(s) may be removed whilst the paintwork is preserved by careful use of a polished spoon and dolly block. Dents which are comparatively larger may be removed whilst the paintwork is preserved by placing a "sandbag" against the outer surface and hammering the inside of the panel with a suitably shaped wooden mallet. A "sandbag" can be made from a piece of 18 in. square leather by folding it and packing it tightly with sand. Finally, finish off using a suitable dolly block and polished spoon as required.

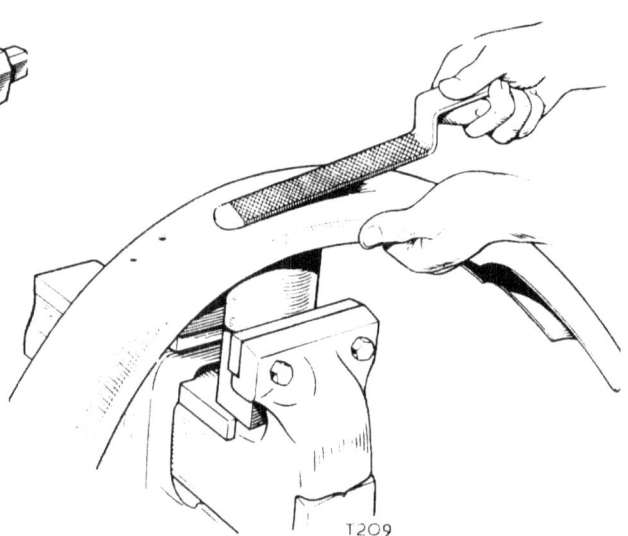

Fig. E19. Removing a dent with a dolly block and spoon

Note.—It is not advisable to use a hammer as hammer-blows tend to stretch the surrounding metal, giving rise to further complications. Also, unless the aim is true, damage of a more serious nature may result.

Where a fuel tank has become damaged the repair work should only be entrusted to a competent panel beater, or preferably, return the tank to the Service Department—Triumph Engineering Company Ltd.

SECTION E16

PAINTWORK REFINISHING

PAINT STRIPPING

Except in cases where a "touch-up" is to be attempted, it is strongly recommended that the old finish is completely stripped and the refinish is carried out from the bare metal. A suitable paint stripper can be obtained from most paint stores and accessory dealers.

The stripper should be applied with a brush and allowed approximately 10 minutes to react. A suitable scraper should be used to remove the old finish, then the surface cleaned with water using a piece of wire wool. Ensure that all traces of paint stripper are removed. If possible, blow out crevices with compressed air.

It is advisable to strip a small area at a time to avoid the stripper drying and also to enable easier neutralizing of the stripper.

Finally, the surface should be rubbed with a grade 270 or 280 emery cloth to give a satisfactory finish then washed off with white spirits or a suitable cleaner solvent.

PRIMING

A thin coat of cellulose primer must be sprayed onto the surface prior to application of an undercoat or stopper. Undercoat and stopper will not adhere satisfactorily to bare metal. It is advisable to thin the primer by adding 1 part cellulose thinners to 1 part primer. Ensure that the primer is dry before advancing further.

APPLYING STOPPER

Imperfections and slight dents in the surface may be filled with stopper, but rubbing down with "wet and dry" should not be attempted until the undercoat or surfacer has been applied.

Apply the stopper with a glazing knife in thin layers, allowing approximately 20 minutes for drying between each layer. After the last layer, allow the stopper about 6 hours (or over-night if possible) to dry. Heavy layers or insufficient drying time will result in risk of surface cracking.

UNDERCOAT (SURFACER)

Most cellulose undercoats also called surfacers, will suffice for a base for TRIUMPH finishes. About two or three coats are required and should be sprayed on in a thinned condition using 1 part cellulose thinners to 1 part undercoat. Allow approximately 20 minutes between each coat.

If stopper has been applied the final layer of undercoat should be sprayed on after smoothing the surface with "wet and dry" abrasive as shown below.

WET AND DRY SANDING

After application of the undercoat, the surface should be rubbed down with 270 or 280 grade abrasive paper used wet. An ideal method is to have a rubber block approximately 3 in. x 2 in. x 1 in. around which to wrap the emery paper. However, this is only recommendable for flat surfaces; where rapid change of sections occur, a thin felt pad is more useful.

The abrasive paper should be allowed to soak in cold water for at least 15 minutes before use. A useful tip is to smear the abrasive surface of the paper with soap prior to rubbing down. This will prevent clogging and should at least treble the useful life of the paper if it is washed thoroughly after each rub-down.

When the surface is smooth enough, wash it thoroughly with water and dry off with a clean sponge.

If smoother surface than this is required it can be given another layer of undercoat and then the rubbing down procedure repeated using 320 or 400 grade of paper depending upon conditions.

FINISHING

Before spraying on the finishing coats the surface must be quite smooth, dry and clean. It is important that conditions are right when finish spraying is to be carried out otherwise complications may occur. Best conditions for outdoor spraying are those on a dry sunny day without wind. Moisture in the atmosphere is detrimental to paint spraying.

FRAME

The first coat should be thinned in the ratio of 50% cellulose thinners to 50% lacquer. Subsequent coats should have a higher proportion of thinners as shown below.

	Cellulose Thinners	Lacquer
1st Coat	50%	50%
2nd Coat	60%	40%
3rd Coat	70%	30%
4th Coat	80%	20%

Between each coat the surface may be flatted by hand with 320 or 400 abrasive paper as required.

Allow at least 10 minutes between each coat and after the final coat leave overnight or 24 hours if possible. For most purposes the 2nd coat of finishing is more than adequate.

POLISHING

The final colour coat must be completely dry before cutting and polishing. Using a clean rag rub down with brass polish or fine cutting paste and burnish to a high gloss using a clean mop before applying a suitable wax polish for protection and shine.

Note.—TRIUMPH supply only the finishing lacquers. These are available in $\frac{1}{4}$ pint tins and aerosol sprays or, for workshop use, 1 gallon tins.

METALLIC FINISHES

Metallic finishes can be applied equally as well to either a white or brown primer, and no base colour is needed. These finishes are as follows:—

Finish	(Ser. Ref.)
Aquamarine	AQU.

SECTION F

WHEELS, BRAKES AND TYRES
2LS
DRUM BRAKES

DESCRIPTION	Section
REMOVING AND REFITTING THE FRONT WHEEL	F1
REMOVING AND REFITTING THE REAR WHEEL	F2
FRONT AND REAR WHEEL ALIGNMENT	F3
BRAKE ADJUSTMENTS	F4
STRIPPING AND REASSEMBLING THE BRAKES	F5
RENEWING BRAKE LININGS	F6
REMOVING AND REFITTING THE WHEEL BEARINGS	F7

WHEELS, BRAKES AND TYRES

SECTION F1
REMOVING AND REFITTING THE FRONT WHEEL

Place the machine with the front wheel approximately six inches off the ground. First, unscrew the handlebar front brake adjuster then disconnect the cable at the actuating lever on the brake plate by removing the spring pin.

To release the cable from the anchor plate it is necessary to remove the split pin at the cable abutment. Unscrew the two wheel spindle cap bolts from the base of each fork leg and remove the wheel.

Refitting the wheel is the reversal of the above instructions but care should be taken to ensure that the anchor plate locates correctly over the peg on the inside of the right fork leg. Tighten the spindle cap bolts evenly a turn at a time, on the left leg firstly, and before tightening the bolts on the right, bounce the fork to correctly align each leg with the spindle.

SECTION F2
REMOVING AND REFITTING THE REAR WHEEL

First unscrew the rear brake adjuster, then disconnect the rear chain. Slacken the bolt at the rear of the chainguard so that the chainguard can be swung upwards. Remove the nut securing the rear brake torque stay to the anchor plate, then slacken the left and right wheel spindle securing nuts. The speedometer cable must be disconnected. The rear wheel is now free to be removed.

To refit the rear wheel first ensure that the spindle nuts are sufficiently unscrewed then offer the wheel to the swinging fork.

Locate the adjuster caps over the fork ends then lightly tighten the wheel spindle nuts. Place the chain around the rear wheel sprocket and connect up the brake anchor plate torque stay. Refitting the chain may necessitate slackening off both the left and right adjusters. It is now necessary to ensure that the front and rear wheels are aligned. This is shown in Section F3 below. Finally, lock up the two spindle nuts, ensure the torque stay securing nut is tight, and reconnect the speedometer cable.

SECTION F3
FRONT AND REAR WHEEL ALIGNMENT

When the rear wheel has been fitted into the frame it should be aligned correctly by using two straight edges or "battens", about 7 feet long. With the machine off the stand the battens should be placed along-side the wheel, one either side of the machine and each about four inches from the ground. When both are touching the rear tyre on both sides of the wheel the front wheel should be midway between and parallel to both battens. Turn the front wheel slightly until this can be seen. Any necessary adjustments must be made by first slackening the rear wheel spindle nuts, then turning the spindle adjuster nuts as required ensuring that rear chain adjustment is maintained. Refer to Fig. F1 for illustration of correct alignment. Note that the arrows indicate the adjustment required.

WHEELS, BRAKES AND TYRES

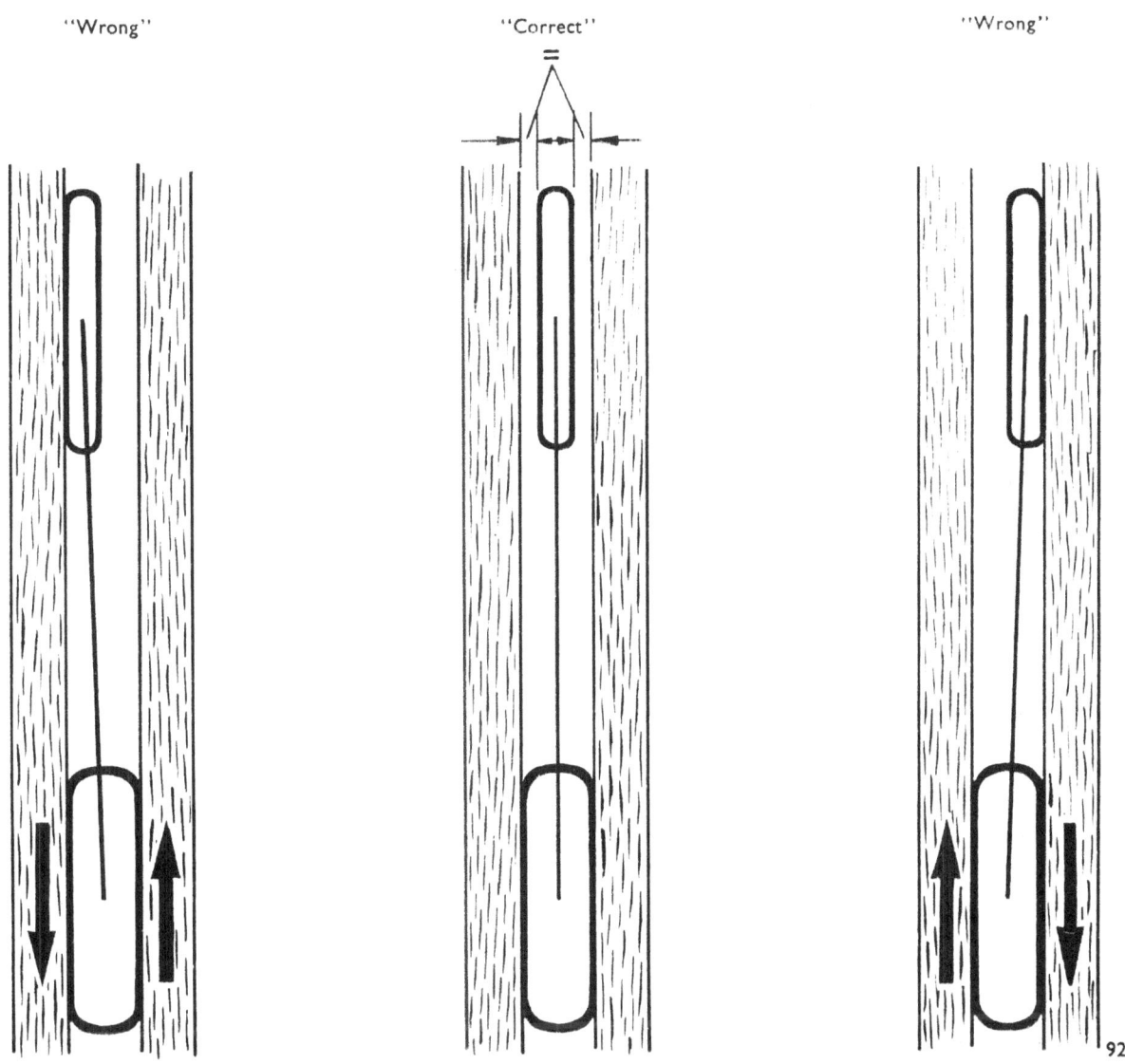

Fig. F1. Aligning the front and rear wheels

SECTION F4
BRAKE ADJUSTMENTS

The front brake being of the two leading shoe variety has the length of the lever adjusting rod pre set during assembly or reset after the brake shoes have been replaced (see Section F5). The shoes are however self centreing on the abutments and are equipped with steel end caps for this purpose. Cable adjustment is by means of the knurled adjuster at the handlebar lever. Turn the knurled nut anti-clockwise to take up the slack in the control cable. The correct adjustment is with not less than $\frac{1}{16}$ in. (1·5 mm.) and not more than $\frac{1}{8}$ in. (3 mm.) slack in the inner cable, at the handlebar lever.

Any wear on the brake shoe lining is indicated by the angular position of the brake operating lever when the brake is fully applied. Fig. F2 illustrates the limiting position before wear is obviously excessive. This applies to both front and rear brake operating levers. In this case the brake should be dismantled and worn parts renewed as shown in Section F5.

The adjustment of the front brake operating mechanism is by means of a knurled adjuster nut incorporated in the handlebar abutment. Turn the nut anti-clockwise to take up the slack in the control cable. The correct adjustment is with not less than $\frac{1}{16}$ in. (1·5 mm.) and not more than $\frac{1}{8}$ in. (3 mm.) slack in the inner cable at the handlebar lever.

The rear brake pedal is adjustable for position and any adjustment for the pedal position to suit the rider should be made before adjusting the free movement. From the static position before the brake is applied there should be about $\frac{1}{2}$ in. (1·2 cm.) of free movement before the brake starts to operate. The actual adjustment is by means of a finger operated nut on the rear end of the brake operated rod. Turn the nut clockwise to reduce the clearance.

Fig. F2. Rear brake operating lever

SECTION F5
STRIPPING AND REASSEMBLING THE BRAKES

FRONT BRAKE—TWO LEADING SHOE

Access to the front brake shoes is gained by removing the wheel (see Section F1). The brake plate is retained by a centre nut. This is recessed into the anchor plate and will require the use of 61-6062 box spanner. The brake plate assembly will then lift away complete. Holding the brake plate with one hand lift up one shoe as in Fig. F3 until it is free. Disconnect one end of each brake return spring and lift away the second shoe. Release the spring clip from the pivot pin at each end of the lever adjustment rod and lift the pivot pins clear. Remove the brake cam nuts and washers and remove the return spring from the front cam. Finally prise off the levers in turn and the brake cams are free to be removed from the back of the anchor plate.

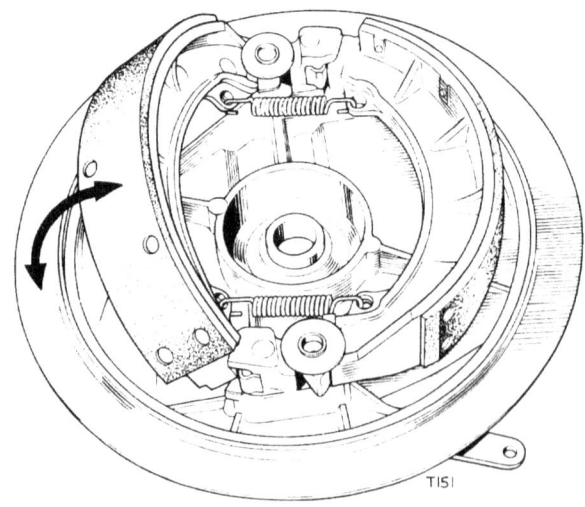

Fig. F3. Removing and replacing shoe on 2LS brake

WHEELS, BRAKES AND TYRES

To reassemble the brake shoes to the front anchor plate first grease the spindles lightly and refit both cams, wedge shape outboard on both. Refit the outside return spring to the front cam and then refit both brake cam levers (at a similar angle) and secure with the plain washers and nuts. Fit the abutment plates to the anchor plate, tag side towards the anchor plate.

Link the two shoes together with the return springs (the narrow end of the shoe abuts to the cam in each case). Both shoes fit with the radiused end to the pivot. Fit the first shoe to both the cam and abutment pad then stretch the springs by grasping the second shoe and fitting it as shown in Fig. F4.

Fig. F5. Showing adjustment of cam lever rod

The complete brake plate is now ready for fitting to the wheel. Replace the anchor plate over the wheel spindle and lock it home with the spindle nut, using spanner 61-6062.

At this stage it may be necessary to adjust the cam lever rod assembly. To do so the rod adjuster nut should be slackened (see Fig. F5) and the rear pivot pin removed. The help of a second operator will be needed at this stage. Each cam lever should be applied until the shoes are in contact with the drum. The easiest method is by fitting a spanner to each cam nut.

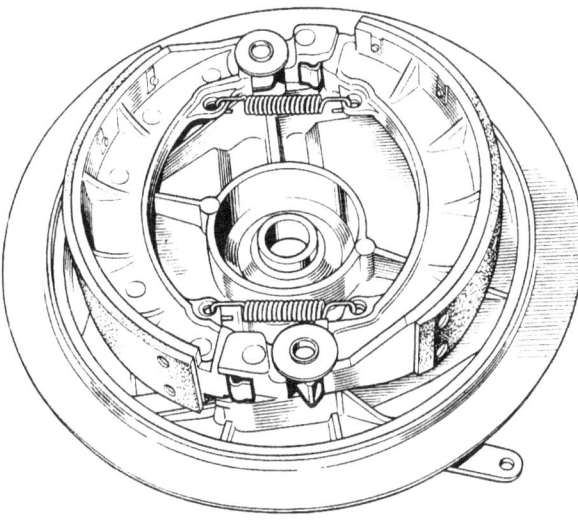

Fig. F4. Brake assembled showing position of shoes

The threaded fork end should be adjusted to accommodate the revised distance between the brake cam levers. The rod assembly should then be refitted, and the locknut retightened. Reconnect the brake cable and adjust as described in Section F4.

WHEELS, BRAKES AND TYRES

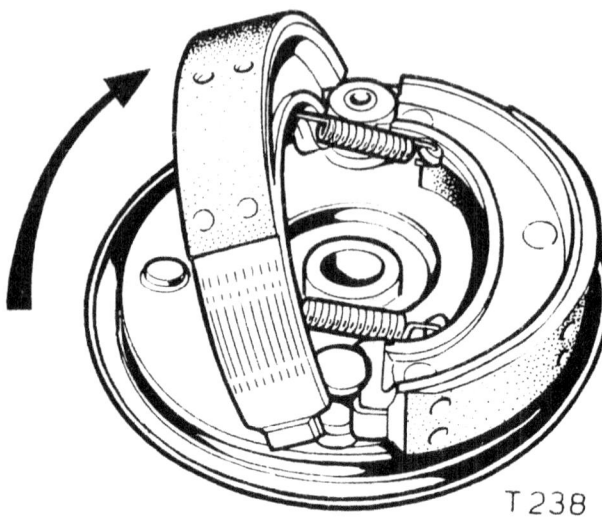

Fig. F6. Removing shoes from rear brakes

REAR BRAKE

Access to the brake shoes is obtained by removing the wheel and unscrewing the central nut which retains the brake anchor plate. If the brake operating lever is then turned to relieve the pressure of the shoes against the drum, the complete brake plate assembly can be withdrawn from the spindle. Slowly release the lever and continue until the return spring can be removed, then take off the brake shoes by the method shown in Fig. F6. Remove the nut and washer securing the brake lever to the cam spindle and remove the lever. The cam spindle can then easily be withdrawn from the plate.

INSPECTION PROCEDURE

(1) Examine the anchor plate for cracks or distortion, particularly in the brake cam housing.

(2) Clean out the grease in the brake cam spindle and remove any rust with a fine emery cloth.

(3) Inspect the return springs for signs of fatigue and distortion. Renew them if necessary.

(4) Examine the brake drum for scoring or ovality. In the case of the rear wheel if the drum requires skimming it should be removed from the wheel. Do not skim more than ·010 in. from the drum. If the diameter exceeds more than that given in "General Data" by more than ·010 in. the drum should be renewed.

In the case of the front wheel drum, scoring or signs of ovality can be removed by similar procedure but a large swing lathe of 18 in. diameter is required.

(5) Examine the brake shoes. The brake linings should be replaced immediately the rivets show signs of having worn level with the linings face, or the linings show signs of cracks or uneven wear. Replacement is described fully in Section F6. Also check that the brake shoes are not cracked or distorted in any way.

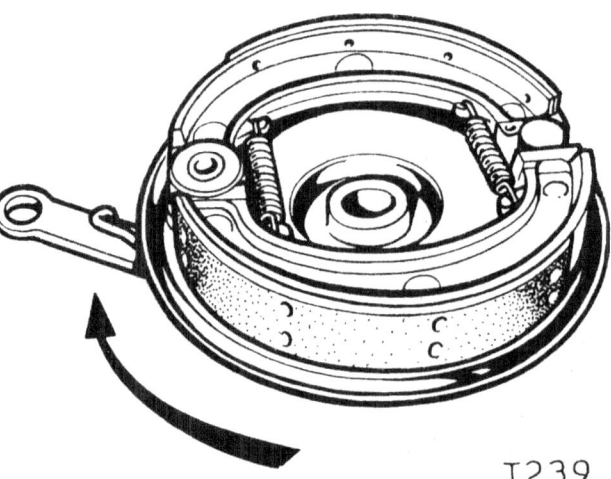

Fig. F7. Correct assembly of shoes onto rear brake plate

WHEELS, BRAKES AND TYRES

To reassemble the brake shoes to the anchor plate first place the two brake shoes on the bench in their relative positions. Fit the return springs to the retaining hooks, hooked ends uppermost, then taking a shoe in each hand (see Fig. F6) and at the same time holding the springs in tension, position the shoes as shown over the cam and fulcrum pin and snap down into position by pressing on the outer edges of the shoes. Rotate the brake lever in an anti-clockwise direction and engage the return spring.

Note.—When replacing the brake shoes, note that the leading and trailing brake shoes are not interchangeable in either the front or rear brake and ensure that they are in their correct relative positions as shown in Fig. F7.

Reassembly then continues by placing the anchor plate over the wheel spindle and locking home with the spindle nut. Refer to Section F4 for final re-alignment of the wheels if this is found to be necessary.

SECTION F6
RENEWING THE BRAKE LININGS

The old linings can be removed by either drilling through the rivets with a suitable sized drill (No. 23 ·154 in. dia.) or chiselling the lining off at the same time shearing through the brass rivet. Drilling is of course preferred and is best undertaken from the inside of the shoe to remove the peened over portion of the rivet.

New linings are supplied ready drilled, counter bored and the correct shape. If no jig is available for riveting, a simple method of spreading the rivet is shown in Fig. F8.

Rivet the linings in the centre holes first, working towards each end: great care must be taken to ensure that the rivets are tight and that the linings do not lift between the rivets. After fitting, all sharp edges of the lining should be chamfered and the leading and trailing edges tapered off to the extent of $\frac{1}{8}$ in. deep x $\frac{1}{2}$ in. long.

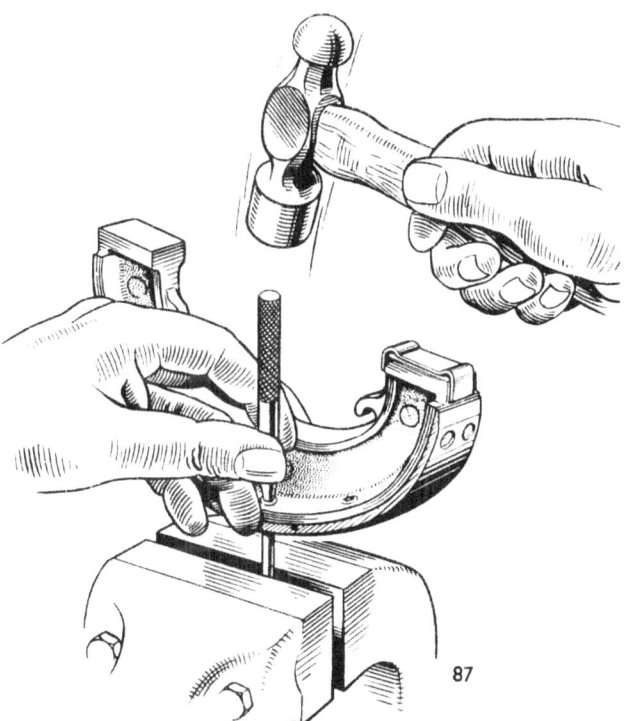

Fig. F8. Riveting lining onto brake shoe

SECTION F7
REMOVING AND REFITTING THE WHEEL BEARINGS

Access to the wheel bearings differs in front and rear wheels and therefore each wheel is dealt with separately in this section.

FRONT WHEEL

Remove the front wheel from the fork and withdraw the brake anchor plate from the brake drum. Unscrew the retainer ring (left hand thread) using service tool 61-3694

The right bearing can be removed by using the spindle and driving through from the left hand side. Withdraw the backing ring and inner retaining disc (note that current wheels use a single part replacing these two). To remove the left bearing, spring out the circlip and insert the spindle from the right side driving the bearing out complete with inner and outer grease retainer plates.

Fully clean all parts in paraffin (kerosene). Clean and dry the bearings thoroughly. Compressed air should be used for drying out the ball races. Test for end float and inspect the balls and races for any signs of pitting. If there is any doubt about their condition, the bearings should be renewed.

To refit the bearings, first insert the left inner grease retainer, bearing, and outer dust cap using a liberal amount of grease (see Section A2). Refit the spring circlip and insert the shouldered end of the wheel spindle from the right, using it as a drift to drive the bearing and grease retainer until they come up to the circlip. Re-insert the spindle the opposite way round and re-fit the right hand grease retainer disc and backing ring. Drive the right bearing into position well smeared with grease, then screw in the retainer ring (left hand thread) until tight.

Finally, tap the spindle from the left to bring the spindle shoulder up against the right bearing. Refer to Fig. F9 for correct layout. Reassembly then continues as the reversal of the above instructions.

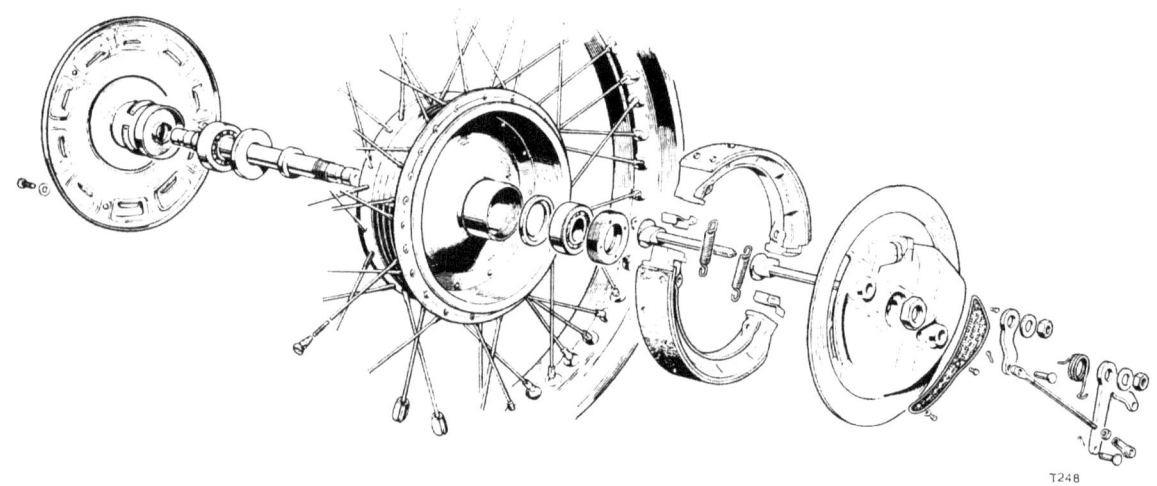

Fig. F9. 2LS wheel arrangement

REAR WHEEL

Remove the rear wheel then unscrew the anchor plate retainer nut and withdraw the brake anchor plate assembly. Withdraw the wheel spindle then unscrew the slotted screw which serves to lock the bearing retainer ring. The retainer ring can then be unscrewed using service tool 61-3694. So that the left bearing can be removed the central distance piece must be displaced to one side to allow a drift to be located on the inner ring of the left bearing. To do this, first insert a drift from the left and move the distance piece to one side so that the grease retainer shim collapses. A soft metal drift should then be inserted from the right and the left bearing driven out. The speedometer drive adaptor must first be unscrewed from the hub before removing the right hand wheel bearing. When this is done, withdraw the backing ring, damaged grease retainer

WHEELS, BRAKES AND TYRES

and distance piece then drive out the right bearing and dust cap using a drift of approximately $1\frac{5}{8}$ in. diameter.

Fully clean all parts in paraffin (kerosene) and clean and dry the bearing thoroughly. Compressed air should be used for drying out if possible. Test the end float and inspect the ball races for any signs of indentation or pitting. If the condition of the bearing is in doubt it should be renewed.

The damaged grease retainer shim usually can be reclaimed for further service by carefully hammering it flat to restore its original shape.

To refit the bearings first drive in the right inner grease retainer disc, the bearing and then press on the outer dust cap ensuring that the bearing and both cavities are well filled with grease. From the left, insert the distance piece, grease retainer shim, backing ring and having packed the bearing with grease, press it in the hub and bring the distance piece into line with the spindle. Screw in the retainer ring and tighten it with service tool 61-3694.

Finally, tighten the locking screw to ensure that the bearing retainer ring is locked in position. Reassembly then continues as a reversal to the above instructions, but do not forget to refit the outer distance piece before assembling the anchor plate and brake shoe assembly.

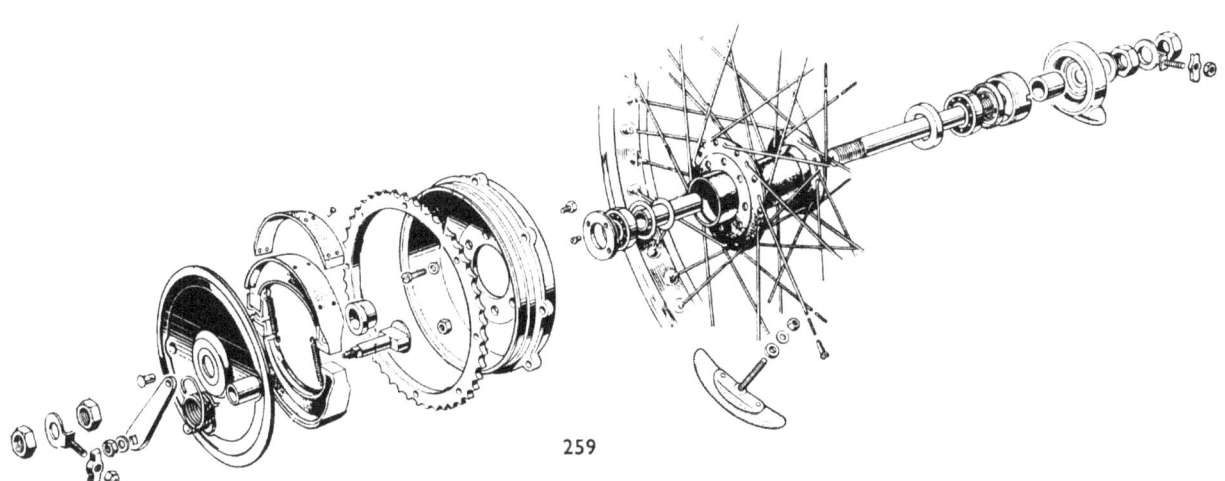

Fig. 10. Rear wheel arrangement

NOTES

SECTION F

WHEELS, BRAKES AND TYRES

DRUM BRAKES

DESCRIPTION	Section
REMOVING AND REFITTING FRONT WHEEL	F1
REMOVING AND REFITTING FRONT WHEEL BEARINGS	F2
STRIPPING AND REASSEMBLING THE FRONT BRAKE	F3
STRIPPING AND REASSEMBLING REAR BRAKE	F4
REAR WHEEL REMOVAL AND REPLACEMENT	F5
REMOVING AND REPLACING REAR WHEEL BEARINGS	F6
BRAKE ADJUSTMENT	F7
REMOVING AND REPLACING THE FRONT BRAKE CABLE	F8
RENEWING BRAKE LININGS (REAR BRAKE)	F9
WHEEL BALANCING	F10
FRONT AND REAR WHEEL ALIGNMENT	F11
WHEEL BUILDING	F12
REAR CHAIN ADJUSTMENT	F13
REMOVING AND REPAIRING TYRES	F14
SECURITY BOLTS	F15
TYRE MAINTENANCE	F16

SECTION F1
REMOVING AND REFITTING THE FRONT WHEEL

Place the machine with the front wheel approximately 6 inches off the ground. First slacken the handlebar front brake adjuster then disconnect the cable at the brake plate. See Section F3 for details. Loosen the anchor plate stud fixing nut and then unscrew the four wheel spindle cap nuts from the base of each fork leg and remove the wheel. When refitting the wheel it is important to note the following instructions otherwise the anchor plate will become distorted.

Place the front wheel assembly into the forks at the same time locating the anchor plate stud into the slot in the right hand fork leg.

Fit the spindle end caps and tighten all the nuts evenly until the cap is 'pinch' tight then slacken all of them half a turn. Pull the wheel to the right hand side of the machine until the anchor plate facing boss touches the mating lug on the fork leg. With the wheel in this position tighten the spindle clamp nuts evenly to the recommended torque figure. (15 lbs. ft.). Check that there is no gap between the anchor plate facing boss and the fork leg. Retighten the anchor plate stud nut. Finally reconnect the front brake cable and readjust.

SECTION F2
REMOVING AND REFITTING THE FRONT WHEEL BEARINGS

Remove the front wheel from the fork (see Section above). Remove the retaining nut and withdraw the front anchor plate from the brake drum. Unscrew the retainer ring (left hand thread) using service tool 61-3694.

The right bearing can be removed by using the spindle and driving through from the left side. Withdraw the inner grease retaining disc. To remove the left bearing, spring out the circlip and insert the spindle from the right side, driving the bearing out complete with inner and outer grease retainer plates.

Fully clean all parts in paraffin (kerosene). Clean and dry the bearings thoroughly. Compressed air should be used for drying out the ball races. Test for end float and inspect the balls and races for any signs of pitting. If there is any doubt about their condition, the bearings should be renewed.

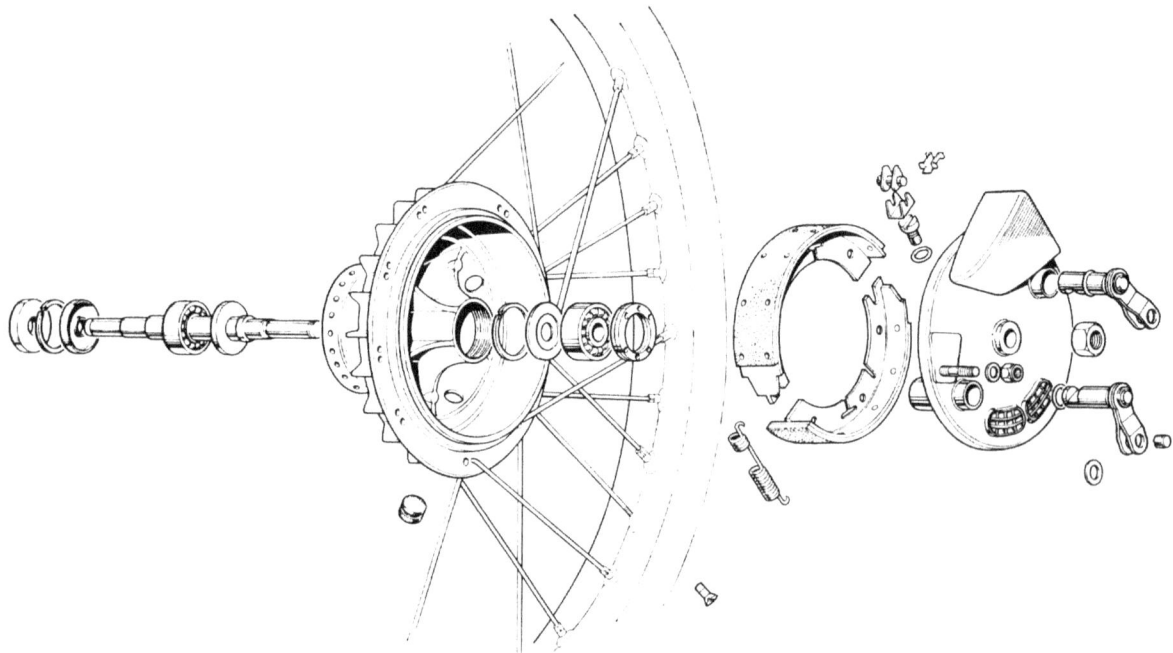

Fig. F1. Exploded view of front wheel bearing arrangement

WHEELS, BRAKES AND TYRES

To refit the bearings, first insert the left inner grease retainer, bearing and outer dust cap, using a liberal amount of grease (see Section A16). Refit the spring circlip and insert the shouldered end of the wheel spindle from the right, using it as a drift to drive the bearing and grease retainer until they come up to the circlip. Re-insert the spindle the opposite way round and refit the right hand grease retainer disc. Drive the right bearing into position well smeared with grease, then screw in the retainer ring (left hand thread) until tight.

Finally, tap the spindle from the left to bring the spindle shoulder up against the right bearing. Refer to Fig. F1 for correct layouts. Reassembly then continues as a reversal of the above instructions.

SECTION F3

STRIPPING AND REASSEMBLING THE FRONT BRAKE

Access to the front brake shoes is gained by removing the wheel (see Section F1). The brake plate is retained by a centre nut. Remove the centre nut and the brake plate assembly will then lift away complete. Pull the leading side of one shoe away from the snail cam and lift it over towards the other brake shoe.

Disconnect the springs and remove shoes. (See Fig. F2).

Remove the brake shoe actuating plungers from their housings on the brake plate. Note the "O"-ring on the tappets. Replace them if suspect. The cam and lever assembly can now be removed from the brake plate. The rubber "O"-ring on the spindle should also be replaced if necessary. Note the assembly of the snail cam adjuster and inspect for wear on the teeth.

INSPECTION PROCEDURE

(1) Examine the anchor plate for cracks or distortion, particularly in the brake cam housing.

(2) Clean out the grease in the brake cam spindle and remove any rust with a fine emery cloth.

(3) Inspect the return springs for signs of fatigue and distortion. Renew them if necessary.

(4) Examine the brake drum for scoring or ovality. In the case of the rear wheel if the drum requires skimming it should be removed from the wheel. Do not skim more than ·010 in. from the drum. If the diameter exceeds more than given in the GENERAL DATA by more than ·010 in. the drum should be renewed.

In the case of the front wheel drum, scoring or signs of ovality can be removed by similar procedure.

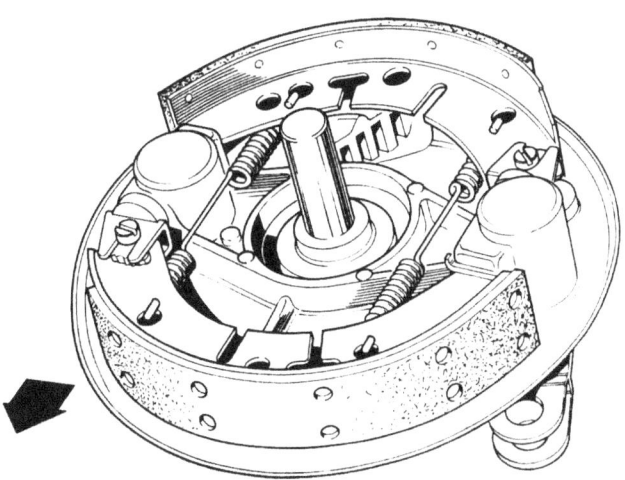

Fig. F2. Removing brake shoes

WHEELS, BRAKES AND TYRES

(5) Examine the brake shoes. The brake linings should be replaced immediately the rivets show signs of having worn level with the linings face, or the linings show signs of cracks or uneven wear. Also check that the brake shoes are not cracked or distorted in any way.

To reassemble the shoes, first grease the cam and the actuating plunger and then assemble them into the brake plate. Assemble the springs onto the brake shoes (as shown in Fig. F2) and holding the shoes apart rest them onto the brake plate with the snail cam adjusters in position. Then force the shoes apart and into their respective locations.

While replacing the shoes the anchor plate can be effectively supported by gripping a spindle of suitable size in a vice and placing the plate onto it (see Fig. F3).

The complete brake plate is now ready for fitting to the wheel. Replace the anchor plate over the wheel spindle and lock it home with the spindle nut.

Finally, refit the wheel and adjust the brake (see Sections F1 and F7).

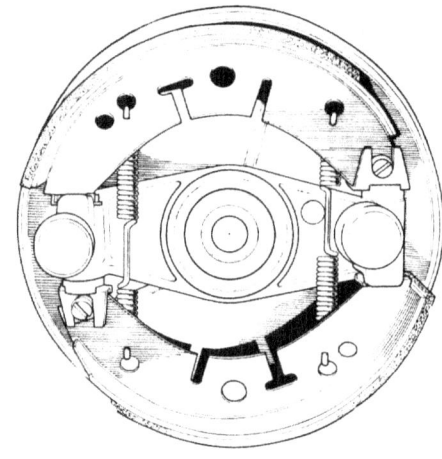

Fig. F3. 2LS brake assembled showing position of shoes

SECTION F4
STRIPPING AND REASSEMBLING THE REAR BRAKE

Access to the rear brake shoes is gained by removing the rear wheel (see Section F5).

Remove the brake shoes by lifting one brake shoe away from the brake plate until the return spring becomes disconnected. (See Fig. F4).

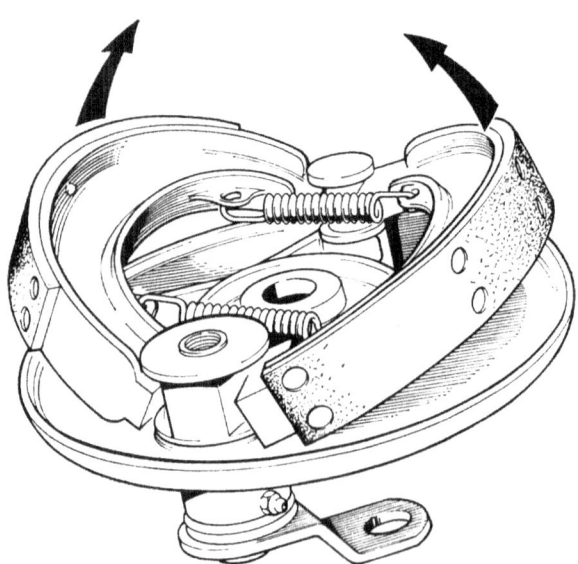

Fig. F4. Removing brake shoes

WHEELS, BRAKES AND TYRES

To re-assemble the brake shoes to the brake anchor plate first place the two brake shoes on the bench in their relative positions. Fit the return springs to the retaining hooks, then taking a shoe in each hand (see Fig. F5) and at the same time holding the springs in tension, position the shoes as shown over the cam and fulcrum pin and snap down into position by pressing on the outer edges of the shoes.

Note. When replacing the brake shoes, note that the leading and trailing brake shoes are not interchangeable and ensure that they are in their correct relative positions as shown in Fig. F5.

The rear brake has a fully floating cam and therefore the shoes are automatically self centralising.

Adjustment of the rear brake is achieved by the wing nut on the rear end of the brake operating rod. Turn the nut clockwise to reduce clearance. From the static position before the brake is applied there should be about ½ in. (1·2 cm.) of free movement before the brake starts to operate.

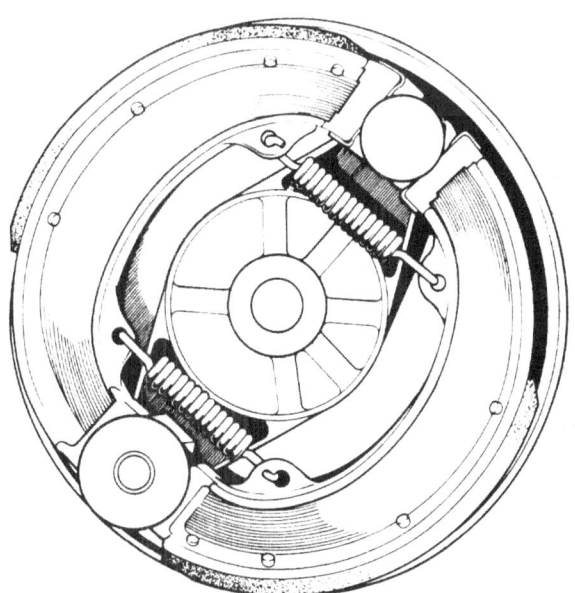

Fig. F5. Position of brake shoes

SECTION F5
REAR WHEEL REMOVAL AND REPLACEMENT

Support the machine on a suitable stand so that the rear wheel is approximately 12 in. clear of the ground. Uncouple the rear chain at its spring link and remove it from the rear wheel sprocket. Leave the chain in position on the gearbox sprocket: this will much simplify replacement. Unscrew and remove the rear brake rod adjuster. Push the rod clear of the brake lever.

Rear Wheel Removal and Replacement

Disconnect the speedometer drive cable at the drive gearbox at the right side of the rear wheel. Disconnect the torque stay at the front attachment lug (on the swinging arm) and at the brake plate then remove the stay from the machine. Remove the left side panels and remove the nut and bolt securing the chainguard to the swinging arm.

Remove the remaining attachment bolt at the rear fork end and withdraw the chainguard. Loosen the wheel spindle nut at the right-hand side and pull the wheel out of the swinging fork and away from the machine. When replacing the wheel check section F10 for front and rear wheel alignment and section F12 for rear chain adjustment.

SECTION F6
REMOVING AND REPLACING THE REAR WHEEL BEARINGS

The hub is fitted with two identical single row ball bearings which are a press fit into the hub.

Remove the speedometer drive ring (left hand thread) from the right side and the bearing retaining ring (right hand thread) from the left side. Use service tool No. 61-3694 to remove bearing retainer.

Using a drift (of the dimensions shown in Fig. F7) knock out the spacer tube contained between the bearings taking one bearing with it. This operation can be carried out from either side of the wheel. See Fig. F8.

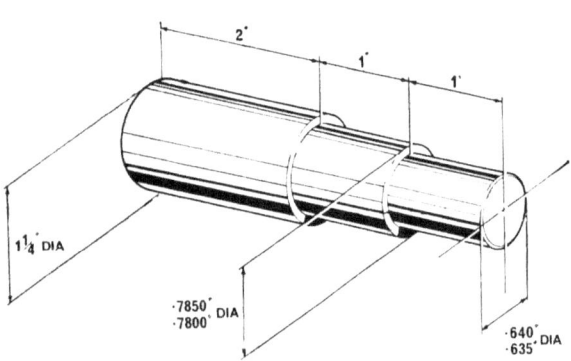

Fig. F7. Wheel bearing drift

If a drift of the correct dimensions is not used then the spacer tube will be damaged and have to be replaced.

The bearing is an interference fit on the spacer tube and should be removed using the same drift as before. The spacer tube and drift can now be used to knock the remaining bearing out of the hub. Remove the bearing from the spacer tube

To examine the bearings, wash thoroughly in paraffin and if possible, blow out with a high pressure air line. Examine each bearing carefully for signs of roughness indicating broken balls or damaged tracks, or excessive play.

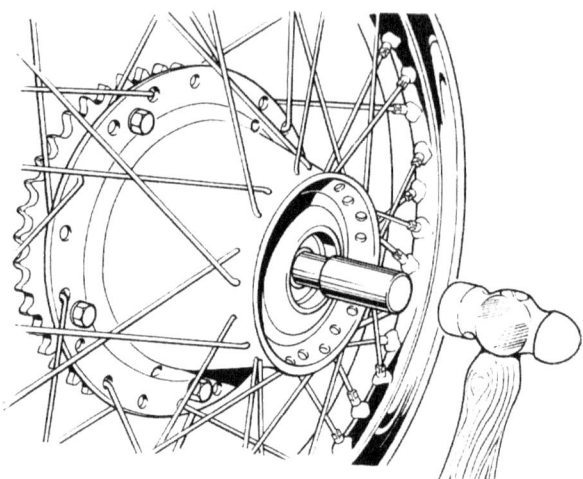

Fig. F8. Drifting the wheel bearings

The grease retainers behind the bearings should not require attention. But if replacement is necessary knock them out using a drift from inside the hub.

Replace the bearing onto the spacer tube and place the assembly into the hub from the left side. Drift the bearing into the housing and down onto the grease retainer with a suitable diameter drift. Force must be applied to the outer ring of the bearing and not the inner ring. If possible use a hand press for replacing these bearings.

Replace the retaining ring and tighten using tool No. 61-3694. Replace the remaining bearing from the right side.

Reassembly of the hub is simply the reverse of the dismantling procedure but, when pressing the bearings in, apply pressure only to the outside ring of the bearing and ensure that the retainer on the left-hand side is quite tight.

WHEELS, BRAKES AND TYRES

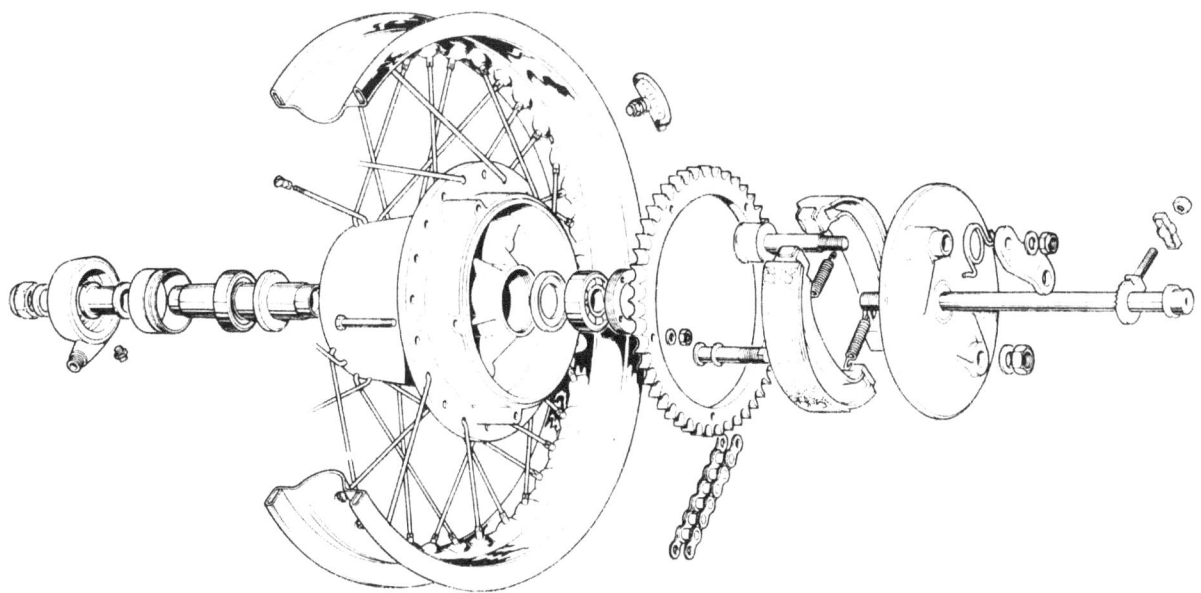

Fig. F9. Exploded view of rear wheel assembly

SECTION F7
BRAKE ADJUSTMENT

The brakes must be adjusted to give maximum efficiency at all times and for this to be maintained, the shoes should be just clear of the drum when the brake is off, and close enough for immediate contact when the brake is applied. The brakes must not be adjusted so closely, however, that they are in continual contact with the drum; excessive heat may be generated, resulting in deterioration of braking efficiency.

On twin leading shoe brakes the expansion of the shoes is equalised by the caliper action of the cam levers. The cable adjuster is combined with the control lever on the handlebar and should be set to eliminate slackness without applying the brakes. After considerable mileage it may be necessary to re-position the shoes within the brake drum.

Individual adjustment of the shoes is provided by a screw at the actuating tappet of each screw. Slacken off the cable adjuster at the handlebar lever and remove the rubber grommet from the hub shell. Rotate the wheel until the aperture is opposite to the adjuster screw. The adjuster turns with a series of clicks and must be rotated in a clockwise direction until it cannot be turned any further. At this point the shoes will be fully expanded against the drum. Now unscrew the adjustor until the wheel is free to rotate and the shoe is just clear of the drum. Turn the wheel through half a revolution and repeat the adjustment on the remaining shoe. Check that the wheel revolves freely. Now adjust the clearance in the cable at the adjuster on the control lever. Turn the knurled nut until there is approximately $\frac{1}{16}$ in. to $\frac{1}{8}$ in. slack in the cable at the lever.

The rear brake is adjusted by turning the self-locking sleeve in a clockwise direction (viewed from the rear of the machine), to shorten the effective length of the brake rod and so open the shoes in the drum.

Note that if maximum efficiency is to be obtained, the angle between the brake cable or rod and the operating lever on the brake plate should not exceed 90° when the brake is fully applied.

The rear brake shoes are of the fully floating type, (i.e. they are not pivoted on a fulcrum) and are therefore self-centralising.

F WHEELS, BRAKES AND TYRES

SECTION F8

REMOVING AND REPLACING THE FRONT BRAKE CABLE

FRONT BRAKE CABLE

Detach the cable at the handlebar lever by fully slackening the adjuster. Note that the nipple is floating but not removable from the cable. Using the slack produced relax the nipple from the front brake lever and withdraw the trunnion. As this is done, two steel washers will be released from the brake lever. Remove the return spring and pull the cable through the remaining trunnion.

To replace the cable, firstly pass the cable through the trunnion in the rear brake lever and ensure that the cable abutment locates correctly in the counterbore. See Fig. F10.

Replace the return spring onto the cable and hold the spring in a compressed position to reveal some clear cable.

Position the end of the cable inner between the fork of the front brake lever and position a steel washer to the outside of the cable. Hold the washer in this position by pressing the cable against the fork. Pass the trunnion through the lever, the washer and over the cable and then push the trunnion fully home through the fork lever. Position the nipple into the counterbore. Finally, replace the cable at the front brake lever and adjust as detailed in Section F5.

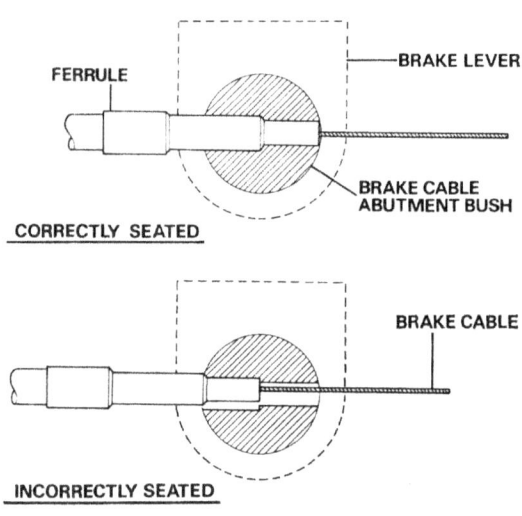

Fig. F10. Correct replacement of cable abutment

SECTION F9

RENEWING BRAKE LININGS (REAR BRAKE)

Hold the shoe firmly in a vice and, using a good sharp chisel, cut off the peened-over portion of the rivet See Fig. F11.

Drive out the rivets with a suitable pin punch and discard the old lining. Reverse the shoe in the vice

and draw-file the face of the shoe to remove any burrs.

Clamp the new lining tightly over the shoes and, using the shoe holes as a jig, drill straight through the lining with a $\frac{5}{32}$ in. diameter drill.

WHEELS, BRAKES AND TYRES

Remove the clamps and, holding the lining carefully in the vice, counterbore or countersink (according to the type of rivet used) each hole to no more than two-thirds the thickness of the lining, i.e., if the lining is $\tfrac{3}{16}$ in. thick, then the counterbore must not be deeper than $\tfrac{1}{8}$ in.

Having prepared the linings for riveting, start at the centre and position the lining with one or more rivets.

Place a suitable mandrel in the vice, clamp the linings to the shoes with either small "G" or tool-makers clamps and peen-over the rivets as shown in Fig. F12, working alternatively outwards from the centre.

The mandrel used in the vice must be flat on the end and the diameter should be no more than that of the rivet head. It will also help to bed the rivet down if a hollow punch is used before peening.

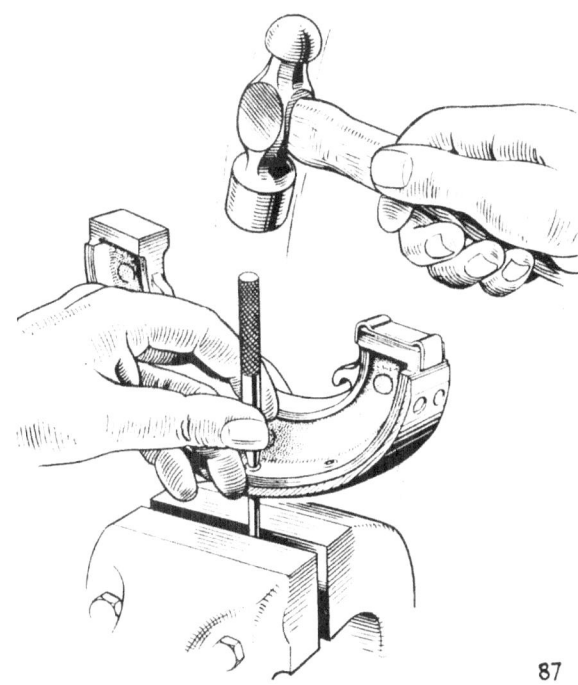

Fig. F12. Punching lining rivets

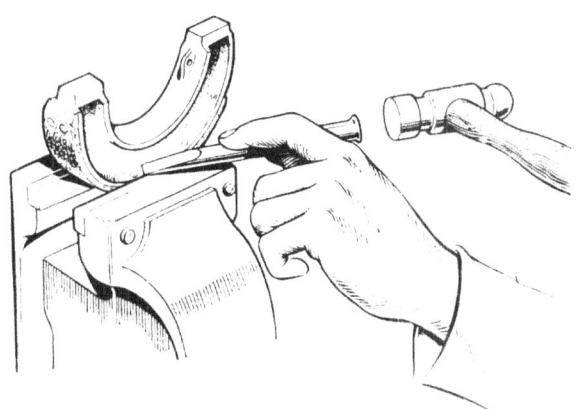

Fig. F11. Chiselling off brake rivets

Note. If the clamps are used correctly, that is, next to the rivet being worked on, the linings can be fitted tightly to the shoe.

If the linings are fitted incorrectly, a gap will occur between the lining and the shoe, resulting in inefficient and "spongy" braking.

When the riveting is completed, file a good chamfer at each end of the lining to approximately half its depth and lightly draw-file the face of the lining to remove any fraze caused by the drilling.

SECTION F10
WHEEL BALANCING

When a wheel is out of balance it means that there is more weight in one part than in another. This is very often due to variation in the tyre and at moderate speeds will not be noticed but at high speeds it can be very serious, particularly if the front wheel is affected.

Wheel balancing can be achieved by fitting standard one ounce and half ounce weights which are readily available, as required. All front wheels are balanced complete with tyre and tube before leaving the factory and if for any reason the tyre is removed it should be replaced with the white balancing "spot" level with the valve. If a new tyre is fitted, existing weights should be removed and the wheel re-balanced, adding weights as necessary until it will remain in any position at rear. Make sure that the brake is not binding while the balancing operation is being carried out.

For normal road use it is not found necessary for the rear wheel to be balanced in this way.

SECTION F11
FRONT AND REAR WHEEL ALIGNMENT

When the rear wheel has been fitted into the frame it should be aligned correctly by using two straight edges or "battens", about 7 feet long. With the machine off the stand the battens should be placed along-side the wheel, one either side of the machine and each about four inches from the ground. When both are touching the rear tyre on both sides of the wheel the front wheel should be midway between and parallel to both battens. Turn the front wheel slightly until this can be seen. Any necessary adjustments must be made by first slackening the rear wheel spindle nuts, then turning the spindle adjuster nuts as required ensuring that rear chain adjustment is maintained. Refer to Fig. F13 for illustration of correct alignement. Note that the arrows indicate the adjustment required.

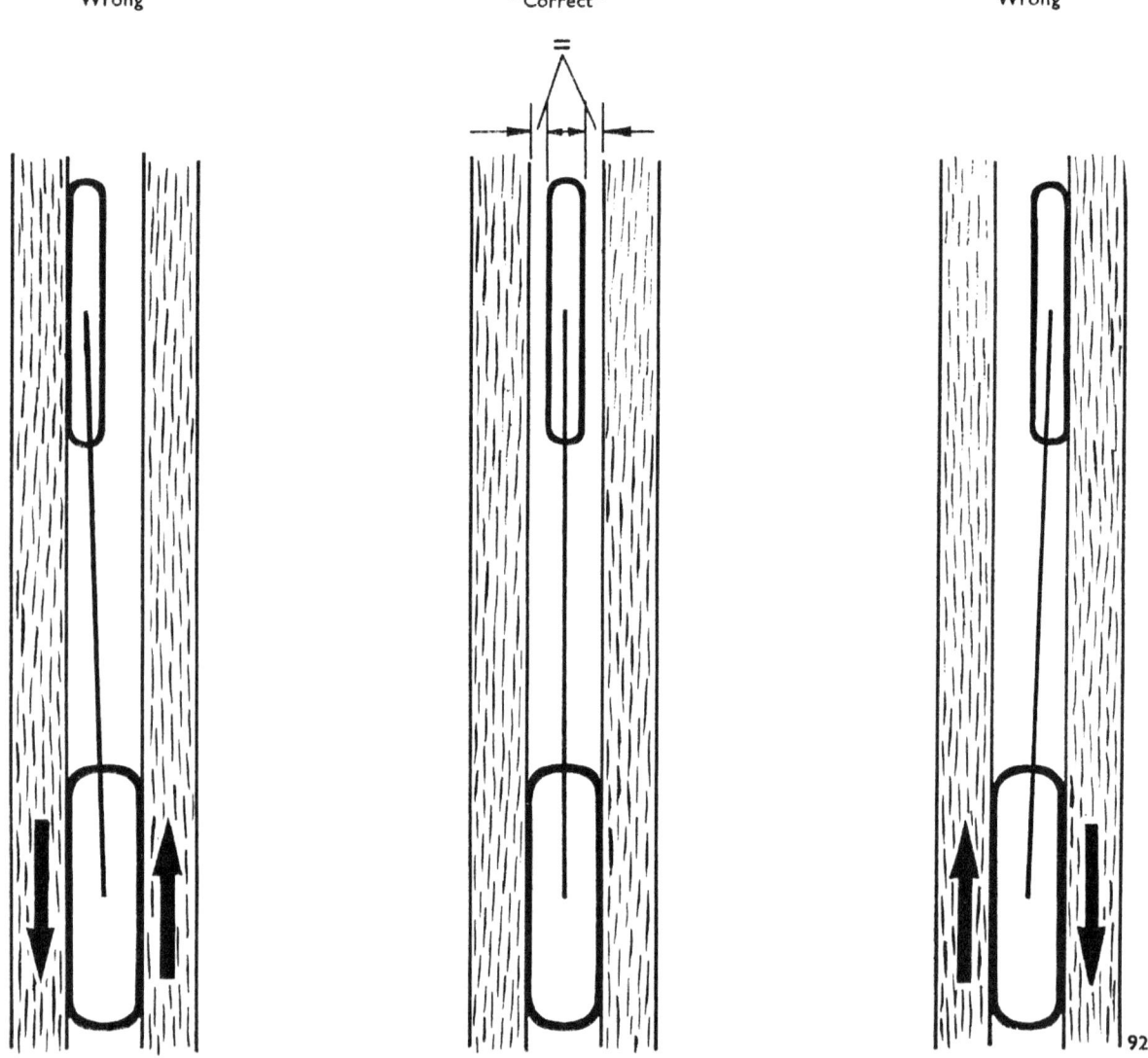

Fig. F13. Aligning the front and rear wheels

WHEELS, BRAKES AND TYRES

SECTION F12
WHEEL BUILDING

Wheel building, or adjustment to the spokes to realign the wheel rim should only be untertaken by a specialist and these notes are for the specialist, to enable him to follow Triumph practice. The main point to remember is that all Triumph wheels are built with the inside spokes on the brake drum side taking the braking strain. This means the inside spokes on the drum side are in tension when the brake is applied in the direction of forward motion.

Wheel	Rim type	Location	Dimensions	
			Inches	mm.
Front: Standard	WM2	Drum	$-\frac{1}{64}$	-0.4
Rear: Standard	WM3	Hub	$1\frac{3}{4}$	44.4

Table of "Dish" Dimensional Settings for Front and Rear Wheels

The front wheel has 40 straight 8/10 gauge butted spokes and is single cross-laced, whilst the rear wheel has 40 8/10 gauge butted spokes, and is double cross-laced.

A checking gauge suitable for Triumph wheels can be made from two pieces of mild steel bar as shown in Fig. F14 and this should be used to register from the edge of the hub or brake drum onto the wheel rim edge giving the relation indicated in the table.

This ensures the correct relation between the hub and rim centre lines.

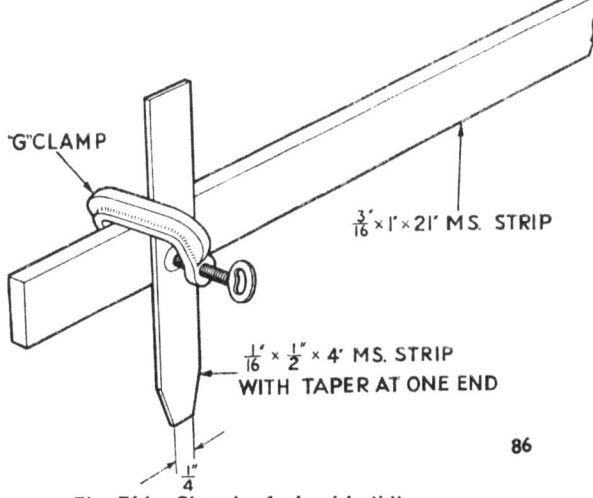

Fig. F14. Sketch of wheel building gauge

SECTION F13
REAR CHAIN ADJUSTMENT

Rear Chain

The adjustment of the rear chain is controlled by draw bolts fitted to each end of the rear wheel spindle. The correct adjustment for the rear chain is $\frac{3}{4}$ in. (1.8 cm.) free movement with the machine on its wheels and the chain at its tightest point or $1\frac{3}{4}$ in. (4.3 cm.) with the machine on the stand and the chain at its slackest point. If the adjustment of chain is outside these limits it should be corrected by loosening the wheel spindle and the nut securing the torque stay to the brake anchor plate and adjusting the draw bolts. Tighten the wheel spindle and check the chain adjustment again. If the wheel alignment was correct originally the adjustment of the nuts by an equal number of turns should preserve that alignment but if you are doubtful whether the rear wheel is in line then you should use a straight edge or piece of string alongside the rear wheel, and then tighten or loosen the draw bolt adjuster on the right side so that the rear wheel lines up with the front wheel. If the rear wheel is not in line the road holding of the machine will be adversely affected and the effect on the rear chain and rear wheel sprocket will cause rapid wear. When the adjustment is satisfactory check the tightness of the wheel spindle, adjuster draw bolts and brake torque stay nut. Finally check the adjustment of the brake operating rod.

A positive oil feed to the rear chain is taken from the return side of the oil tank. Provision for adjusting the rate of flow is made by removing the oil tank cap and operating a screw which will be observed in the oil tank neck. Turn the screw clockwise to reduce the flow and anti-clockwise to increase it.

SECTION F14
REMOVING AND REPAIRING TYRES

To remove the tyre first remove the valve cap and valve core, using the valve cap itself to unscrew the core. Unscrew the knurled valve securing nut and then place all parts where they will be free from dirt and grit. It is recommended that the cover beads are lubricated with a little soapy water before attempting to remove the tyre. The tyre lever should be dipped in this solution before each application. First, insert a lever at the valve position and whilst carefully pulling on this lever, press the tyre bead into the well of the rim diametrically opposite the valve position (see Fig. F15). Insert a

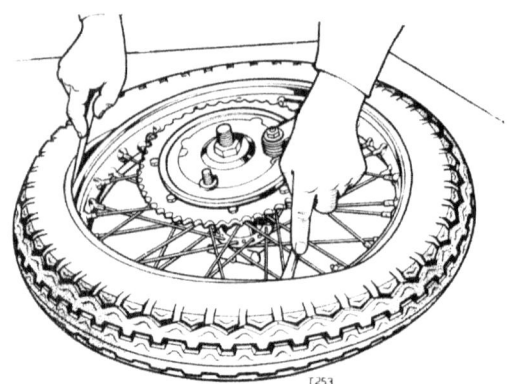

Fig. F16. Removing the first bead of the tyre, using two tyre levers

Fig. F15. Removing the first bead of the tyre. Lever inserted close to valve, whilst bead is pressed into well on opposite side of wheel

second lever close to the first and prise the bead over the rim flange. Remove the first lever and reinsert a little further round the rim from the second lever. Continue round the bead in steps of two to three inches until the bead is completely away from the rim. Push the valve out of the rim and then withdraw the inner tube. To completely remove the tyre first stand the wheel upright and then insert a lever between the remaining bead and the rim. The tyre should be easily removed from the rim as shown in Fig. F16.

REFITTING THE TYRE

First place the rubber rim band into the well of the rim and make sure that the rough side of the rubber band is fitted against the rim and that the band is central in the well. Replace the valve core and inflate the inner tube sufficiently to round it out without stretch, dust it with french chalk and insert it into the cover with the valve located at the white "balancing spot" leaving it protruding outside the beads for about four inches either side of the valve. At this stage it is advisable to lubricate the beads and levers with soapy water (see Fig. F17).

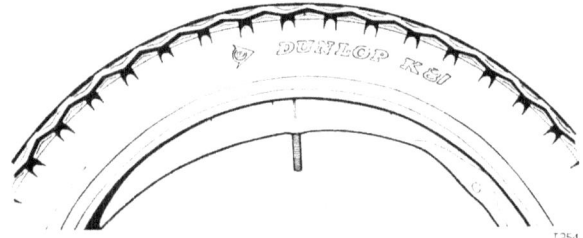

Fig. F17. Cover and tube assembled ready for fitting to the wheel

Squeeze the beads together at the valve position to prevent the tube from slipping back inside the tyre and offer the cover to the rim, as shown in Fig. F18 at the same time threading the valve through the valve holes in the rim band and rim. Allow the first bead to go into the well of the rim and the other bead to lie above the level of the rim flange.

WHEELS, BRAKES AND TYRES   F

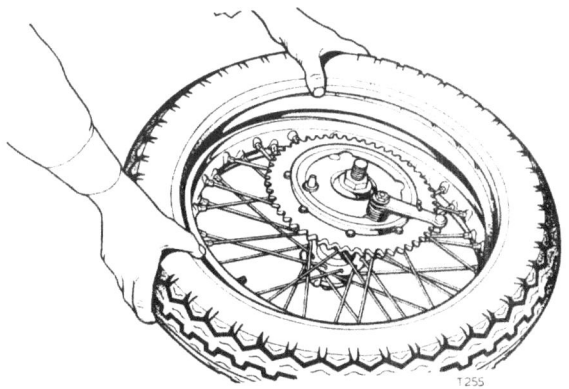

Fig. F18. Refitting the tyre to the wheel. Note valve engaged in rim hole

Working from the valve, press the first bead over the rim flange by hand, moving forward in small steps and making sure that the part of the bead already dealt with, lies in the well of the rim. If necessary use a tyre lever for the last few inches, as shown in Fig. F19. During this operation continually check that the inner tube is not trapped by the cover bead.

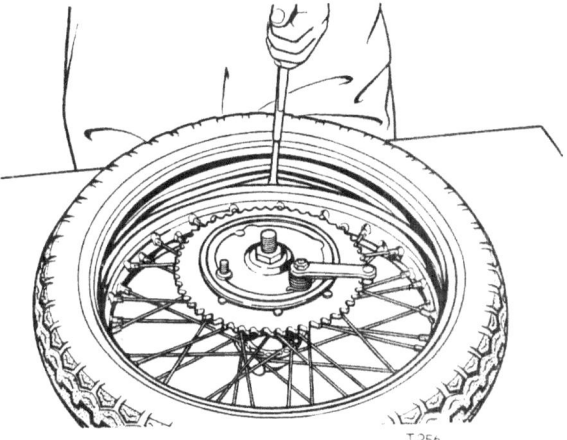

Fig. F19. Levering the first bead onto the rim

Press the second bead into the well of the rim diametrally opposite the valve. Insert a lever as close as possible to the point where the bead passes over the flange and lever the bead into the flange, at the same time pressing the fitted part of the bead into the well of the rim. Repeat until the bead is completely over the flange, finishing at the valve position (see Fig. F20).

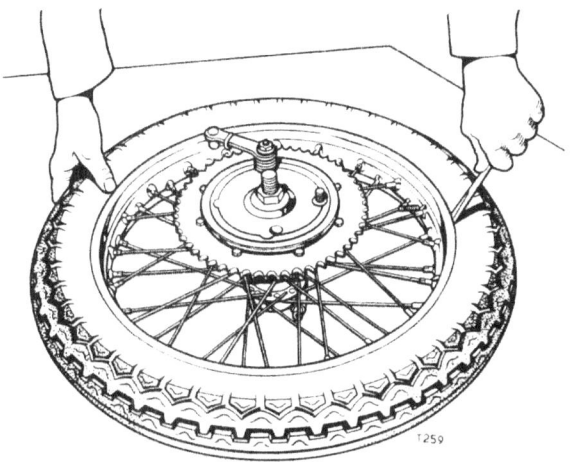

Fig. F20. Refitting the second bead over the wheel rim. Care must be taken not to trap inner tube

Push the valve inwards to ensure that the tube near the valve is not trapped under the bead. Pull the valve back and inflate the tyre. Check that the fitting line on the cover is concentric with the top of the rim flange and that the valve protrudes squarely through the valve hole. Fit the knurled rim nut and valve cap. The tyre pressure should then be set to the figure given in General Data.

SECTION F15
SECURITY BOLTS

Security bolts are fitted to the rear wheel to prevent the tyre "creeping" on the rim when it is subjected to excessive acceleration or braking. Such movement would ultimately result in the valve being torn from the inner tube. There are two security bolts fitted to the rear wheel, which are equally spaced either side of the valve and thereby do not affect the balance of the wheel.

Note: The security bolt nuts must not be overtightened, otherwise excessive distortion may occur.

WHEELS, BRAKES AND TYRES

Where a security bolt is fitted the basic procedure for fitting and removing the tyre is the same, but the following instructions should be followed:—

(1) Remove the valve cap and core as described.

(2) Unscrew the security bolt nut and push the bolt inside the cover.

(3) Remove the first bead as described.

(4) Remove the security bolt from the rim.

(5) Remove the inner tube as described.

(6) Remove the second bead and tyre.

For refitting the tyre and inner tube:—

(1) Fit the rim band.

(2) Fit the first bead to the rim without the inner tube inside.

(3) Assemble the security bolt into the rim, putting the nut onto the first few threads (see Fig. F21).

(4) Partly inflate the inner tube and fit it into the tyre.

(5) Fit the second bead but keep the security bolt pressed well into the tyre, as shown in Fig. F22 and ensure that the inner tube does not become trapped at the edges.

(6) Fit the valve stem nut and inflate the tyre.

(7) Bounce the wheel several times at the point where the security bolt is fitted and then tighten the security bolt nut.

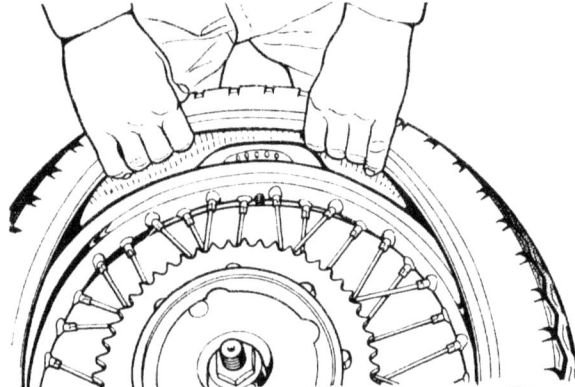

Fig. F21. Placing the security bolt in position

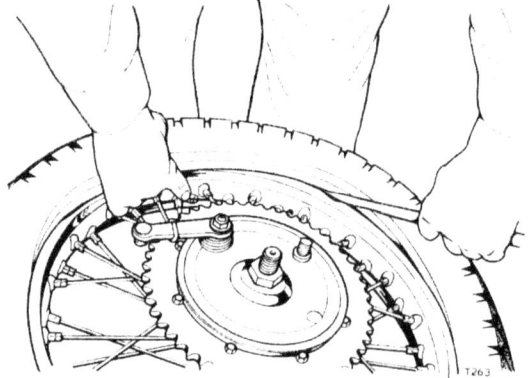

Fig. F22. Refitting the second bead with the security bolt in position

SECTION F16

TYRE MAINTENANCE

To obtain optimum tyre mileage and to eliminate irregular wear on the tyres it is essential that the recommendations governing tyre pressures and general maintenance are followed. The following points are laid out with this in mind.

(1) Maintain the correct inflation pressure as shown in "General Data". Use a pressure gauge frequently. It is advisable to check and restore tyre pressures at least once per week. Pressures should always be checked when tyres are cold and not when they have reached normal running temperatures.

(2) When a pillion passenger or additional load is carried, the rear tyre pressure should be increased appropriately to cater for the extra load.

(3) Unnecessary rapid acceleration and fierce braking should always be avoided. This treatment invariably results in rapid tyre wear.

(4) Regular checks should be made for flints, nails, small stones etc., which should be removed from the tread or they may ultimately penetrate and damage the casing and puncture the tube.

(5) Tyres and spokes should be kept free of oil, grease and paraffin. Regular cleaning should be carried out with a cloth and a little petrol (gasoline).

(6) If tyres develop irregular wear, this may be corrected by reversing the tyre to reverse its direction of rotation.

Disc Brake Supplement

750cc (45cu.in.) Three Cylinder

SECTION F

WHEELS, BRAKES and TYRES

	Section
DESCRIPTION (F17)	
BRAKE ADJUSTMENTS	F18
BRAKE FLUID LEVEL	F19
BRAKE PAD AND LINING	F20
BLEEDING THE HYDRAULIC SYSTEM	F21
FLUSHING THE HYDRAULIC SYSTEM	F22
FLEXIBLE BRAKE HOSES	F23
MASTER CYLINDER	F24
STRIPPING AND REASSEMBLING THE BRAKE CALIPER	F25
BRAKE DISCS	F26
REMOVING AND REFITTING THE FRONT WHEEL	F27
REMOVING AND REFITTING THE FRONT WHEEL BEARINGS	F28

(DISC FRONT BRAKE)

BRAKES, WHEELS AND TYRES

DESCRIPTION

All machines are fitted with a Lockheed hydraulic disc brake on the front wheel. (See Fig. F24). The disc brake assembly consists of a high quality cast iron disc (hard chrome plated) attached to the front wheel hubs and a cast iron brake caliper attached to the left fork leg. The brake caliper houses two co-axially aligned pistons (Fig. F23) and a pair of brake pads the latter being retained by two split pins.

The pistons and their bores are protected by dust seals fitted in the open ends of the bores. (See Fig. F23). Application of the front brake lever generates hydraulic pressure within the system and brake caliper causing the pistons (Fig. F23) to apply equal and opposite pressure on the brake pads (Fig. F23) which in turn move into contact with the rotating brake disc. The operation of the master cylinder and hydraulic flow is detailed in Section F24.

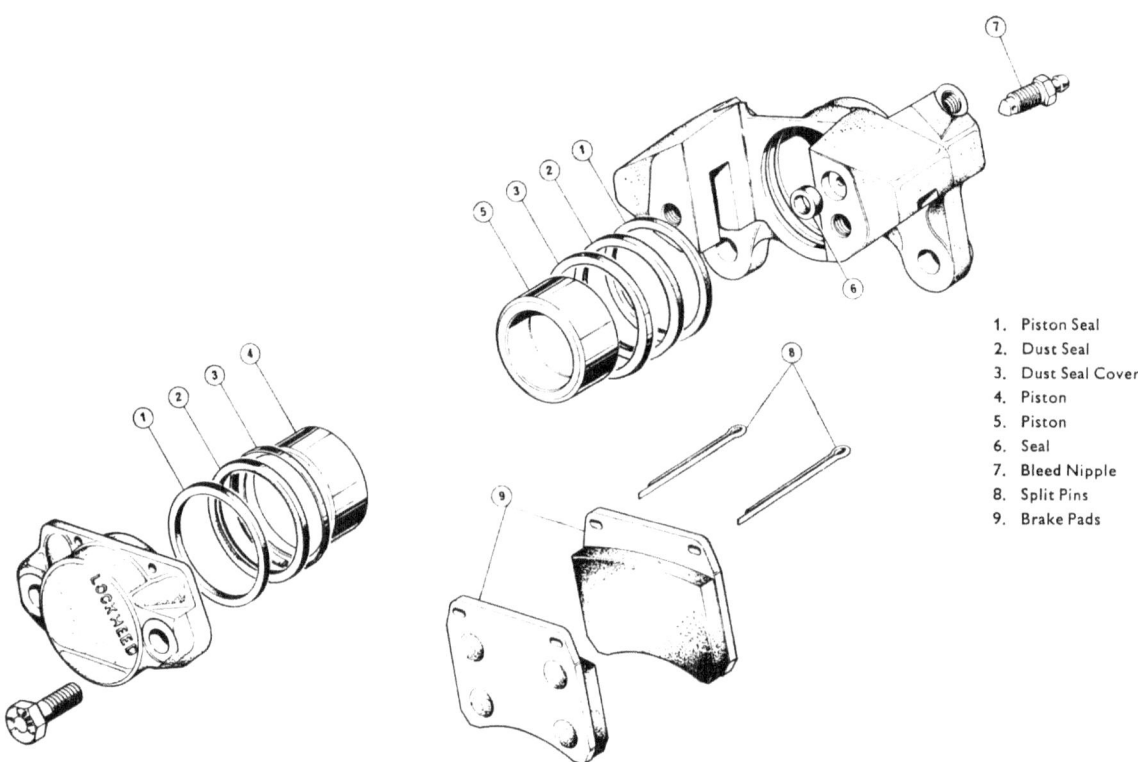

1. Piston Seal
2. Dust Seal
3. Dust Seal Cover
4. Piston
5. Piston
6. Seal
7. Bleed Nipple
8. Split Pins
9. Brake Pads

Fig. F23. Front brake caliper

BRAKES, WHEELS AND TYRES

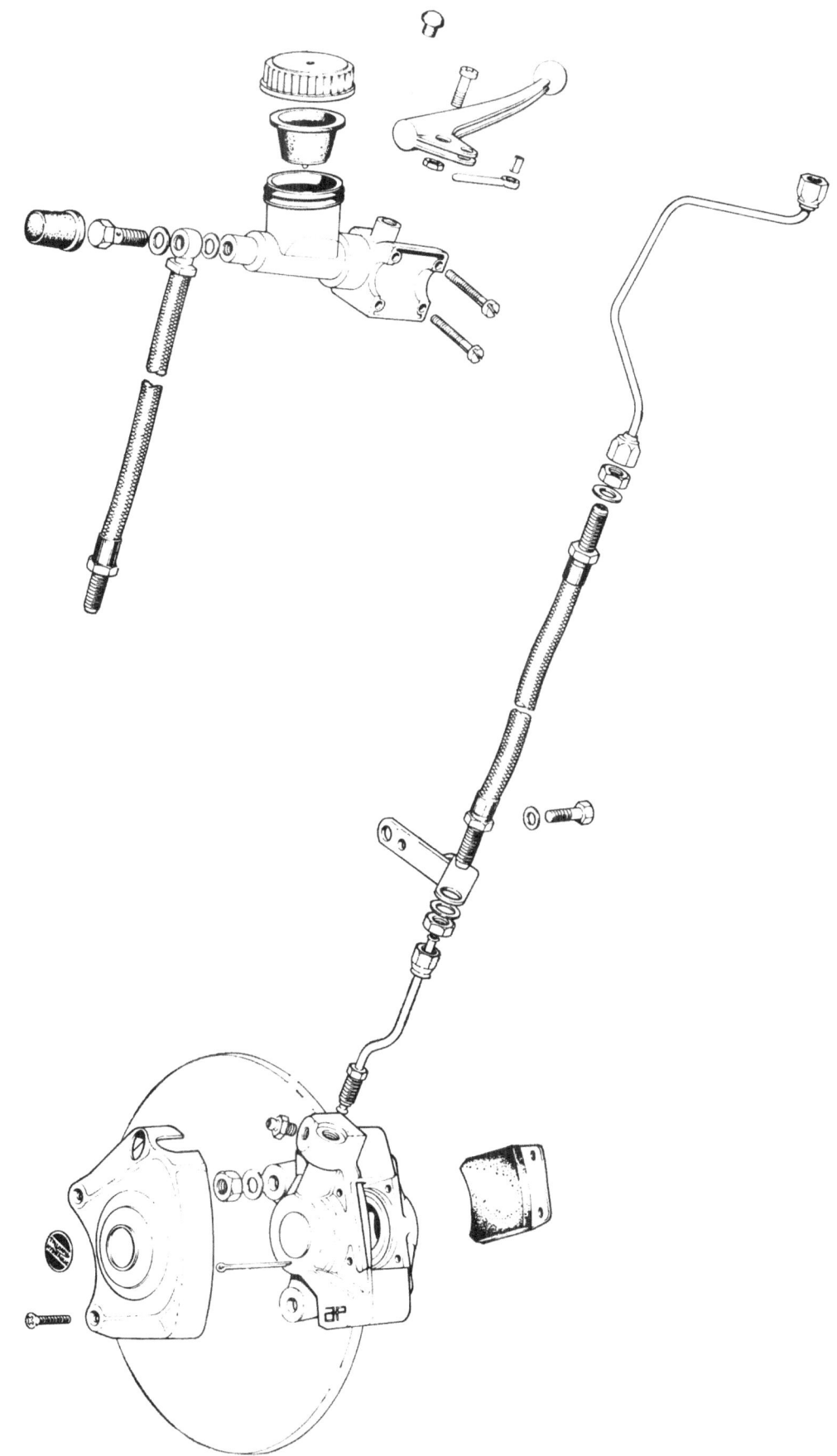

Fig. F24. Front brake components

SECTION F18

BRAKE ADJUSTMENTS

The brake pads of the disc brake will require no adjustment as the reducing thickness of the friction material is automatically cancelled out by the displacement of hydraulic fluid in the system (See Section F24).

SECTION F19

BRAKE FLUID LEVEL

The brake fluid level in the master cylinder reservoir should be as shown in Fig. F25. (F). There is a mark running around the inside periphery of the reservoir about $\frac{1}{4}''$ (6·35 mm) from the top. During the life of the brake pads it will not be necessary to maintain the maximum fluid level in the master cylinder. The level will drop slightly as the pads wear and when new pads are fitted the fluid will return to the original level provided no leakage has occurred.

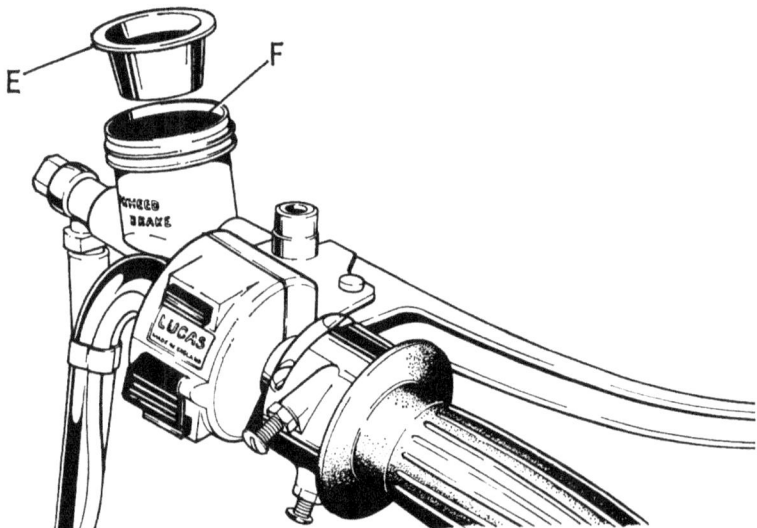

Fig. F25. Showing the brake reservoir fluid level and cap.

BRAKES, WHEELS AND TYRES

SECTION F20

BRAKE PAD LINING

The front brake pads should be examined at regular intervals for wear. The pads will require replacement when the lining thickness reaches a minimum of $\frac{1}{16}$ in. (1·6 mm). This can be easily determined by removing the pad from the caliper. Firstly detach the aluminium cover from the caliper by removing the two cross-head screws. Then remove both split pins "B" (See Fig. F26) and pull out both the pads "D".

The brake pad friction material is bonded to the pressure plate of the brake pad and therefore can only be renewed by the fitting of complete brake pad assemblies. New split pins are advisable when fitting new or replacing used brake pads.

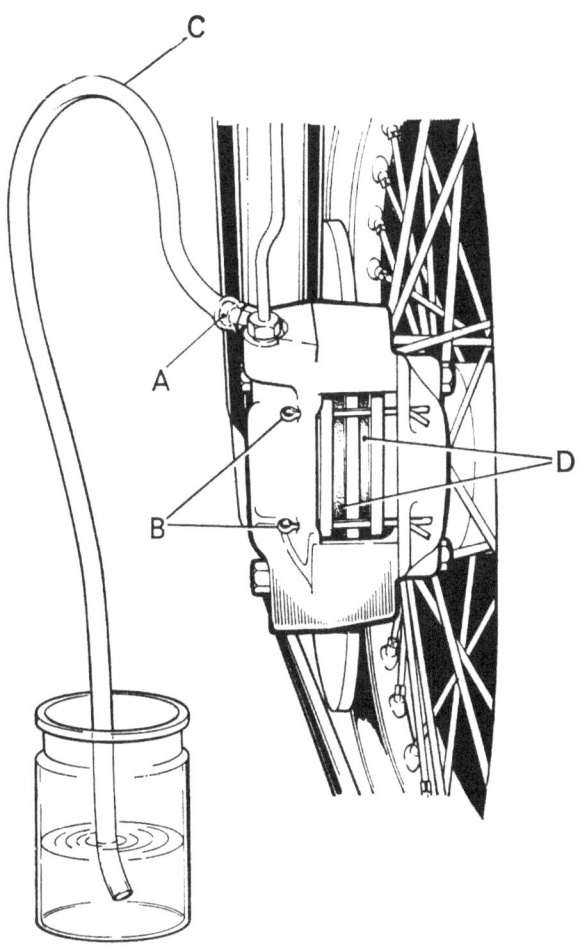

Fig. F26. Showing arrangement for bleeding the front brake.

SECTION F21

"BLEEDING" THE HYDRAULIC SYSTEM

If at any time it has been found necessary to disconnect a part of the hydraulic system (for repair etc.) it will be necessary to replenish the master cylinder reservoir and "bleed" the system free of trapped air pockets. "Bleeding" (or expelling air from) the hydraulic system is not a routine maintenance operation. Always keep a careful check on the fluid level in the reservoir during "bleeding". It is most important that it is kept at least half full, otherwise air may be drawn into the system necessitating a fresh start.

Fluid drained from the system should not be used again unless it is perfectly clean and free from air bubbles. The fluid should not be used again in any case if it has been in use for some time. To ensure that the fluid is completely free of air bubbles it should be allowed to stand for several hours before use.

Use only the specified type of brake fluid for topping up the reservoir. See General Data.

Procedure for "bleeding" is as follows:—

Connect a suitable sized rubber "pipe" "C" Fig. F26 to the bleed nipple "A" Fig. F26 and suspend the free end of the tube in a glass jar with the open end immersed in at least ½ in. (12·7 mm) of brake fluid. Remove the screwed cap from the master cylinder reservoir and take out the rubber diaphram "E" Fig. F25. Now slacken the bleed nipple ½ to ¾ of a turn, (with the bleed pipe still attached).

Ensure that the master cylinder is full of the correct fluid before commencing further. Now pull the front brake lever firmly to the handlebar holding it in that position for a few seconds. Air in the system will now be expelled through the rubber tube and will be observed in the form of bubbles rising in the jar. Release the brake lever and repeat the operation until air bubbles are no longer seen to escape. As a safeguard to prevent any air being drawn back into the system when the lever is released, loop the "bleed" pipe as shown in Fig. 26. This ensures that a "head" of fluid is maintained between the top of the loop and the "bleed" nipple.

When the flow of air bubbles ceases hold the brake lever in the fully "on" position and retighten the bleed nipple (with the "bleed" pipe still connected).

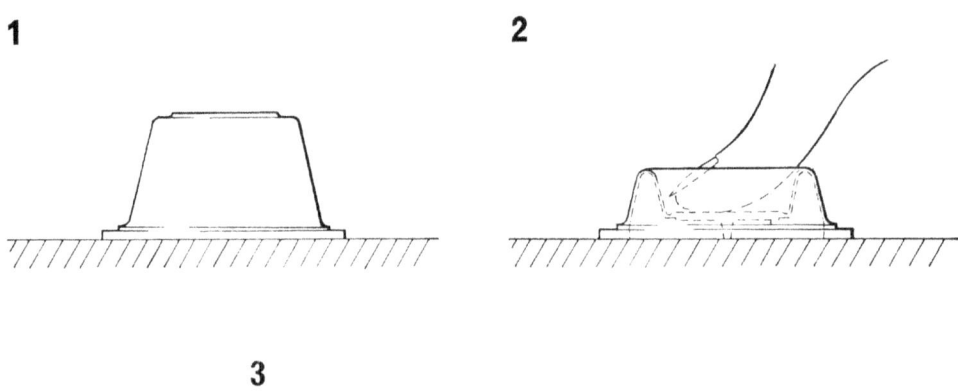

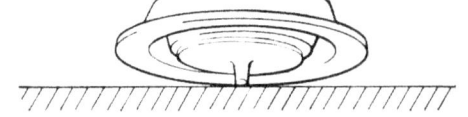

Fig. F27. Folded condition of rubber diaphram

BRAKES, WHEELS AND TYRES   F

Remember to maintain the level of hydraulic fluid in the master cylinder during the entire operation. The correct level for the fluid is shown in Fig. F25 at "F". This will be the correct level when the brake pads are NEW. When replacing the rubber diaphram (Fig. F25 "E") it will be easier to replace the cap with the diaphram in a folded condition. See Fig. F27.

Hold the diaphram upside down on a flat surface and push the middle section down until it touches the surface it is resting on. It will now remain in that position and the diaphram can now be replaced into the reservoir and the cap refitted. Do not forget the paper washer that is fitted between the cap and the diaphram. When fitting the cap make sure it is retightened firmly and make sure that the air vent is unobstructed.

If at any time it has been necessary to replenish the system with hydraulic fluid during the life of one set of brake pads, remember that when new pads are fitted the fluid level spill will rise appreciably in the cylinder and may spill onto the gas tank. Therefore the level will have to be corrected to that shown in Fig. F25 (Hydraulic fluid instantaneously corrodes cellulose paintwork and great care should be exercised when handling this fluid).

SECTION F22

FLUSHING THE HYDRAULIC SYSTEM

If the hydraulic system has been contaminated by foreign matter or other fluids it should be flushed out and refilled with new fluid as described below. The system should be flushed out, in any case, once every three years.

Firstly, pump all the fluid out of the system by opening the bleed screw (connect a pipe to the bleed screw and safely collect in a container) and operating the front brake lever. Fill the master cylinder reservoir with methylated spirit and pump out through the bleed screw in a manner similar to that described above. Having ensured that all the methylated spirit has passed through the bleed screw replenish the master cylinder reservoir with the specified grade of Lockheed brake fluid (see General Data). "Bleed" the brake as described in Section F21.

IMPORTANT NOTE: If the system has been contaminated by a mineral oil, all rubber parts including flexible hoses must be replaced.

SECTION F23

FLEXIBLE BRAKE HOSES

Remove the union nut at the fork top lug and then unscrew the locknut and withdraw the rubber hose. See Fig. F24 for assembly details. Similarly disconnect the remaining pipe and hoses from the middle lug, left fork leg and caliper. Note that the pipe junction at the middle lug is mounted in such a fashion that the rubber hose that hence travels down to the left fork leg is splayed outwards and away from the wheel when the front forks are compressed. See Fig. F28 for detail drawing. To reset the angle as shown simply loosen the bolt clamping nut and alter the position of the bolt accordingly.

Be careful not to overtighten the union nuts as their threads may be easily stripped. When re-fitting the hoses "bleed" the system as described in Section F21. Check that no chafing of the hoses or pipes occurs when the handlebars are turned from left lock to right lock and when the front forks are fully compressed.

The brake hoses should be checked at regular intervals for leakage, chafing or general deterioration. Do not attempt to clear the bore of a flexible hose by probing. If a hose is choked or perished, fit a replacement.

Hoses may be replaced as follows:- Firstly drain the system of its fluid See Section F22. Unscrew the fixing bolt from the end of the master cylinder and detach the union (U.S.A. models only). Note the copper sealing washers at the front and back of the union. These sealing washers must be annealed if they are to be re-used and this is effected by heating the washers to a cherry red colour and plunging them into cold water. (Other export models with low handlebars have a feed hose that screws directly into the master cylinder and this hose should be disconnected at the fork top lug first and then unscrewed from the master cylinder).

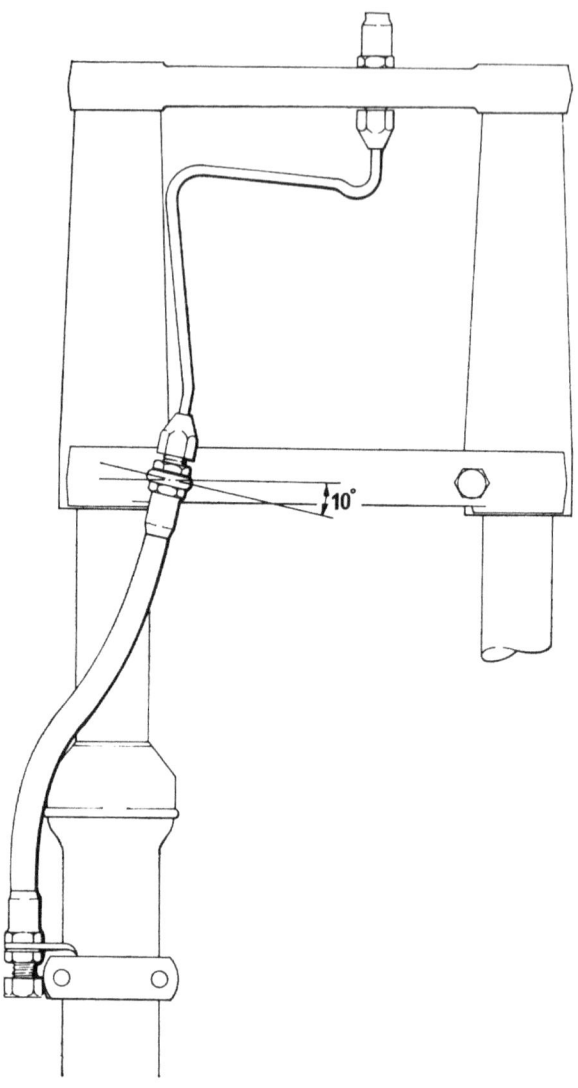

Fig. F28. Showing brake pipe installation

BRAKES, WHEELS AND TYRES

SECTION F24

MASTER CYLINDER

The master cylinder is mounted in the right hand handlebar electrical switch. It consists of a fluid reservoir bolted to a cylinder body containing a piston, seals and other parts as shown in Fig. F29 With reference to the hydraulic flow diagram (Fig. F30) and the exploded view (Fig. F29) the operation of the cylinder is as follows:— When the front brake lever is pulled on the push rod (1) moves the piston (2) down the bore. The displaced fluid in front of the piston is forced through holes in the check valve (3) lifting the rubber seal clear of the holes to provide an unblocked passage to the wheel cylinders. On releasing the front brake lever the return spring (4) thrust the piston (2) back faster than the fluid is able to return from the wheel cylinders. This creates a partial vacuum in the cylinder which causes fluid to be drawn past the lip of the primary seal (5) from the main reservoir via the main feed port (A) and the small feed holes in the head of the piston (2).

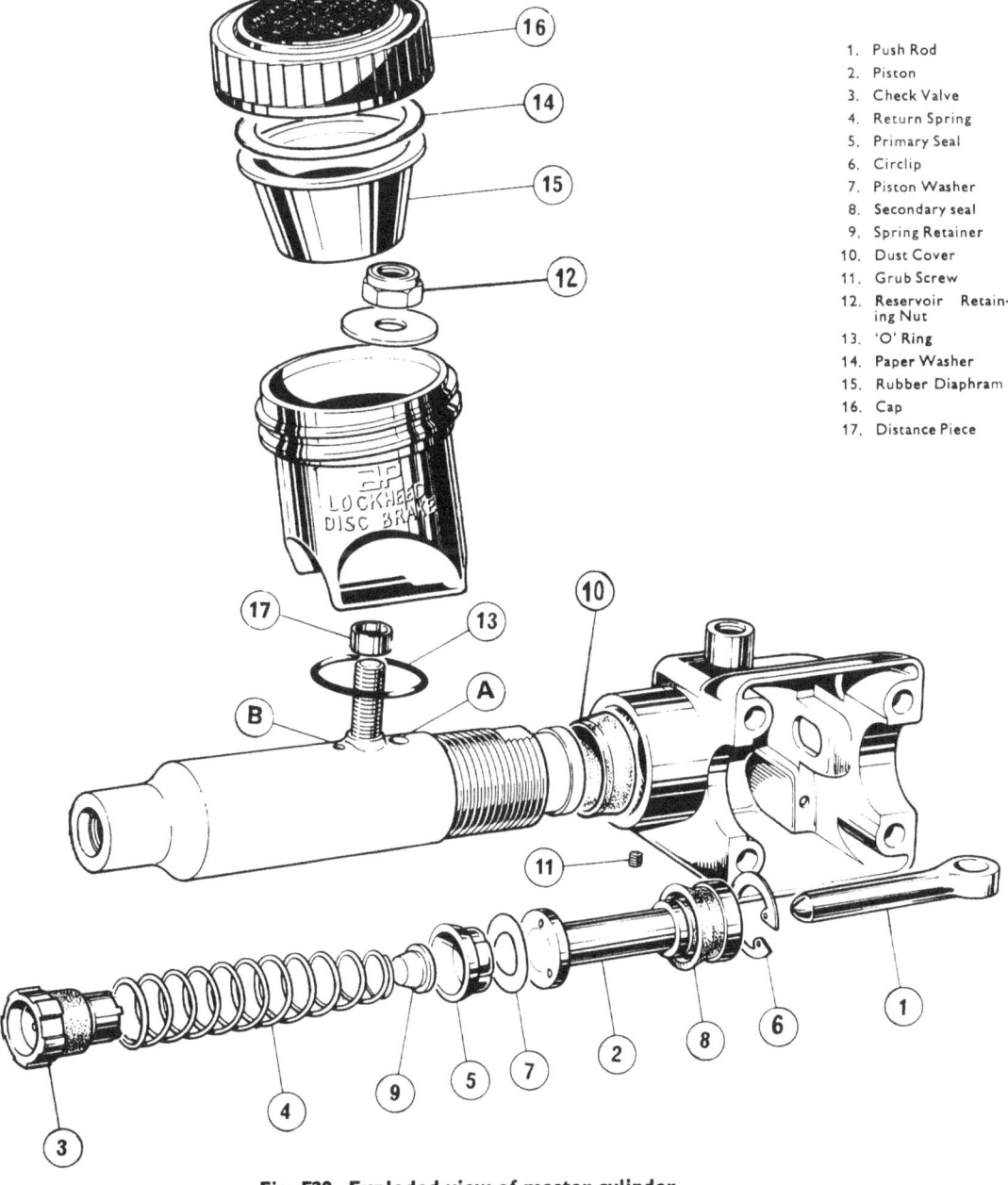

1. Push Rod
2. Piston
3. Check Valve
4. Return Spring
5. Primary Seal
6. Circlip
7. Piston Washer
8. Secondary seal
9. Spring Retainer
10. Dust Cover
11. Grub Screw
12. Reservoir Retaining Nut
13. 'O' Ring
14. Paper Washer
15. Rubber Diaphram
16. Cap
17. Distance Piece

Fig. F29. Exploded view of master cylinder

BRAKES, WHEELS AND TYRES

Meanwhile fluid returning from the wheel cylinder lifts the check valve (3) away from its seat and re-enters the cylinder. When the piston has fully returned a small breather port (B) is uncovered which allows a release of excess fluid to the reservoir and also compensates for contraction and expansion of the fluid due to changes in temperature. The purpose of the check valve (3) is to prevent the re-entry into the master cylinder of fluid pumped into the line during the "bleeding" operation, thus ensuring a fresh charge of fluid at each stroke of the lever.

Removal and dismantling procedure of the cylinder is as follows:— Firstly drain the system of fluid. See Section F22. Remove the rubber hose from the wheel cylinder. Remove the brake lever and push rod by unscrewing the pivot bolt. Unscrew the four retaining screws that retain the right switch console and remove the master cylinder from the handlebar. Detach the reservoir bowl from the cylinder by removing the attachment nut from the inside (See Fig. F29). Note assembly of washer, spacer and 'O' ring. Remove the grub screw that locks the cylinder in position in the switch housing (See Fig. F29) and then unscrew the cylinder. Detach the rubber boot from the end of the cylinder. Using the push rod (1) depress the piston in the cylinder to relieve the load on the spring and remove the circlip (6). Remove the piston (2) piston washer (7), primary seal (5), return spring (4) and check valve (3). The removal of the primary seal (5) may be simplified by applying gentle air pressure to the pipe connection at the end of the cylinder.

Remove the secondary seal (8) by stretching it over the flange of the piston. Renew all seals and check the bore of the cylinder for deep score marks. If such damage is apparent a new cylinder should be fitted.

It is important that all parts are meticulously cleaned with brake fluid before assembly. Do not use petrol, trichlorethylene or any other similar cleaning agents to wash the parts.

Fit the secondary seal (8) onto the piston (2) so that the lip of the seal faces towards the head (drilled end) of the piston. See Fig. F29. Gently work the seal around the groove with the fingers to ensure that it is properly seated. Fit the spring retainer (9) onto the small end of the spring (4) and the check valve (3) onto the large end. Insert the spring assembly onto the cylinder bore, large end first. Insert the primary seal (5) into the cylinder bore, lip foremost (See Fig. F29), taking care not to damage or turn back the lip. Insert the piston washer (7) into the barrel with the dished side towards the primary seal (5) (See Fig. F30) followed by the piston, head (drilled end) innermost, see Fig. F29. Push the piston inwards with the end of the push rod and refit the circlip (6). Make sure that the circlip beds evenly in its groove. Refit the boot (10) by stretching it over the barrel. Refit the reservoir bowl, not forgetting the 'O' ring and test the cylinder by filling the reservoir and pushing the push rod and piston inwards and allowing it to return unassisted. After a few applications fluid should flow from the outlet connection at the cylinder head.

BRAKES, WHEELS AND TYRES   F

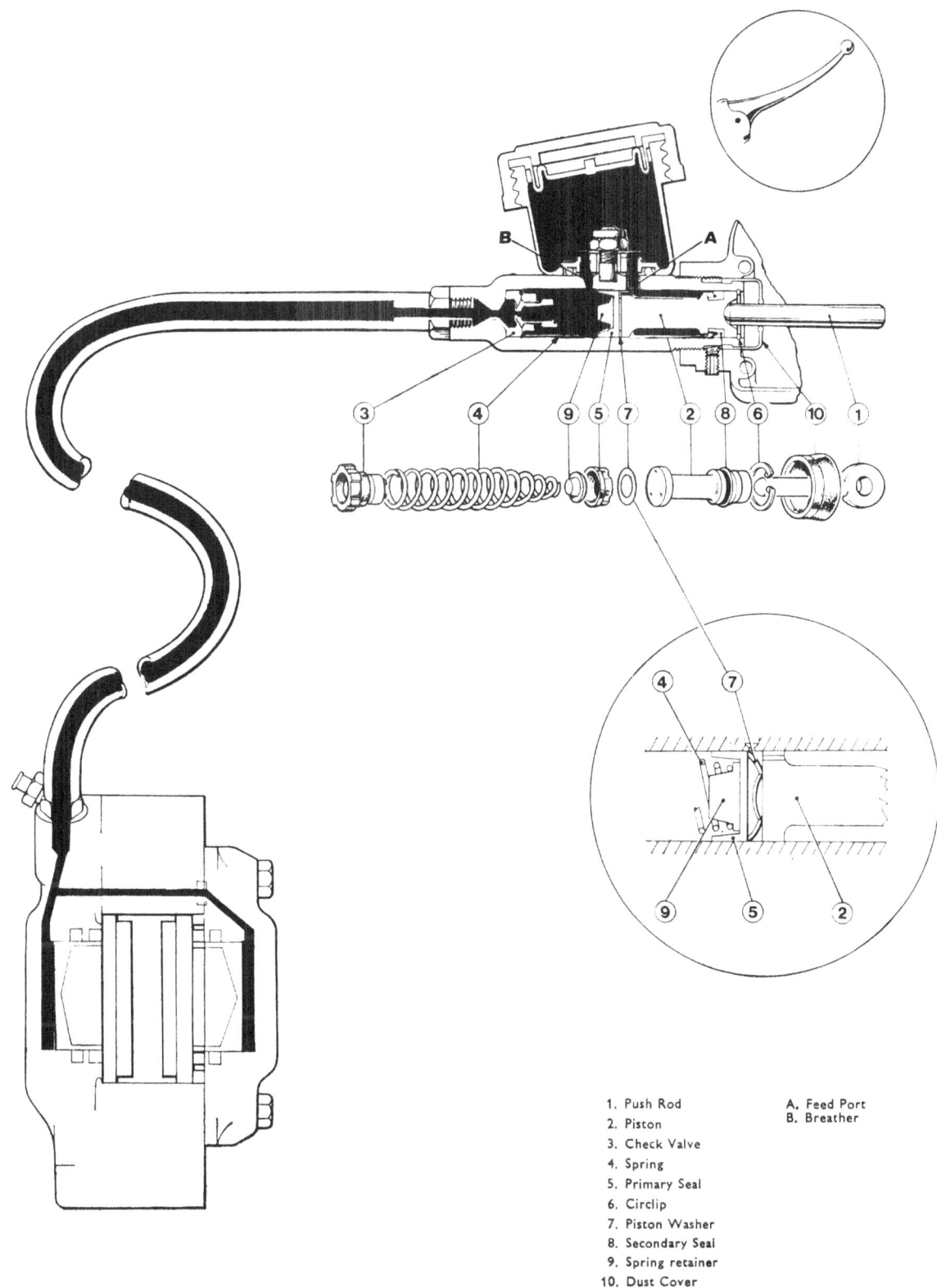

1. Push Rod
2. Piston
3. Check Valve
4. Spring
5. Primary Seal
6. Circlip
7. Piston Washer
8. Secondary Seal
9. Spring retainer
10. Dust Cover

A. Feed Port
B. Breather

Fig. F30. Hydraulic flow diagram

If necessary refit the return spring. Empty the cylinder of fluid and proceed to re-assemble the cylinder barrel into the switch housing. At this stage the final position of the cylinder barrel in the housing must be determined. Here reference must be made to Fig. F30 (i). It will be observed from Fig. F30 (i) that the lip of the primary seal (5) must be 1/16 of an inch behind the breather port and the reservoir set at an angle of 10° to the vertical. The milled flats on the threaded end of the cylinder are machined relative to the 10° position and the appropriate one must be used when assembly takes place.

The following method can be used to determine the correct linear position of the cylinder barrel.

(1) Remove the reservoir from the cylinder.
(2) Re-assemble the front brake lever and push rod to the switch housing.
(3) Screw the cylinder barrel into the switch housing whilst holding the brake lever in the closed position until it will screw no further.

(4) Place one finger over the main feed port (A) Fig. F29 and by blowing through the outlet end of the cylinder it will be observed that no air will escape from the breather port (B) Fig. F29.

(5) Now unscrew the cylinder barrel until air is heard to escape from the breather port (B). At this point the port will have just become uncovered.

(6) Unscrew the barrel one complete turn and set the angle to 10° as shown in Fig. 31. The milled flat on the threaded end of the barrel must be located when the grub screw (Fig. F29) is being re-tightened and will set the angle automatically.

Re-assemble the master cylinder to the handlebar replenish the reservoir with fluid and "bleed" the system as described in Section F24.

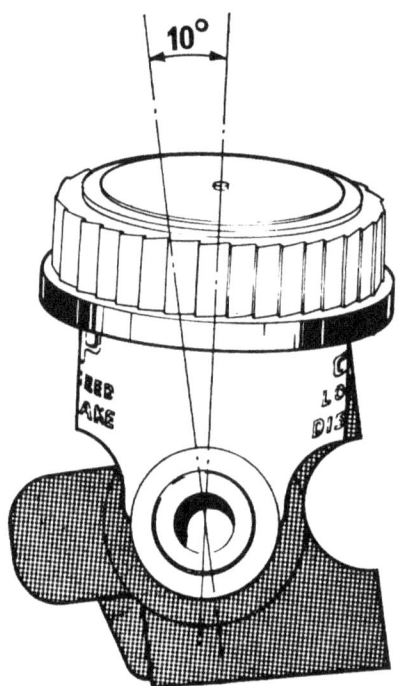

Fig. F31. Showing angle of brake reservoir

SECTION F25

STRIPPING AND REASSEMBLING THE BRAKE CALIPER

Detach the protection cover from the caliper by removing the two crosshead screws. (See Fig. F23 for exploded view). Drain the system of fluid. See Section F22. Detach the feed pipe from the caliper and remove the two securing nuts at the fork leg and withdraw the caliper from its mounting studs. Remove the two split pins that retain the brake pads and pull them out.

No attempt should be made to remove the caliper bridge bolts jointing the two halves of the caliper. There is no necessity to do so and all the servicing can be carried out without splitting the halves, and in addition the bolts are tightened to a critical torque loading.

If in an emergency, the brake caliper has been split and in event of the fluid channel seal being undamaged, the caliper and bridge bolts should be thoroughly cleaned, dried and reassembled and the bridge bolts tightened to a torque loading of 35–40 ft. lbs. (4.8 to 5.5 Kg.m). After reassembling, the brake caliper should be checked for fluid tightness under maximum brake lever pressure.

It should be understood that this procedure will only provide a temporary remedy and the caliper should be returned to the manufacturers for overhaul at the first opportunity. Service the rubber seals as follows:- (read in conjunction with Fig. F23).

A rubber sealing ring (1) is fitted in a groove machined in each pistons bore to seal off the hydraulic fluid. A "U" shaped rubber dust seal (2) having two wiping edges and housed in a metal container (3) is pressed into the open end of the piston bore to prevent the ingress of dust from the brake pads.

The dust seal (2) together with its retainer (3) must be renewed each time they are removed from the piston bore. When the rubber seal (1) is worn or damaged it must be renewed. Before installation the seals should be lubricated with Lockheed disc brake lubricant. The movement of the pistons (4) and (5) within their respective bore extrude the rectangular rubber seal (1) from its groove. On releasing the brake lever the hydraulic pressure collapses and the rubber seal (1) retracts the pistons (4) and (5) a pre-determined amount, thus maintaining a constant clearance between the brake pads and the brake disc when the brakes are not in use.

To remove rubber seals:- Prise out and discard the dust seal (2) and (3) from the open end of each piston bore by inserting a blade of a blunt screwdriver between the seal and retainer. Eject each piston from their bores by applying compressed air to the fluid inlet. Lift out and discard the sealing rings (1) from the grooves in the piston bores by inserting a blunt screwdriver under each ring taking care not to damage the grooves.

Dry the new sealing rings (1) and smear them with Lockheed disc brake lubricant and refit them into the groove of each piston bore so that the large side is nearer the open end of the piston bore. Gently work the sealing rings into their respective grooves with the fingers to ensure correct seating. Dry the pistons and coat with Lockheed disc brake lubricant. Offer up the pistons, closed end first squarely to the bores in the caliper and press the pistons fully home. Dry the dust seals and coat with Lockheed disc brake lubricant.

Fit a dust seal into a metal retainer and position both squarely into the mouth of one piston bore with the dust seal facing the bore. Press the dust seal into the mouth of the piston bore using a "G" clamp and support plate, until its outer edges are flush with the bore. Repeat with the second dust seal and retainer. Fit new brake pads (See Section F20). Refit the brake caliper to the fork leg. Reconnect the hydraulic feed pipe and "bleed" the system as in Section F21. Refit the protection cover.

SECTION F26

BRAKE DISCS

The brake disc will require no maintenance other than when re-newal becomes necessary due to damage or becoming excessively scored. If this occurs the disc must be checked for run-out using a dial test indicator. The maximum reading should not exceed 0.0035 ins. (·089 mm)

To replace the disc, firstly remove the front wheel. See Section F27. Unscrew the four securing nuts and detach the disc. Fit new disc and tighten the nuts diagonally opposite to each other to the torque figure given in General Data.

Replace the wheel into the forks and attach a dial test indicator to the fork leg and check the run-out to the figure previously quoted. If it is outside the limit the disc should be repositioned in an attempt to obtain a more satisfactory combination of machining limits.

Excessive run-out of the brake disc moves the pistons back into the bores and creates excessive lever travel when the brake is applied thus the run-out must be kept to the specified minimum.

SECTION F27
REMOVING AND REFITTING THE FRONT WHEEL

Place the machine on the centre stand or support so that the front wheel is clear of the ground.
Unscrew the eight fork cap nuts and remove both caps and withdraw the front wheel. Do not apply the front brake while the wheel is out of the forks. To replace the wheel engage the disc between the brake pads in the caliper and replace the fork caps tightening the four nuts of the left hand fork leg before finally tightening the right hand leg. This will enable the spindle to align correctly with the left fork leg. (See General Data for correct torque figures for the cap nuts).

SECTION F28
REMOVING AND REFITTING THE FRONT WHEEL BEARINGS

Remove the front wheel (See Section above). Unscrew the wheel spindle fixing nut from the left hand side and then unscrew the retaining ring with service tool 61-3694 (Right hand thread). The left hand bearing can now be removed by driving the wheel spindle through from the right hand side. Withdraw the inner grease retaining disc from the left hand side. To remove the right hand side bearing, spring out the circlip and insert the wheel spindle from the left hand side and drive the bearing out complete with inner and outer grease retaining plates.

Fully clean all parts in paraffin (kerosene). Clean and dry the bearings thoroughly. Compressed air should be used for drying out the ball races. Test for end float and inspect the balls and races for any signs of pitting. If there is any doubt about their condition, the bearings should be renewed.

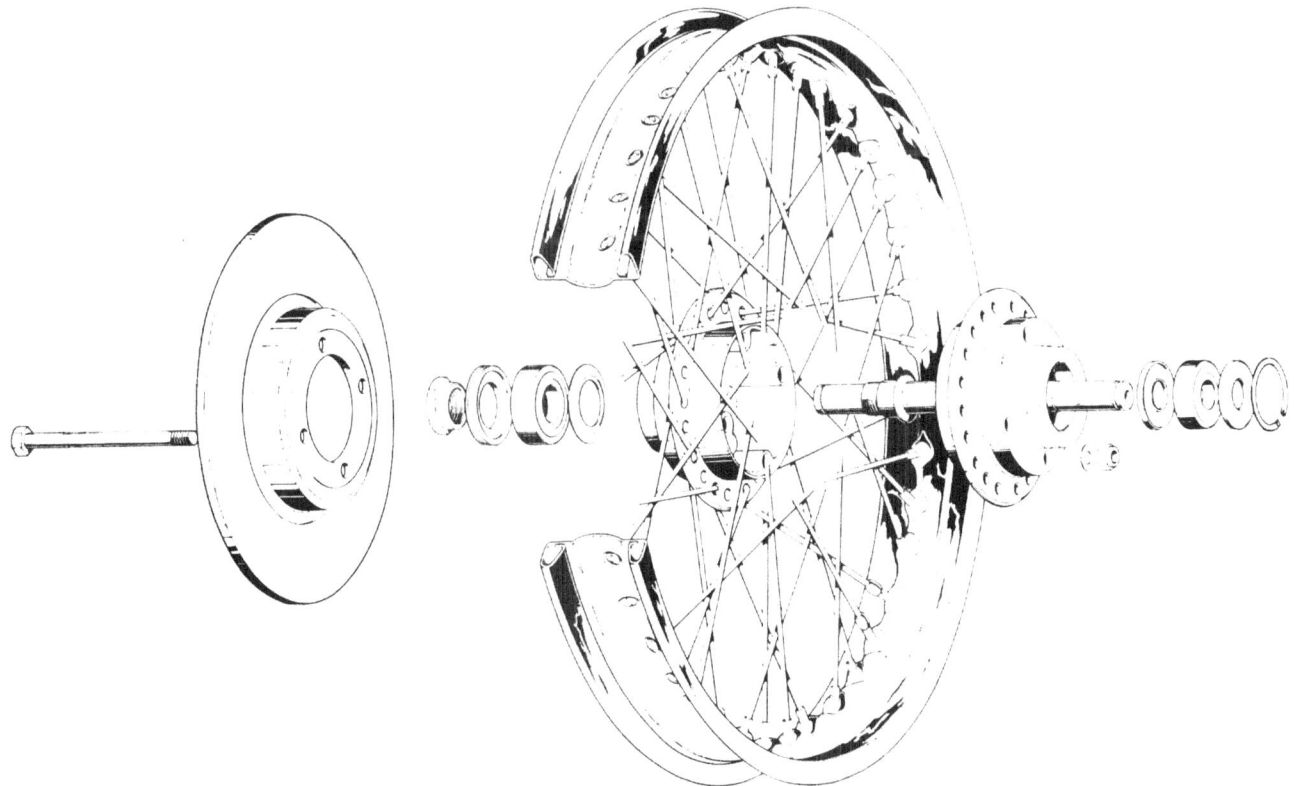

Fig. F32. Exploded view of front wheel bearing arrangement

BRAKES, WHEELS AND TYRES

To refit the bearings first insert the right grease retainer, bearing and outer dust cap, using a liberal amount of grease (See Section A2). Refit the spring circlip and insert the shouldered end of the wheel spindle from the left and using it as a drift drive the bearing and grease retainer until they come up to the circlip. Re-insert the spindle the opposite way round and refit the left hand grease retainer disc. Drive the left bearing into position well smeared with grease then screw in the retainer ring (right hand thread) until tight. Using Service tool No. 61-3694. Tap the spindle from the right to bring the spindle shoulder up against the left bearing Replace the spindle fixing nut and re-tighten firmly. (Refer to Fig. F32 for layout and identification).

SECTION G

TELESCOPIC FORKS

DESCRIPTION:

	Section
REMOVING THE TELESCOPIC FORK UNIT	G1
REMOVING AND REPLACING THE INSTRUMENT BINNACLE	G2
DISMANTLING THE TELESCOPIC FORK	G3
INSPECTION AND REPAIR OF FORK COMPONENTS	G4
RENEWING THE STEERING HEAD RACES	G5
RENEWING THE FRONT OIL SEALS	G6
REASSEMBLING AND REFITTING THE FORK UNIT	G7
TELESCOPIC FORK ALIGNMENT	G8
ADJUSTING THE STEERING HEAD RACES	G9
CHANGING THE FRONT FORK MAIN SPRINGS	G10

G TELESCOPIC FORKS

DESCRIPTION

The front fork assembly is of the telescopic type, using turned steel stanchions, ground over the sliding portion of their length.

The fork bottom members slide on sintered bronze bushes, the lower ones being secured to the bottom of each stanchion, and the top ones being shouldered to rest on the top of the fork bottom members, where they are secured by chromium-plated dust excluder sleeve nuts.

External main springs are fitted, these being supported at the lower ends by the dust excluder sleeve nuts which contain garter type oil seals. Oil is contained in the fork bottom members, this being used for damping purposes and also for lubrication. These stanchions have drilled bleed holes, and shuttle valves which are fitted to the lower end of each stanchion, and retained by circlips. Cone-shaped restricters are secured inside the bottom members by hexagonally headed bolts, recessed into the spindle cutaway.

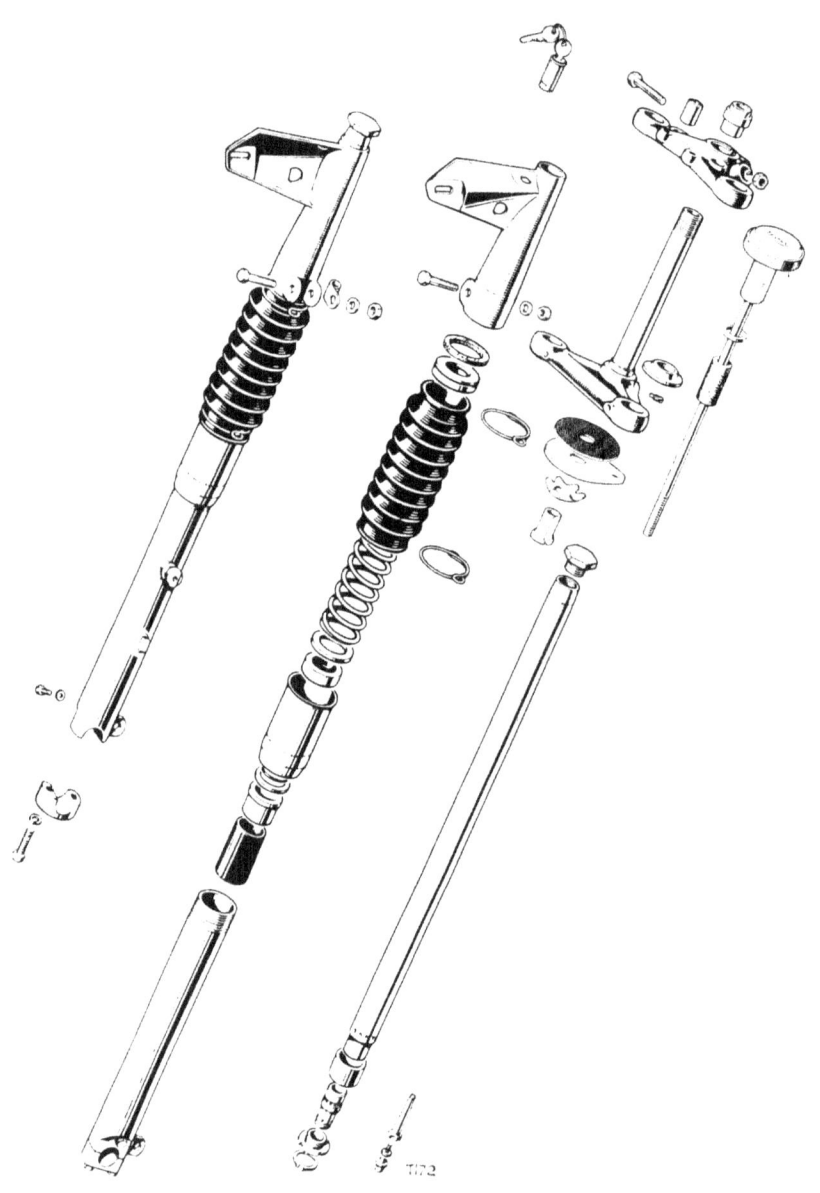

Fig. G1. Exploded view of telescopic front fork

SECTION G1

REMOVING THE TELESCOPIC FORK UNIT

Removal of the front forks is best achieved by detaching the fork as a unit, removing the top lug only whilst the stanchions and middle lug assembly is lower than the frame.

First, unscrew the small drain plugs at the bottom of the fork legs, adjacent to the wheel spindle lug, and drain the oil by pumping the fork up and down several times.

Place a strong wooden box beneath the engine, so that the front wheel is about 6 in. clear of the ground. Remove the front wheel and mudguard as in Section F1. Detach the headlamp unit, Section H10, and detach the throttle cable and air control cable. The handlebar can then be removed by unscrewing the two self-locking nuts which secure the eye bolts beneath the top lug.

Remove the steering damper knob, and slacken the top lug pinch bolt and unscrew the sleeve nuts. Remove the left and right stanchion top nuts, using spanner D779.

Remove the Zener Diode "Lucar" connector, and also the earth (ground) wire from the mounting bolts. Remove the fork pinch bolts, to enable the fork shrouds, headlamp and binnacle to remain in position.

Support the fork and then give the top lug a sharp tap on the underside until it is released from the stanchion locking tapers. The stanchions and middle leg assembly can then be lowered from the frame head lugs. If care is taken the top ball race can be left undisturbed, and the lower race balls collected when the clearance is sufficient.

ALTERNATIVE METHOD
Alternatively, fork stanchions can be removed whilst the middle lug, top lug and head races are left undisturbed. To facilitate extraction of the stanchions from the top of middle lugs in this space, service tool 61-3824 will be required. Remove the top nuts, slacken the middle lug pinch bolts, and screw in 61-3824 drift. Drive the stanchion downwards until it is free to be withdrawn from the middle lug, as shown in Fig. G2.

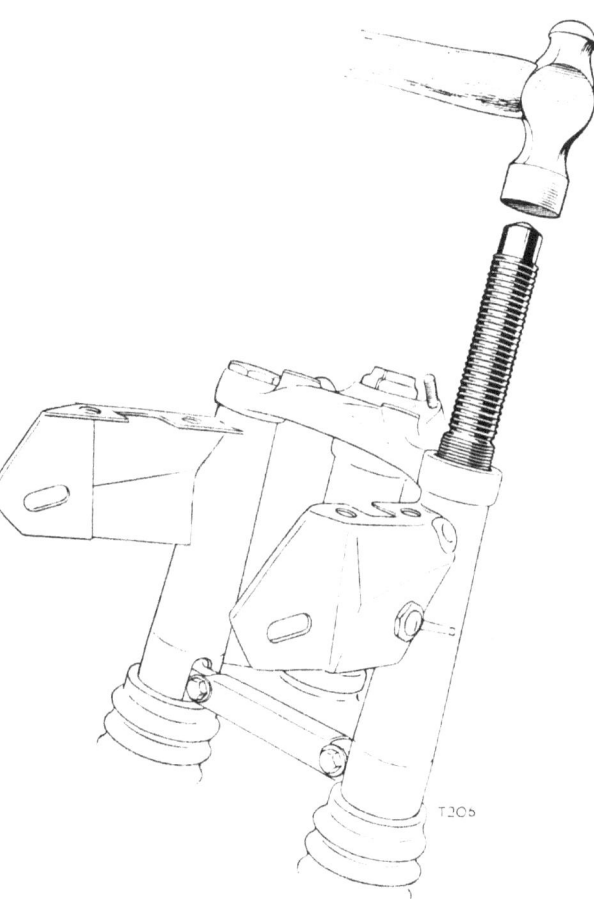

Fig. G2. Extracting a stanchion using service tool 61-3824

SECTION G2

REMOVING AND REPLACING THE INSTRUMENT BINNACLE

Remove the headlamp as in Section H10, and disconnect the speedometer and tachometer drive cables from the instrument heads. Withdraw the "Lucar" connectors from both the ignition switch and light switch, and withdraw the Lucar connector and disconnect the earth (ground) tag from the Zenner Diode heat sink. Withdraw the snap connectors for the instrument illumination lamps, and also the binnacle warning lights, also disconnect two red earth (ground) wires at their snap connectors. Finally, withdraw the cut-out button and dip switch/horn push from the snap connectors.

Remove four nuts and plain washers from the binnacle securing studs, and withdraw the binnacle from the fork shrouds.

The reassembly procedure is the reversal of the above, reference being made to the wiring diagram in Section H17.

SECTION G3

DISMANTLING THE TELESCOPIC FORK

Remove the front fork from the frame head lug as described in Section G1. Grip the middle lug firmly in a vice, and remove the top and bottom gaiter securing clips. Screw service tool 61-3824 into the top of the stanchion (use an old cap nut in the absence of the correct tool) and drive the stanchions out of the middle lug. When the stanchions are removed, collect the spring abutments, springs, gaiters and clips (if fitted). At this stage, the fork top shrouds can be removed. It is advisable to renew the sealing washer when reassembling the forks.

Removal of the dust excluder sleeve nuts is facilitated by service tool 61-6017, which should be attached to the sleeve nut whilst the wheel spindle lug is held firmly in a vice. The sleeve nut has a right hand thread and should unscrew easily once the nut has been initially loosened by giving the spanner a sharp tap with a mallet.

When the dust excluder nut is removed, a few sharp pulls should release the stanchion, bush and shuttle valve assembly from the bottom member.

If it is required to remove the cone-shaped restricter from the bottom member, merely release the securing bolts. The hexagon headed restricter securing bolt, counter-bored into the wheel spindle lug, is sealed by means of an aluminium washer which should be withdrawn from the counter-bore when the bolt is removed, and placed in storage and refitted on assembly.

The shuttle valves are retained in the bottom end of each stanchion by the bottom bearing retaining nuts. Circlips are also fitted to prevent the shuttle valves recessing into the stanchions (see Fig. G3).

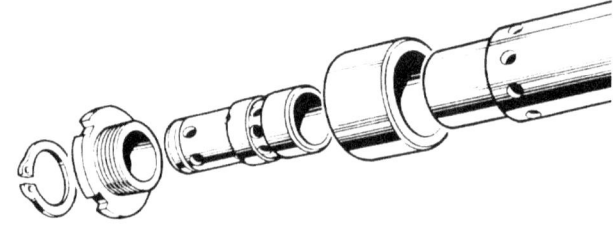

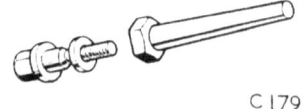

Fig. G3. Exploded view of shuttle valve

SECTION G4

INSPECTION AND REPAIR OF FORK COMPONENTS

Telescopic fork components which have received minor damage may possibly be repaired without the need of new parts. The stanchions are the most vulnerable part to damage and correction is often possible if the damage is within the limits described below. The top lug and middle lug are malleable stampings and slight misalignment can be corrected as described in the paragraphs below. The tools required in order that a throrough check of the various alignments can be made are an engineer's checking table, set square, adjustable calipers and a height gauge.

(1) Check the stanchions for truth by rolling them slowly on a flat checking table. A bent stanchion may be realigned if the bow does not exceed $\frac{5}{32}$ in. maximum. To realign the stanchion, a hand press is required. Place the stanchion on two swage "V" blocks at either end and apply pressure to the raised portion of the stanchion. By means of alternately pressing in this way and checking the stanchion on a flat table the amount of bow can be reduced until it is finally removed.

(2) Inspect the top lug by fitting both stanchions (if true) with the cap nuts tightened in position as shown in Fig. G4. Check that the stanchions are parallel to each other in both planes by laying the assembly on a checking table and taking caliper readings as shown. Using a set square, check that the stanchions are at right angles to the top lug.

Check the middle lug and stem for alignment by inserting the stanchions until $6\frac{1}{2}$ in. (16·5 cm.) of the top of the stanchion protrudes shown in Fig. G5. Fit and tighten the pinch bolts in position and then lay the assembly on the checking table and with calipers check that the stanchions lie parallel in the middle lug.

The stanchions should also be checked for being parallel in the other plane by sighting along the checking table top. A set square should be used to check that the stanchions are at right angles to the middle lug.

The middle lug stamping is malleable and provided that the lug is not excessively distorted, it can be trued quite easily. Each time a distortion correction is carried out check that the assembly is true in both planes.

(3) When the stanchions and middle lug assembly has been trued, the top lug can be used to check the position of the stem relative to the middle lug. For this purpose, the distance between the middle lug and top lug should be the same on either side and to achieve this the stanchions should be set in the middle lug to the figure given in Fig. G6. When the top lug is fitted the stem should be central in the top lug hole. If it is not a long tube can be placed over the stem and used to press the stem in the correcting direction. When this is achieved, re-check the fork assembly to ensure that the original alignment has not been adversely effected.

Fig. G4. Checking the top lug for alignment

G TELESCOPIC FORKS

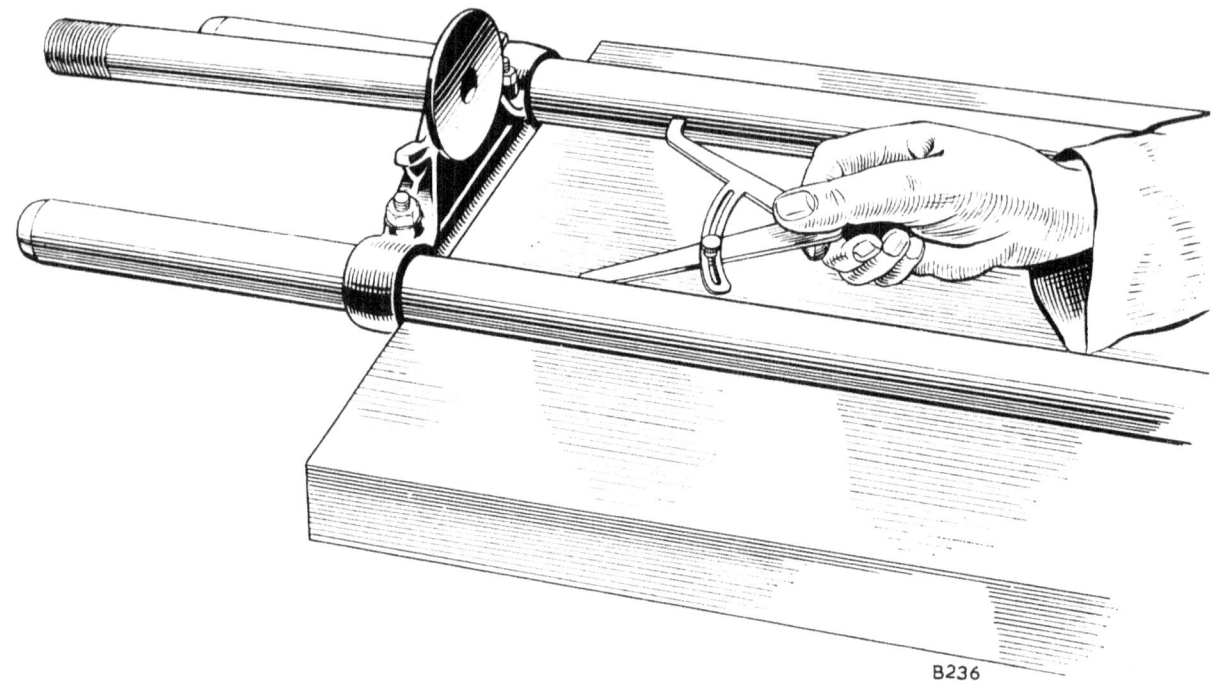

Fig G5. Checking the stanchions and middle lug for alignment

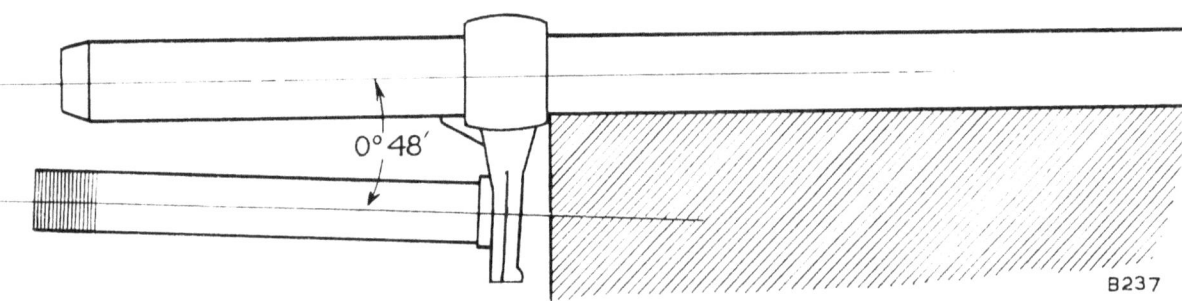

Fig. G6. Showing the correct angle and positioning between the stanchion and middle lug and stem

Check the stanchion bearing surfaces for wear. It is permissible to polish the stanchions with the fine emery cloth to remove roughness.

(4) Check that the bottom members are not dented or damaged in any way by inserting the stanchion and bottom bush assembly and feeling the amount of clearance of the bush within the bore of the bottom member. Any restriction on movement indicates that the bottom member is damaged and requires renewing. The wheel spindle lug can be checked for being at right angles to the bottom member by machining a one $\frac{1}{4}$ in. wide groove in a $\frac{11}{16}$ in. diameter bar and bolting it in position in the wheel spindle lug. A square may then be used to check that the bar is perpendicular to the bottom member. If the degree of error is excessive, no attempt should be made to realign the wheel spindle lug, the bottom member should be renewed.

(5) Examine the top and bottom bushes for Wear by measuring the bore diameter of the top bush and the outside diameter of the bottom bush and comparing them with the figures given in GENERAL DATA. Also, the bushes can be checked against their respective mating surfaces: put the top bush over the stanchion and at about eight inches from the bottom of the stanchion check the diametral clearance at the bush. An excessive clearance indicates that the bush requires renewing. As described above, the bottom bush can only be checked by fitting it to the stanchion and inserting the stanchion into the bottom member to a depth of about eight inches whilst the diametral clearance is estimated from the amount of "play".

(6) Examine the main springs for fatigue and cracks and check that both springs are of approximate equal length and within $\frac{1}{4}$ in. of the original length. The figures for the original length are given in GENERAL DATA.

(7) Inspect the cups and cones for wear in the form of pitting or pocketing. This will appear as a series of small indentations in the ball tracks and indicates that both the races and the balls require renewing.

The cups should be a tight interference fit into the frame headlug. Slackness there usually indicates that the headlug cup seatings are distorted. The bottom cone should be a tight fit onto the middle lug stem and the top cone and dust cap assembly should be a close sliding fit over the stem. Slackness of the cone on the stem indicates that the steering races have not been in correct adjustment. In this case, if the new cone is not a tight fit over the stem, then either the stem and middle lug assembly should be renewed or in certain cases a proprietary sealant may be used to secure the cone in position.

SECTION G5

RENEWING THE STEERING HEAD RACES

The cups can be driven out of the headlug from the inside by inserting a long narrow drift and locating it on the inner edge of the cups. When the cups are removed the bore of the headlug should be cleaned thoroughly and the new cups driven in by using a hammer and aluminium drift or a piece of hard wood interposed to check the blow. Care should be taken to ensure that the cup enters into the headlug squarely and that no burrs are set up due to misalignment.

The bottom cone can easily be removed from the stem by inserting levers on either side and prising the cone upwards. When it has been removed, clean the stem and remove any burrs with a fine grade file before fitting the new cones. To ensure that the new cone is driven on squarely service tool number D2218 should be used. To assist in the assembly of the cone a small amount of grease may be smeared on the middle lug stem. If the service tool is not available a suitable drift can be made from a piece of $1\frac{1}{16}$ in. (2·7 cm.) inside diameter tube 9 in. long. Note that when new cups and cones are fitted, new balls must also be used. The correct quantity is 40 off $\frac{1}{4}$ in. diameter balls— 20 top race and 20 bottom race.

SECTION G6

RENEWING THE FRONT FORK OIL SEALS

On the front fork the oil seal is pressed into the dust excluder sleeve nut and is freely accessible from both sides. The oil seal can be driven out by inserting a suitable drift and locating it on the oil seal at one of the peripheral slots.

The new oil seal should be pressed in with the lip and spring side facing the threaded end of the sleeve nut and a check should be made to ensure that it is fully and squarely engaged.

A rubber 'O' ring seal is fitted into the thread of the chrome dust excluder. It is advisable to remove the 'O' ring which will almost certainly be compressed and to fit a new one to each dust excluder.

SECTION G7

REASSEMBLING AND REFITTING THE TELESCOPIC FORK UNIT

Assemble the bottom bush to the stanchion, fit the shuttle valve, large diameter uppermost and secure with the bearing retaining nut. Fit the circlip to prevent the shuttle valve sliding back into the stanchion (see Fig. G3).

If the cone-shaped restrictor has been removed, it must be refitted to the bottom member at this stage, being retained by the hexagonally headed bolt, and aluminium sealing washer fitted into the wheel spindle cutaway recess. To hold the restrictor in position whilst the bolt is fitted, use the stanchion complete with shuttle valve as a guide.

Offer the stanchion bottom bush assembly into the bottom member and refit the top bush. Offer the dust excluder sleeve complete with 'O' ring and seal over the stanchion which should be lightly smeared with oil. Tighten the dust excluder in position over the bottom member, using a spanner 61-6017. Lower the spring into position over the stanchion, followed by the gaiters, top spring abutment and cork washer. (The gaiters should be secured top and bottom with the clips over the top abutment, and dust excluder, on early machines).

Thoroughly clean the head race cups and cones and smear the ball tracks with the recommended grease (see Section A2). Place the ball bearings in the cups (20 top, 20 bottom) using grease to hold them in position. Offer the middle lug and stem assembly to the headlug and lower the top cone and dust cover assembly into position. Refit the top lug and sleeve nut, tighten the sleeve nut until all the slack is taken up. Refit the sleeve nut pinch bolt finger tight and align the middle lug and top lug. Align the top and middle lug. Fit the left and right fork top shrouds and insert the middle lug pinch bolts and nuts finger tight.

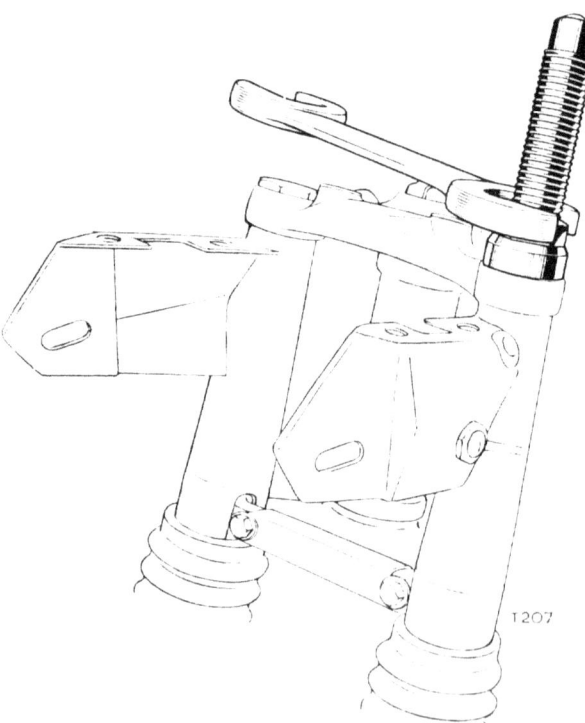

Fig. G7. Refitting the fork stanchion assemblies using service tool 61-3824

TELESCOPIC FORKS

Offer the right stanchion assembly (with welded boss for front brake anchor plate location) and engage as much of the stanchion as possible in the middle lug. To pull the stanchion up to the top lug, service tool 61-3824 is required, which should be inserted into the top lug and the plug adaptor screwed into the stanchion top. The stanchion can be easily drawn up to the required level and when this is achieved, temporarily tighten the pinch bolt, remove the tool and screw in the cap nut until several threads are engaged (see Fig. 67).

Repeat this procedure for the left stanchion assembly and then remove both cap nuts and pour one third of a pint (200 c.c.) of the recommended grade of oil (see Section A2) into each fork leg.

Refit the cap nuts until several threads are engaged, and slacken off the middle lug pinch bolt and fully tighten the cap nuts with a spanner, D779. When this is achieved, adjust the steering head races as described in Section G9 and then tighten the sleeve nut pinch bolt and two middle lug pinch bolts, until the required torque figures as given in GENERAL DATA.

Reassembly continues as the reversal of the dismantling procedure, referring to Section H17 for the wiring diagram, and Section H9 to align the headlamp main beam.

HANDLEBAR FIXING

Eyebolts are employed for fixing the handlebars. Metalastic bushes are fitted into the fork top lug. Note that the hemispherical washers (see Fig. G8) should be fitted with the rounded side towards the headlug.

Solid bushes are available if a handlebar mounted windscreen is to be fitted. This arrangement dispenses with the metalastic bushes in the headlug. It is not necessary to use the hemispherical washers.

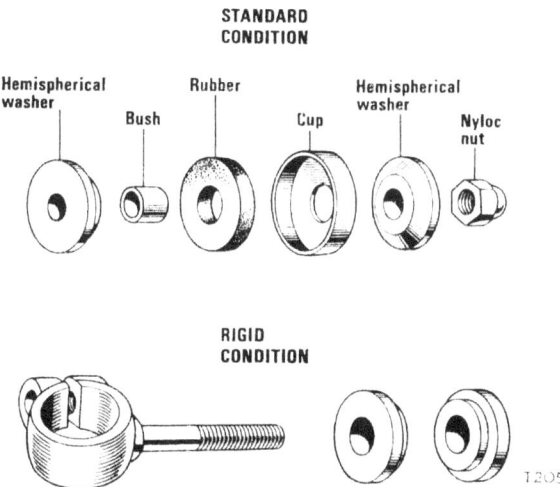

Fig. G8. Handlebar mountings

SECTION G8

TELESCOPIC FORK ALIGNMENT

To facilitate checking the alignment of the telescopic fork legs there is available service tool 61-6025 the dimensions of which are shown in Fig. G9.

To check the front fork alignment, the front wheel and mudguard must be removed and a spare wheel spindle bolted in position. If a spare spindle is not available use the one removed from the front wheel as described in Section F7.

G TELESCOPIC FORKS

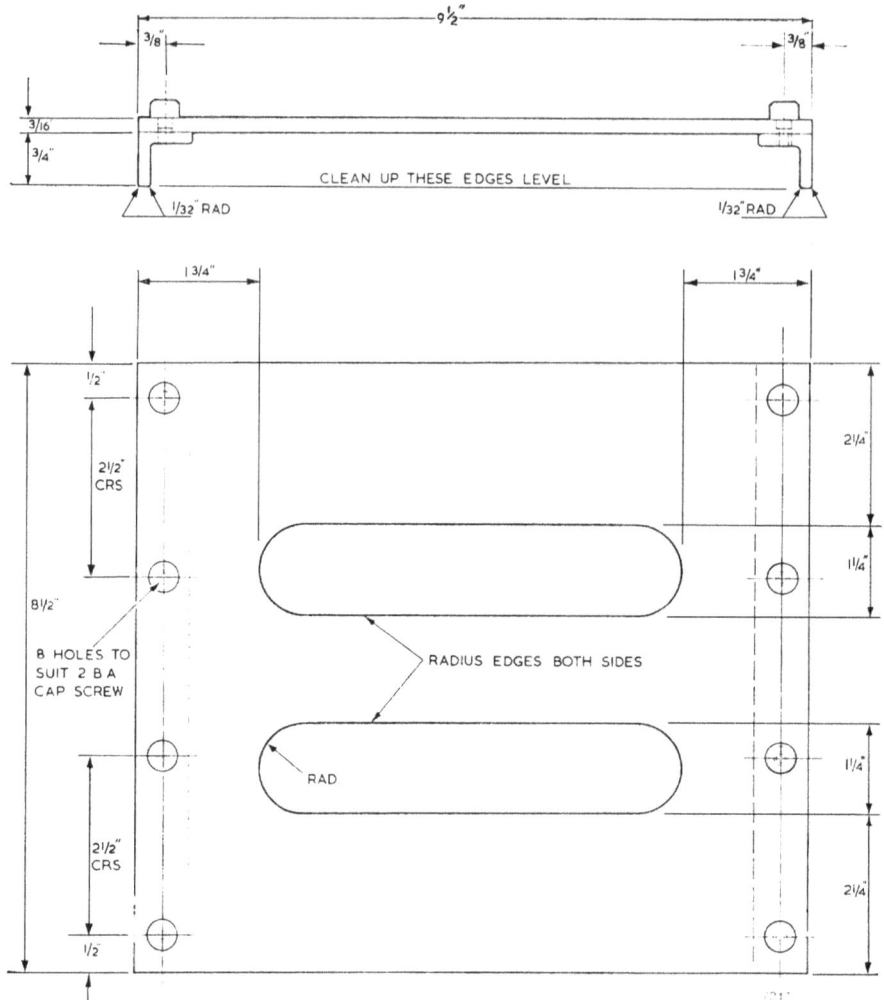

Fig. G9. Telescopic fork leg alignment gauge, service tool 61-6025

Hold the alignment gauge firmly against the fork legs as shown in Fig. G10 and check that the gauge contacts at all four corners. If the gauge does not make contact at point A then this indicates that point B is too far forward. To remedy this, slacken off the two middle lug pinch bolts and the stem sleeve nut pinch bolt and give the top lug above point 'A', a sharp blow using a hide mallet or a hammer used in conjunction with a soft metal drift.

Check the alignment again with the gauge and again give correcting blows in the above mentioned manner until the amount of rock at any one corner does not exceed $\frac{1}{64}$ in. When this is achieved, tighten all three pinch bolts and then finally apply the gauge to check that tightening has not caused distortion.

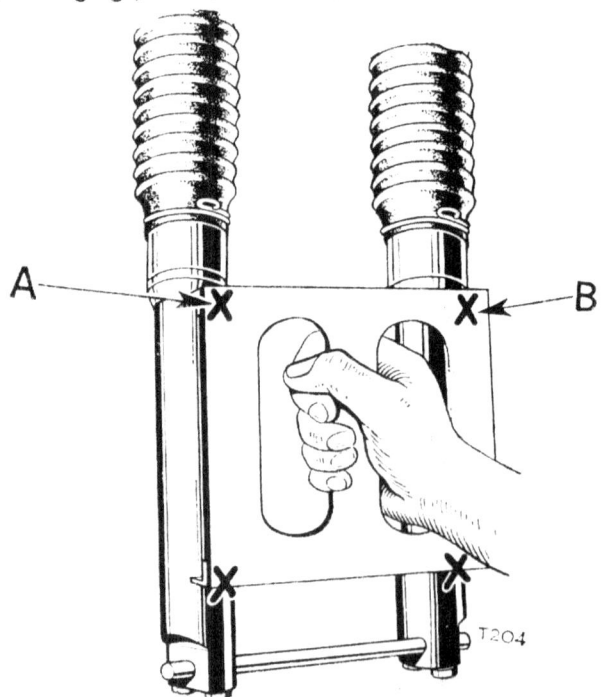

Fig. G10. Checking the telescopic fork leg alignment with service tool 61-6025

TELESCOPIC FORKS

SECTION G9

ADJUSTING THE STEERING HEAD RACES

When a new machine has covered the 500 miles (running-in period) it will be necessary to check the steering head races for excessive play due to the balls, cups and cones bedding down.

Also, after long periods, the head races may require adjusting to compensate for any wear that may have taken place. The working clearance of the balls in the tracks of the cups and cones is controlled by the fork stem sleeve nut which is locked in position by means of a pinch bolt at the rear of the top lug. When the pinch bolt is slackened the sleeve nut can be turned to increase or decrease the head race working clearance.

Mount the machine with the front wheel clear of the ground and balance the front fork so that both the front and rear wheels are aligned. When the fork is tilted to either side of its central position it should just fall to its full lock position. If the fork will do this then the head races are not over tight and conversely to check that they are not too loose, hold the top lug with the left hand and hold the top portion of the front mudguard in the right hand and then attempt to "rock" the fork. If there is any "rock" in evidence, then tighten the stem sleeve nut $\frac{1}{4}$ turn and check again. Continuing this way until the fork will not rock but will turn from lock to lock easily. When this is achieved, re-tighten the stem sleeve nut pinch bolt.

SECTION G10

CHANGING THE FRONT FORK MAIN SPRINGS

First, place a strong box underneath the engine so that the motorcycle is mounted with the front wheel off the ground.

Removing the springs necessitates withdrawing the complete fork leg assemblies, leaving the top and middle lugs in the frame. This is accomplished by removing the top nuts using spanner D779. The pinch bolts should be slackened and the leg assemblies driven out with tool 61-3824.

The springs can then be lifted off over the stanchions. Reassembly can then be undertaken by offering up the stanchions as in Section G7.

When the cap nuts are refitted, they must be fully retightened. If necessary use a piece of tubing which will increase the leverage to about 12 in. to finally tighten the nuts. Reassembly then continues as a reversal of the dismantling procedure.

NOTES

SECTION GG

TELESCOPIC FORKS

INDEX

	Section
DESCRIPTION	—
STEERING HEAD ADJUSTMENTS	GG1
RENEWING HEAD RACES	GG2
STRIPPING AND REASSEMBLING THE FORK LEGS	GG3
FORK ALIGNMENT	GG4
HYDRAULIC DAMPING	GG5

TELESCOPIC FORKS

DESCRIPTION

The front fork is of the telescopic type using high grade steel tube stanchions. They are ground to a micro finish and hard chromium plated over their entire length.

The alloy bottom members are precision bored and provide the bearing for the stanchion. Internal main springs are fitted and locate on the damper tube.

An oil seal is contained in the top lip of each bottom member and is protected by a rubber dust cover.

Oil is contained in each bottom member and serves the dual purpose of damping and lubrication. Oil is added by removal of the fork cap nuts and cap screws and drained at the plugs provided.

SECTION GG1

STEERING HEAD ADJUSTMENT

It is important that the steering head bearings are always correctly adjusted.

Place a strong support underneath the engine so that the front wheel is raised clear of the ground then, standing in front of the wheel, attempt to push the lower fork legs backwards and forwards. Should any play be detected, the steering head must be adjusted.

If possible, ask a friend to place the fingers of one hand lightly round the head lug, whilst the forks are being pulled back and forth. Any play will be felt quite easily by the fingers.

It should be possible to turn the forks from side to side quite smoothly and without any "lumpy" movement. If the movement is "lumpy", the rollers are indented into the races or broken. In either case the complete bearing should be renewed.

To adjust the steering head assembly, slacken the clamp nut B, Fig. GG1 and the top yoke adjuster nut A then tighten down the adjuster nut until adjustment is correct. There should be no play evident in the races but great care must be taken not to over-tighten, or the rollers will become indented into the races, making steering extremely difficult and dangerous.

Having carried out the adjustment, tighten the clamp nuts and the top yoke pinch bolt securely. Re-check the adjustment.

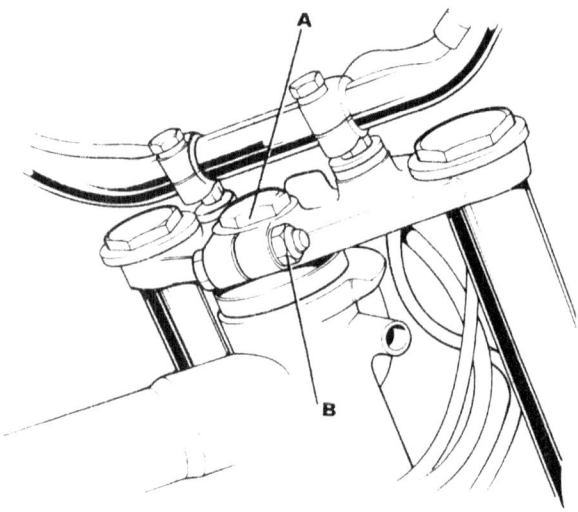

Fig. GG1. Steering head adjustment

SECTION GG2

RENEWING HEAD RACES

Place a strong support underneath the engine so that the front wheel is raised-clear of the ground. Remove the front wheel (see Section F1). Remove the front mudguard (see Section E14).

The steering head can be dismantled without stripping the forks. First, disconnect the hydraulic brake pipe from the top and middle lug. See section KK6

Disconnect the two wires from the Zener Diode and remove by unscrewing the bolt that holds it to the middle lug.

Remove the headlamp. See section H10. Detach the handle bar complete by unscrewing the two self locking nuts which secure the two eye bolts in the top lug. See fig. GG2. Remove fork cap nuts. Place the speedometer and tachometer to one side after first disconnecting the drive cables and illuminating lights.

Slacken the top lug pinch bolt (A) fig. GG1 and remove adjuster nut (B). Loosen both the top and middle lug stanchion pinch bolts with an allen key. Slide fork leg and stanchion from the machine.

Using a raw-hide mallet strike the undersides of the top lug alternately to release if from the stanchions.

Place the yolk to one side and withdraw the steering stem out of the head lug. The ball race bearings can now be removed from the stem and the top lug for cleaning and inspection. Check for pitting and fracture of the roller surface. The bearings must be replaced if any of these faults are in evidence.

The steering head outer races have a very long serviceable life and should not need replacement for a very considerable mileage. If however their replacement is deemed necessary the races can be removed using a suitable drift from inside the head lug. Replacement of the new race is effected by using service tool 61-6121. Do not forget to re-fit the bearing abutment rings behind the outer races.

Reassembly is the reverse of the above procedure. Note that the head of both the top lug and stanchion must be flush leaving the head of the inner retaining plug standing proud. Care must be taken to ensure that the headlamp shrouds are located correctly in the prespective recesses in the top lug.

Note that when refitting the plastic dust cover ensure that it sits square to allow the adjuster nut to locate on the bearing. Readjust the steering head bearing as in Section GG1. Reassemble the hydraulic system as described in Section KK6.

SECTION GG3

STRIPPING AND REASSEMBLING THE FORK LEGS

Before commencing work on the forks it is advisable to have the following tools and replacements available:

(a) Oil seal for dust excluder (2)

(b) Oil seal for damper valve (1)

(c) Service tool (61-6113)

Remove small drain plug at the bottom of each fork adjacent to the wheel spindle and drain out the oil by pumping the forks up and down. Support the machine on a box with the front wheel clear of the ground. Remove front wheel as described in Section FF1. Remove front mudguard.
Detach the handlebar complete by unscrewing the two self locking nuts which secure the two eye bolts in the top lug. Remove fork cap nuts. Place the speedometer and tachometer to one side after first disconnecting the drive cable and illuminating lights.
Disconnect the hydraulic brake pipe at middle lug and fork leg to stanchion (See Section KK6). Remove caliper and place carefully to one side. Unscrew the two allen pinch bolts at the back of the top head lug. Remove alluminium cap screws with suitably sized allen key.

Remove the internal fork springs. Using service tool 61-6113 placed down into the stanchion; hold the valve assembly while the retaining allen screw is being unscrewed at the base of the fork leg.

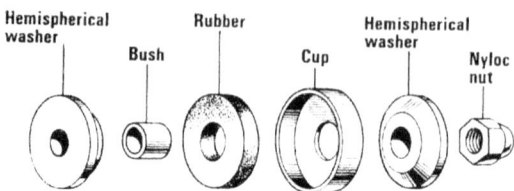

GG2. Handlebar mountings

At this stage it will be possible to remove the fork leg by sliding it from the stanchion. Remove the stanchions by slackening the pinch bolts on the bottom yolk and withdrawing the stanchions. When refitting tighten the pinch bolts to 18/20 lbs./ft.

The dust cover on the fork leg can easily be prised off by hand.

The damper valve assembly is retained in the bottom of the stanchion by an aluminium nut which should be carefully removed with a ring spanner or similar.

TELESCOPIC FORKS GG

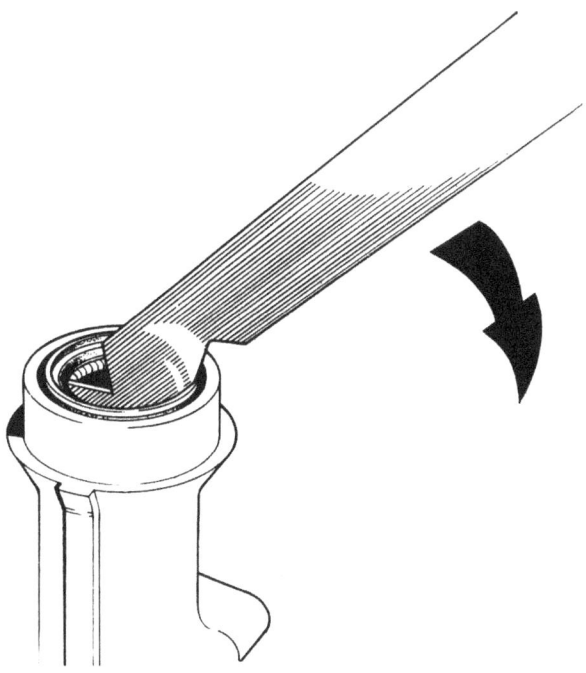

Fig. GG3. Removing oil seal

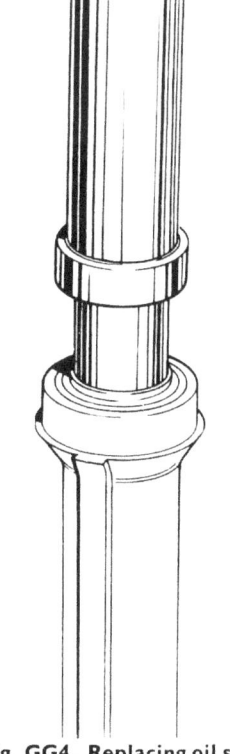

Fig. GG4. Replacing oil seal

Place the stanchion into the fork leg and place a small polythene bag over the top lip of the stanchion. Push the oil seal over the stanchion and down into position on the fork leg. It is important that the polythene is used because the lip of stanchion has a sharp edge that may easily scratch or damage the precision edge of the seal. Even a scratch that may not be readily visible to the eye will cause leakage at the seal. A drift will be required to replace the oil seal into the housing. This can be simply fabricated from an early type steel fork outer member. A turned shoulder will have to be machined and brazed or welded to one end of the fork leg. See Fig. GG5 for details. It is important to assemble the oil seal with the stanchion in position because the seal **must** sit squarely in the counterbore otherwise leakage will occur.

The stanchion used as a guide can now be removed. Check all components for cleanliness and wash in fuel if necessary. Examine the bore of the stanchion and clean with a cloth pushed into the bore.

Reassembly of the fork leg is a reversal of the dismantling procedure. Replace the valve into the bottom of the stanchion. Apply some red loctite to the aluminium nut and tighten to a torque of 25 ft./lbs.

Check that the small "Dowty" sealing washer is located in the well in the base of the fork leg. (If this washer shows signs of damage or wear it must be replaced).

Push the rubber dust cover onto it's location groove on the fork leg and then replace the leg on the stanchion.

As the leg is refitted onto the stanchion the stem of the damper valve assembly must be located on top of the "Dowty" sealing washer. If difficulty is encountered during this operation, service tool 61-6113 which is used to retain the valve assembly while it is being removed may be used to navigate the damper valve onto its location.

The allen screw can then be replaced into the bottom of the fork leg and tightened as described above.

Replace fork leg and stanchion by sliding it up through the rubber stop, middle lug, headlamp bracket and top lug until the top of the stanchion and the surface of the top lug lie exactly flush. Retighten top lug and middle lug pinch bolts to a torque setting of 20 ft/lbs.

Replace the fork springs and refill the fork legs with the correct quantity of oil. See section GD.

Coat the threads of the Cap screw with well seal jointing compound and refit, tightening to a torque of 40 ft/lbs. Reconnect the speedometer drive cable illuminating lights.

Refit caliper on fork leg and reassemble the hydraulic brake system as described in Section KK6.

Replace the handlebars Replace the front mudguard. Refit the front wheel (see section FF1).

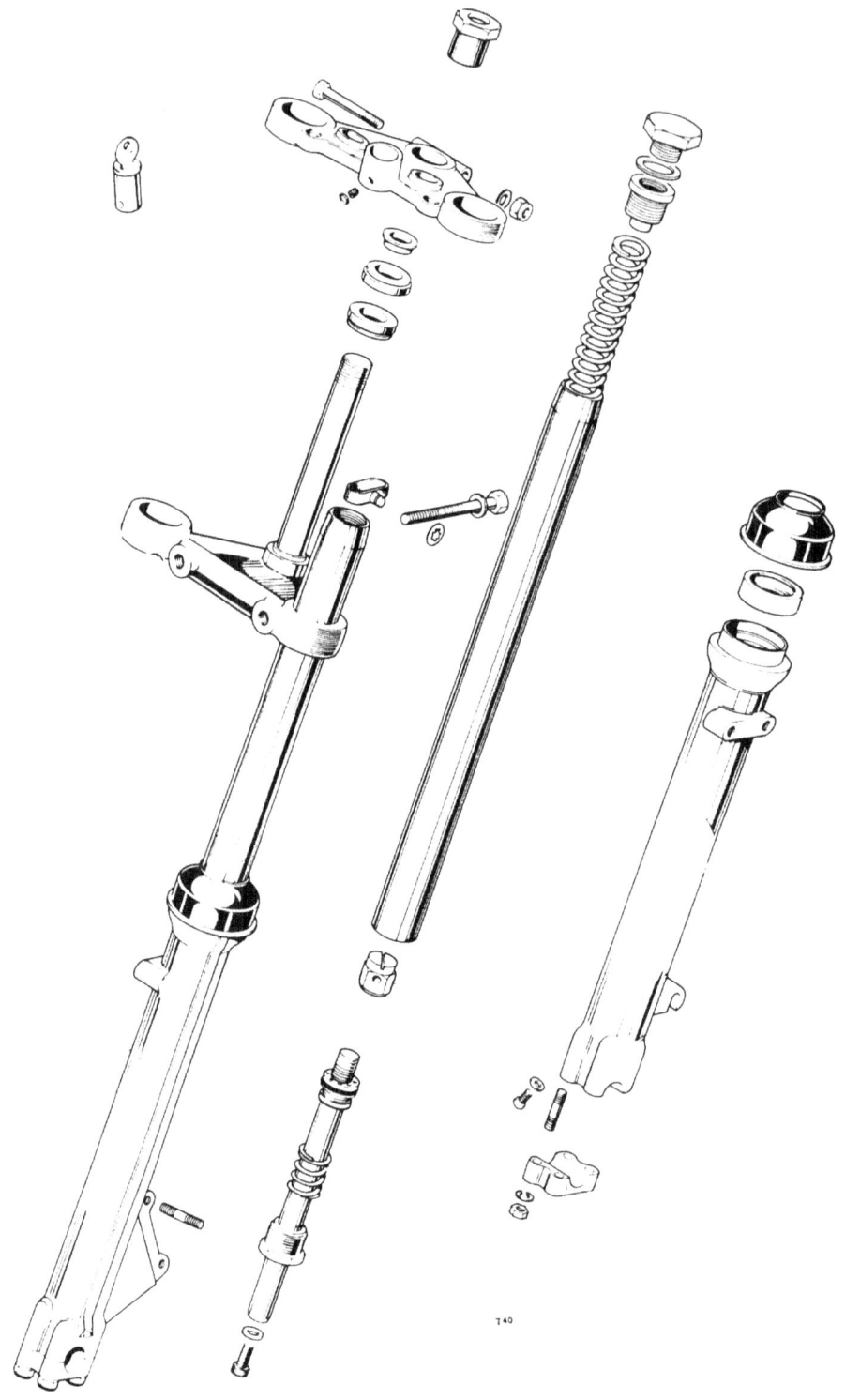

Fig. GG5. Fork assembly details

TELESCOPIC FORKS   GG

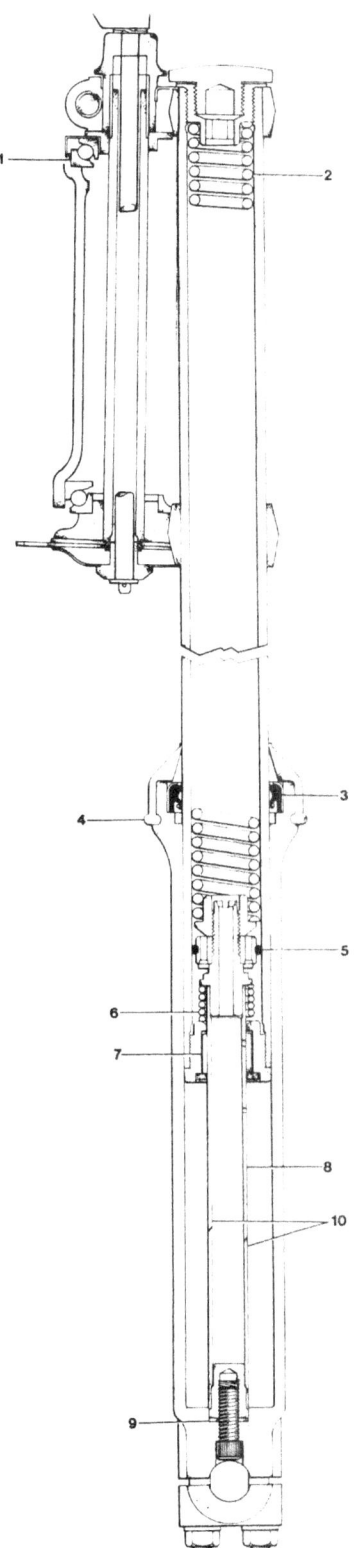

1. Head bearings
2. Main spring
3. Outer member oil seal
4. Scraper sleeve
5. Damper valve 'O' ring
6. Recoil spring
7. Plastic sleeve
8. Damper tube
9. Damper tube cap screw
10. Bleed holes—damper tube

Fig. GG6. Sectional view of assembled fork leg

SECTION GG4
FORK ALIGNMENT

After replacing the fork legs, mudguard and wheel, it may be found that the fork is incorrectly aligned.

To rectify this, the fork wheel spindle cap nuts must first be screwed up tight on the right-hand leg and the spindle cap on the left-hand leg slackened off. Also loosen the top caps and the pinch bolts in both the bottom and top yokes. The forks should now be pumped up and down several times to line them up and then tightened up from bottom to top, that is, wheel spindle, bottom yoke pinch bolts, top caps and finally, the steering stem pinch bolt in the top yoke.

If, after this treatment, the forks still do not function satisfactorily then either the fork stanchions are bent or one of the yokes is twisted.

The stanchions can only be accurately checked for straightness with special equipment such as a surface plate. Special gauges are also required to check the yokes. It is possible, however, to make a reasonable check of the stanchions by rolling them on a surface plate or flat surface such as a piece of plate glass, but it is not a simple operation to straighten a bent tube, and a new part may be necessary.

Check the stanchions for truth by rolling them slowly on a flat checking table. A bent stanchion may be realigned if the bow does not exceed $\frac{5}{32}$ in. maximum. To realign the stanchion, a hand press is required. Place the stanchion on two swage "V" blocks at either end and apply pressure to the raised portion of the stanchion. By means of alternately pressing in this way and checking the stanchion on a flat table the amount of bow can be reduced until it is finally removed.

Having checked the stanchions for straightness and reset as necessary, the top and bottom yokes can now be checked. First, assemble the two stanchions into the bottom yoke so that a straight edge across the lower ends is touching all four edges of the tubes, then tighten the pinch bolts. Now view them from the side; the two stanchions should be quite parallel. Alternatively, the lower 12 in. of the stanchions can be placed on a surface plate, when there should be no rocking.

To reset, hold one stanchion in a vice (using soft clamps) and reposition the other stanchion, using a longer and larger diameter tube to obtain sufficient leverage. Having checked the stanchions this way, check the gap between them on the ground portion.

The next step is to place the top yoke in position over the stanchions, when the steering stem should be quite central.

The final step is to check if the tubes are parallel when assembled into the top yoke only. In this case the bottom yoke can be fitted loosely on the tubes, acting as a pilot only.

Though it is permissible to rectify slight errors in alignment by resetting, it is much safer to replace the part affected especially when there is excessive misalignment. Works reconditioned units are available to owners in the United Kingdom through the dealer network.

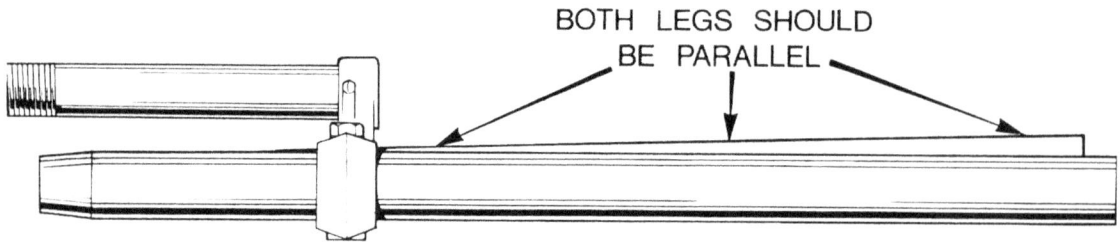

Fig. GG7. Fork leg alignment

SECTION GG5

HYDRAULIC DAMPING

Note the valve assembly which is retained in the bottom of the fork leg. Bleed holes are contained in the valve stem and in a sub-assembly at the top of the stem. This particular valve operates in conjunction with a damper valve which acts as a restrictor.

Oil is contained in the bottom member the level of which is always above the valve assembly. On compression the oil is forced through bleed holes in the valve stem. As the travel increases the bleed holes are progressively sealed off by a plastic sleeve and the damping increases until finally the stanchion is trapped on a cushion of oil which acts as the final bump stop. During this operation a vacuum is created in the space formed between the bottom of the stanchion and the damper valve, hence oil is transferred into this compartment through the eight bleed holes in the valve.

On expansion the oil in this newly formed compartment is compressed, the damper valve closes and the oil is bled through four small holes in the damper valve itself and then progressively through the holes in the valve stem. While this operation is being executed, oil is transferred back into the bottom member in readiness for the next compression.

NOTES

SECTION H

ELECTRICAL SYSTEM

INTRODUCTION

BATTERY INSPECTION AND MAINTENANCE ... H1
    DESCRIPTION
    (a) ROUTINE MAINTENANCE
    (b) MAXIMUM PERMISSABLE ELECTROLYTE TEMPERATURES DURING CHARGING

CAPACITOR PACK ... H2

COIL IGNITION SYSTEM ... H3
    DESCRIPTION
    (a) CHECKING THE LOW TENSION CIRCUIT FOR CONTINUITY
    (b) FAULT FINDING IN THE LOW TENSION CIRCUIT
    (c) IGNITION COILS
    (d) CONTACT BREAKER
    (e) CHECKING THE HIGH TENSION CIRCUIT

SPARKING PLUGS ... H4

CHARGING SYSTEM ... H5
    DESCRIPTION
    (a) CHECKING THE D.C. OUTPUT AT THE RECTIFIER
    (b) CHECKING THE ALTERNATOR OUTPUT
    (c) RECTIFIER MAINTENANCE AND TESTING
    (d) CHECKING THE CHARGING CIRCUIT FOR CONTINUITY
    (e) MAKING A 1 OHM LOAD RESISTOR

ZENER DIODE CHARGE CONTROL AND TEST PROCEDURE ... H6

ZENER DIODE LOCATION ... H7

ELECTRIC HORNS ... H8

HEADLAMP ... H9
    DESCRIPTION
    BEAM ADJUSTMENTS

HEADLAMP REMOVING AND REFITTING ... H10

TAIL AND STOPLAMP UNIT ... H11

FUSES ... H12

IGNITION SWITCH ... H13

IGNITION CUT-OUT BUTTON ... H14

WARNING LAMPS ... H15

CAPACITOR IGNITION (Model 2MC) ... H16
    IDENTIFICATION OF CAPACITOR TERMINALS
    STORAGE LIFE OF MODEL 2MC CAPACITOR
    TESTING
    WIRING AND INSTALLATION
    SERVICE NOTES
    BASIC MOTORCYCLE CIRCUIT

WIRING DIAGRAM ... H17

H ELECTRICAL SYSTEM

INTRODUCTION

The electrical system is supplied from an alternating current generator contained in the timing cover and driven from the crankshaft. The generator output is then converted into direct current by a silicon diode bridge connected rectifier. The direct current is supplied to a 12 volt 8 ampere/hour battery with a Zener Diode in circuit to regulate the battery current.

The current is then supplied to the ignition system which is controlled by a triple contact breaker driven direct from the exhaust camshaft. The contact breaker feeds three ignition coils, one for each cylinder, and the three capacitors are mounted seperately in a waterproof pack. The battery supplies current for the headlamp, tail lamp and instruments and warning light in the binnacle. An ammeter is fitted. Twin tone horns are used with a relay.

The routine maintenance needed by the various components is set out in the following sections. All electrical components and connections including the earthing points to the frame of the machine must be clean and tight.

No emergency start facility is provided. On these models there is however sufficient voltage to start the machine when a discharged battery is in circuit.

SECTION H1
BATTERY INSPECTION AND MAINTENANCE

The battery containers are moulded in translucent polystyrene through which the acid level can be seen. The battery top is so designed that when the cover is in position, the special anti-spill filler plugs are sealed in a common venting chamber. Gas from the filler plugs leaves this chamber through a vent pipe union at the side of the top. The vent at the other side of the top is sealed off. Polythene tubing is attached to the vent pipe union to lead corrosive fumes away from parts of the machine which may otherwise suffer damage.

To prepare a dry-charged battery for service, first discard the vent hole sealing tape and then pour into each cell pure dilute sulphuric acid of appropriate specific gravity to THE COLOURED LINE. (See table in Part A). Allow the battery to stand for at least one hour for the electrolyte to settle down, thereafter maintain the acid level at the coloured line by adding distilled water. The battery should then receive an initial charge of 1 Ampere for approximately 3 hours prior to fitting to the machine.

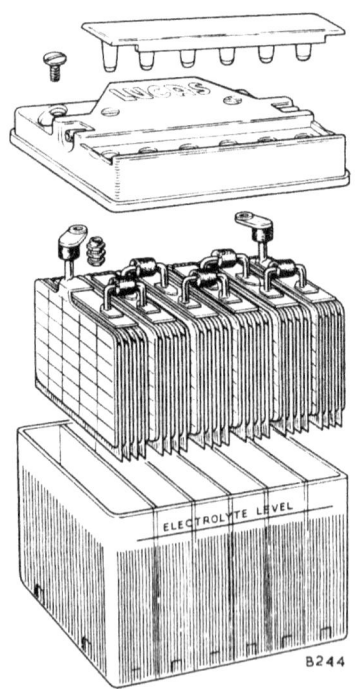

Fig. H1. Exploded view of battery

ELECTRICAL SYSTEM   H

H1. PART A. ROUTINE MAINTENANCE

Every week examine the level of the electrolyte in each cell. Lift the battery out of the carrier so that the coloured filling line can be seen. Add distilled water until the electrolyte level reaches this line.

Note.—On no account should the battery be topped up to the separator guard but only to the coloured line.

With this type of battery, the acid can only be reached by a miniature hydrometer, which would indicate the state of charge.

Great care should be taken when carrying out these operations not to spill any acid or allow a naked flame near the electrolyte. The mixture of oxygen and hydrogen given off by a battery on charge, and to a lesser extent when standing idle, can be dangerously explosive.

The readings obtained from the battery electrolyte should be compared with those given in table (a). If a battery is suspected to be faulty it is advisable to have it checked by a Lucas Service Centre or Agent.

SPECIFIC GRAVITY OF ELECTROLYTE FOR FILLING THE BATTERY

U.K. and Climates normally below 90°F (32·2°C)		Tropical Climates over 90°F (32·2°C)	
Filling	Fully charged	Filling	Fully charged
1·260	1·280/1·300	1·210	1·220/1·240

Every 1,000 miles (1,500 km.) or monthly, or more regularly in hot climates the battery should be cleaned as follows. Remove the battery cover and clean the battery top. Examine the terminals: if they are corroded scrape them clean and smear them with a film of petroleum jelly, such as vaseline. Remove the vent plugs and check that the vent holes are clear.

H1. PART B. MAXIMUM PERMISSABLE ELECTROLYTE TEMPERATURE DURING CHARGE

Climates normally Below 80°F (27°C)	Climates between 80–100°F (27–38°C)	Climates frequently above 100°F (38°C)
100°F (38°C)	110°F (43°C)	120°F (49°C)

Notes.

The specific gravity of the electrolyte varies with the temperature. For convenience in comparing specific gravities, they are always corrected to 60°F., which is adopted as a reference temperature. The method of correction is as follows:

For every 5°F. below 60°F. deduct ·020 from the observed reading to obtain the true specific gravity at 60°F. For every 5°F. above 60°F., add ·020 to the observed reading to obtain the true specific gravity at 60°F.

The temperature must be indicated by a thermometer having its bulb actually immersed in the electrolyte and not the ambient temperature. To take a temperature reading tilt the battery sideways and then insert into the electrolyte.

ELECTRICAL SYSTEM

SECTION H2
CAPACITOR PACK

The capacitors are located on the coil mounting plate beneath the twinseat, being mounted on a common bracket and protected from water by a rubber cover. Each capacitor is connected into the low tension circuit by means of a "Lucar" connector.

To remove any one of the condensers, disconnect the low tension lead, remove the rubber cover, remove the nut and shakeproof washer and withdraw the capacitor.

Reassembly is undertaken in the reverse order.

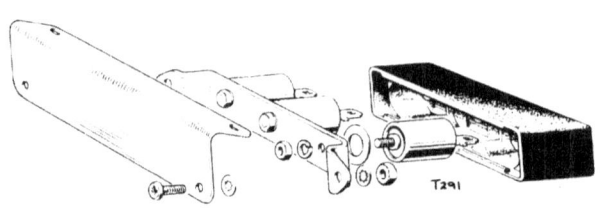

Fig. H2. Exploded view of capacitor pack

SECTION H3
COIL IGNITION SYSTEM

The coil ignition system comprises a 7CA contact breaker in the timing cover driven by the exhaust camshaft feeding three ignition coils fitted with vibration proof rubber rings into the mounting plate beneath the hinged twinseat.

The capacitors are fitted into a rubber covered pack also mounted on the plate beneath the twinseat. Attention to the contact breaker is covered by Section H3 part D. The ignition coils can be removed, for testing as in Section H3 part C, merely by disconnecting the terminals and grasping each coil in turn and lifting it firmly away from the rubber mounting ring.

The capacitor pack is secured to the plate by two small screws and nuts and after removal and disconnecting of the spade terminals the rubber cover can be pulled away, leaving only the capacitors, each of which is secured by a serrated washer and nut. The coils and capacitors require no attention beyond keeping them clean and the terminals sound.

The best method of approach to a faulty ignition system is that of first checking the low tension circuit for continuity as shown in H3 Part A, and then following the procedure laid out in H3 Part B to locate the fault(s).

Failure to locate a fault in the low tension circuit indicates that the high tension circuit or sparking plugs are faulty and the procedure detailed in H2 Part E must be followed. Before commencing any of the following tests, however, the contact breaker and sparking plugs must be cleaned and adjusted to eliminate these possible sources of faults.

ELECTRICAL SYSTEM H

H3 PART A. CHECKING THE LOW TENSION CIRCUIT FOR CONTINUITY

Note.—Lucas coils are marked 'S.W.' and 'C.B.', SIBA coils are marked '1' instead of 'S.W.' and '15' instead of 'C.B.'.

To check whether there is a fault in the low tension circuit and to locate its position, the following tests should be carried out:—

Lift the twinseat and remove the white lead which connects the 'S.W.' terminals of the three ignition coils. Then, with the wiring harness white lead connected to the 'S.W.' terminals of one coil only, turn the ignition switch to the "IGN" position. Slowly crank the engine and at the same time observe the ammeter needle, which should fluctuate between zero and a slight discharge, as the contacts open and close respectively.

Change the white lead over from S.W. of one coil to the next, repeating the test in turn for the other two coils.

If the ammeter needle does not fluctuate in the described way then a fault in the low tension circuit is indicated.

First, examine the contact breaker contacts for pitting, piling or presence of oxidation, oil or dirt etc. Clean and ensure that the gap is set correctly to ·014 in.–·016 in. (·35–·40 mm.) as described in Section B31.

H3 PART B. FAULT FINDING IN THE LOW TENSION CIRCUIT

To trace a fault in the low tension wiring, turn the ignition switch on and then place a piece of insulating material between all sets of contacts whilst the following test is carried out.

Note. Disconnect the Zener Diode before the test is carried out. To do this remove the brown/white lead from the Diode centre terminal.

For this test, it is assumed that the twinseat is lifted and the wiring is fully connected as shown in the appropriate wiring diagram, Section H24. With the aid of a 0-15 range D.C. voltmeter and 2 test-prods, make a point to point check along the low tension circuit starting at the battery and working right through to the ignition coils, stage by stage, in the following manner, referring to the relevant wiring diagram in Section H24.

(1) First, establish that the battery is earthed correctly by connecting the volt meter across the battery negative terminal and the machine frame earth. No voltage reading indicates that the red earthing lead is faulty. Check the fuse in the main negative lead. Also, a low reading would indicate a poor battery earth connection or a discharged battery.

(2) Connect the voltmeter in turn between each ignition coil S.W. terminal and earth on all three coils. No voltage reading indicates a breakdown between the battery and the coil S.W. terminal, or that the switch connections or ammeter connections are faulty.

(3) Connect the voltmeter between both of the ammeter terminals in turn and earth. No reading on the "feed" side indicates that either the ammeter is faulty, there is a bad connection along the brown and blue lead from the battery or the fuse has blown and a reading on the "battery" side only indicates a faulty ammeter.

(4) Connect the voltmeter between ignition switch input terminal and earth. No reading indicates that the brown and white lead has faulty connections. Check for voltage at the brown/white lead connections at rectifier and ammeter.

(5) Connect the voltmeter across ignition switch output terminal and earth. No reading indicates that the ignition switch is faulty and should be replaced. Battery voltage reading at this point but not at the ignition coil S.W. terminals indicates that the white lead has become "open circuit" or become disconnected.

(6) Connect the voltmeter across the C.B. terminal of each coil and earth in turn. No reading on the voltmeter between any one coil and earth indicates that the coil primary winding is faulty and a replacement ignition coil should be fitted.

(7) With insulating material between the three sets of contacts, connect the voltmeter across each set of contacts in turn. No reading between any one set of contacts and earth indicates that there is a faulty connection or the internal insulation has broken down in one of the capacitors.

If a capacitor is suspected then a substitution should be made and a re-test carried out.

H5

(8) Finally, reconnect the Zener Diode brown/white lead and then connect the volt meter between the Zener Diode centre terminal and earth. The volt meter should read battery volts. If it does not the Zener Diode is faulty and a substitution should be made. Refer to Section H6 (page H13) for the correct procedure for testing a Zener Diode on the machine. Ignition coil check procedure is given in Section H3, part C.

H3 PART C. IGNITION COILS

The ignition coils consist of primary and secondary windings wound concentrically about a laminated soft iron core, the secondary winding being next to the core. The primary winding consists of 280-372 turns of enamel covered wire and the secondary, some 19,000 turns of much finer wire, also enamel covered. Each layer is paper insulated from the next in both primary and secondary windings.

To test the ignition coils on the machine, first ensure that the low tension circuit is in order as described in H3 Part A then disconnect the high tension leads from each of the sparking plugs. Turn the ignition switch on and crank the engine until the contacts (those with the black/white lead from the ignition coil) for the right (No. 1) cylinder are closed having removed the insulation from between the contacts. Flick the contact breaker lever open a number of times whilst the high tension lead from the ignition coil with the black and white lead is held about $\frac{3}{16}$ in. away from the cylinder head. If the ignition coil is in good condition a strong spark should be obtained. If no spark occurs this indicates the ignition coil to be faulty.

Repeat this test in turn for each of the other coils ensuring that the contacts for the coil being tested are closed. The lead colours at the coils are of course the same at the contacts.

Before a fault can be attributed to an ignition coil it must be ascertained that the high tension cables are not cracked or showing signs of deterioration, as this may often be the cause of mis-firing etc. It should also be checked that the ignition points are actually making good electrical contact when closed and that the moving contact is insulated from earth (ground) when open. (See Test H3 Part B). It is advisable to remove the ignition coils and test them by the method described below.

BENCH TESTING THE IGNITION COIL

Connect the ignition coil into the circuit shown in Fig. H4 and set the adjustable gap to 8 mm.

Using a single lobe contact breaker running at 600 r.p.m. and the coil in good condition, not more than 5% missing should occur at the spark gap over a period of 15 seconds. The primary winding can be checked for short-circuit coils by connecting an ohmeter across the low tension terminals. The reading obtained for the 17M12 coil at 20°C should be within 3·3 ohms minimum and 3·8 ohms maximum.

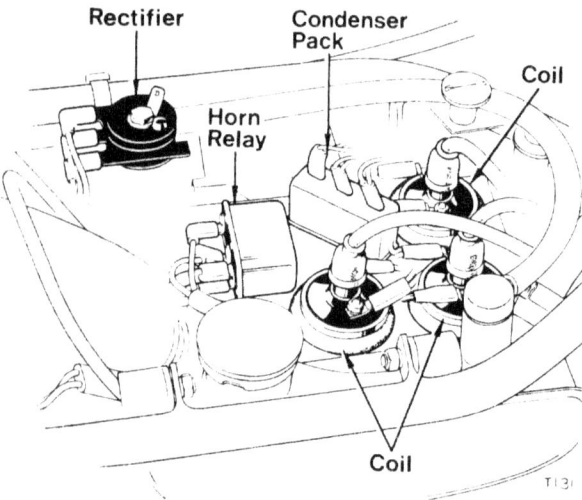

Fig. H3. Electrical components in position beneath twinseat

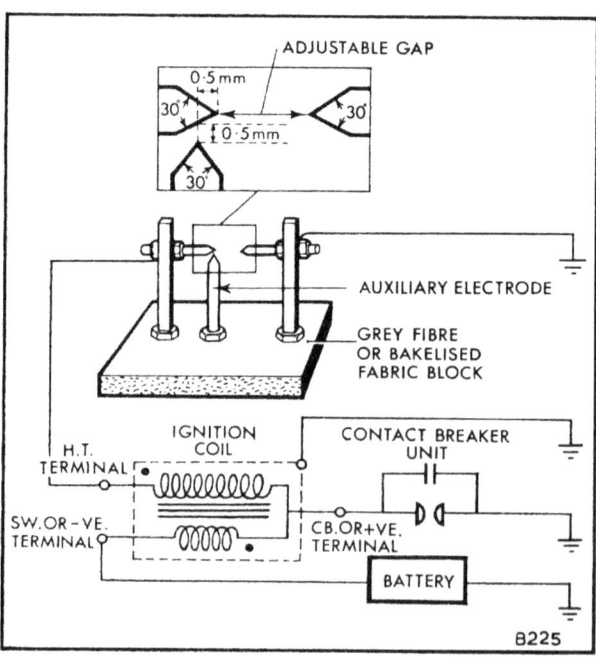

Fig. H4. Ignition coil test rig

ELECTRICAL SYSTEM

H3 PART D. CONTACT BREAKER

Faults occurring at the contact breaker are in the main due to, incorrect adjustment of the contacts or the efficiency being impaired by piling, pitting or oxidation of the contacts due to oil etc. Therefore, always ensure that the points are clean and that the gap is adjusted to the correct working clearance as described in Section B25.

To test for a faulty capacitor, first turn the ignition switch on and then take voltage readings across each set of contacts in turn with the contacts open. No reading indicates that the capacitor internal insulation has broken down. Should the fault be due to a capacitor having a reduction in capacity, indicated by excessive arcing when in use, and overheating of the contact faces, a check should be made by substitution.

Particular attention is called to the periodic lubrication procedure for the contact breaker which is given in Section A11. When lubricating the parts ensure that no oil or grease gets onto the contacts.

If it is felt that the contacts require surface grinding then the complete contact breaker unit should be removed as described in Section B24 and the moving contacts removed by unscrewing the nut which secures the low tension lead, removing the lead and nylon bush. The spring and contact point can be removed from the pivot spindle. Repeat this procedure for the other contact points.

Grinding is best achieved by using a fine carborundum stone or very fine emery cloth, afterwards wiping away any trace of dirt or metal dust with a clean petrol (gasoline) moistened cloth. The contact faces should be slightly domed to ensure point contact. There is no need to remove the pitting from the fixed contact.

When reassembling, the nylon bush is fitted through the low tension connection tab, and through the spring location eye. Apply a smear of grease to the C.B. cam and moving contact pivot post. Every 3,000 miles and/or contact replacement, apply two drops of clean engine oil to the rear of the three lubricating felt wicks.

H3 PART E. CHECKING THE HIGH TENSION CIRCUIT

If ignition failure or mis-firing occurs, and the fault is not in the low tension circuit, then check the ignition coils as described in Part C. If the coils prove satisfactory, ensure that the high tension cables are not the cause of the fault.

If a good spark is available at the high tension cable, then the sparking plug suppressor cap or the sparking plug itself may be the cause of the fault. Clean the sparking plug and adjust the electrodes to the required setting as described in Section H4 and then re-test the engine for running performance. If the fault recurs then it is likely the suppressor caps are faulty and these should be renewed.

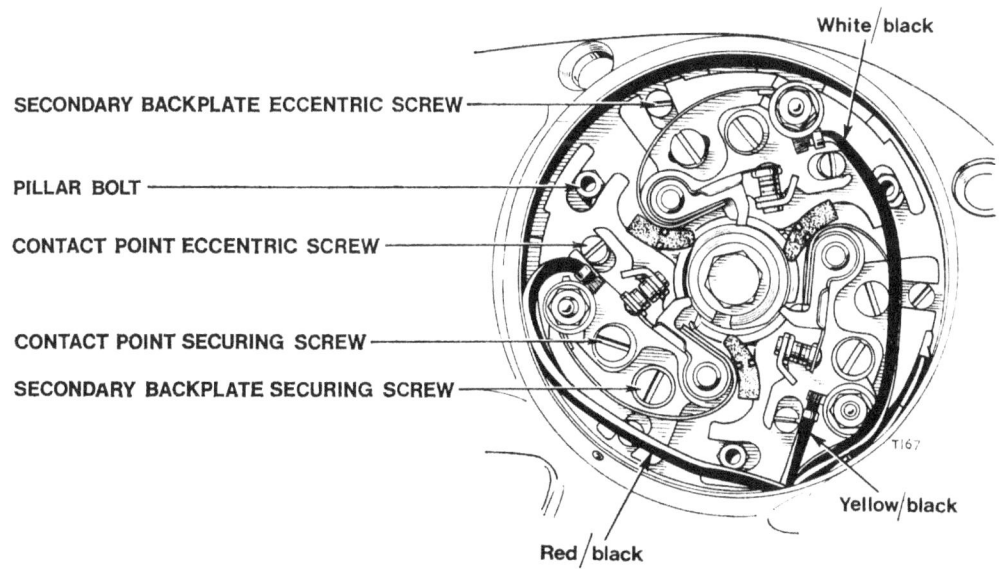

Fig. H5. Contact breaker assembly type 7CA

ELECTRICAL SYSTEM

SECTION H4
SPARKING PLUGS

It is recommended that the sparking plugs be inspected, cleaned and tested every 3,000 miles (4,800 km.) and new ones fitted every 12,000 miles (20,000 km.).

To remove the sparking plugs a box spanner ($\frac{13}{16}$ in. (19·5 mm.) across flats) should be used and if any difficulty is encountered a small amount of penetrating oil (see lubrication chart Section A2) should be placed at the base of the sparking plug and time allowed for pentration. When removing the sparking plugs identify each plug with the cylinder from which it was removed so that any faults revealed on examination can be traced back to the cylinder concerned.

Examine all plugs for signs of oil fouling. This will be indicated by a wet, shiny, black deposit on the central insulator. This is caused by excessive oil in the combustion chamber during combustion and indicates that the piston rings or cylinder bores are worn.

Next examine the plugs for signs of petrol (gasoline) fouling. This is indicated by a dry, sooty, black deposit which is usually caused by over-rich carburation, although ignition system defects such as a discharged battery, faulty contact breaker, coil or capacitor defects, or a broken or worn out cable may be additional causes. To rectify this type of fault the above mentioned items should be checked with special attention given to carburation system.

Over-heating of the sparking plug electrodes is indicated by severely eroded electrodes and a white, burned or blistered insulator. This type of fault is usually caused by weak carburation, although plugs which have been operating whilst not being screwed down sufficiently can easily become over-heated due to heat that is normally dissipated through to the cylinder head not having an adequate conducting path. Over-heating is normally symptomised by pre-ignition, short plug life, and "pinking" which can ultimately result in piston crown failure. Unnecessary damage can result from over-tightening the plugs and to achieve a good seal between the plug and cylinder head a torque wrench should be used to tighten the plugs to the figure quoted in "General Data".

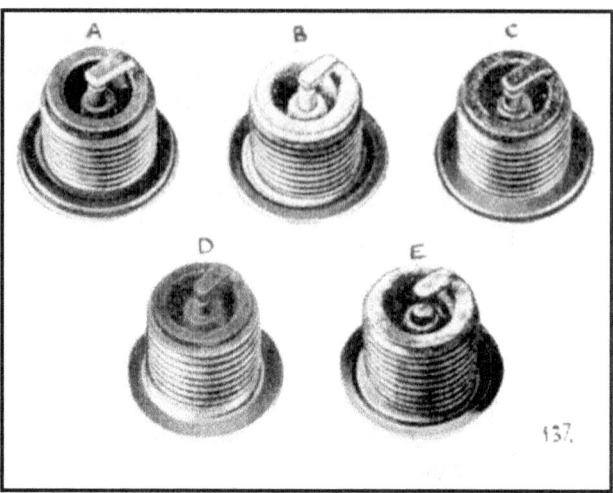

Fig. H6. Sparking plug diagnosis

A plug of the correct grade will bear a light flaky deposit on the outer rim and earth electrode, and these and the base of the insulator will be light chocolate brown in colour. A correct choice of plug is marked A. B shows a plug which appears bleached, with a deposit like cigarette ash; this is too 'hot-running' for the performance of the engine and a cooler-running type should be substituted. A plug which has been running too 'cold' and has not reached the self-cleaning temperature is shown at C. This has oil on the base of the insulator and electrodes, and should be replaced by a plug that will burn off deposits and remove the possibility of a short-circuit. The plug marked D is heavily sooted, indicating that the mixture has been too rich, and a further carburation check should be made. At illustration E is seen a plug which is completely worn out and badly in need of replacement.

To clean the plugs it is preferable to make use of a properly designed proprietary plug cleaner. The maker's instructions for using the cleaner should be followed carefully.

When the plugs have been carefully cleaned, examine the central insulators for cracking and the centre electrode for excessive wear. In such cases the plugs have completed their useful life and new ones should be fitted.

ELECTRICAL SYSTEM

Finally, before re-fitting the sparking plugs the electrodes should be adjusted to the correct gap setting of ·020 in. (·5 mm.). Before refitting sparking plugs the threads should be cleaned by means of a wire brush and a minute amount of graphite grease smeared onto the threads. This will prevent any possibility of thread seizure occurring.

If the ignition timing and carburation settings are correct and the plugs have been correctly fitted, but over-heating still occurs then it is possible that carburation is being adversely affected by an air leak between the carburetter, manifold and the cylinder head. This possibility must be checked thoroughly before taking any further action. When it is certain that none of the above mentioned faults are the cause of over-heating then the plug type and grade should be considered.

Normally the type of plugs quoted in "General Data" are satisfactory for general use of the machine but in special isolated cases, conditions may demand a plug of a different heat range. Advice is readily available to solve these problems from the plug manufacturer who should be consulted.

Note—If the air filter has been removed it will affect the carburation of the machine and hence may adversely affect the grade of sparking plugs fitted.

SECTION H5
CHARGING SYSTEM

DESCRIPTION

The charging current is supplied by the three lead alternator, but due to the characteristics of alternating current the battery cannot be charged direct from the alternator. To convert the alternating current to direct current a full wave bridge silicon type rectifier is connected into the circuit. The alternator gives full output, all the alternator coils being permanently connected across the rectifier.

Excessive charge is absorbed by the Zener Diode which is connected across the battery. Always ensure that the ignition switch is in the "OFF" position whilst the machine is not in use, to prevent overheating of the ignition coils, and discharging the battery.

To locate a fault in the charging circuit, first test the alternator as described in H5 Part B. If the alternator is satisfactory, the fault must lie in the charging circuit, hence the rectifier must be checked as given in Section H5 Part C (page H10) and then the wiring and connections as shown in Section H5 Part D (page H12).

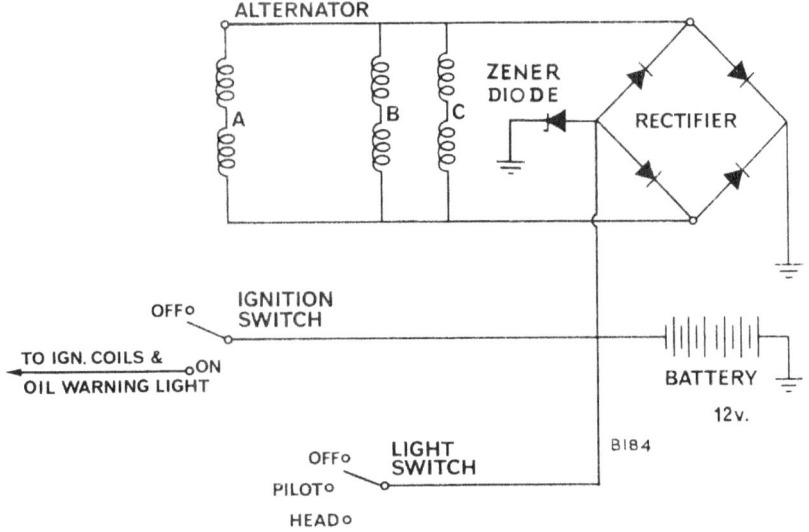

Fig. H7. Schematic diagram of 12 volt charging circuit with Zener Diode

H5 PART A. CHECKING THE D.C. OUTPUT AT THE RECTIFER

For this test the battery must be in good condition and a good state of charge, therefore before conducting the test ensure that the battery is up to the required standard, or alternatively fit a good replacement battery. Disconnect the brown/blue centre lead at the rectifier, connect a D.C. ammeter (0-15 AMP.) in series between the centre terminal and the main brown/blue lead, start the engine and run at approximately 3,000 r.p.m. (equivalent to 45 m.p.h. in top gear).

Note.—Ensure that the ammeter is well insulated from the surrounding earth points otherwise a short circuit may occur.

A single charge rate is used and irrespective of switch positions the minimum D.C. output from the rectifier at 3,000 r.p.m. should be no less than 9·5 amperes.

H5 PART B. CHECKING THE ALTERNATOR OUTPUT

Disconnect the three alternator output cables underneath the engine and run the engine at 3,000 r.p.m. (equivalent to 45 m.p.h. in top gear).

Connect an A.C. voltmeter (0-15 volts) with 1 ohm load resistor in parallel with each of the alternator leads in turn as shown in the table, Fig. H8, and observe the voltmeter readings. A suitable 1 ohm load resistor can be made from a piece of nichrome wire as shown in Section H5 Part E.

From the results obtained, the following deductions can be made:—

(i) If the readings are all equal to or higher than those quoted then the alternator is satisfactory.

(ii) A low reading on any group of coils indicates either that the leads concerned are chafed or damaged due to rubbing on the chains or that some turns of the coils are short circuited.

(iii) Low readings for all parts of the test indicates either that the green/white lead has become chafed or damaged due to rubbing on the chain(s) or that the rotor has become partially demagnetised. If the latter case applies, check that this has not been caused by a faulty rectifier or that the battery is of incorrect polarity, and only then fit a new rotor.

	Alternator output minimum A.C. volts @ 3,000 r.p.m.		
RM20 stator 47209 (12 volt)	green/white and green/black connected 5·0	green/white and green/yellow connected 8·0	green/white green/black and green/yellow connected 10·0

Fig. H8. Alternator output figures

(iv) A zero reading for any group of coils indicates that a coil has become disconnected, is open circuit, or is earthed.

(v) A reading obtained between any one lead and earth indicates that coil windings or connections have become earthed.

If any of the above mentioned faults occur, always check the stator leads for possible chain damage before attempting repairs or renewing the stator.

H5 PART C. RECTIFIER MAINTENANCE AND TESTING

The silicon bridge rectifier requires no maintenance beyond checking that the connections are clean and tight, and that the nut securing the rectifier to the frame is tight. It should always be kept clean and dry to ensure good cooling, and spilt oil washed off immediately with hot water.

Note.—The nuts clamping the rectifier plates together must not be disturbed or slackened in any way.

When tightening the rectifier securing nut, hold the spanner as shown in Fig. H9, for if the plates are twisted, the internal connections will be broken. Note that the circles marked on the fixing bolt and nut indicate that the thread form is $\frac{1}{4}$ in. U.N.F.

ELECTRICAL SYSTEM

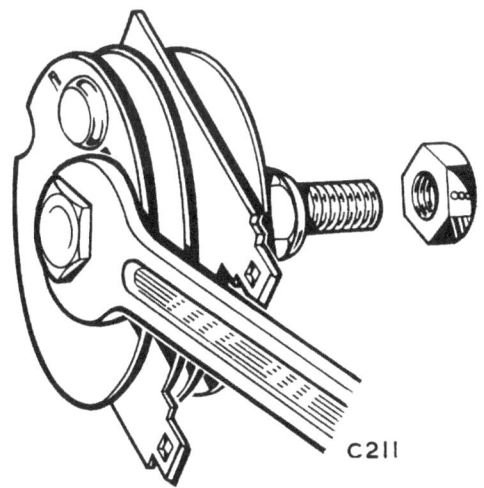

Fig. H9. Refitting the rectifier

TESTING THE RECTIFIER

For test purposes disregard the end earth (ground) terminal on latest rectifiers

To test the rectifier, first disconnect the brown/white lead from the rectifier centre terminal and insulate the end of the lead to prevent any possibility of a short circuit occurring, and then connect a D.C. voltmeter (with 1 ohm load resistor in parallel) between the rectifier centre terminal and earth.

Note.—Voltmeter positive terminal to frame earth (ground) and negative terminal to centre terminal on rectifier.

With the engine running at approximately 3,000 r.p.m. (approximately 45 m.p.h. in top gear) observe the voltmeter readings. The reading obtained should be at least 7·5V minimum.

(i) If the reading is equal to or slightly greater than that quoted, then the rectifier elements in the forward direction are satisfactory.

(ii) If the reading is excessively higher than the figures given, then check the rectifier earthing bolt connection.

(iii) If the reading is lower than the figures quoted or zero readings are obtained, then the rectifier or the charging circuit wiring is faulty and the rectifier should be disconnected and bench tested so that the fault can be located.

Note.—All of the above conclusions assume that the alternator A.C. output figures were satisfactory. Any fault at the alternator will, of course, reflect on the rectifier test results. Similarly any fault in the charging circuit wiring may indicate that the rectifier is faulty. The best method of locating a fault is to disconnect the rectifier and bench-test it as shown below:

BENCH TESTING THE RECTIFIER

For this test the rectifier should be disconnected and removed. Before removing the rectifier, disconnect the leads from the battery terminals to avoid the possibility of a short circuit occurring.

Connect the rectifier to a 12 volt battery and 1 ohm load resistor, and then connect the D.C. voltmeter in the V2 position, as shown in Fig. H10. Note the battery voltage (should be 12V) and then connect the voltmeter in V1 position whilst the following tests are conducted.

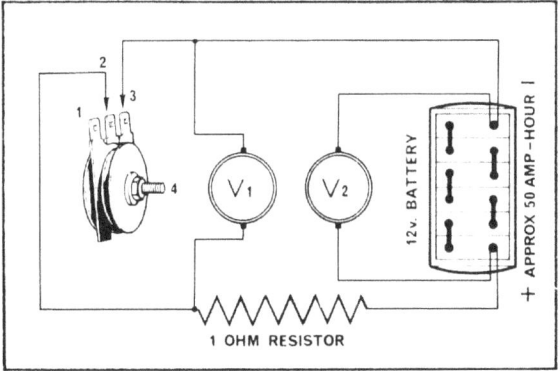

Fig. H10. Bench testing the rectifier

A voltmeter in position V1 will measure the volt drop across the rectifier plate. In position V2 it will measure the supply voltage to check that it is the recommended 12 volts on load.

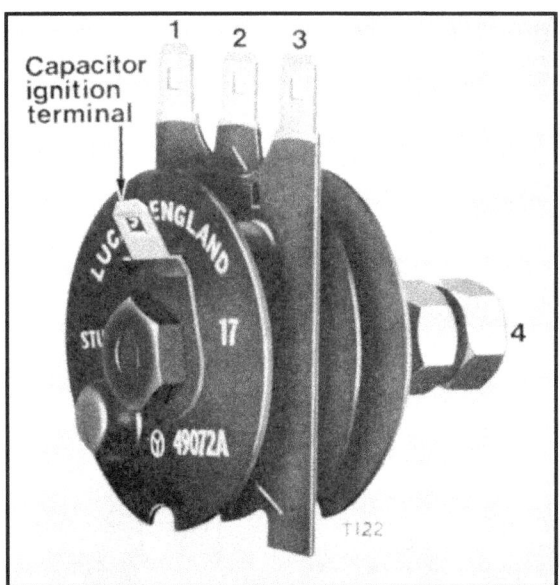

Fig. H11. Rectifier—showing terminal connections for bench tests 1 and 2

TEST 1 CHECKING FORWARD RESISTANCE

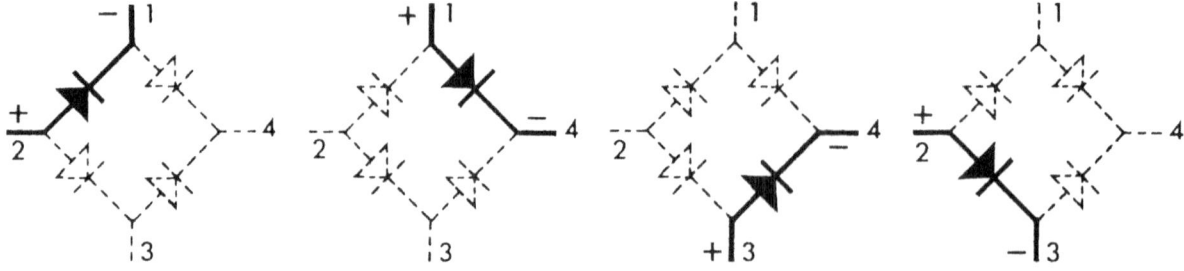

TEST 2 CHECKING BACK LEAKAGE

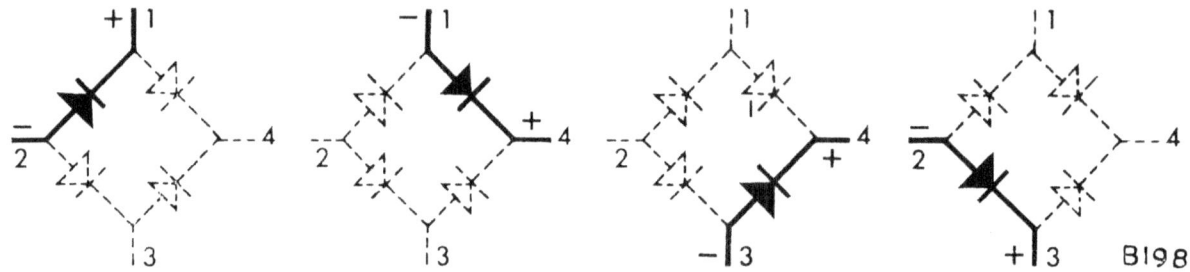

Fig. H12. Rectifier test sequence for checking forward resistance and back leakage

Test 1. With the test leads, make the following connections but keep the testing time as short as possible to avoid overheating the rectifier cell: (a) 1 and 2, (b) 1 and 4, (c) 3 and 4, (d) 3 and 2. Each reading should not be greater than 1·5 volts with the battery polarity as shown.

Test 2. Reverse the leads or battery polarity and repeat Test 1. The readings obtained should be battery voltage (V_2).

If the readings obtained are not within the figures given, then the rectifier internal connections are faulty and the rectifier should be renewed.

H5 PART D. CHECKING THE CHARGING CIRCUIT FOR CONTINUITY

Check that there is voltage at the battery and that it is correctly connected into the circuit +ve earth (ground). Ensure that the fuse has not blown.

(1) First, check that there is voltage at the rectifier centre terminal by connecting a D.C. voltmeter, with a 1 ohm load resistor in parallel, between the rectifier centre terminal (not the end terminal and earth (remember (+ve) positive earth (ground)). The voltmeter should read battery volts. If it does not, disconnect the alternator leads (green/black, green/white and green/yellow) at the snap connectors under the engine unit.

(a) Fit a jumper lead across the brown/white and green/yellow connections at the rectifier, and check the voltage at the snap connector. This test will indicate whether the harness alternator lead is open circuit, or the fuse has blown.

(b) Repeat this test at the rectifier for the white/green lead.

(2) If no voltage is present at the rectifier central terminal (brown/white), check the voltage at the ammeter terminal. If satisfactory, it indicates that the brown/white wire is open circuit. If not, the ammeter is open circuit.

(3) If no voltage is present at either ammeter terminal, then the brown/blue wire from the battery (−ve) is open circuit.

H5 PART E. CONSTRUCTING A ONE-OHM LOAD RESISTOR

The resistor used in the following tests must be accurate and constructed so that it will not overheat otherwise the correct values of current or voltage will not be obtained.

A suitable resistor can be made from 4 yards (3¾ metres) of 18 S.W.G. (·048 in. (i.e. 1·2 mm.) dia.) NICHROME wire by bending it into two equal parts and calibrating it as follows:—

(1) Fix a heavy gauge flexible lead to the folded end of the wire and connect this lead to the positive terminal of a battery.

ELECTRICAL SYSTEM

(2) Connect a D.C. voltmeter (0–15V) across the battery terminals and an ammeter (0–10 amp) between the battery negative terminal and the free ends of the wire resistance, using a crocodile clip to make the connection.

(3) Move the clip along the wires, making contact with both wires until the ammeter reading is numerically equal to the number of volts indicated on the voltmeter. The resistance is then 1 ohm. Cut the wire at this point, twist the two ends together and wind the wire on an asbestos former approximately 2 inches (5 cm.) dia. so that each turn does not contact the one next to it.

SECTION H6
ZENER DIODE CHARGE CONTROL

DESCRIPTION

The Zener Diode output regulating system uses all the coils of the 6-coil alternator connected permanently across the rectifier, provides automatic control for the charging current. It will only operate successfully where it is connected in parallel with the battery as shown in the wiring diagram (Section H17 Fig. H25). The Diode is connected direct to the centre terminal of the rectifier.

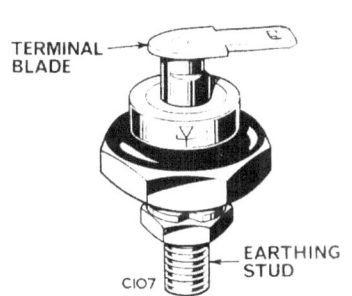

Fig. H13. Zener Diode

Assuming the battery is in a low state of charge its terminal voltage (the same voltage is across the Diode) will also be low, therefore the maximum charging current will flow into the battery from the alternator. At first none of the current is by-passed by the Diode because of it being non-conducting due to the low battery terminal volts. However, as the battery is quickly restored to a full state of charge, the system voltage rises until at 13·5 volts the Zener Diode is partially conducting, thereby providing an alternative path for a small part of the charging current. Small increases in battery voltage results in large increases in Zener conductivity until, at approximately 15 volts about 5 amperes of the alternator output is by-passing the battery.

The battery will continue to receive only a portion of the alternator output as long as the system voltage is relatively high.

Depression of the system voltage, due to the use of headlamp or other lighting equipment, causes the Zener Diode current to decrease and the balance to be diverted and consumed by the components in use.

If the electrical loading is sufficient to cause the system voltage to fall to 13·5 volts, the Zener Diode will revert to a high resistance state of non-conductivity and the full generated output will go to meet the demands of the battery.

With the specially designed heat sink the Zener Diode is able to absorb the full output of the alternator.

MAINTENANCE

Provided a firm flat "metal to metal" contact is maintained between the base of the Diode and the surface of the heat sink, to ensure adequate heat flow, no maintenance will be necessary. Ensure that the earth connection to the diode is a good one.

—ZENER DIODE—
—CHARGING REGULATOR
—TEST PROCEDURE

(Procedure for Testing on the Machine)

The test procedure given below can be used when it is required to check the performance of the Zener Diode type ZD715 whilst it is in position on the machine. It is essential that the battery is in a fully charged state, otherwise the tests below will not be accurate. If in doubt, substitute a battery that is fully charged.

Good quality moving coil meters should be used when testing. The voltmeter should have a scale 0–18, and the ammeter 0–5 amps min. The test procedure is as follows:—

(A) Disconnect the cable from the Zener Diode and connect ammeter (in series) between the diode Lucar terminal and cable previously disconnected. The ammeter red or positive lead must connect to the diode Lucar terminal.

(B) Connect voltmeter across Zener Diode and heat sink. The red or positive lead must connect to the heat sink which is earthed to the frame of the machine by its fixing bolts and a separate earth lead. The black lead connects to the Zener Diode Lucar terminal.

(C) Start the engine, ensure that all lights are off, and gradually increase engine speed while at the same time observing both meters:—

(i) The series connected ammeter must indicate zero amps, up to 12·75 volts, which will be indicated on the shunt connected voltmeter as engine speed is slowly increased.

(ii) Increase engine speed still further, until Zener current indicated on ammeter is 2·0 amp. At this value the Zener voltage should be within 13·5 volts to 15·3 volts.

TEST CONCLUSIONS:—

If the ammeter in test (i) registers any current at all before the voltmeter indicates 12·75 volts, then a replacement Zener Diode must be fitted.

If test (i) is satisfactory but in test (ii) a higher voltage than that stated is registered on the voltmeter, before the ammeter indicates 2·0 amp, then a replacement zener diode must be fitted.

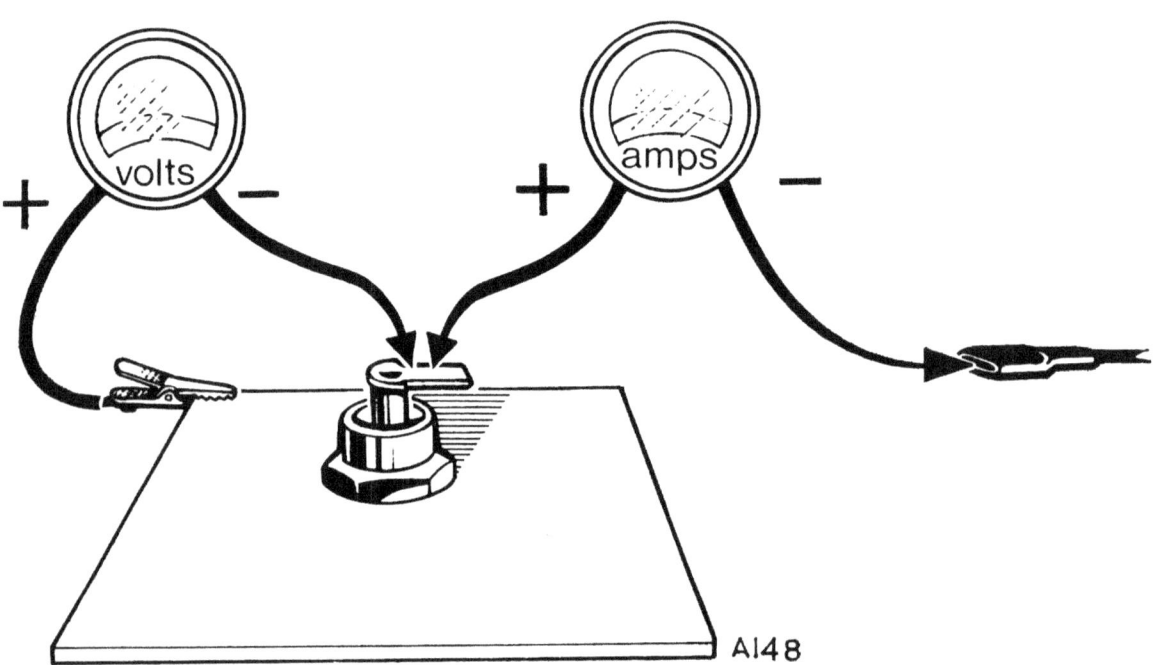

Fig. H14. Showing ammeter and voltmeter connections for test purposes

ELECTRICAL SYSTEM

H

SECTION H7
ZENER DIODE LOCATION

The Zener Diode is mounted on a bracket below the headlamp, the bracket being bolted to the fork middle lug. The aluminium heatsink is finned to assist cooling. The order of assembly is shown in Fig. H15.

To remove diode only, disconnect the brown/white double "Lucar" connector from the diode. Remove the black plastic plug from the heat sink (See Fig. H15) and unscrew the "nyloc" nut which secures the Diode. When refitting, the Diode nut must be tightened with extreme care. (Maximum tightening torque 22/28 lb./in.)

To remove the finned heat sink, remove the front bolt from the retaining bracket. A double red earth (ground) wire is attached at this point.

DO NOT ATTACH THE EARTH (GROUND) LEADS BETWEEN THE DIODE BODY AND HEATSINK

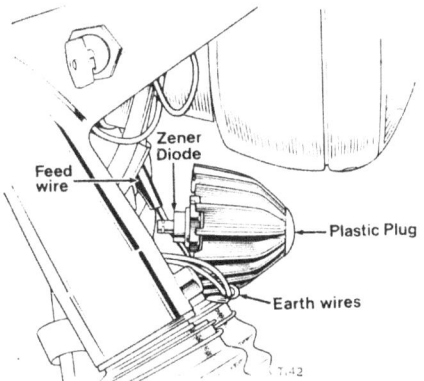

Fig. H15. Finned heatsink

SECTION H8
ELECTRIC HORN

Twin windtone horns are fitted together with a relay to absorb the considerable voltage drop which would otherwise overload the circuit wiring when the horns are used. The method of operation is that twin electro-magnets attract a steel diaphragm. The magnetic circuit is made self-interrupting by contacts which can be adjusted externally. As the points close, the diaphragm reverts to its original position causing the note to be emitted. The tone is improved by the trumpet-shaped sound chamber.

If the horns fail to work, check that the mountings are secure and check the horn wiring connections. Check the battery for state of charge, since a low supply voltage at the horn will affect adversely the horn performance. Ensure that the relay connections are sound (the relay is mounted beneath the twinseat, adjacent to the coils) test the horn relays as follows:—

(1) Eliminate the horn push circuit by earthing W1-terminal (See Fig. H16) with a temporary wire. If the horns then operate, check the horn push and associated wiring.

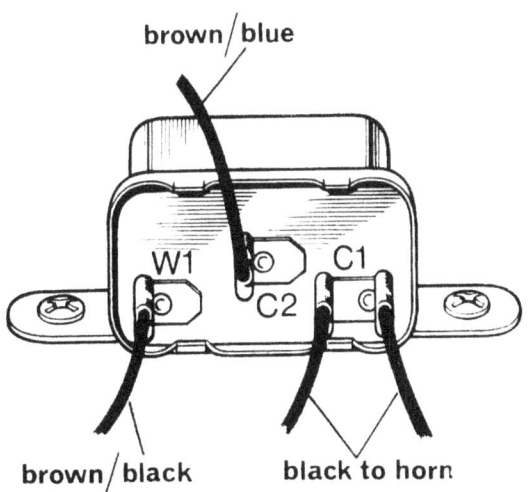

Fig. H16. Horn relay showing terminals

H15

H   ELECTRICAL SYSTEM

(2) Having carried out test one and the horns still fail to operate, apply a direct feed to the horns with a temporary link between relay terminals C1 and C2. If the horns then operate, a faulty 6RA relay is indicated.

If the above checks are made and the fault persists, then adjust the horns as follows:—

HORN ADJUSTMENT

During adjustment it is advisable to depress the horn push for only a fraction of a second at a time.

It is not necessary to remove the horns for adjustment. There is a plastic domed cover, secured by two Phillips-headed screws, on each horn. These covers must be removed to gain access to the adjustment screw. This is clarified by Fig. H17.

Turn the screw clockwise or anti-clockwise a quarter turn at a time until the loudest clear note is delivered. The operation should be repeated for the second horn. Finally, refit both covers and screws.

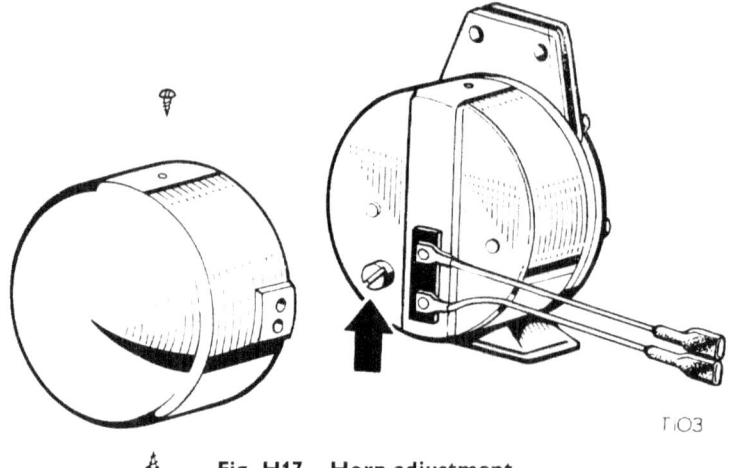

Fig. H17. Horn adjustment

SECTION H9
HEADLAMP

DESCRIPTION

The headlamp incorporates the metal and glass type light unit and access is gained to the bulb and bulb holder by withdrawing the rim and light unit assembly. To do so, slacken the screw at the top of the headlamp and prise off the rim and beam unit assembly.

The bulb can be removed by first pressing the cylindrical cap inwards and turning it anticlockwise. The cap can then be withdrawn and the bulb is free to be removed.

When fitting a new bulb, note that it locates by means of a cutaway and projection arrangement. Also note that the cap can only be replaced one way, the tabs being staggered to prevent incorrect reassembly. Check the replacement bulb voltage and wattage specification and type before fitting. Focusing with this type of light unit is unnecessary and there is no provision for such.

BEAM ADJUSTMENTS

The beam must in all cases be adjusted as specified by local lighting regulations. In the United Kingdom the Transport Lighting Regulations read as follows:—

A lighting system must be arranged so that it can give a light which is incapable of dazzling any person standing on the same horizontal plane as the vehicle at a greater distance than twenty five feet from the lamp, whose eye level is not less than three feet—six inches above that plane.

The headlamp must therefore be set so that the main beam is directed straight ahead and parallel with the road when the motorcycle is fully loaded. To achieve this, place the machine on a level road pointing towards a wall at a distance of 25 feet away, with a rider and passenger, on the machine, slacken the two pivot bolts at either side of the headlamp and tilt the headlamp until the beam is focused at approximately two feet six inches from the base of the wall. Do not forget that the headlamp should be on "full beam" lighting during this operation.

ELECTRICAL SYSTEM H

SECTION H10
REMOVING AND REFITTING THE HEADLAMP

Disconnect the battery at the fuseholder. Remove the pivot bolts and washers and collect the plastic spacers. The headlamp complete can then be lifted away from the fork and the four leads parted at the snap connectors. Note for refitting that the leads connect colour to colour. The headlamp is now free to be removed.

When refitting, set the headlamp main beam as in Section H9 and tighten the headlamp pivot bolts to the torque setting given in "GENERAL DATA".

SECTION H11
TAIL AND STOP LAMP UNIT

Access to the bulbs in the tail and stop lamp unit is achieved by unscrewing the two slotted screws which secure the lens. The bulb is of the double-filament offset pin type and when a replacement is carried out, ensure that the bulb is fitted correctly.

Check that the two supply leads are connected correctly and check the earth (ground) lead to the bulb holder is in satisfactory condition.

When refitting the lens, do not overtighten the fixing screws or the lens may fracture as a result.

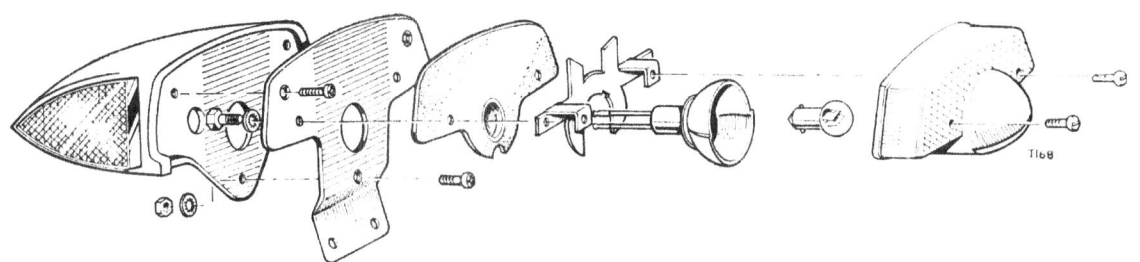

Fig. H18. Tail lamp exploded

SECTION H12
FUSES

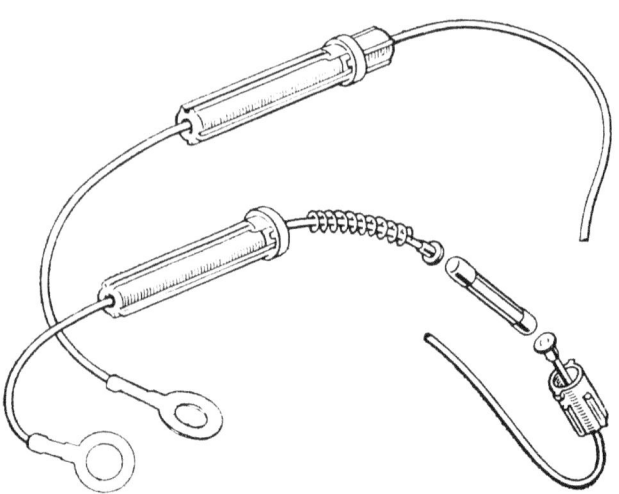

Fig. H19. Exploded view of fuseholder assembly

The fuse is to be found on the brown/blue live lead from the battery negative terminal. It is housed in a quickly detachable shell and is of 35 amp fuse rating.

Before following any fault location procedure always check that the fuse is not the source of the fault. A new fuse-cartridge should be fitted if there is any doubt about the old one.

The fuse rating must not under any circumstances be above 35 amp. rating.

SECTION H13
IGNITION SWITCH

The 45SA ignition switch incorporates a "barrel" type lock. These locks use individual "Yale" type keys and render the ingition circuit inoperative when the switch is turned off and the key removed. It is advisable for the owner to note the number stamped on the key to ensure a correct replacement in the event of the key being lost.

Three Lucar connectors are incorporated in the switch and these should be checked from time to time to ensure good electrical contact. The switch body can be released from the headlamp bracket by removing the large nut retaining the switch and the switch pushed out. The battery leads should be removed before attempting to remove the switch to avoid a short circuit.

The lock is retained in the body of the switch by a spring loaded plunger. This can be depressed with a pointed instrument through a small hole in the side of the switch body and the lock assembly withdrawn after the lock and switch together have been detached from the machine.

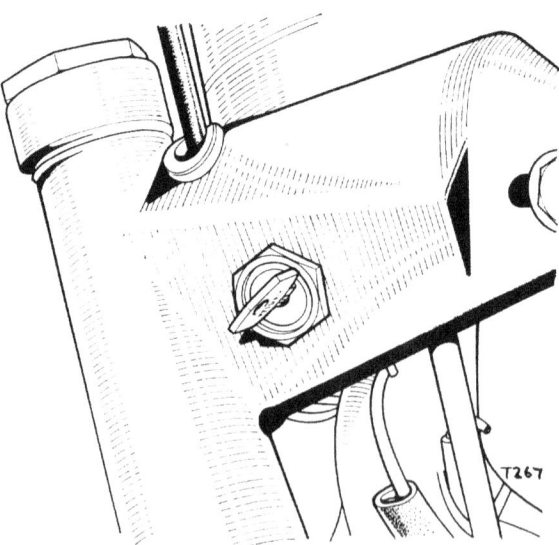

Fig. H20. Showing the ignition switch

SECTION H14
IGNITION CUT-OUT ("KILL") BUTTON

An emergency cut-out (kill) button is provided. This is mounted on the right handlebar and can be used to stop or "kill" the engine. Always ensure that the ignition is turned off after the engine is stopped in this fashion. Although the Trident uses only one type of cut-out button, other models use a button of identical appearance but with internal connections arranged differently. It is therefore essential for the correct replacement to be used, this being ordered by reference to the replacement parts catalogue.

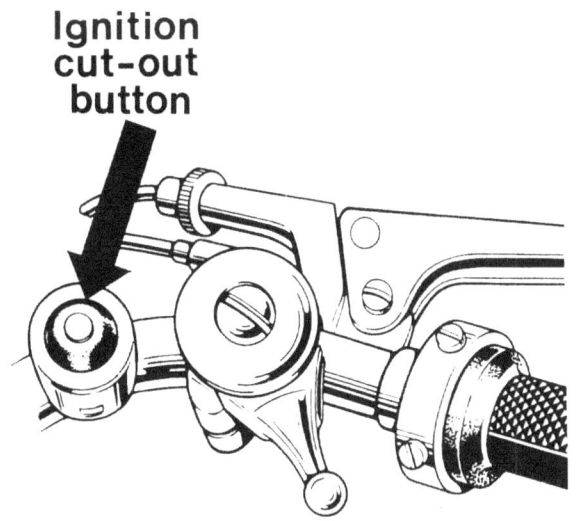

Fig. H21. Ignition cut-out button

SECTION H15
WARNING LAMPS AND AMMETER

The green warning light is used to indicate headlamp high beam and the red, a lack of oil pressure though it acts also as an ignition warning. The latter is operated by a pressure switch screwed into the crankcase below the rear of the oil filter compartment. The pressure switch is a sealed unit requiring no attention. There is no simple way of testing the function of the switch other than by substitution. The red light should extinguish at 7 lb. sq. in. pressure. If it is required to change a warning light bulb, access is most easily gained by releasing the headlamp from its brackets (Section H10) whereupon the bulbholder can be pulled gently downwards and the bulb changed. The warning light bodies are a push fit into the binnacle.

Note that the leads for the high beam warning light are blue/white and for the oil pressure warning light red/green.

The ammeter is merely pushed home into the binnacle and only the leads need to be disconnected prior to removal.

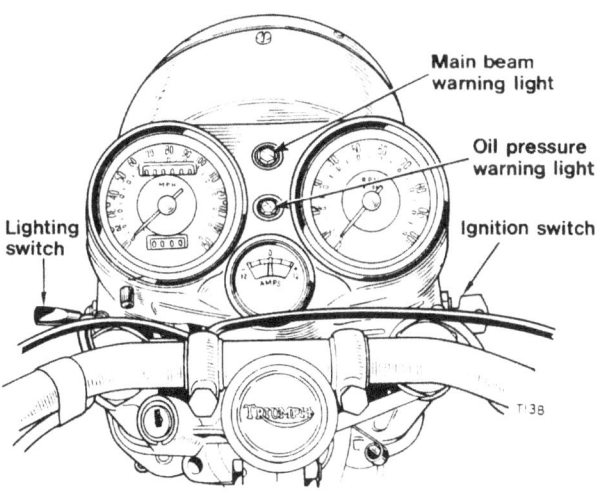

Fig. H22. Showing position of warning lamps

SECTION H16

CAPACITOR IGNITION (MODEL 2MC) ALTERNATIVE SYSTEM

The Lucas motor cycle capacitor system has been developed to enable machines to be run with or without a battery. The rider therefore has the choice of running with normal battery operation or running without battery if desired (e.g. competing in trials or other competitive events) and for emergency operation in case of battery failure.

Machines can readily be started without the battery and run as normal with full use of standard lighting. When stationary, however, parking lights will not work unless the battery is connected. The capacitor system also has the advantage of being less critical with regard to alternator timing.

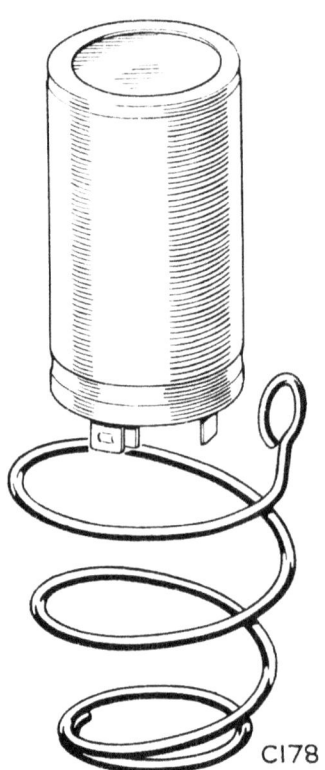

Fig. H23. Capacitor and spring

The system utilises the standard 12-volt battery-coil ignition equipment with the Zener diode charging regulator mounted on an efficient heat sink, plus a spring mounted high capacity electrolytic capacitor (Model 2MC), of a special shock-resistant type.

The energy pulses from the alternator are stored by the capacitor to ensure that sufficient current flows through the ignition coil at the moment of contact opening, thus producing an adequate spark for starting. When running, the capacitor also helps to reduce the D.C. voltage ripple.

Also with this system alternator timing is less critical. Provided the centres of the rotor and stator poles are roughly in line in the fully retarded position (i.e. as normal battery) emergency start condition which is 30° past magnetic neutral) satisfactory starting will be obtained. Furthermore any auto-advance angle and speed characteristics may be used and perfect running ignition performance achieved.

IDENTIFICATION OF CAPACITOR TERMINALS

The 2MC capacitor is an electroclytic (polarised) type and care must be taken to see that the correct wiring connections are made when fitting. Spare Lucar connectors are supplied to assist in connecting up. Looking at the terminal end of the unit it will be seen that there are two sizes of Lucar connector. The small $\frac{3}{16}$ in. Lucar is the *positive* (earth) terminal the rivet of which is marked with a spot of red paint. The double $\frac{1}{4}$ in. Lucar forms the *negative* terminal.

Fig. H23 shows the spring and capacitor. The capacitor should be positioned with its terminals pointing downwards. When fitting the spring to the capacitor, insert the capacitor at the widest end of the spring and push it down until the small coil locates in the groove on the capacitor body.

STORAGE LIFE OF MODEL 2MC CAPACITOR

The life of the 2MC is very much affected by storage in high temperatures. The higher the temperature the shorter its shelf life. At normal temperature i.e. 20°C. (68°F.) it will have a shelf life of about 18 months. At 40°C. (86°F.) about 9 to 12 months. Therefore, storing in a cool place will maintain their efficiency

TESTING

The efficiency of a stored capacitor can be determined fairly accurately with the aid of a voltmeter

ELECTRICAL SYSTEM

(scale 0–12 volts) connected to the terminals of a charged capacitor and the steady, not instantaneous, reading on the meter noted. The procedure is as follows:—

(a) Connect the capacitor(s) to a 12-volt supply and leave connected for 5 seconds. Observe carefully the polarity of connections, otherwise the capacitor may be ruined.

(b) Disconnect the supply leads and allow the charged capacitor to stand for at least 5 *minutes*.

(c) Connect the voltmeter leads to the capacitor and note the steady reading. This should not be less than 9·0 volts for a serviceable unit.

If the reading is less than 9·0 volts, the capacitor is leaking and must be replaced.

If a voltmeter is not available a rough check can be made by following the procedures in (a) and (b) and using a single strand of copper wire instead of the voltmeter to short-circuit the capacitor terminals. A good spark will be obtained from a serviceable capacitor at the instant the terminals are shorted together.

WIRING AND INSTALLATION

The capacitor is fitted into the spring and should be mounted with its terminals downwards. The capacitor negative terminal *and* Zener Diode must be connected to the rectifier centre (D.C.) terminal (brown/white), and the positive terminal must be connected to the centre bolt earthing terminal (see capacitor ignition diagram Fig. H24).

The mounting spring should be attached to any convenient point near the battery carrier.

SERVICE NOTES

Before running a 2MC equipped machine with the battery disconnected it is essential that the *battery negative lead be insulated* to prevent it from reconnecting and shorting to earth (frame of machine). Otherwise, the capacitor will be ruined. This can be done by removing the fuse from its holder and replacing it with a length of $\frac{1}{4}$ in. dia. dowel rod or other insulating medium.

A faulty capacitor may not be apparent when used with a battery system. To prevent any inconvenience arising, periodically check that the capacitor is serviceable by disconnecting the battery to see if the machine will start and run in the normal manner, with full lighting also available.

A capacitor kit is available under part number C.P.210.

Do not run the machine with the Zener Diode disconnected, as the 2MC capacitor will be damaged due to excessive voltage.

Should the engine fail to start without the battery, substitute a new 2MC capacitor. If the engine still refuses to start, check the wiring between the capacitor and rectifier for possible open or short circuit conditions. Also check the earth connections.

If difficulty is encountered in starting with a battery fitted, disconnect the 2MC capacitor to eliminate the possibility of a short circuit.

ELECTRICAL SYSTEM

BASIC MOTORCYCLE CIRCUIT
Using Large Capacitor
For operating with or without battery

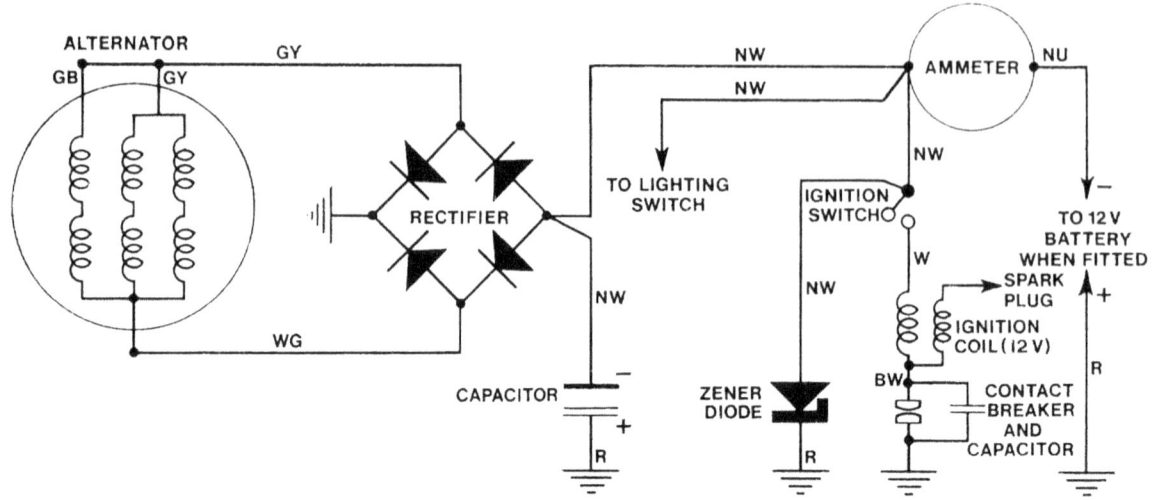

Fig. H24. Capacitor ignition diagram

2MC Capacitor ... ... Part No. 54170009
Mounting Spring (Horizontal Bolt Fixing) ,, 54483156
Mounting Spring (Vertical ,, ,,) ,, 54483155

CABLE COLOUR GUIDE

G	Green
B	Black
R	Red
Y	Yellow
N	Brown
W	White
U	Blue

ELECTRICAL SYSTEM

SECTION H17
WIRING DIAGRAM

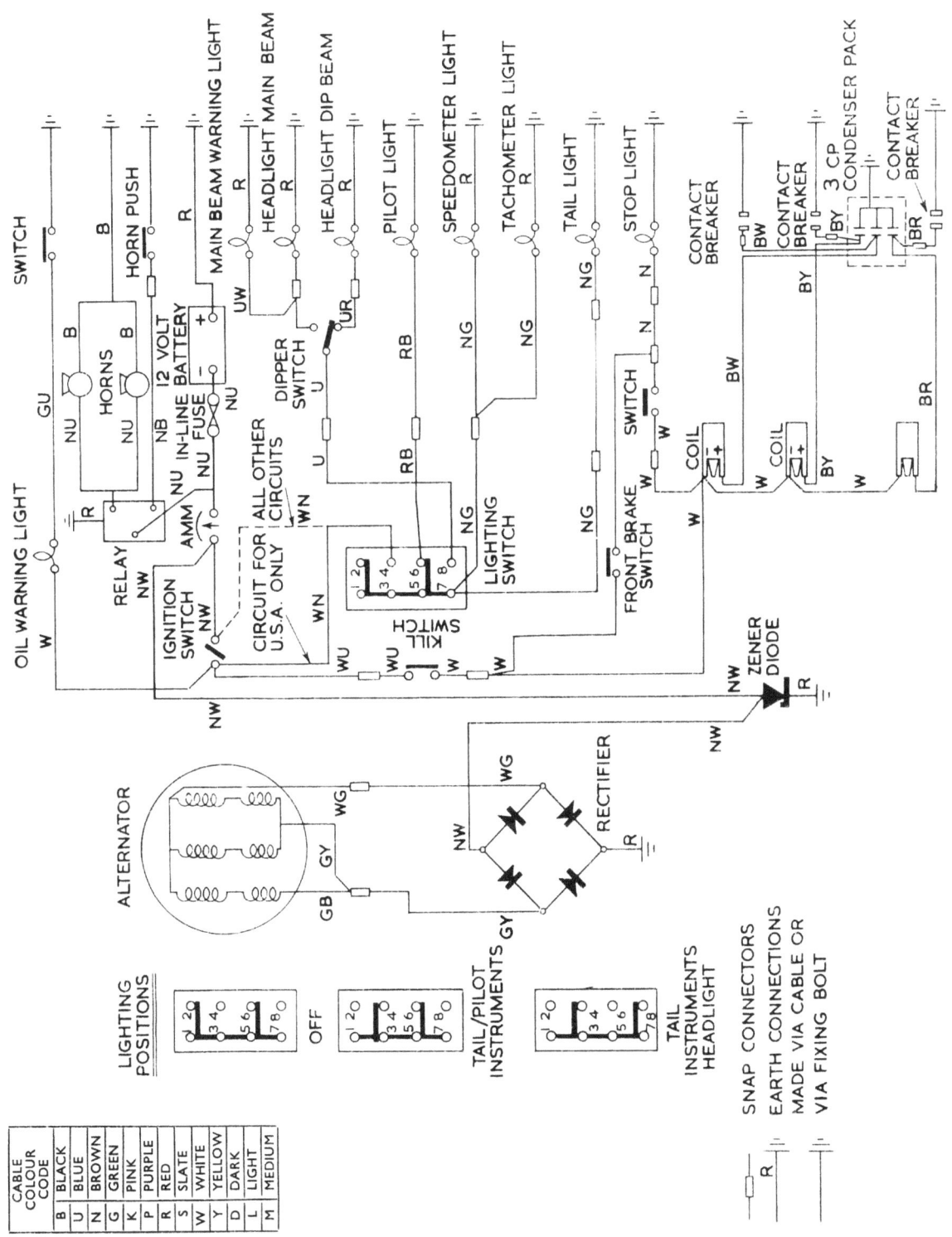

Fig. H25. Wiring diagram all conditions. Note that the front stop switch only appears on later models

NOTES

SECTION HH

ELECTRICAL SYSTEM

DESCRIPTION	Section
Zener diode location	HH7
Removing and refitting the headlamp	HH10
Ignition Switch	HH13
Stop Lamp Switches	HH16
Wiring diagram	HH19
Wiring diagram	HH24

SECTION HH7

ZENER DIODE LOCATION

The Zener Diode is mounted on a bracket below the headlamp, the bracket being bolted to the fork middle lug. The aluminium heatsink is finned to assist cooling. The order of assembly is shown in Fig. H13.

To remove diode only, disconnect the brown/blue double "Lucar" connector from the diode. Remove the black plastic plug from the heat sink (See Fig. H13) and unscrew the "nyloc" nut which secures the Diode. When refitting, the Diode nut must be tightened with extreme care. (Maximum tightening torque 22/28 lb./in.)

To remove the finned heat sink, remove the front bolt from the retaining bracket. A double red earth (ground) wire is attached at this point.

DO NOT ATTACH THE EARTH (GROUND) LEADS BETWEEN THE DIODE BODY AND HEATSINK

SECTION HH10

REMOVING AND REFITTING THE HEADLAMP

Disconnect the leads from the battery terminals then slacken the light unit securing screws at the top of the headlamp. Prise the rim of the light unit free.

Disconnect the two red earth wires from their copper holders, one on the main bulb retaining cap and the other from the bottom of the inside shell. Remove all connectng wires from the six snap connectors and those positioned on the light switch.

Remove the three warning lights from the shell, and the pilot light from the light unit. Withdraw the harness from the headlamp through the appropriate grommets after bending back the harness retaining clips.

Reassembly is the reversal of the above procedure, but reference should be made to the wiring diagram. See section H19. Finally set the headlamp main beam. As described in Section H9.

ELECTRICAL SYSTEM

HH

SECTION HH13

IGNITION SWITCH

All models are fitted with an ignition switch incorporating a "barrel" type lock. These locks use individual "Yale" type keys and render the ignition circuit inoperative when the switch is turned off and the key removed. It is advisable for the owner to note the number stamped on the key to ensure a correct replacement in the event of the key being lost.

Three Lucar connectors are incorporated in the switch and these should be checked from time to time to ensure good electrical contact.

The ignition switch is positioned on the left side headlamp bracket. To detach first remove the rubber cover and the lucar connectors at the back of the switch and then the large retaining nut.

The battery leads should be removed before attempting to remove the switch to avoid a short circuit.

The lock is retained in the body of the switch by a spring loaded plunger. This can be depressed with a pointed instrument through a small hole in the side of the switch body and the lock assembly withdrawn after the lock and switch together have been detached from the machine.

SECTION HH16

STOP LAMP SWITCHES

A rear stop light switch is fitted to both front and rear braking systems and operate independantly.

The rear brake switch is fitted to the frame behind the rear brake pedal and is controlled by adjusting the short bolt and locknut mounted at the pedal pivot. Adjustment should be such that the rear brake light becomes illuminated immediately the brake is applied. Other than checking the terminals for cleanliness and security the unit will require no further maintainance.

The front brake stop switch is contained in the right hand handle-bar switch housing and is actuated by a push rod situated in the brake lever. The push rod length is adjusted by means of a small screw found in the hollow of the lever.

To make the adjustment slacken the screw with the lever in the closed position until the rear stop light becomes illuminated. Now screw in the adjuster until the rear light is extinguished. The rear stop light should now operate as soon as the front brake is applied. The internal electrical connections are all soldered and will require no maintainance.

HH ELECTRICAL SYSTEM

SECTION HH19
WIRING DIAGRAM

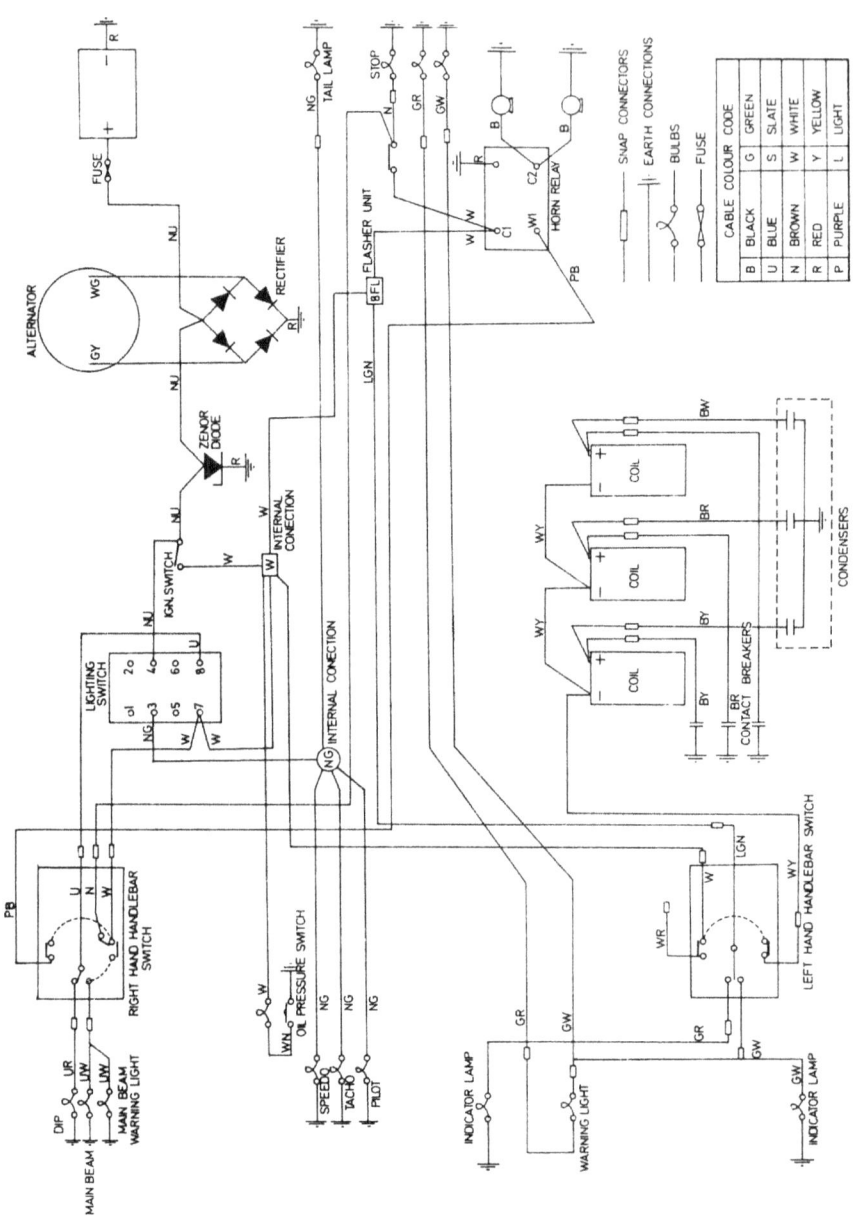

HH19 Wiring Diagram.

ELECTRICAL SYSTEM

SECTION HH24
WIRING DIAGRAM

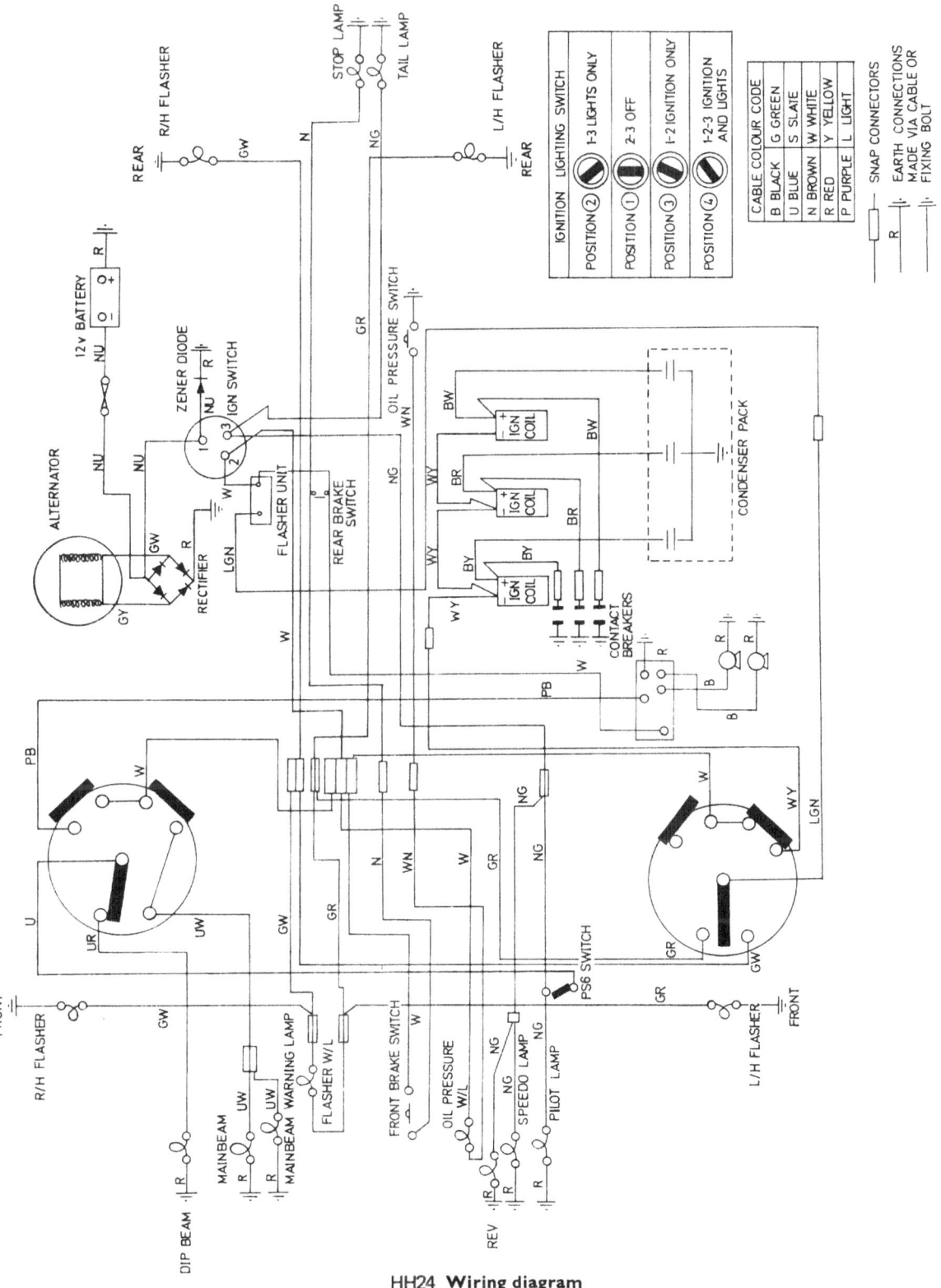

HH24 Wiring diagram

VELOCEPRESS MANUALS – MOTORCYCLE BY MAKE

AJS 1932-1948 SINGLES & TWINS 250cc THRU 1000cc (BOOK OF)
AJS 1945-1960 SINGLES 350cc & 500cc MODELS 16 & 18 (BOOK OF)
AJS 1955-1965 SINGLES 350cc & 500cc (BOOK OF)
AJS 1957-1966 FACTORY WSM - ALL SINGLES & TWINS
ARIEL UP TO 1932 (BOOK OF)
ARIEL 1932-1939 PREWAR MODELS (BOOK OF)
ARIEL 1933-1951 (WORKSHOP MANUAL)
ARIEL 1939-1960 4 STROKE SINGLES (BOOK OF)
ARIEL 1958-1964 LEADER & ARROW (BOOK OF)
BMW R26 R27 (1956-1967) FACTORY WORKSHOP MANUAL
BMW R50 R50S R60 R69S (1955-1969) FACTORY WORKSHOP MANUAL
BRIDGESTONE 90 SERIES FACTORY WSM & PARTS CATALOGUE
BRIDGESTONE 175 SERIES FACTORY WSM & PARTS CATALOGUE
BRIDGESTONE 350 SERIES FACTORY WSM & PARTS CATALOGUES
BSA SERVICE SHEETS MASTER CATALOGUE ALL MODELS 1945-1967
BSA BANTAM D1 TO D7 1948-1966 FACTORY SERVICE SHEETS MANUAL
BSA BANTAM ALL MODELS FROM 1948 ONWARDS (BOOK OF)
BSA DANDY FACTORY WORKSHOP MANUAL (COMPILATION)
BSA SINGLES & V-TWINS UP TO 1927 (BOOK OF)
BSA SINGLES & V-TWINS UP TO 1930 (BOOK OF)
BSA SINGLES & V-TWINS UP TO 1935 (BOOK OF)
BSA SINGLES & V-TWINS 1936-1939 (BOOK OF)
BSA C10, C11 & C12 1945-1958 FACTORY SERVICE SHEETS MANUAL
BSA OHV & SV SINGLES 250-600cc 1945-1959 (BOOK OF)
BSA C15 & B40 1958-1967 FACTORY SERVICE SHEETS MANUAL
BSA OHV & SV SINGLES 250cc (ONLY) 1954-1970 (BOOK OF)
BSA B31, B32, B33 & B34 1945-60 FACTORY SERVICE SHEETS MANUAL
BSA OHV SINGLES 350 & 500cc 1955-1967 (BOOK OF)
BSA M20, M21 & M33 1945-1963 FACTORY SERVICE SHEETS MANUAL
BSA TWINS A7 & A10 1948-1962 FACTORY SERVICE SHEETS MANUAL
BSA TWINS A7 & A10 1948-1962 (BOOK OF)
BSA TWINS A50 & A65 1962-1965 FACTORY WORKSHOP MANUAL
BSA TWINS A50 & A65 1962-1969 (SECOND BOOK OF)
DOUGLAS 1929-1939 PREWAR ALL MODELS (BOOK OF)
DOUGLAS 1948-1957 POSTWAR ALL MODELS FACTORY SHOP MANUAL
DUCATI 160cc, 250cc & 350cc OHC MODELS FACTORY SHOP MANUAL
HONDA 50 ALL MODELS UP TO 1970 INC MONKEY & TRAIL (BOOK OF)
HONDA 90 ALL MODELS UP TO 1966 (BOOK OF)
HONDA 50-65-70-90cc OHC SINGLES 1959-1983 FACTORY WSM
HONDA 125-150cc TWINS C/CS/CB/CA FACTORY WORKSHOP MANUAL
HONDA 125-160-175-200cc TWINS 1964-1980 WORKSHOP MANUAL
HONDA 250-305 TWINS C/CS/CB 1959-1967 FACTORY WSM
HOHDA 250-350 TWINS CB/CL/SL 1968-1973 FACTORY WSM
HONDA 450 CB/CL 1965-1974 K0 TO K7 WORKSHOP MANUAL
HONDA C100 SUPER CUB FACTORY WORKSHOP MANUAL
HONDA C110 SPORT CUB 1962-1969 FACTORY WORKSHOP MANUAL
HONDA TWINS & SINGLES 50cc THRU 305cc 1960-1966 (BOOK OF)
HONDA TWINS ALL MODELS 125cc THRU 450cc UP TO 1968 (BOOK OF)
INDIAN PONYBIKE, BOY RACER & PAPOOSE ILL PARTS LIST & SALES LIT
J.A.P. ENGINES 1927-1952 & MOTORCYCLES 1934-1952 (BOOK OF)
MATCHLESS 1931-1939 ALL MODELS 250cc THRU 990cc (BOOK OF)
MATCHLESS 1945-1956 350 & 500cc SINGLES (BOOK OF)
MATCHLESS 1955-1966 350 & 500cc SINGLES (BOOK OF)
MATCHLESS 1957-1966 FACTORY WSM - ALL SINGLES & TWINS
NEW IMPERIAL ALL SV & OHV FROM 1935 ONWARDS (BOOK OF)
NORTON 1932-1939 PREWAR MODELS (BOOK OF)
NORTON 1932-1947 (BOOK OF)
NORTON 1938-1956 (BOOK OF)
NORTON 1955-1963 MODELS 19, 50 & ES2 (BOOK OF)
NORTON 1955-1965 DOMINATOR TWINS (BOOK OF)
NORTON 1960-1970 TWIN CYLINDER FACTORY WORKSHOP MANUAL
NORTON 1970-1975 COMMANDO 850 & 750cc FACTORY WSM
NORTON 1975-1978 MK 3 COMMANDO 850 cc FACTORY WSM
PANTHER 1932-1958 LIGHTWEIGHT MODELS 250 & 350cc (BOOK OF)
PANTHER 1938-1966 HEAVYWEIGHT MODELS 600 & 650cc (BOOK OF)
RALEIGH MOTORCYCLES 1919-1933 (BOOK OF)
ROYAL ENFIELD 1934-1946 SINGLES & V TWINS (BOOK OF)
ROYAL ENFIELD 1937-1953 SINGLES & V TWINS (BOOK OF)
ROYAL ENFIELD 1946-1962 SINGLES (BOOK OF)
ROYAL ENFIELD 1958-1966 250cc & 350cc SINGLES (SECOND BOOK OF)
ROYAL ENFIELD 736cc INTERCEPTOR FACTORY WORKSHOP MANUAL
RUDGE 1933-1939 (BOOK OF)
SUNBEAM 1928-1939 (BOOK OF)
SUNBEAM 1946-1957 S7 & S8 (BOOK OF)
SUZUKI 50cc & 80cc UP TO 1966 (BOOK OF)
SUZUKI T10 1963-1967 FACTORY WORKSHOP MANUAL
SUZUKI T20 & T200 1965-1969 FACTORY WORKSHOP MANUAL
SUZUKI TWINS 1962 ONWARDS 125-500cc WORKSHOP MANUAL
TRIUMPH 1935-1949 SINGLES & TWINS (BOOK OF)
TRIUMPH 1937-1951 (WORKSHOP MANUAL)
TRIUMPH 1945-1955 FACTORY WORKSHOP MANUAL
TRIUMPH 1945-1959 TWINS (BOOK OF)
TRIUMPH 1956-1969 TWINS (BOOK OF)
TRIUMPH 1963-1970 UNIT CONSTRUCTION 650cc FACTORY WSM
TRIUMPH 1968-1974 TRIDENT T150 & T150V FACTORY WSM
VELOCETTE 1925-1970 ALL SINGLES & TWINS (BOOK OF)
VILLIERS ENGINE UP TO 1959 INC. 3 WHEELERS (BOOK OF)
VILLIERS ENGINE UP TO 1969 (BOOK OF)
VINCENT 1935-1955 (WORKSHOP MANUAL)
YAMAHA 1961-1967 YA5 & YA6 (WORKSHOP MANUAL & ILL PARTS LIST)
YAMAHA 1971-1972 JT1& JT2 (WORKSHOP MANUAL & ILL PARTS LIST)

VELOCEPRESS TECHNICAL BOOKS – MOTORCYCLE

1930'S BRITISH MOTORCYCLE CARBS & ELEC COMPONENTS (BOOK OF)
1930'S BRITISH MOTORCYCLE ENGINES (OVERHAUL & MAINTENANCE)
1930'S BRITISH MOTORCYCLE GEARBOXES & CLUTCHES (BOOK OF)
CATALOG OF BRITISH MOTORCYCLES (1951 MODELS)
LUCAS ELECTRONICS BRITISH M/CYCLES REPAIR & PARTS (1950-1977)
MOTORCYCLE ENGINEERING (P.E. Irving)
MOTORCYCLE ROAD TESTS 1949-1953 (Motor Cycle Magazine UK)
SPEED AND HOW TO OBTAIN IT (Motor Cycle Magazine UK)
TUNING FOR SPEED (P.E. Irving)
WIPAC (COMBO) MANUAL NUMBER 3 + M/CYCLE & SCOOTER MANUAL

VELOCEPRESS MANUALS – SCOOTERS BY MAKE

BSA SUNBEAM SCOOTER WORKSHOP MANUAL 1959-1965
BSA SUNBEAM SCOOTER 1959-1965 (BOOK OF)
LAMBRETTA 1947-1957 ALL 125 & 150cc MODELS (BOOK OF)
LAMBRETTA 1957-1970 LI & TV MODELS (SECOND BOOK OF)
NSU PRIMA 1956-1964 ALL MODELS (BOOK OF)
TRIUMPH TIGRESS SCOOTER WORKSHOP MANUAL 1959-1965
TRIUMPH TIGRESS SCOOTER (BOOK OF)
VESPA 1951-1961 (BOOK OF)
VESPA 1955-1963 125 & 150cc & GS MODELS (SECOND BOOK OF)
VESPA 1955-1968 GS & SS (BOOK OF)
VESPA 1963-1972 90, 125 & 150cc (THIRD BOOK OF)

VELOCEPRESS MANUALS – MOPEDS & MOTORIZED BICYCLES

CYCLEMOTOR (BOOK OF)
NSU QUICKLY 1953-1963 ALL MODELS (BOOK OF)
PUCH MAXI N & S MAINTENANCE & REPAIR (3 MANUAL COMPILATION)
RALEIGH MOPEDS 1960-1969 (BOOK OF)

VELOCEPRESS MANUALS - THREE WHEELER'S

BOND MINICAR THREE WHEELER 1948-1967 (BOOK OF)
BMW ISETTA FACTORY WORKSHOP MANUAL
BSA THREE WHEELER (BOOK OF)
RELIANT REGAL THREE WHEELER 1952-1973 (BOOK OF)
VINTAGE MORGAN THREE WHEELER (BOOK OF)

VELOCEPRESS MANUALS – AUTOMOBILE BY MAKE

ALFA ROMEO GIULIA WORKSHOP MANUAL 1300 TO 2000cc 1962-1975
ALFA ROMEO GIULIA TECH MANUAL CARBURETED CARS FROM 1962
ALFA ROMEO GIULIA TECH MANUAL FUEL INJECTED CARS FROM 1969
ALFA ROMEO GIULIETTA & GIULIA 750 & 101 SERIES 1955-1965 WSM
AUSTIN-HEALEY SPRITE & MG MIDGET WORKSHOP MANUAL 1958-1971
BMW 600 LIMOUSINE FACTORY WORKSHOP MANUAL
BMW 600 LIMOUSINE OWNERS HAND BOOK & SERVICE MANUAL
BMW 2000 & 2002 1966-1976 WORKSHOP MANUAL
CORVAIR 1960-1969 WORKSHOP MANUAL
CORVETTE V8 1955-1962 WORKSHOP MANUAL
FIAT 500 FACTORY WORKSHOP MANUAL 1957-1973
FIAT 600, 600D & MULTIPLA FACTORY WORKSHOP MANUAL 1955-1969
JAGUAR E-TYPE 3.8 & 4.2 SERIES 1 & 2 WORKSHOP MANUAL
JAGUAR MK 7, 8, 9 & XK120, 140, 150 WORKSHOP MANUAL 1948-1961
METROPOLITAN FACTORY WORKSHOP MANUAL
MGA & MGB OWNERS HANDBOOK & WORKSHOP MANUAL
MG MIDGET TC, TD, TF & TF1500 WORKSHOP MANUAL
PORSCHE 356 1948-1965 WORKSHOP MANUAL
PORSCHE 911 2.0, 2.2, 2.4 LITRE 1964-1973 WORKSHOP MANUAL
PORSCHE 911 2.7, 3.0, 3.2 LITRE 1973-1989 WORKSHOP MANUAL
PORSCHE 912 WORKSHOP MANUAL
TRIUMPH TR2, TR3, TR4 1953-1965 WORKSHOP MANUAL
VOLKSWAGEN TRANSPORTER, TRUCKS & WAGONS 1950-1979 WSM
VOLVO 1944-1968 ALL MODELS WORKSHOP MANUAL

VELOCEPRESS TECHNICAL BOOKS - AUTOMOBILE

FERRARI OWNER'S HANDBOOK
HOW TO BUILD A FIBERGLASS CAR
HOW TO BUILD A RACING CAR
HOW TO RESTORE THE MODEL 'A' FORD
MASERATI OWNER'S HANDBOOK
PERFORMANCE TUNING THE SUNBEAM TIGER
SOUPING THE VOLKSWAGEN
SOLEX CARBURETORS (EMPHASIS ON UK & EU AUTOMOBILES)
SU CARBURETORS (EMPHASIS ON UK AUTOMOBILES)
WEBER CARBURETORS (EMPHASIS ON ALFA & FIAT)

VELOCEPRESS BOOKS & GUIDES - AUTOMOBILE

COMPLETE CATALOG OF JAPANESE MOTOR VEHICLES
FERRARI 308 SERIES BUYER'S AND OWNER'S GUIDE
FERRARI BROCHURES AND SALES LITERATURE 1968-1989
FERRARI SERIAL NUMBERS PART I - ODD NUMBERS TO 21399
FERRARI SERIAL NUMBERS PART II - EVEN NUMBERS TO 1050
HENRY'S FABULOUS MODEL "A" FORD
MASERATI BROCHURES AND SALES LITERATURE

VELOCEPRESS BOOKS – RACING

CARRERA PANAMERICANA - MEXICAN ROAD RACE (BOOK OF)
DIALED IN - THE JAN OPPERMAN STORY
VEDA ORR'S NEW REVISED HOT ROD PICTORIAL

AUTOBOOKS WORKSHOP MANUALS

FOR A COMPLETE LISTING OF THE AUTOBOOKS WORKSHOP MANUALS
THAT WE CURRENTLY HAVE AVAILABLE, PLEASE VISIT OUR WEBSITE.
www.VelocePress.com

www.ingramcontent.com/pod-product-compliance
Lightning Source LLC
Chambersburg PA
CBHW060248240426
43673CB00047B/1891